NORTH CAROLINA
STATE BOARD OF COMMUNITY COLLEGES
LIBRARIES
CAPE FEAR COMMUNITY COLLEGE

D1801884

Critical Essays on
KINGSLEY AMIS

CRITICAL ESSAYS ON BRITISH LITERATURE

Zack Bowen, General Editor
University of Miami

Critical Essays on
KINGSLEY AMIS

edited by
ROBERT H. BELL

G. K. Hall & Co.
An Imprint of Simon & Schuster Macmillan
New York

Prentice Hall International
London   Mexico City   New Delhi   Singapore   Sydney   Toronto

Copyright © 1998 by G. K. Hall & Co.

All rights reserved. No part of this book may be reproduced or transmitted in any form or by any means, electronic or mechanical, including photocopying, recording, or by any information storage and retrieval system, without permission in writing from the Publisher.

G. K. Hall & Co.
An Imprint of Simon & Schuster Macmillan
1633 Broadway
New York, NY 10019

Library of Congress Cataloging-in-Publication Data

Critical essays on Kingsley Amis / edited by Robert H. Bell.
    p. cm. — (Critical essays on British literature)
    Includes bibliographical references and index.
    ISBN 0-7838-0039-8 (alk. paper)
    1. Amis, Kingsley—Criticism and interpretation. I. Bell, Robert H. (Robert Huntley), 1946– . II. Series.
PR6001.M6Z6 1998
828'.91409—dc21   98-35290
                                                              CIP

This paper meets the requirements of ANSI/NISO Z3948-1992 (Permanence of Paper).

10 9 8 7 6 5 4 3 2 1

Printed in the United States of America

dedicated with love for my daughters,
Kaitlin and Amanda
"They endured."

Contents

General Editor's Note	xi
Publisher's Note	xiii
Acknowledgments	xv
Introduction: Kingsley Amis in the Great Tradition and in Our Time ROBERT H. BELL	1

ESSAYS AND ARTICLES

Real and Made-up People KINGSLEY AMIS	23
Kingsley Amis and *The Situation of the Novel* BERNARD BERGONZI	28
The Modern, the Contemporary, and the Importance of Being Amis DAVID LODGE	40
"No, Not Bloomsbury": The Comic Fiction of Kingsley Amis MALCOLM BRADBURY	60
The Language of Kingsley Amis NORMAN MACLEOD	76
Appreciating Kingsley Amis WILLIAM H. PRITCHARD	103
The Anti-Egotist: Kingsley Amis, Man of Letters PAUL FUSSELL	111
Ending Up with Amis LAWRENCE GRAVER	130

Seriocomic Amis and True Comic Edge: *Lucky Jim* and *You Can't Do Both* Robert H. Bell	141
Traditional Comedy and the Comic Mask in Kingsley Amis's *Lucky Jim* Bruce Stovel	158
What Are Little Girls Made Of? Jeremy Treglown	170
When the Curse Begins to Hurt: Kingsley Amis and Satiric Confrontation D. R. Wilmes	176
Looking Back on *Lucky Jim* David Lodge	187
Jim, Jake, and the Years Between: The Will to Stasis in the Contemporary British Novel Keith Wilson	193
Kingsley Amis Patrick Swinden	205
Entertaining Amis William H. Pritchard	229
The Old Devil James Wolcott	237
A Touch of Class Terry Teachout	243
Kingsley's Ransom James Wolcott	257
An Interview with Kingsley Amis Dale Salwak	266
The Curious Theodicy of Kingsley Amis Lawrence Graver	281
Kingsley and the Women John McDermott	285
Jake and Lolly Opt Out John Updike	293
The Old Devil Gabriele Annan	296

Kingsley and the Women HERMIONE LEE	299
Amis Lite CHARLES MCGRATH	304
Closing Time DAVID LODGE	309
Kingsley Amis V. S. PRITCHETT	315
Amis Behavin' WILLIAM H. PRITCHARD	319
Do Not Go Sober JAMES WOLCOTT	323
London *Times* Obituary: Sir Kingsley Amis	327
Can a Feminist (Still) Read Kingsley Amis? SHARI BENSTOCK	332
Index	339

General Editor's Note

◆

The Critical Essays on British Literature series provides a variety of approaches to both classical and contemporary writers of Britain and Ireland. The formats of the volumes in the series vary with the thematic designs of individual editors and with the amount and nature of existing reviews and criticism, augmented, where appropriate, by original essays by recognized authorities. It is hoped that each volume will be unique in developing a new overall perspective on its particular subject.

In his introduction Robert Bell sets the stage comparing Kingsley Amis's work with that of his classical predecessor, Henry Fielding, and then proceeds with a tour de force of the major Amis novels. He indicates how Amis's vices and views become the virtues of his pungent, eminently quotable, delightfully splenetic language. Along the way Bell treats the acerbic, often misogynist opinions and habits of many of Amis's protagonists, and the response of the critics they offended.

Bell's selection of essays includes overviews of Amis's work, as well as treatments of individual works in roughly chronological order. Acknowledging Amis's popularity among a wide, informed reading public as well as academics, there is a healthy reliance on reviews (three by David Lodge over a span of years) as well as selections from book-length works. Three new essays, by Lawrence Graver, the editor himself, and Shari Benstock, were written especially for this volume.

University of Miami
ZACK BOWEN

Publisher's Note

◆

Producing a volume that contains both newly commissioned and reprinted material presents the publisher with the challenge of balancing the desire to achieve stylistic consistency with the need to preserve the integrity of works first published elsewhere. In the Critical Essays series, essays commissioned especially for a particular volume are edited to be consistent with G. K. Hall's house style; reprinted essays appear in the style in which they were first published, with only typographical errors corrected. Consequently, shifts in style from one essay to another are the result of our efforts to be faithful to each text as it was originally published.

Acknowledgments

♦

It's a pleasure to express my appreciation to several people who supported my research and writing. David L. Smith, Dean of the Faculty at Williams College, provided generous funding and warm encouragement. Heather Pierce worked long and hard, always with remarkable reliability and good cheer. Williams College librarians were wonderfully helpful; thanks to Lee Dalzell, Peter Giordano, and JoAnn Irace. Larry Graver and I have been reading, enjoying, and discussing Amis's work for 26 years; while my general debts to him are incalculable, on this project he has been a particular catalyst as well as a major contributor. Thanks to the authors who gave permission to reprint their writing. Particular thanks to William Pritchard of Amherst College, one of our very best readers of Amis and of much else. I am very grateful to Zack Bowen, a great Joycean and an ideal editor. Finally, thanks again and always to Ilona.

Introduction: Kingsley Amis in the Great Tradition and in Our Time

ROBERT H. BELL

> Kingsley Amis
> Is famous. His fame
> Is partly due to his writing like an average bloke
> With ordinary feelings. His joke.
> —James Michie

The writings of Kingsley Amis provide unique pleasures and pose persistent challenges. Early and late, Amis is a virtuoso stylist, creating the inflections, accents, and idioms that define and expose characters. He revels in linguistic follies and endows ordinary language with vitality. His forte is cant and cliché, especially the descent into banality or stupidity. Despite his enduring reputation as a comic novelist, few Amis novels after *Lucky Jim* are purely or even predominantly comic. In most of his books, circumstances are gloomy, fate unconsoling. People live in a precarious Hobbesian state, vulnerable to mortal woes, prey to awful forces. The world of Amis is more disturbing and painful than amusing or reassuring. The funniest writer of our time is also one of the most troubling.

Amis's best novels—I'd cite *Lucky Jim; Take a Girl like You; Girl, 20; Ending Up; Jake's Thing; The Old Devils;* and *You Can't Do Both* as the works of highest distinction and permanent interest—are richly entertaining and subtly provocative.[1] In many ways he is a traditional moralist, exploring the demands of decency and the power of appetite. Yet Amis is also a twentieth-century writer alert to complexities of evaluation, loath to simplify moral problems. His great vexing issue is sex—its origins in individual psychology, its perpetual implications for personal identity and relationships. Nothing is

---

This essay was written specifically for this volume and is published here for the first time by permission of the author.

more characteristic of an Amis hero than the difficulties caused by his sexual desire and conduct. Though most of his protagonists would do better if they could, rarely do they reform. More likely the resolution is a feeling of uncertainty, ambivalence, or confusion produced by the hero's inadequacy to the situation's complexity. While the characters remain ambivalent, our perceptions of them differ and shift. Typically an Amis hero precipitates notoriously mixed reactions—volatile blends of compassion and indignation. The hero may have no more than vacillating sympathy for himself. Struggling fitfully, Amis characters achieve only partial self-awareness and may never grow substantially: their capacity for introspection and change is limited. Many of Amis's heroes are notable sham detectors, mockers of fools, phonies, and bastards; they may themselves also be, and remain, egregious bastards.

Amis's fiction has always provoked criticism, including some serious objections to his personal prejudices and his inability to transcend them in his art. The question of identification between author and characters—some of them objectionable, some obnoxious—has animated responses to Amis from the outset of his career. In many of his narratives Amis seems massively ubiquitous, his characters articulating the author's likes and dislikes. The multiplicity of experience is not always rendered or dramatized. In his expressed wish to tell "believable stories about understandable characters in a reasonably straightforward style," Amis depletes his imaginative resources and restricts his range of effects. His characters are sometimes flat, reduced to cartoon dimensions, viewed from the outside, with little sense of their subjectivity or interiority. Too often they appear deprived or incapable of agency.

In his intriguing mix of remarkable virtues and significant limitations, Kingsley Amis rewards comparison with the novelist he praised most often and most highly, Henry Fielding, "whose realism two hundred years have not dimmed and whose humor is closer to our own than that of any writer before the present century."[2] Considering all that comes between neoclassicism and modernism, Amis and Fielding share a surprising number of values, traits, and inclinations. Both were vitally engaged with contemporary issues and zesty, pugnacious combatants in the cultural wars. Amis cherished Fielding's "moral seriousness . . . without the aid of evangelical huffing and puffing."[3] They shared the classical conviction that literature should be *dulce et utile,* and they believed that, in Amis's words, "the satirist's laughter is valid as a gesture—a gesture on the side of reason."[4] Their traditional values prized candor, kindness, magnanimity, charity, and generosity of spirit. They enjoyed and represented camaraderie once termed robust or "manly," now more often regarded warily as "masculinist." Both mix high intellect with low tastes. They espouse clarity, accessibility, "a reasonably straightforward technique." Their craftsmanship was always precise, meticulous, and elegant. Both novelists were humorists as well as moralists, stressing human folly, especially our appetitive passions and self-exonerations. Their wit was inexhaustible and unsparing. Both Fielding and Amis eagerly, frankly entertained; neither refused to play the fool. Both highlight farcical antics, feature picaresque plots, and love to parody anything ludicrous, especially figures of pretense and fatuity. Amis and Fielding disorient readers with consistent ethical problems and lively irreverence toward authority, piety, and righteousness. Both affirm common sense and ordinary decency in ways sometimes regarded as too sentimental or simplified. And neither Fielding nor Amis conveys a convincing sense of sublime possibility or extraordinary capacity beyond the creation of the novel.

Both Fielding and Amis had remarkable early success. *Lucky Jim* (1954) is a perpetual fount of pleasures. It has pleased many and pleased long—enough in our fragmented times to declare it a classic. A great deal of the pleasure is provided by Jim Dixon, and it is frankly guilty. He is, as his adversaries declare, Philistine, unscrupulous, disgraceful. Incorrigibly adolescent, he painstakingly forges a letter to his enemy Johns in the voice of an outraged boyfriend of the secretary Johns has been eyeing, but he works and plays at foolishness with such precision, gusto, and joy! *"This is just a freindly letter and I am not threatenning you, but you just do as I say else me and my palls from the Works will be up your way and we sha'nt be coming along just to say How do you can bet. . . ."*[5] Just as characteristic of Jim as the forgery, made by holding the pencil like a butter knife, is the nasty delight he takes in his own cleverness: "He read it through, thinking how admirably consistent were the style and orthography. Both derived in large part, from the essays of some of his less proficient students" (*Lucky*, 158). Some of what Jim wants and likes is disreputable. He is the Laureate of Liquor, but even more notable than his love of beer is his hangover, a paragraph devoted Amis fans recite from memory: "His mouth had been used as a latrine by some small creature of the night, and then as its mausoleum" (*Lucky*, 64).

Part of what redeems Jim, or at least maintains our interested regard, is that in all his silliness he is surrounded by more profoundly objectionable fools whose outrages are hilariously revealed. There is Professor Welch, serving Jim "the smallest drink he'd ever been seriously offered" (*Lucky*, 61), or discoursing professorially: "I expect you know his book on medieval Cwmrbydyceirw" (*Lucky* [London: Penguin, 1961], 81). And Bertrand, whose speech is annoying in more ways than you'd think possible: "And I happen to like the arts, you sam" (*Lucky*, 53). Or Margaret, in her intimate mode: "All the barriers are down at last, aren't they?" (*Lucky*, 27). And like a holy fool there is Jim Dixon, the hero of language, whose witty responses are uttered mainly to himself, for the sake of survival. "He's such a queer mixture." Christine says of Bertrand. "Naming to himself the two substances of which he personally thought Bertrand a mixture" (*Lucky*, 143), Jim muses. Above all, Jim is an infallible boredom detector, alert to any solemn pomposity, as when he hears Margaret pretending to restrain herself "like a great actress demonstrating the economical conveyance of strong emotions" (*Lucky*, 114).

The permanent pleasure and abiding virtue of *Lucky Jim* are its verbal wit, its richly textured observations and conversation, and its merciless cruelty, sparing nothing, least of all Jim himself. Though Jim is enabled by his wit, he is also hindered by his humorous instincts and attitudes, even when he is being very funny, reflecting on the strangely neglected topic of his article. His wit is too reckless and too nimble to be contained or focused; animosities invariably spill over, and frequently rebound upon himself. Jim is excessive, out of control, and beyond the pale: if Jim is a humorous hero, *Lucky Jim* is also a rogue's progress. The hero, like the novel, overflows with vitality: "As he left the bar with Christine at his side, Dixon felt like a special agent, a picaroon, a Chicago war-lord, a hidalgo, an oil baron, a mohock" (*Lucky,* 117).

So engaging is Jim, so amply endowed with Amis's verbal resources, that one hesitates to condemn his impropriety, laziness, and tastelessness, or to emphasize the novel's evident deficiencies. Problems exist, including plot contrivances, an overly convenient deus ex machina, narrow narrative empathy, prismatic perspectives, simplification of motives, and exterior or one-dimensional characterizations. But as Henry James said of Tom Jones, Jim Dixon has so much life "that it amounts, for the effect of comedy and the application of satire, almost to his having a mind, that is to his having reactions and a full consciousness."[6] It may be argued, as James implies, that the limitations of *Tom Jones* and of *Lucky Jim* are intrinsic to comedy. While Henry James, F. R. Leavis, and I would not include *Lucky Jim* in the great tradition of English fiction, one could do worse—could one do better?—than to begin a course on English comic fiction with *Tom Jones* and to end it with *Lucky Jim*.

That Uncertain Feeling (1955) resembles *Lucky Jim* in several ways but is markedly less ebullient, far more reflective. The protagonist, John Lewis, is a restless, horny librarian who truly values his marriage to Jean and really craves an affair with Elizabeth Gruffydd-Williams, an older, married lady of means and pretensions. He recounts his difficulties with some detachment, regret, and gusto: "why did I like women's breasts so much? I was clear on why I liked them, thanks, but why did I like them *so much?*"[7] There are some splendid satirical elements, especially the wicked parody of Dylan Thomas in the person of Gareth Probert, who "sounded like an actor pretending with fair success on the whole, to be Owain Glyndwr in a play on the Welsh Children's Hour" (*Feeling,* 40), and the hero's farcical escape from the lady's boudoir disguised as a Welshwoman. Like Jim Dixon, John Lewis is woefully, ludicrously misplaced and miscast whenever he is in more privileged circles. Overall, though, *That Uncertain Feeling* is neither persistently amusing nor especially compelling. Notable is Amis's lifelong theme, the volatile, vexing nature of relations between men and women, and how, in a mixed, muddled character such as John Lewis, sincere compunctions compete with hypocritical self-justification. He vacillates, "feeling a tremendous rakehell, and not much liking myself for it, and feeling rather a good chap for not liking myself for it, and not liking myself for feeling rather a good chap" (*Feeling,* 93). While John, resolving to mend his ways, does return to home and family, his future is dubious. The best he can imagine is, "Since I seemed to have piloted myself into the position of being both immoral and moral at the same time, the thing was to keep trying not to be immoral, and then to keep trying might turn into a habit" (*Feeling,* 239–40). Amis leaves it to us to correct his hero's deficient, refracted perspective and to speculate about his fate; some readers resist and resent such uncertainty, and fault either the novelist's dereliction of duty or Amis's reluctance to separate himself from the protagonist.

I Like It Here (1958), a potpourri of picaresque adventures, travelogue, mystery, and satire, is regarded by nearly everyone including Amis as his least successful novel. It is most sympathetically seen as a self-reflexive, parodic text in the tradition of *Tristram Shandy* and *Pale Fire*. Writer Garnet Bowen, another put-upon, plain-speaking fellow, spends a fellowship year in Portugal, disliking and mocking most of what he experiences, except for an inspirational visit to the tomb of Henry Fielding, where he is reminded of what is most lovable and admirable in the grand old tradition of the English novel, "a moral seriousness that could be made apparent without the aid of evangelical puffing and blowing" (167).[8] Too often the plot seems to be a contrivance for hanging chips on shoulders and Bowen appears a mere mouthpiece for the author, a pale copy of Jim Dixon, grumping about "furrin" parts, occasionally scoring a palpable hit: "A couple of months [in Portugal] would be like learning to drive or making a determined start of *Finnegans Wake*—an experience bound in itself to be arduous and irritating" (*Here,* 23). Though critics like Norman MacLeod have found *I Like It Here* a subtle satire, exposing Bowen's bluff English xenophobia, for most readers the novel does not travel well or endure vitally.

Take a Girl like You (1960) is a provocative, challenging, entertaining novel, a seriocomic treatment of sexual fidelity and promiscuity. There is an admirable ambition in this novel to investigate contemporary morality, to understand what is inherited and what can and should be forged anew; Amis regards morality as a problem. *Take a Girl like You* recalls Samuel Richardson's novel *Clarissa,* in dramatizing the seduction of Jenny Bunn, a provincial virgin who is pursued by Patrick Standish, a winning, amoral rake, devoted to Eros but prematurely haunted by Thanatos. Patrick's ploys sometimes have authorial resonance if not sanction, as when he schools Jenny:

> These ideas of yours. Jolly sound in 1880 and everything.... There are two sorts of men today, those who do—you know what I mean—and those who don't. All the ones you're ever going to really like are the first sort, and all the ones those ideas of yours tell you you ought to have are the second sort. Oh, there wouldn't be any problem of temptation there. The problem would come on the wedding night. And on all the nights after that. There used to be a third sort, admitted. The sort that could, but didn't—not with the girl he was going to marry, anyway. You'd have liked him all right, though, and he wouldn't have given you any trouble trying to get you into bed before the day. The snag about him is he's dead. He died in 1914 or thereabouts. He isn't ever going to turn up, Jenny, that bloke with the manners and the respect and the honour and the bunches of flowers *and* the attraction.[9]

Patrick, like Richardson's Lovelace, is presented vividly, from the inside, with considerable sympathy, and he displays a persuasive fluency. But Patrick's charm and eloquence hardly exempt him from ethical scrutiny, though he escapes hanging. He is often, one would think manifestly, self-indulgent, rapacious, and malicious, and even his fellow rakes condemn his methods as reprehensible when, "tired of fairness" (*Take,* 304), Patrick takes Jenny while she is drunk and defenseless. But he becomes increasingly (if inadequately) aware of his selfishness, often questioning and criticizing himself, experiencing at least "a tiny wisp of remorse". It is unclear why lack of explicit authorial evaluation, so typical of modern fiction, an absence of "evangelical huffing and puffing", disorients and dismays some readers. *Take a Girl like You* is remarkably even-handed, devoting more than half its attention to Jenny's point of view, endowed with innocence and goodness, but also vigorous force. We come to know both characters as they see themselves and as they are perceived by each other. A number of women reviewers noted the novel's scrupulous regard for the heroine. The open-endedness of *Take a Girl like You* surely inclines us toward sympathy for Jenny, regret for her fate, and apprehensions for her future: "Well," says Jenny, "those old Bible-class ideas have certainly taken a knocking, haven't they?" Patrick: "They were bound to, you know, darling, with a girl like you. It was inevitable." Jenny has the last rueful word: "Oh, yes, I expect it was. But I can't help feeling it's rather a pity" (*Take,* 317).

One Fat Englishman (1963) presents another flagrantly unappealing hero, Roger Micheldene, an obese old-school/old-boy publisher and a fish out of water, beached and bitching in America.[10] At Budweiser College in pursuit of his former lover Helene Bang, Micheldene meets her linguist husband and is plagued by Irving Macher, a young Jewish writer. Though he himself is tellingly humorless, Micheldene's dyspeptic reactions are amusingly hyperbolic and occasionally imposing: "Of the seven deadly sins, Roger considered himself qualified in gluttony, sloth, and lust but distinguished in anger."[11] Like several subsequent Amis novels centered around offensive figures, *One Fat Englishman* appeals to readers entertained by the hero's nasty perceptions and/or persuaded that such nastiness is at least intermittently exposed rather than endorsed. (Studies in the psychology of laughter indicate that racist humor appeals to both the *most* and the *least* bigoted audiences). If Roger Micheldene, "his mammary development . . . acceptable only if he could have shed half his weight as well as changing his sex" (*One,* 8), collecting women as trophies, conjugating Greek verbs to delay climax, cannot be judged more sinned against than sinning, at least he is nearly as pained as he is abusive. His quest for Helene Bang is sabotaged by his own orneriness and horniness. Losing at Scrabble to a child, he deliberately upsets the board, and later in retaliation discards one of the boy's favorite toys. Most critics find *One Fat Englishman* disappointing, though a reader as canny as Christopher Ricks, perhaps thinking of *Paradise Lost,* admires the way the narrative tricks the reader into misguided sympathy for Micheldene in order to shame and teach us. Amis has said that his protagonist is "a bastard to a very large extent, and he understands it and yet he can't be different. One isn't asking for sympathy for him exactly, but we all have our crosses to bear and realizing it is a kind of cross which he bears."[12]

At one point Amis regarded his 1966 metaphysical spy story *The Anti-Death League* as "my favorite of my own books. Partly because of being more ambitious than anything before."[13] Overtly grander in subject and scope yet severe in style, *The Anti-Death League* sustains narrative suspense and complicated relationships with no humorous filigrees or farcical interludes. The MacGuffin, the mysterious Operation Apollo, is deadly serious, potentially fatal. There is little comfort to be found, certainly not with psychiatrists like Dr. Best, one of a bad lot. As the hero says, "You've probably heard of those things they call lethal nodes.... Well, we're in a lethal node now, only it's one that works in time instead of space."[14] God or Providential Design is relentlessly harsh, overseeing gratuitous suffering and not sparing even hapless L. S. Caton, that shadowy figure who has flitted through every previous Amis narrative until he is dispatched for good in this one. In this lethal node, a decent bloke like Moti Naidu is an unheeded Cassandra, and James Churchill's genuine love for Catherine Casement is vulnerable, a feeble gesture against despair. Anthony Burgess characterizes *The Anti-Death League* as a "masque of ultimate bitterness." After this novel, Amis is never simply comic, and when he is predominantly humorous, it is to illustrate the closeness of the comic to the cosmic, or the similarity between humor and horror. Increasingly Amis creates nightmare worlds and individuals subjected to malign forces.

I Want It Now (1968) is almost an exception. It does recall *Lucky Jim* in its endearingly romantic plot and thoroughly enjoyable, merciless vivisections. Amis's cherished targets include smarmy television personalities, swinging 60s London, the southern United States, "the Ritz people,"[15] the idle, vacuous young, and other ridiculous annoyances. Ronnie Appleyard begins as a hypocritical, young Lochinvar of the airwaves, though "to be fair, he had no feelings for old people as such beyond a mild dislike, never wasted his time sweating about the H-bomb, and would not have cared a curse if the British army were to set about re-occupying the Indian subcontinent" (*Now,* 11). His project, to procure "fame and money, with a giant's helping of sex thrown in" (*Now,* 14), is gradually and quite persuasively transformed into a benevolent mission. Ronnie saves Simona Quick (usually called Simon or Mona) from her tyrannical mother, Lady Baldock; marriage to the loathsome Student Mansfield; and a life of promiscuity and frigidity. In rescuing Simon, Ronnie learns a surprising amount, enjoys being nice to someone, and is redeemed by love. "I was a shit when I met you," Ronnie says to Simon. "I still am in lots of ways. But because of you I've had to give up trying to be a dedicated full-time shit" (*Now,* 254). For the last time in an Amis narrative, the wicked are exposed and the redeemable rewarded by love and, wondrous to tell, good sex. Malcolm Bradbury explains, "Some moral explorations have to be conducted before gratification comes. So, just as *Take a Girl like You* depends on the principle of procrastinated rape, *I Want It Now* depends on the notion of deferred orgasm."[16] Satire, comedy, and romance blend fluently in this sprightly and altogether appealing narrative. *I Want It Now* is a social comedy enriched by its explorations of individual decency and responsibility. Most fans of Amis put *I Want It Now* on the Amis A-list.

One would be mistaken to dismiss *The Green Man* (1968) as a potboiler or expendable genre work. A satisfying unsettling ghost story, it is altogether serious and highly engrossing—painstakingly realistic, densely plotted, and psychologically intriguing. Maurice Allington is our narrator, the proprietor of an inn called the Green Man, who drinks, ruminates, and conducts or misconducts an affair with the wife of his best friend. He seriously dislikes women, and uses sex as an antidote to the tedium of domesticity and the terror of mortality. Alcoholic, loveless, haunted by death, Allington is visited by the evil spirit of Dr. Thomas Underhill. The threat to Allington's teenage daughter compels the distant father to look deeper into his own heart of darkness and to recognize something familiar in Underhill's spirit. Like many Amis bastard-heroes, Allington is diagnosed harshly and aptly by his wife as she leaves him. There is also a climactic exorcism and something of a purgation. *The Green Man* is a gripping, frightening tale, admired by many readers and several critics. When *The Green Man* became a popular British television series in 1990, the book enjoyed renewed popularity.

Girl, 20 (1971) is a triumphant return to the world of *I Want It Now*. In his element and on his home turf, Amis gleefully demolishes all he surveys. The hero is a trendy lefty composer, Sir Roy Vandervane, avidly pursuing teenage girls like Sylvia Meers, who is sexually attractive, utterly vacuous, and unfeeling. Our point of view is provided by the narrator, Douglas Yandell, a music critic and a man of uncertain views and partial reliability. Yandell sensibly disapproves of Sir Roy's conduct, politics, and style yet reluctantly abets his adulterous capers while caring for the man, his wife and family, and his art. Though Yandell's viewpoint is insufficient, it is a complicated mixture of sympathy, impatience, amusement, exasperation, and outrage. Yandell has his own problems, including a mistress he regularly, willingly shares with another bloke, one indication of his problematic detachment. Certainly exceptional, Yandell's narrative angle of vision is always engaging. *Girl, 20* depicts hilariously awful characters whose follies and fates compel our attention. Particular delights are Sir Roy's fatuous idiom ("arse-creeping the young 'be people,'" "deploring the old 'have people'") his ludicrous exclamations ("Oh Puck-like theme!" "School of thought!").[17] His foolishness, intermittently silly and grievous, culminates in an experimental composition titled "Erection 9," performed at the Pig's Out concert, where the eminent composer is booed and his beloved Stradivarius is trashed. Douglas

Yandell laments disgustedly, "this lot positively disliked the idea of the difficult made to seem easy, seem anything at all, exist in any form . . . what they liked was the easy seeming easy" (*Girl*, 226). A richly textured, tragic satire, *Girl, 20* is one of Amis's finest novels: it evokes laughter and pity for desperate, bleak, and terrible lives.

The savage indignation of *Girl, 20* is surpassed by Amis's short satiric masterpiece, *Ending Up* (1974). This is a book, wrote John Betjeman, "to make one want to cut one's throat before getting old."[18] Tupenny-hapenny Cottage is the idyllic name of a grotesque hell inhabited by five connected but estranged septuagenarians. Worst of the sorry lot is Bernard Bastable, one of the vilest bastards in Amis's gallery of rogues, scheming to make his mates appear incontinent. Other members of this motley crew are somewhat less antipathetic, more truly pathetic. Adela is a woman capable of loving but denied the chance "as the result of her extreme ugliness."[19] Marigold speaks cutesy-wutesy baby talk, while aphasic George can't think of nouns. Ultimately, everyone in Tupenny-hapenny Cottage dies, victims of malicious fate and individual malevolence. Amis's language, always incisive, is here especially sharp, cutting like a butcher's knife close to the bone. Told in 40 brief, interlocking vignettes, *Ending Up* is a virtuoso performance, blending horrific comedy and satiric fervor. In this world, the quality of mercy is that the hateful Bernard, pursuing his cruel operations, brings about his own death before cancer claims him. Like Swift, another merciless satirist raging against the human condition, Amis provoked psychological diagnoses as well as literary criticism: "such a brutal and pointless apocalypse," opined the *New York Times*, makes it "difficult to avoid psychoanalytic speculations about the source of Mr. Amis's animosity." If we read *Ending Up* not as pathology but as satire, we may perceive how, as D. R. Wilmes comments, "we've been made to laugh, then made to realize that we've laughed with and at the dragon, who really isn't very funny. . . . The curse is directed at us, and it hurts."[20] *Ending Up* was a finalist for the Booker Prize.

The Alteration (1976) is a counterfeit world, defined by one of its character as "a class of tale set more or less at the present date, but portraying the results of some momentous change in historical fact."[21] What if the Reformation never had happened? Imagine instead that Henry VIII's elder brother survived and spawned heirs with Katherine of Aragon, the Spanish Armada won a Holy Victory, and Martin Luther became the crude Pope Germanian I. In the world thus altered, Europe is still a Holy Roman Empire, England a totalitarian state, Jean-Paul Sartre a Jesuit theologian and Heinrich Himmler a papal envoy. A neat twist on science fiction is that this is a world without science. The drama is largely from the view of Hubert Anvil, a boy soprano whom clergymen wish to "alter" for the greater glory of God. *The Alteration*, at first droll, becomes a pretty exciting adventure, and a somber meditation on fate and free will. It won the Campbell Award for the year's best science fiction.

Jake's Thing was violently attacked when it appeared in 1978. It now seems to provide more delights and richer contemplation than was originally thought possible. What infuriated many readers was the suspicion that the author endorsed Jake's male chauvinism. It is probably true but only partially pertinent that Jake Richardson is less than kind and more than kin with his author. In character traits as well as name, he recalls Amis's first hero (Jakes/Jim, Richardson/Son of Dick/Dixon). Jake's "thing" is, variously, his penis, his malaise, his impotence, his obsessions, and his particular, peculiar forte. He inhabits a deteriorating London that provides little comfort but much grist for his dismal, acute observations: "You got your coffee out of a machine, and having done that you couldn't get it back in again." Commuting to Oxford to lecture on Classics, Jake shares the train "with younger persons for the most part, undergraduates, junior dons, petty criminals".[22]

If life is unlivable, Jake is unlovable—an easily irritated, profoundly irritating figure: the satirist satirized. His favorite targets are women, especially intellectual women, yawn-enforcing academics, psychiatrists, Americans, snobs, the idle rich, the undeserving poor. "If there's one word that sums up everything that's gone wrong since the War, it's Workshop. After Youth, that is" (*Jake*, 149). Anyone who likes this sort of thing can enjoy *Jake's Thing*—without condoning Jake, who gives misogyny and misanthropy a bad name. The urgent intensity of Jake's perspective raises questions: Is Jake the source or the object of satiric scrutiny? Is he both? How sympathetic should one be toward what Jake himself terms his "contempt, hatred, weariness, and malicious hilarity" (*Jake*, 222)? *Jake's Thing*, like several Amis novels, works dually or contradictorily, as Malcolm Bradbury notes: "it can be seen as a punishment vested on a presumptuous male chauvinist and a hero of prejudice, but also as a reverse satire, assaulting the modernization of the world."

As often in Amis, the plot of *Jake's Thing* is less important than its examination of character under stress. Jake's marriage to Brenda is threatened by his sexual indifference and antipathy. Once a notable visitor of ladies, amusingly admired by Ernie the Porter as "a ruddy uncraned king you were" (*Jake*, 104), Jake at 59 has fallen mightily. He now undergoes grimly hilarious sexual therapy with stupid doctors who dispense smothering jargon and casually humiliating treatment (nudity in front of strangers, "nocturnal mensurators" to measure erections, if any, during sleep). In a speech supposedly espousing coeducation to the Oxford faculty, Jake abandons text and sense to present a resoundingly classical antifeminist diatribe even for a classicist: "They don't mean what they say, they don't use language for discourse but for extending their personality, they take all disagreement as opposition, yes they do, even the brightest of them, and that's the end of the search for truth which is what the whole thing's supposed to be about" (*Jake*, 210–211).

Eventually Jake realizes he is not incapable so much as uninterested, a recognition that enables him to forswear women forever:

Jake did a quick run-through of women in his mind, not of the ones he had known or dealt with in the past few months or years so much as all of them: their concern with the surface of things, with objects and appearances, with their surroundings and how they looked and sounded in them, with seeming to be better and to be right while getting everything wrong, their automatic assumption of the role of injured party in any clash of wills, their certainty that a view is the more credible and useful for the fact that they hold it, their use of misunderstanding and misrepresentation as weapons of debate . . . their fondness of general conversation and directionless discussion, their preemption of the major share of feeling, their exaggerated estimate of their own plausibility, their never listening and lots of other things like that, all according to him (*Jake*, 285).

In determining that nasty things can be nicer than nice things, Jake repudiates Jim Dixon's pleasure principle and chooses to live outside the circle and beyond the pale. His wife Brenda, bailing out at last, gets her say, but however accurate her diagnosis of Jake's problems, it somehow isn't as *quotable* as Jake's excoriations. This book solidified Amis's reputation as a Tory terror and a truly difficult old sod. Even admirers of Amis connected this novel to the author's psyche: Malcolm Bradbury said that *Jake's Thing* was "written in what seems a masochistic rage." Short-listed for the Booker, *Jake's Thing* remains a vital novel, and a disturbing work likely to endure.

Stanley and the Women (1984) presents an even more odious viewpoint than *Jake's Thing*. According to widespread reports, this book so troubled female editors at U.S. publishing houses that it could not for some time find a publisher. Stanley Duke, a protagonist in dire straits, seems quite obviously unreliable, but his misogynist rantings were confidently identified with Kingsley Amis's personal views. (Included in this collection are several reviews of *Stanley and the Women*.) "The root of the trouble," says Stanley, is that "we want to fuck them, the pretty ones, women I mean. . . . And if you don't want to she fucks you up anyway for not wanting to. . . . [Women today] seem to feel they can get on with the job of fucking you up any time they feel like it. That's what Women's Lib is for."[23] Conspicuously missing from *Stanley and the Women* is the voice of any plausible female. All are ridiculous or unbalanced, especially Trish Collins, the psychiatrist treating Stanley's insane son Steve. Most of the story dramatizes the effects of Steve's mental illness on Stanley and his first wife, Nowell (Steve's mother); his second wife, Susan; and his mother-in-law Lady Daly. Like Swift's Gulliver, Stanley has had what feels to him like a blinding illumination—but as with Gulliver he may simply be blinded. A notorious passage in the novel is Dr. Nash's response to one of Stanley's rare moments of doubt: " 'Not enough of a motive?' His voice had gone very high. 'Fucking up a man? Not enough of a motive? What are you talking about? Good God, you've had wives, haven't you?' " (*Stanley*, 246–247).

The Old Devils (1986) is Amis at his best and most congenial. William Pritchard's review in the *New York Times* was headed "Amis Behavin'." The novel was awarded the Booker Prize and garnered enthusiastic praise. Certainly the tone of *The Old Devils* is less sardonic outrage than mellow equanimity, though it is by no means sentimental, and its female characters are treated more considerately and tenderly than its male figures. This broadened, richened, and deepened view rewards multiple readings and sustained consideration. The action begins with a return.

Alun Weaver, the BBC's professional Welshman, a "frightful shit," and his beautiful, appealing wife, Rhiannon, have retired from London's whirligig and returned to Wales, which, he declares, means "Many things grave and gay and multi-colored but one above all: I'm coming home . . . and the heart of a Welshman."[24] What it means really is an amazing amount of alcohol; Charles McGrath says, "Amis is to booze what DeQuincey was to opium."[25] The Weavers' return reactivates an extremely complicated history of sexual relationships; every male falls in love with Rhiannon and nearly every female is bedded or propositioned by the goatish Alun. *The Old Devils* is an ensemble without one dominating figure. The other sixtyish couples in South Wales are Charlie and Sophy Norris, Malcolm and Gwen Cellan-Davies, Peter and Muriel Thomas, Percy and Dorothy Morgan, and Garth and Angharad Pumphrey.

The Old Devils has an elegiac or autumnal tone, suggesting that life, even with abundant mortifications and inevitable infirmities, is not nearly so terrible as depicted in *Ending Up*. Still, no one could say the presiding old devil has gone soft. Here is bilious Alun in a pub: " 'What is the vintage port?' asked Alun. 'Port is a fortified wine from Portugal,' said the waiter, having perhaps misheard slightly, 'and the vintage port is made from—' 'I didn't ask for a bloody lecture on vinification, you horrible little man.' Alun laughed a certain amount as he spoke. 'Tell me the shipper and the year and then go back to your hole and pull the lid over it' " (*Devil*, 64). Drinking early and steadily, one old sod muses, "Soon it might cease to be one of those days that made you sorry to be alive" (*Devil*, 13). There is plenty of gloom and terror but withal a suprising degree of light and tenderness. Poor Peter Thomas may be too fat to cut his own toenails, and dear Rhiannon can't even remember the most exquisitely romantic moment of her former suitor's life, but one makes do with sharp toenails and dim memories. Like very few Amis heroines, including Jenny Bunn and Catherine Casement, Rhiannon remains attractive, decent, and wise. It's better for her that her husband drops dead. And the heroine is in a way eternized by Malcolm's adaptation of an old Welsh epic with an interpolated Rhiannon, Malcolm's tribute to "the only woman who'd ever cried for him" (*Devils*, 294). The story ends with Rhiannon in an improved situation, attending her daughter Rosemary's reassuringly lovely wedding. But Amis never lets any such consolation pass completely unexamined or unscathed. Peter remarks of Alun's sudden death, "Oh fabulous. . . . Well, that certainly softens the blow and no mistake. Blessing in disguise, really, looked at in that light" (*Devils*, 261). David Lodge says of *The Old Devils*, "Although the surface texture of the novel is amused and amusing, one feels that it is a very fragile integument covering an appalling abyss of pain, desperation, and anxiety ... not so far removed from the bleak vision of Samuel Beckett as it might think, or as Mr. Amis might like to think."[26]

Difficulties with Girls is the only book by Amis that revisits characters from an earlier novel. Here we return to, or rather follow, Jenny Bunn and Patrick Standish, who were mated and matched, equivocally, at the end of *Take a Girl like You*. Now it is seven years later, deep in the swinging '60s, or Amis's heart of darkness: they are still married, uneasily, with Patrick working in publishing and Jenny teaching part-time in a children's hospital. Older, wiser, sadder, unable to conceive the child she desperately wants, Jenny is the picture of "resignation, disappointment, and loneliness."[27] She continues to be an attractive and appealing person, almost saintly in her endurance and compassion. Patrick has fared much less well. He's easily, quickly bored, which provides him sufficient justification for adultery, and he mollifies his guilt by trying to manipulate Jenny into an affair she doesn't really want. Jenny's voice is sharp, clear, and potent, most markedly when she exposes Patrick's selfish games and manipulations.

Jenny speaks as it were with Fielding on her side or with comparable authority. Here she cites passages Patrick had marked in his copy of *Tom Jones*:

> "Uncanny, isn't it. Really gets you to a T. . . . I bet you imagined old Henry Fielding winking at you when he said that. But now for the clincher. It looks as though you've underlined it heavier than the others, but there's probably nothing in that. 'Though he did not always act rightly, yet he never did otherwise without feeling and suffering for it.' "

She adds, "So that's all right, isn't it, Patrick." When Patrick asks, "What am I to do," she replies, "Well, for a start you could try reading some different books" (*Girls*, 239).

Sexual relations, actions, feelings, and sufferings continue to be Amis's precious lode or mine field, and not because he has many funny things or only one boring thing to say. At times, his sense of the ridiculous is sublime indeed. Has anyone been more outrageously amusing about the cost of sex, what Patrick terms the "cock tax"? Here is Wendy Porter-King's postcoital blither and Patrick's reaction: " 'The sky is blue, and I feel gay.' She never knew how close she came to losing her front teeth for that. Taken off guard again, Patrick again spoke too quickly. 'Are you an American?' " (*Girls*, 120). Sex in Amis is often dear and rarely valuable. Difficulties with girls, or sex troubles generally, are endemic (in a porn shop, the clerk inquires, "was it bondage, sir?"). Another character who endures them, for quite different reasons, is Tim Valentine, a likable chap but a darling dodo flimflammed by his therapist into believing he must be suppressing his homosexuality. Another relationship under severe strain is that of the gay neighbors, where the fem member of the homosexual couple causes the difficulty, according to Erik, the butch member: "it's the clash between male and non-male that causes all the trouble. They're different from us. More like children. Crying when things go wrong. Making difficulties, just so as to be a person" (*Girls*, 256).

For me *Difficulties with Girls* is a good book, limited not so much by its imbalanced sexism or programmatic rigidity as by its relative lack of humor. It's a savage assault on male egocentricity and men's terrible treatment of women. In the end, Patrick's obliviousness cannot conceal the truth, even if it protects him from realizing it. Jenny has finally become pregnant. "How wonderful," he said. "For us both. . . . You clever little thing. . . . You've done it. Changed everything. You've saved us" (*Girls*, 276). Patrick is incorrigible and self-deluded, which even dear Jenny recognizes as she concentrates her loving attention on her child-to-be: "Jenny was happy. She was going to have him all to herself for at least three years, probably more like five, and a part of him for ever, and now she could put it all out of her mind" (*Girls*, 276). That's about as sad as anything one could say.

By the 1990s Amis had become, depending on one's values, either an English institution or an outrageous anachronism. Knighted in 1990, renowned or notorious, Amis continued to produce lively fiction regularly until his death in 1995. *The Folks That Live on the Hill* (1990) is a version of his life in his seventies, when, oddly but apparently satisfactorily all around, he moved into the home of his first wife, Hilly, and her third husband, where he found friendship, creature comforts, and quiet stability. The hero of *The Folks That Live on the Hill* is Harry Caldecote, a retired librarian content to be involved in the lives of family, friends, and acquaintances, mindful that while marriage has some advantages, "Many or even most of them . . . seemed to be at least adequately supplied by having one's widowed sister housekeep for one."[28] Shepherd's Hill in North London is jarring, cacophonous, reliably awful. Here lives a houseful of unhappy souls related or connected to avuncular Harry: The widowed sister is Clare; Fiona Carr-Stewart, an alcoholic; Bunty Streatfield, Harry's daughter, a gay woman separated from her husband, Desmond, and now involved with Popsy; Freddy Caldecote and his virago wife, Desirée, with no secrets or discretion; and Harry's son Piers. At the center of this circle is a recognizably Fieldingesque good man, Harry Caldecote—not only decent but actively benevolent. Or, to compare Harry to another eighteenth-century figure, he resembles Samuel Johnson, minding his Streatham menagerie of old, infirm, and pathetic people. More remarkable still, Harry's beneficence is recognized and appreciated. Though much of what Harry hears is infuriating, or confounding, or ridiculous (the pub keeper describes himself as "A dime breed. Dine out like the dinosaurs" (*Folks*, 35), and most people neither realize nor care how they sound, one thing Amis always affirms is the power of language. A telling contrast between early and late Amis is the comparison between Jim Dixon's game endurance of a hangover and Fiona's dreadful description of alcoholism.

The Russian Girl (1992) is the story of another unexceptionable, decent man, Richard Vaisey. Now in his forties, a professor of Russian literature in the London Institute of Slavonic Studies, Vaisey has been married for a decade to rich, loathsome Cordelia (pronounced by her as "Nggornndelia"). A fine twist is that the Gonerilian Cordelia, besides supporting Richard in the manner to which he has become accustomed, is terrific in bed. Their sex life reminds Richard of "a wartime Resistance chief in German occupied France and the local Gestapo commandant who, finding they shared a love of Mozart's operas, had met periodically to play the gramophone records under a mutual guarantee of safe conduct that was never broken."[29] Many good writers could labor a lifetime without producing such a sentence. With this awful human being, if she is a human being, Richard copes in Amisian ways: eventually Richard ceased noticing Cordelia's preposterously affected accent, "more than a couple of times a day, and for years had given up speculating what speech-sounds she might make if, for example, he were to creep up behind her and fire a loaded revolver past her ear" (*Russian,* 13). Into this volatile situation comes the Russian girl, Anna Danilova, a visiting Russian poet and dissident. Anna's mission is to organize English protest on behalf of her imprisoned brother, and of course to discombobulate Vaisey's life. He is deeply torn, not so much between desire and duty as between true love and authentic taste, for though Anna is a warm, lovable person, she is a wretched poet. Their love affair is dramatized with keen satire and affectionate warmth. What to do with his unbearable wife and his poetic principles, especially when Anna urges him to sign a petition falsely characterizing her as a major Russian poet, is Richard Vaisey's dilemma and our delight. His ordeal includes a farcical vengeance taken by his irate, forsaken wife ("Vug of, uzz haul," says Nggornndelia the areezdongrannd). *The Russian Girl* is a thoroughly enjoyable, admirable blend of humor and realism.

You Can't Do Both (1994) is by any standard a remarkable achievement, a novel I rate among Amis's top six or eight. Evidently if not frankly autobiographical, it is the story of Robin Davies. Like Amis, Robin grows up in a modest London suburb in the 1930s, excels at school, wins a scholarship to Oxford, pauses for military service in World War II, and returns to Oxford, marriage, and an academic career. What distinguishes *You Can't Do Both* is extraordinary precision in evoking that Jamesian quality of "felt life," the texture of daily experience, and a subtle, fascinating account of a sexually errant hero who usually means well and rarely does well for long. Partly because the novel is dedicated to Hilly, and partly because its details are so obviously autobiographical, one can't help seeing it as a sort of apologia, an interpretation I find ingratiating but inadequate to the book's complexities, as I argue in my contribution to this volume.

The Biographer's Mustache (1996) is Amis's last publication, and another artful use of and comment upon life. Amis had authorized a biography by an acquaintance named Eric Jacobs, and the results were a workmanlike life story and strained relations between author and subject. Typically, Amis's response was to make another novel, *The Biographer's Mustache,* zestfully caricaturing the rather dull biographer and satirizing even more savagely the pompous, second-rate author who is more devoted to aristocrats' parties than literary endeavors. There is also an engaging sexual triangle involving the author's decidedly U wife and the non-U, younger biographer. This is a thoroughly enjoyable and intelligent novel, treated shamefully by British reviewers, some of whom seemed impatient for Amis to hush and die like a good chap.

Amis published his *Memoirs* in 1991, and it is a great pity that it is not truly worthy of the author. Even by Amis's standards of provocative egocentricity it is an odd performance, a series of disconnected essays and portraits, with hardly anything on writing or his work. The Old Devil in his anecdotage does continue to entertain, exasperate, and appall. He discloses that Margaret Thatcher excited his amorous propensities. He debunks and dispatches nearly everybody he's ever encountered, with a few notable exceptions like Philip Larkin and Anthony Powell. He delivers some breathtaking hyperbole: "Freudianism has probably been instrumental in fewer deaths than Naziism or Marxism, though it is surely one of the great pernicious doctrines of our century with its denial of free will and personal responsibility."[30] Too often, though, his targets are fish in a barrel, famous people who are too cheap to stand drinks. When Amis aims his sights on ephemeral writers like Leo Rosten, he seems to be attacking mosquitoes with automatic weapons. There is precious little about Amis beyond his childhood and youth. He explains that "I have already written an account of myself in twenty or more volumes, most of them called novels" (*Memories,* xv).

Amis had always, or at least intermittently, acknowledged the connections between his personal experiences and his art: "All my heroes, and other principal figures, have a great deal of me in them."[31] But he also regularly insisted that readers naively overestimate the degree of identification between author and characters. He stressed that not only the heroes but any character may have bits or elements of Amis in them. What seems true and most important to a consideration of Kingsley Amis, humorist and moralist, is that rarely if ever is the voice or perspective of the protagonist, however powerfully presented, permitted unchallenged sovereignty; competing viewpoints rise and shine. Even when a figure such as Jim Dixon or Jake Richardson dominates the discourse, he is subject to irony or vulnerable to critique. If such made-up people are to some extent authorial agents, they are also vehicles of self-criticism. In his essay, "Real and Made-up People," Amis says, "by that very act of distancing, by projecting himself into an entity that is part of himself and yet not himself, he may be able to see more clearly, and judge more harshly, his own weaknesses and follies" [p. 25, this collection]. While that formulation may be too tidy and affable a version of more elusive, contrary personal reactions, it is a fairly complicated and nearly aptly equivocal comment on two things that will surely endure: human folly and the fiction of Kingsley Amis.

Notes

1. This introduction focuses on Amis's novels. Among his many other publications, several deserve mention. *New Maps of Hell* (1960/1961) is the series of science fiction lectures Amis delivered at Princeton. *My Enemy's Enemy* (1962) is a volume of seven short stories, most notably the title story, set (like others) in noncombatant military life. *Collected Short Stories* (1980) reprints 16 short stories, the best of which are drawn from *My Enemy's Enemy*. Another collection, *Mr. Barrett's Secret and Other Stories,* appeared in 1993. Amis published four volumes of poetry: *Bright November* (1947), *A Case of Samples: Poems 1946–1957, A Look Round the Estate: Poems 1957–1967,* and finally *Collected Poems 1944–1979*. Amis also wrote feisty, engaging literary criticism, available in *What Became of Jane Austen? And Other Questions* (1970) and in the larger *Amis Collection: Selected Non-Fiction 1954–1990*. Other novels by Amis include *The Egyptologists,* written in 1965 in collaboration with Robert Conquest, which depicts contemporary Englishmen who form a "Metropolitan Egyptological Society" as a front to escape their wives and chase other women. There are sundry complications, some labored farce, a de rigueur reversal, and many better books by Amis. *Colonel Sun* is a James Bond adventure published under the pseudonym of "Robert Markham" in 1968. Amis plays Ian Fleming with evident delight, considerable finesse, and cheerful gloominess: "No, said Bond again. We're prisoners. But let's enjoy our captivity when we can" (*Colonel Sun* [London: Jonathan Cape, 1968], 147). *Russian Hide-and-Seek* (1980) imagines England 50 years after being occupied and subjugated by the Soviet Union. *The Crime of the Century* (1987) was first published as a summer-holiday serial in six installments in *The Sunday Times* in 1975. It is a run-of-the-mill "tec yarn." *The Riverside Villas Murder* (1973) recreates and spoofs detective stories. It grips and tickles quite successfully. Peter Furneaux, like the author, lives in South London in 1936, a period and place rendered fully and fondly. As in his earlier genre pieces, Amis adds an intensely metaphysical and psychological dimension to the generic format, so that *The Villas Murder* becomes a painful coming-of-age for 14-year-old Peter.
2. Kingsley Amis, "Laughter's to Be Taken Seriously," *The New York Times Book Review,* (July 7, 1957), 1. Hereafter referred to as *Laughter*.
3. Garnet Bowen's tribute to Fielding in *I Like It Here*.
4. Amis, *Laughter* (July 7, 1957), 1.
5. ———, *Lucky Jim* (New York: Viking Compass, 1958), 158. Hereafter referred to as *Lucky*.
6. Henry James, in the preface to *The Princess Casamassima* (New York: Charles Scribner's Sons, 1908), xiv.
7. Amis, *That Uncertain Feeling,* (London: Penguin, 1985), 60. Hereafter referred to as *Feeling*. Speaking of women's breasts, Amis and his characters speak frequently of women's breasts. In a 1975 interview with Dale Salwak, Amis remarks that he and Jim Dixon "have taken a lot of stick and a lot of bad mouthing for being Philistine, aggressively Philistine, and saying, 'Well, as long as I've got me blonde and me pint of beer and me packet of fags and me seat at the cinema, I'm all right.' I don't think either of us would say that. It's nice to have a pretty girl with large breasts rather than some fearful woman who's going to talk about Ezra Pound and hasn't got large breasts and probably doesn't wash much" (Dale Salwak, An Interview with Kingsley Amis).
8. ———, *I Like It Here* (London: Penguin, 1968), 167. Hereafter referred to as *Here*.
9. ———, *Take a Girl like You* (London: Penguin, 1962), 160. Hereafter referred to as *Take*.
10. He bears a family resemblance to another fat Englishman stateside, John Self in Martin Amis's *Money: A Suicide Note* (New York: Viking, 1984).

11. ———, *One Fat Englishman* (London: Penguin, 1966), 10. Hereafter referred to as *One*.
12. Dale Salwak, in "An Interview with Kingsley Amis," in this volume.
13. Clive James, "Kingsley Amis—A Profile," *The New Review* 4 (July 1974), 25.
14. Amis, *The Anti-Death League* (New York: Harcourt, Brace, 1966), 193.
15. ———, *I Want It Now* (London, Jonathan Cape, 1968), page 37. Hereafter referred to as *Now*.
16. Malcolm Bradbury, " 'No, Not Bloomsbury': The Comic Fiction of Kingsley Amis," in this volume.
17. Amis, *Girl, 20* (New York: Harcourt, Brace, Jovanovich, 1972), page 86. Hereafter referred to as *Girl*.
18. Cited by Dale Salwak in *Kingsley Amis: Modern Novelist* (New York: Harvester, 1992), 187.
19. A. R. Wilmes in "When the Curse Begins to Hurt: Kingsley Amis and Satiric Confrontation," in this volume.
20. Amis, *Ending Up* (London: Jonathan Cape, 1974), 13.
21. ———, *The Alteration* (New York: Carroll & Graf, 1988), 26.
22. ———, *Jake's Thing* (London, Hutchinson, 1978), 98. Hereafter referred to as *Jake*.
23. ———, *Stanley and the Women* (New York: Summit Books, 1985), 254. Hereafter referred to as *Stanley*.
24. ———, *The Old Devils* (New York: Summit Books, 1987), 42. Hereafter referred to as *Devils*.
25. Charles McGrath, "Amis Lite," in this volume.
26. David Lodge, "The Modern, the Contemporary, and the Importance of Being Amis," in the volume.
27. Amis, *Difficulties With Girls* (New York: Summit, 1989), page 267. Hereafter referred to as *Girls*.
28. ———, *The Folks That Live on the Hill* (London: Penguin, 1991), 14. Hereafter referred to as *Folks*.
29. ———, *The Russian Girl* (New York: Viking Penguin, 1994), 115. Hereafter referred to as *Russian*.
30. ———, *Memoirs* (London: Penguin, 1992), 117. Hereafter referred to as *Memoirs*.
31. ———, "Real and Made-up People," in this volume.

Works Cited

The introduction refers to the following books by Kingsley Amis. Unless otherwise specified, all quotations are from these editions and are identified in the introduction by parenthetical numerals.

Amis, Kingsley. *Bright November*. London: Fortune Press, 1947.
———. *A Case of Samples: Poems 1946–1957*. New York: Harcourt, Brace, 1957.
———. *New Maps of Hell*. New York: Harcourt, Brace, 1960.
———. *My Enemy's Enemy*. London: Victor Gollancz, 1962.
———. *A Look Round the Estate: Poems 1957–1967*. London: Jonathan Cape, 1967.
———. *Colonel Sun*. London: Jonathan Cape, 1968.
———. *The Green Man*. London, Cape, 1969.

———. *What Became of Jane Austen? And Other Questions*. New York: Harcourt, Brace, 1971.
———. *The Riverside Villas Murder*. London, Jonathan Cape, 1973.
———. *Collected Poems 1944–1979*. New York: Viking, 1980.
———. *Collected Short Stories*. London: Hutchinson, 1980.
———. *Russian Hide-and-Seek*. London: Hutchinson, 1980.
———. *That Uncertain Feeling*. London: Penguin, 1985.
———. *The Crime of the Century*. London, J. M. Dent, 1987.
———. *Amis Collection: Selected Non-Fiction 1954–1990*. London: Hutchinson, 1990.
———. *Mr Barrett's Secret and Other Stories*. London: Penguin, 1994.
———. *You Can't Do Both*. London: Hutchinson, 1994.
———. *The Biographer's Moustache*. London: Flamingo, 1995.
Amis, Kingsley, with Robert Conquest. *The Egyptologists*. London: Jonathan Cape, 1965.

ESSAYS AND ARTICLES
◆

Real and Made-up People

KINGSLEY AMIS

All fiction is autobiographical in the sense that its writer cannot truly invent anyone or anything, can only edit his experience, and cannot, poor fellow, represent ideas that have never entered his head. Let us at once discard this trifling and tautological sense, and notice the plain distinction between action based on what the writer has made up and that based on what has actually happened to him. The distinction is not always sharp, but in practice we usually know where we are. Treatment of character is the surest guide.

The second kind of writer only arrived on the scene about 1900. We are told that Dickens put something of his father into Mr. Micawber, but he is not writing about his father. Maggie Tulliver is rather the same sort of person as George Eliot, but the latter is not writing about herself in *The Mill on the Floss,* nor about what actually happened to her, and Dorothea Brooke is not to any interesting extent the same sort of person as she. (Mr. Casaubon may look like a different case, one I will return to.) Then D. H. Lawrence started writing about himself, people he knew and what there was of what had actually happened to him, and his knowing or unknowing heirs are all around us today. They have raised the ghosts of long-dead Philistines who thought the poet a liar and history the only truth, and Katherine Mansfield is called "the most autobiographical of writers" in unadorned commendation (admittedly on television).

This is not a polemical piece; we have plenty of room for two, or two dozen, kinds of novelist. But the autobiographical kind works under severe limitations. The writer whose direct experience gives him one satisfactory novel (as opposed to a short or a very short story) in fifty years is very lucky. The rest of the time, thinness, repetitiousness, poverty of incident, scarcity of character supervene. If, in life, his marriage breaks down, he takes off with somebody else, has difficulties with her and with his children and finally returns home, or stays away, he has little hope, even with the aid of a fictitious charwoman or taxi-driver here and there, of writing about that experience and those people and coming through with a novel. As my friend George MacBeth put it to me the other day, such a novelist is simply not doing enough.

Copyright © 1973 Kingsley Amis. Reprinted by kind permission of Jonathan Clowes Ltd., London, on behalf of the Literary Estate of Sir Kingsley Amis.

The writer who makes things up is on the face of it much freer. I make things up, make my characters up, not out of superior virtue but through something deeper than conscious choice. I did once, out of laziness or sagging imagination, try to put real people on paper and produced what is by common consent my worst novel, *I Like It Here*. There were fictitious characters and incidents in it too, and it is only those that I dare to allow to cross my conscious mind nowadays. Real people are interesting enough, but everybody is what he does, and to portray a man doing what he actually did do means holding up the whole show while he does it. By what is either a paradox or a truism, the closer the likeness of the real interesting person, the less interesting he will be in the novel.

I learnt my lesson in the course of setting out to repeat my mistake. Old Jock MacDonald, I thought (the name and all details are changed)—here is somebody so unconsciously funny that I must "put him into a book." But I liked Jock and could not offend him; so he became Welsh instead of Scotch, an architect instead of a stockbroker, a bachelor instead of a married man. And then, as the plot took shape, I needed Jock to do things he not only had not actually done, but never would have done, so there was very little left of him in the result. Later Jock told me he had particularly enjoyed the portrayal of that Welsh architect fellow. Had he seen? Had he not seen? Most likely he had seen without knowing he had seen.

So where, since those days, do those characters come from? Me, in the first instance. All my heroes, and other principal figures, have a great deal of me in them. No doubt the heroes, at least, show some family likeness, but I am not writing about different, or similar, bits of me. Nor, incidentally, am I writing about me mixed up, as camouflage or for fun, with some real person. "Who were you getting at in that television chap in your last one? Robin Frost? David Day?" Nobody; I made him up.

But to resume: even intelligent readers, even those who might consciously reject the concept of fiction as experience with style sauce, much overestimate the degree of identification between author and central character. I treasure the memory of being introduced to the amiable Marghanita Laski not long after the publication of my first novel, *Lucky Jim*. On hearing my name, she looked at me and about her in something not far from panic. She was wondering which I would do first: pour my pint of bitter over her or assault her sexually. To this day, on hearing that I was born in South London, people will murmur that they always thought I was a Yorkshireman; Jim in fact came from Lancashire, but only a close reading shows that.

Either origin would have done to produce the distancing that, through that deep instinct, I felt I needed: he must not come from anywhere near London, teach English, be married, admire Mozart, be much too law-abiding —or cowardly—to appear drunk on the lecture platform or hijack a professor's taxi, as in my own case. And, again incidentally, to polish up my non-autobiographical claims, the whole basic situation of that novel was clear in my mind before I ever thought of teaching at a university, let alone had started to do so.

Yes, but there is still some sort of identification: all my heroes start from me and in a sense stay with me, even when there are half a dozen of them occupying the same book, as in *The Anti-Death League*. This bond is at least as strong when the protagonist is unpleasant. Roger Micheldene of *One Fat Englishman* is, at least in intention, unlike me in various radical ways, starting with his gluttony about food, a substance my own gluttonies do not touch (curries excepted). I strongly disapprove of nearly everything Roger is and does, and yet the critic who wrote, "I can't help feeling that the author likes the character," had seen the truth, not that it is a very surprising one. We all like people we disapprove of: one of the injustices of life that at the same time help to make it bearable. And it is doubly hard to dislike one's child. That worn and sentimentalising metaphor does still give a hint of the strength of the attachment in question.

The novelist's heroes, or central characters, are clearly meant to do more than just go round being close or distant relatives of him. As between him and them in the first place, they are vehicles of his self-criticism—an important function of poetry too. By that very act of distancing, by projecting himself into an entity that is part of himself and yet not himself, he may be able to see more clearly, and judge more harshly, his own weaknesses and follies; and, since he must know that no failings are unique, he may be helped to acquire tolerance for them in others. In the second place, if the novel comes off at all, the reader will perhaps accompany the writer in some parallel process of self-discovery.

But that is still not enough; in an age that increasingly likes to view art as occupational therapy for the artist, it may even be too much. What about the character working in the novel? For me, the novel works on the character, at any rate rough-hews the character. It is not the case that a fully-formed hero goes stalking about in search of situations in which he can be effectively arrogant or incompetent or spiteful or pathetic or even decent, though he may very likely fall as if by chance into a couple of such in the course of being written about. The central situation comes first in every sense.

Here I must be unabashedly personal to show what I mean. *Lucky Jim* originally quickened in the womb of time when I spent a few minutes in the senior common-room of a provincial university (not Swansea). I thought at once, "Christ, somebody ought to do something about *this*." What followed can most easily, and accurately, be put in note form. University shags. Provincial. Probably keen on culture. Crappy culture. Fellow who doesn't fit in. Seems anti-culture. Non-U. Non-Oxbridge. Beer. Girls. Can't say what he really thinks. Boss trouble. Given chores. Disasters. Boring boss (a) so boring girl (b). Nice girl comes but someone else's property. Whose? etc.

This may be too articulate or logical and in the wrong order here and there, but not in the wrong order overall. Those who remember the novel will see that a large amount of Jim's character is already there, stated or implied, and reflection may suggest that even what could seem quite accidental quirks of behaviour are logical extensions of that same character. The various faces Jim makes to himself, for instance, are the covert protests and tension-reducers of a man in enemy territory without effective allies. Not that I saw them as that when I first thought of them; it took a critic to point the connection out to me. So much of all this takes place at some non-conscious level that almost any account of it must be riddled with unintended rationalisations and false links.

Jim, and *Jim,* took literally years to emerge even half-formed from those depths. Not practice but good fortune saw to it that, on one later occasion, the situation-cum-character complex appeared in a twinkling. I was in search of a taxi in Tottenham Court Road, saw one with its light on, hailed it, saw that a small brown man nearer it had done the same, cursed, was astonished when it passed the brown man and stopped at my side. I got in without demur, but a voice not my own was saying at top volume in my head, "Turn round and go back and pick up that other chap, you racialist!" So was born Sir Roy Vandervane of *Girl, 20,* and his randy girlfriend who would have to be there to give the incident an edge, and his views, and the fix he would be in and what he would do, and, somehow or other, the knowledge that he would be hero but not narrator.

I suspect that the "creation" of minor characters is subject to the same kind of process, though with them there is often a sense of wider choice, or the illusion of it. Here, the novelist may well start from a real person, as George Eliot may have started Mr. Casaubon from Mark Pattison. But then he became Mr. Casaubon, because he had to do things Mark Pattison did not do. I read (parts of) the recent long correspondence in the *Times Literary Supplement* about whether or not Pattison "was meant to be"—or even "was" Casaubon—or the other way round—with incredulity. Even if it were a real question, any answer could have been of no more literary interest than some supposed identification of Shakespeare's Dark Lady. George Eliot *made up* Casaubon, and Pattison, to compare great things with small, went the way of Jock MacDonald.

One last run of personal examples: about halfway through writing *I Want It Now,* I found I needed a character who was rich, boring, revolting, rude, egotistical, stupid and a figure of fun, needed him for a vital turn in the plot: to compete almost successfully with the hero as a suitor of the heroine. He (Student Mansfield by name) was already there, had been hanging about the place for dozens of pages, passing himself off as a mere illustration of the awful kind of people who surrounded the heroine. A little later, I found I needed another character for another vital turn in the plot: to assist in the public humiliation of the heroine's mother. He (Bill Hamer by name) had been about the place even longer, pretending to be no more than an illustration of the awful kind of people who surrounded the hero. In each case, nothing had to be trimmed from the figure as he had already taken shape, and very little added.

A third character in that novel, an even more minor character, on the scene for a mere ten pages altogether, is my favourite in anything I have written, George Parrot by name. Trying to regard each as a real person, I am fonder of James Churchill in *The Anti-Death League,* see Brian Leonard in that same book as a much more decent man, would far rather have a drink (no more, thank you) with Patrick Standish of *Take a Girl Like You.* But George, who is as unreal a person as any of the others is or started as, remains my favourite because, in making him up, I thought I was for once cutting quite free of the demands of the plot. All he had to do, I thought, was be rich, disclose some information and make his car available at a crucial point.

So it seemed I tried to make George, got to the end of making George, a fool at first sight but formidable very soon thereafter, chivalrous, vengeful, sensitive, cynical, hot-tempered, snobbish, naïve, distrustful, intelligent, lazy and acutely aware of linguistic niceties. Not, of course, that I had compiled any sort of list of traits and ticked them off as each was supposedly realised; George simply turned out to be such a person. But did he? After I had quite done with him, I saw that he had to be everything he was, except perhaps linguistically aware; at that point, ordinary, authorial fears of being unentertaining may have taken over, though I doubt it. I probably value George because, longer than anyone else, he kept me in the dark about what he was doing in my book.

It does rather look as though the freedom I attributed to the non-autobiographical novelist is indeed illusory. But, if he is confined, he is at least confined by something outside the narrow twists and turns of his own real existence. How that something comes into being I have very little idea. The process may be neither grand nor significant but it is rather mysterious.

Kingsley Amis and the Situation of the Novel

BERNARD BERGONZI

A writer who has established a comparable reputation to Angus Wilson's in the last fifteen years is Kingsley Amis: like Wilson's, his fiction is marked by an acute comic sense, a finely responsive eye and ear for social nuance, concern about the difficulties of behaving decently, and an intermittent sense of nightmare. Admittedly these qualities, which occur in Amis's fiction in roughly the order in which I have set them down here, assume a different pattern of frequency in Wilson's work; one does not regard him primarily, as one still tends to regard Amis, as a comic novelist. Even so, to describe Amis in this way may surprise those who still think of him only as the author of *Lucky Jim* and a founding father of the Angry Young Men. But it is over fifteen years since *Lucky Jim* came out, and in that time Amis has published seven more novels, a collection of short stories and two books of poems, together with critical studies of science fiction and the writings of Ian Fleming. One thing that this sizeable œuvre makes clear is that the comic spirit in Amis's work has become steadily less dominant since Jim Dixon made his carefree debut. Amis admirably refused to repeat his initial success (although a quite recent novel, *I Want it Now,* does look uncomfortably like an attempt to do just that) in a way which disconcerted readers who were eager for more of the same thing, and who were disinclined to pursue the interesting mixture of comedy and seriousness in Amis's subsequent fiction. There are also those who claim that Amis is not worth anyone's serious attention, that *Lucky Jim* is at worst a crude and childish farce, and at best no more than a faded relic of the taste of the early fifties. Nevertheless *Lucky Jim* remains, for me, a comic masterpiece, the funniest English first novel since Anthony Powell's *Afternoon Men* appeared in 1931, and a work that is surpassed only by the very best of Waugh and Powell. One would like to think that it will retain its appeal, just as their early books have, even when its sociological implications, of which so much was made in the fifties, have dwindled into a historical footnote.

On its first appearance *Lucky Jim* was assumed to inherit the comic manner of the early Waugh; but some readers also related it to famous works of Edwardian comic fiction, like Wells's *Kipps* or Arnold Bennett's *The Card.* (Jerome K. Jerome's *Three Men in a Boat* is another possible antecedent.)[1]

Reprinted from *The Situation of the Novel* (London: Macmillan, 1970), 161–174, with the kind permission of Bernard Bergonzi.

This critical perspective seems to me largely correct, although it needs a certain qualification. In the remarks about fiction scattered about his reviews and other critical writings—conveniently summarised in Ruben Rabinovitz's book—Amis has shown himself to be assertively anti-modern, anti-experimental, anti-cosmopolitan, to at least the same degree as Snow or William Cooper; indeed his tastes are narrower, since he does not share Snow's admiration for Proust. Yet his way of writing fiction suggests that he has undergone, no matter how unwillingly, the influence of the Modern Movement, at least in his reliance on linguistic effect; style functions actively in Amis's comic writing, as it does in Powell's. John Gross has remarked on the way in which many of Amis's comic effects originate in his linguistic finesse rather than in the comedy of situation. Throughout his novels there is a steady preoccupation with language; we see it in characters such as Julian Ormerod in *Take a Girl Like You* or Harry Bannion in *I Like it Here,* compulsive and singular verbalisers, who are regarded by their creator with considerable affection. In *That Uncertain Feeling,* John Lewis, in the midst of his troubles, finds time to reflect on his children's speech habits: "'Yas, she said. This lowering of the *e*-phoneme is widespread, I've noticed, in childish dialect." In *One Fat Englishman* the Danish philologist Ernest Bang keeps up a running commentary on the way the other characters talk. This concentration on verbal effects shows that Amis believes that fiction, whatever else it may be made of, is also made of words; this implicit conviction places him as a post-Joycean novelist, and distinguishes him not only from Edwardian comic writers such as Bennett or Wells or Saki, but from contemporaries such as Snow or Cooper. The stylistic dimension in Amis has been discussed at some length by David Lodge in his book *Language of Fiction,* and he gives good reasons for seeing Amis as a novelist worth serious critical attention, no matter how flawed his output might be. Although Amis writes what can be regarded as a traditional, uncomplicated narrative, he differs from the Edwardians in his degree of concentration; there are no loose, low-pressure transitional passages of the kind that one finds in Wells or Bennett, and although Jim Dixon resembles their heroes, he also exhibits an exacerbated sensitivity akin to that of Stephen Dedalus.

Even in *Lucky Jim,* which remains the most light-hearted and innocent, and certainly the funniest, of Amis's novels, there are casual references that would seem savage if it were not for the tone and the stylistic controls which preserve it: Jim dreams of stuffing Professor Welch down the lavatory, or of beating him about the head and shoulders with a bottle until he explains why he gave his sons French names; at one angry moment he is tempted to push a bead up Margaret Peel's nose. In the later novels these fantasies of hostility and aggression are more frequent and less controlled. And traces of nightmare are quite apparent in Amis's other writings. His poems, which are mostly deft, glum and *borné,* afford some relevant insights: one thinks, for instance, of "The Box of Friends" and "Dirty Story" from *A Case of Samples,* or "Out-Patient" and "Nothing to Fear" from *A Look Round the Estate:*

> it's a dead coincidence
> That sitting here, a bag of glands
> Tuned up to concert pitch, I seem to sense
> A different style of caller at my back,
> As cold as ice, but just as set on me.

The latter volume also includes "Science Fiction," which explains Amis's own interest in that literary genre. This is one of Amis's best poems; the first stanza talks of the attraction of finding "simpler versions of disaster," like "a ten-clawed monster" or some other traditional horror; but the second stanza turns to contemporary apocalyptic imaginings:

> In him, perhaps, we see the general ogre
> Who rode our ancestors to nightmare,
> And in his habitat their maps of hell.
> But climates and geographies soon change,
> Spawning mutations none can quell
> With silver sword or necromancer's ring,
> Worse than their sires, of wider range,
> And much more durable.

One of Amis's own occasional ventures into science fiction, the story called "Something Strange" is a pure exercise in nightmarish mystification.

Nostalgia, which I see as the opposite pole to nightmare, is also evident, though in a more subdued form. In *Lucky Jim* the past is regarded as a matter for suspicion: Jim Dixon has no commitment to the history he is supposed to teach, and he loathes Professor Welch's bogus attempts to revive the past by means of handicrafts and madrigal singing. Indeed, when he is forced to give a public lecture on "Merrie England", Jim turns it into a virulent hymn of hate against all the more obvious forms of cultural nostalgia. Nevertheless Amis's attachment to a central thread of English insular nonconformism, and his distaste for cosmopolitan modernism, were sufficiently pronounced for Martin Green, in his book *A Mirror for Anglo-Saxons,* to place Amis in a select pantheon representative of the traditional English virtues, the other heroes being Lawrence, Leavis and Orwell. In so far as Amis's basic ideas about novel-writing are traditional—both as stated in his criticism and implicitly expressed in his fiction—then it is a tradition whose roots lie closer to the robustness and moral simplicity of the eighteenth century than to the high Victorian seriousness admired and to some extent imitated by Snow or Wilson. The point is made explicitly in Amis's third novel, *I Like it Here,* when Garnet Bowen, on visiting Fielding's tomb at Lisbon, falls into a vein of unexpected seriousness:

> Perhaps it was worth dying in your forties if two hundred years later you were the only non-contemporary novelist who could be read with unaffected and wholehearted interest, the only one who never had to be apologised for or

excused on the grounds of changing taste. And how enviable to live in the world of his novels, where duty was plain, evil arose out of malevolence and a starving wayfarer could be invited indoors without hesitation and without fear. Did that make it a simplified world? Perhaps, but that hardly mattered beside the existence of a moral seriousness that could be made apparent without the aid of evangelical puffing and blowing.

In *Take a Girl Like You* Amis seems to have turned to Richardson rather than Fielding for his inspiration: its plot is remarkably close to *Clarissa* in outline, and offers much the same kind of interest in a long-deferred rape. Will Patrick Standish, an engaging, rakish grammar-school master of thirty, succeed in laying the delectable Jenny Bunn, a virgin infant-school teacher, just down from the backward reaches of the North of England? In the end he succeeds, but not before a very long pursuit, and only when Jenny is drunk. *Take a Girl Like You* has many entertaining passages, but it is heavily padded, and it suffers from the incoherence at its centre. Patrick Standish is shown as an agreeable and gay fellow; he may be irascible and a bit promiscuous, but this is forgiven easily, just as it is with Tom Jones. Nevertheless the final rape is *not* a good thing to have done. Patrick feels badly about it, of course, but perhaps Jenny was really to blame for hanging onto her old-fashioned ideas about sex and giving him such a rotten time. The novel circles uneasily around these unresolved dilemmas, and the result is not merely ambivalence but moral and artistic incoherence. As a character Patrick is interesting, but not in focus. He is full of fears about cancer and impotence and death, which he tries to keep at bay by thinking about sex most of the time. He regards most of the world with unrelieved hostility, particularly the ugly or the tiresome: thus when driving in the rain he gets immense satisfaction when he is "lucky enough to send the greater part of a puddle over a sod in ragged clothes who was doing his level best to blow his nose into the gutter." Patrick and his friend Graham concoct an elaborate fantasy directed against Jenny's landlord, Dick Thompson; they imagine that Dick is naked and they are pursuing him with syringes filled with acid or a solution of itching powder; admittedly Dick's meanness and boringness are unpleasant characteristics, yet this seems an over-compensated reaction. "But bang's the way to get things done," writes Amis in the last line of his poem, "Mightier than the Pen," and the lesson is applied late in *Take a Girl* when Dick is wounded by a shotgun. The world of Amis's fiction is basically Hobbesian, where mutual hostility is the normal relationship between the inhabitants. Patrick, we have to assume, is verbally aggressive, obsessed and sexually attractive; yet we never see him objectively, for the author's sympathy covers him with a protective mantle of charm. To have made him fully convincing would have required a kind of characterisation closer to Stiva Oblonsky than to Tom Jones.

Yet although *Take a Girl Like You* is an imperfect and indeed annoying novel, it remains a remarkably interesting book. It is an incisive anatomy of the England of rising affluence in the late fifties, yet it is shot through with a sense of other values which are fast disappearing. In chapter 2 there is a striking paragraph, which not only characterises Jenny but sets out some of the dominant themes of the novel. In presenting Jenny's impressions Amis shows a remarkable mimetic sense, which recalls, even if it is not intended to, the consciousness of Gertie MacDowell in *Ulysses:*

> They had been walking slowly over to the corner of the playground, where a church of no particular coloured stone was to be seen on the far side of the road. The sight of it depressed Jenny. There was a lot about it that reminded her of what it had been like to go out for walks with her parents when she was a child. These walks now seemed to have always taken place on cloudy Sunday evenings at about this time of the year, they had always gone through a street where, so it was said (and she could well believe it), a famous mass murderer had done his stuff, and they had always ended up at her grandma's, where in semi-darkness—the old lady had not cared much for switching on what she called the electric—Jenny had had to keep Robbie quite while hymns of the sort that made you want to do away with yourself had been sung: *The King of Love My Shepherd Is* and *There is a Green Hill Far Away.* Over the road now an elaborately got-up notice-board advertised forthcoming attractions in gilt on black and a wayside-pulpit placard told her that there would not always be a tomorrow on which to do better than yesterday. A draught of cold air—the evenings were turning chilly about now—passed up her spine. She longed for the sight of cheerful modern colours, the cover of a new copy of *Woman's Domain,* the yellow or blue label of a record on the top twenty, somebody passing in scarlet jeans and luminous socks.

Young Jenny has left the dull and backward North, where her father is, appropriately enough, a hearse-driver, for the bright lights and gay consumer-goods of the corrupt and affluent South. She has left behind, however, not only the grime of decaying industrialism, but family pieties and evangelical religion. She sees these values—the traditional positives of Richard Hoggart's England—as wholly negative, remembered as hymns that made you "want to do away with yourself" and the gloom of her grandma's house, the whole picture haunted by the ghost of a famous murderer. Elsewhere in Amis's fiction, however, these values are treated in a more positive way: in *That Uncertain Feeling* they are embodied in John Lewis's admirable father, a colliery clerk; at the end of that novel John Lewis flees from the corrupt society symbolised by Mrs. Gruffydd-Williams to go back to the mining town where his father lives. This retreat into a grimy pastoral is not at all convincing, but it has affinities with the conviction expressed in Raymond Williams's two novels, *Border Country* and *Second Generation,* that a proper loyalty to the traditions of the labour movement is inextricably involved with having the right attitude to one's father. (Richard Hoggart has remarked that at twenty-five the mature scholarship boy should be able to smile at his father with his whole face (*Uses of Literacy,* 1957: p. 239).

In *Take a Girl*, however, Jenny puts all that behind her, and commits herself to a new and lively world, without a fixed sense of values: "people down her bothered less about there being a time and a place for everything than the people at home." On rereading, when one knows how the story will end, the novel looks like a prolonged proleptic elegy for Jenny's lost virginity, itself a symbol for traditional pieties. At one point an exasperated Patrick accuses her of harbouring nostalgic sexual fancies:

> There are two sorts of men today, those who do—you know what I mean—and those who don't. All the ones you're ever going to really like are the first sort, and all the ones those ideas of yours tell you you ought to like are the second sort. Oh, there wouldn't be any problem of temptation there. The problem would come on the wedding night. And on all the nights after that. There used to be a third sort, admitted. The sort that could, but didn't—not with the girl he was going to marry, anyway. You'd have liked him all right, though, and he wouldn't have given you any trouble trying to get you into bed before the day. The snag about him is he's dead. He died in 1914 or thereabouts. He isn't even going to turn up, Jenny, that bloke with the manners and the respect and the honour and the bunches of flowers *and* the attraction.

At the end of the novel a deflowered Jenny resignedly observes, "Well, those old Bible-class ideas have certainly taken a knocking, haven't they?" To which Patrick replies that, given a girl like her, it was inevitable. Jenny agrees, but the novel ends with the words, "But I can't help feeling it's rather a pity." The ideals of provincial rectitude give a last faint flicker before being lost for ever in the swinging scene of the top twenty and somebody's scarlet jeans.

The hero of Amis's next novel, the short and sour *One Fat Englishman*, is as far on in unpleasantness from Patrick Standish as Patrick was from Jim Dixon, though he has affinities with both of them. Roger Micheldene, the fat Englishman, is a publisher searching for literary talent in the neighbourhood of an American university. He is an old-world, upper-class Englishman with a classical education: he makes no secret of the way in which he despises Americans (and, for that matter, most Englishmen). He is a snuff-taker, a frank glutton—he reflects that "outside every fat man there was an even fatter man trying to close in"—and a fastidious connoisseur of cigars. His principal vices, in addition to greed, are lechery (frequently frustrated by circumstances) and anger. He is also a lapsed Catholic who at intervals prays in the Augustinian spirit of "Make me chaste, Lord, but not yet." Roger is both a snob and an oaf, with an instant line in gratuitous rudeness and no respect at all for anyone's feelings. Apart from a certain sympathy with Roger's fleshly failings, Amis's earlier nonconformist, *déclassé* heroes would certainly have loathed him. And so, one assumes, does Amis: at the end of the book Roger gets everything he has been asking for in the way of retribution. And yet the same ambivalence that was apparent in the treatment of Patrick Standish is even more apparent. If Amis does not endorse Roger's odious attitudes, they are not very energetically distanced or disowned. Although Kingsley Amis, as an enthusiastic supporter of the American cause in Vietnam, would not endorse Roger's anti-Americanism, it may well be that, in Amis's present rightist stance, some of Roger's generally anti-progressive sentiments may have caught up with him.

There are a number of ways in which *One Fat Englishman* amplifies the preoccupations of the earlier novels. One of them is the natural oppugnancy between man and objects, and another, closely related, is the idea that the organisation of the universe is not random, but that man and things are in the grip of a malign but perversely intelligent force. In this respect Amis is at the opposite pole to Alain Robbe-Grillet, who posits man and objects as existing in icy mutual indifference, in a cool, neutral universe without plan or design. The difference can, I think, be neatly shown in the different ways in which they are both interested in the minute delineation of material objects. Here, for instance, is a paragraph from *Jealousy:*

> The furnishings of this room are very simple: files and shelves against the walls, two chairs, the massive desk. On one corner of the latter stands a little mother-of-pearl inlaid frame with a photograph taken at the seaside, in Europe. A . . . is sitting on the terrace of a large café. Her chair is set at an angle to the table on which she is about to set down her glass.

And so on, with a detailed account of everything in the photograph, implicitly emphasising its total detachment from the observer. We can compare it with a passage from *Lucky Jim*. Jim Dixon is having breakfast in his digs, and is joined by his tough, silent friend Bill Atkinson:

> He halted contemptuously at his chair, clicking his tongue and sighing histrionically like one kept waiting in a shop. His dark, mysterious eyes ran round the walls, making leisured halts at each photograph, summing up adversely Miss Cutler's nephew in the uniform of a Pay Corps lance-corporal, Miss Cutler's cousin's two little girls, Miss Cutler's former employer's country house with a gig at the portico, Miss Cutler vehemently dressed as a bridesmaid in the fashions of the First World War. He was perhaps engaged in whittling down the huge volume of abuse evoked by each of these sights into four tiny toxic gouts of hatred, one for each photograph.

Amis, one must admit, is trying to be funny, whilst Robbe-Grillet is not. Yet one notices at once the marvellous accuracy of social observation that is Amis's principal strength as a novelist; how many of us have found in similar establishments, if not precisely those photographs, others scarcely distinguishable from them? And Amis's characteristic verbal irony is evident in the deliberate use of the cliché, "dark, mysterious eyes." But this passage also shows that while Amis can rival Robbe-Grillet in the precise delineation of objects, *his* objects do not exist in cold indifference to human beings; they are, rather, actively hostile to them, triggers to set off ever-present reserves of hatred and resentment.

As I have remarked, mutual hostility is the usual relationship between the inhabitants of Amis's world. And things join in enthusiastically on the side of their owners, like Professor Welch's car, where a broken spring rips open Jim's trousers, or the terrifying geyser in Dick Thompson's bathroom which intimidates Jenny Bunn in the opening chapter of *Take a Girl Like You*. Robbe-Grillet would, no doubt, regard this as deplorably superstitious, and in a way he would be right. For there is something profoundly animistic about Amis's universe: it may not contain a God, but its characters are constantly in the toils of a powerful and malign governing force. Patrick Standish refers to this as "Bastards' H.Q.," and this phrase seems to be a part of Amis's personal terminology. In *That Uncertain Feeling* John Lewis, swallowing a mouthful of tea-leaves after entertaining adulterous thoughts, reflects, "Life, that resourceful technician, had administered a typical rebuke." Dixon obtains a book he wants from a library "with almost sinister promptitude." A few pages later there is an elaborate example of this quasi-magical attitude. Jim, riding in Welch's car, sees a fat man walking with lustful intent towards two pretty girls at a pillar-box. A little later he notices a cricket match in which the batsman, another fat man, is violently hit in the stomach by a ball. Jim is "uncertain whether this pair of *vignettes* was designed to illustrate the swiftness of divine retribution or its tendency to mistake its target." It would be paradoxical to call Amis a religious writer; but he is undoubtedly a superstitious one.

In my chapter on American fiction I referred to the possibility of imagining the real world as though it were a novel, in which case the "plot" of conventional fiction would seem like a "plot" of a conspiratorial kind, full of sinister coincidences and parallels. Thomas Pynchon, as I have suggested, is interested in this possibility; and John Barth has said that "God wasn't too bad a novelist, except he was a Realist." Amis, too, has become increasingly interested in it. He has, for instance, a poem called "The Huge Artifice," in which human history, seen as a novel written by God, is subject to a long and adverse review:

> Enough of this great work has now appeared
> For sightings to be taken, the ground cleared,
> Though the main purpose—*what it's all about*
> In the thematic sense—remains in doubt.
> We can be certain even at this stage,
> That seriousness adequate to engage
> Our deepest critical concern is not
> To be found here. First: what there is of plot
> Is thin, repetitive, leaning far too much
> On casual meetings, parties, fights and such,
> With that excessive use of coincidence
> Which betrays authorial inexperience.

In *One Fat Englishman* Roger Micheldene finds himself being manipulated in a quasi-fictional way by his arch-enemy, the young hipster novelist Irving Macher, who intervenes in Roger's life like an accredited representative of Bastards' H.Q., making things difficult for him out of disinterested curiosity.

The preoccupation with malign purpose is fully exploited in *The Anti-Death League*, which is Amis's blackest and most obsessed novel, with few pretensions to the comic. In this novel Jim Dixon's cheerful conviction that "nice things are nicer than nasty ones" is replaced by a death's head and the traditional injunction *memento mori*. The world is irretrievably in the power of Bastards' H.Q., which is now starkly identified with God. The story opens with three army officers going to visit another officer who is undergoing a cure for alcoholism in a mental hospital. One of them, James Churchill, is struck by a girl he sees in the grounds of the hospital, and with whom he subsequently falls in love. Most of the action is divided between the hospital and the near-by army camp, both institutional settings where life is inevitably depersonalised, and in *The Anti-Death League* Amis has written a more generalised kind of fiction, with more clearly symbolic implications, than in any of his earlier novels. There is still a trace of sardonic humour, and his ear remains alert to the placing details of individual speech; but Amis has here abandoned the incisive social mimicry, the memorable responses to the specificity of a person's appearance or the look of a room that have previously characterised his fiction. The military establishment may, in one way, recall the army stories in *My Enemy's Enemy*, but it is less human and more portentously sinister; it also recalls "Special Welfare Research Station No. 4" in "Something Strange" from the same book. This anonymous establishment, concealed by a security blanket, reflects those aspects of the real world which already overlap with the more serious forms of science fiction: blank, closely guarded structures, which could equally well conceal a centre for experimenting with new and ever more frightful kinds of warfare, or for the liquidation of human beings. There is an apocalyptic passage by Marcuse which seems relevant here:

> Auschwitz continues to haunt, not the memory but the accomplishments of man—the space flights; the rockets and missiles; the "labyrinthine basement under the Snack Bar"; the pretty electronic plants, clean, hygienic and with flower beds; the poison gas which is not really harmful to people; the secrecy in which we all participate. This is the setting in which the great human achievements of science, medicine, technology take place; the efforts to save and ameliorate life are the sole promise in the disaster. (*One-Dimensional Man*, 1964: p. 247)

The apocalypticism is not misplaced. Although the camp in *The Anti-Death League* seems, at first, to house nothing more alarming than a new type of atomic tactical rifle, we subsequently learn that some of the officers there are being trained for a project called Operation Apollo, which is designed to meet a threatened Chinese invasion of India by spreading a particularly horrible form of plague through the Chinese army (Apollo being, in addition to his more familiar roles, the god of disease). At the end of the book we learn, in fact, that the whole scheme was an elaborate bluff, to deceive the Chinese intelligence and force them to abandon the invasion. At a superficial level *The Anti-Death League* is something of a spy story, in the morally depressed, double- and treble-crossing vein of Len Deighton and John Le Carré, with little to remind us of Amis's admiration for Ian Fleming, apart from a spot of implausible gunplay. But this level is very superficial indeed, and the thriller elements are so feebly handled as to be easily disposed of; in essence *The Anti-Death League* is a novel of ideas, and its theme is the inevitability of death. The ideas dominate the action, and tend to lead us away from the novel as "felt life" towards the moral fable, or even the Platonic dialogue (there is a remarkable amount of slightly flat conversation in the book). This novel differs from Amis's previous books in not being told through the consciousness of one or two central characters; here we follow the fortunes of several at once: the young lieutenant, James Churchill; Catherine Casement, the girl he falls in love with; the chaplain, Ayscue; the ineffectual security officer, Brian Leonard; and the alcoholic, Max Hunter. Churchill is, however, closest to the moral centre of the narrative, and what is most noticeable about him is that he has the two-dimensional thinness of an allegorical hero; as a novelistic character he remains wholly unrealised. Until he meets Catherine, Churchill has been loyally performing his duties as a serving officer, including his part in Operation Apollo. But Catherine, who has been driven temporarily insane by a sadistic husband, and who is soon to be threatened by cancer, makes him conscious of the universal reality of arbitrary suffering and death. He revolts angrily against whatever God could have made such a world, and harries the unfortunate clergyman Ayscue with bitter questions (although Ayscue, as we are to discover, is a secret unbeliever). An anonymous anti-religious poem sent to the camp magazine, and a subversive circular inviting the formation of an "anti-death league," show that Churchill is not alone in his sentiments.

Churchill's attacks on God are not new—for they occur, in similar terms, in the Book of Job—and as a response to the casual cruelty of the universe they are not unjustified; at least, as attacks on the detached manipulator of a purely rationalistic theology. The Christian concept of an incarnate God who himself underwent suffering and death may afford a greater insight into, though not a solution of, the mystery of suffering, although Amis has expressed his dissatisfaction with Christ in his poem "New Approach Needed." But such protests are themselves religious; they are meaningful only if they come from a believer, for whom reconciling belief in a good and all-powerful God with the manifest evil of the world is likely to be most agonizing—as Dostoievsky, for instance, showed. An atheist would not waste his time in railing against "God." In a television interview after the novel was published Amis suggested that by "God" he intends a metaphor for "the way things are." To revolt against the nature of reality, and in particular the inevitability of death, is an extreme but tenable philosophical position, and one which has been explored by Camus, but the only way in which the revolt can be fully expressed is by an Empedoclean suicide. Amis does not carry the argument so far, though he perhaps approaches it when Churchill decides to have nothing more to do with the army, the supreme death-dealing mechanism, and retires to his bed in a cataleptic state, from which only Catherine can arouse him.

The other anti-death crusader, Max Hunter, is a more interesting character. As a practising homosexual and an alcoholic, he recalls the monumental self-indulgence of Roger Micheldene. When we first see him in a hospital bed he is surrounded by all the characteristic amenities of earlier Amis heroes:

> He was lying back against advantageously arranged pillows within reach of various comforts: non-glossy illustrated magazines, paperback novels on the covers of which well-developed girls cringed or sneered, a comparatively hardback work on how to win at poker, a couple of newspapers folded so as to reveal half-completed crossword puzzles, a tin jug containing a cloudy greyish fluid, packets of French cigarettes and an open box of chocolates.

Later, Max confesses: "I've never been particularly keen on having to think about things. And on things that make you think about things. You know, like music and all that. Love's another one. I joined the Army specially to get away from them." But, he continues, the imponderable realities of love and death have caught up with him, and shown the insufficiency of this carefree view of the world. So he, too, is in revolt against death and God. *The Anti-Death League* is enough of a moral fable for one to feel that Amis is close to the attitudes of his anti-death crusaders, so that Max Hunter's rejection of his past can be seen as a valediction to Lucky Jim. One is not, of course, certain whether Amis would endorse all the ideas expressed in the novel; as, for instance, when Churchill tells Catherine: "If there were no such thing as death the whole human race could be happy." The Tithonus myth is surely a potent reminder of the ills of immortality. The essential difficulty Amis faces in *The Anti-Death League* is that it is intensely concerned with the questions that lead to tragedy—death, cruelty, loss of every kind—while lacking the ontological supports—whether religious or humanistic—that can sustain the tragic view of life. And to this extent it is representative of contemporary attitudes.

Considered as an anti-theological novel of ideas, *The Anti-Death League* is provocative and intelligent, even though it may ultimately lack the courage of its philosophical convictions. It represents Amis's immersion in the nightmare that flickers at the edges of his earlier fiction. It is a brave book, for in writing it Amis surrendered a great deal of the novelistic territory in which he is most at home, and got very little in exchange; considered as a novel in the everyday sense, *The Anti-Death League* is feeble and unconvincing, and the supererogatory spy story jars against the novel's deeper preoccupations. Yet it is a work of impressive seriousness and marks a crucial point in Amis's development.[2]

Notes

1. One critic who pointed out the parallel was John Holloway, in *The Charted Mirror* (1960). In an essay on Amis published in the *London Magazine* for January 1964 I dismissed any possible similarities between his work and Edwardian fiction; wrongly, as I now think.

2. Amis's latest novel *The Green Man* is thematically a direct development from *The Anti-Death League*. There is the same obsession with death and evil, and an explicitly religious frame of reference. The book is entertaining though ambiguous in its attempt to combine the ghost story and the moral fable.

The Modern, the Contemporary, and the Importance of Being Amis

David Lodge

As far as English literature is concerned, the important modern novelists were James, Conrad, Joyce, Lawrence, Forster, and Virginia Woolf. They are still the important modern novelists, although all but Mr. Forster are dead, and most of them had written their best work by 1924. "Modern" has, in fact, become a qualitative rather than a chronological term; and to any one with an elementary knowledge of recent literary history it is obvious that, in Britain, "the contemporary novel is no longer 'modern' "[1]—whether one takes "contemporary" to include the work of authors such as Graham Greene or Evelyn Waugh, who established their reputations before the war (as does the critic I quote), or restricts the term to those writers who have emerged in the last decade.

This distinction between the modern novel and the contemporary novel is a commonplace of current criticism; but it has been given a new dimension by Stephen Spender in his recent book, *The Struggle of the Modern* (1963), in which he emancipates "contemporary" as well as "modern" from a chronological significance. He observes that all through twentieth-century literature there have been two kinds of writers. On the one hand there are those who engage in a direct, prosaic way with their social and political circumstances, and who, if they protest against these circumstances, do so with some degree of revolutionary optimism in the possibility of amelioration, an amelioration that literature can help to bring about. These Spender calls "contemporaries," and he includes among them such writers as Shaw, Wells, and Bennett. Orwell too, though Spender does not, I think, mention him, would fit very well into this category.

On the other hand there are those who distrust or detest their circumstances, to the extent of abandoning the hope of acting on them in a practical way. Instead, such writers seek a radical transformation of conventional forms of communication, through which to express poetically an inner crisis of sensibility, a crisis which often manifests itself in the search for a tradition which

Reprinted from *The Language of Fiction: Essays in Criticism and Verbal Analysis of the English Novel,* by David Lodge. Copyright © 1966 by Columbia University Press. Reprinted with permission of the publisher.

has been lost or broken. These are "moderns": T. S. Eliot, James Joyce, and Virginia Woolf, for example. Spender draws attention to various significant literary quarrels and controversies which illuminate the differences between these two groups: the quarrel between Wells and James; Virginia Woolf's attack on Bennett, and Lawrence's on Galsworthy. Lawrence, of course, as Spender acknowledges,[2] does not fit neatly into the "modern" category. Like all such broad classifications, Spender's distinction between the "modern" and the "contemporary" is open to qualification; but I think it is a useful one.

It is clear that, today, the English novel is dominated by "contemporaries," in Spender's sense. While the "modern" tradition is carried on in America, France and Germany, in Britain only William Golding, Iris Murdoch, and Lawrence Durrell, of the novelists who have produced any considerable body of work, can be intelligibly placed in this perspective, and then with important reservations.

It is possible to take two views of this situation. Anyone who has had a literary education, who has experienced the work of the great moderns instructed by such education, will tend to feel dissatisfied with "contemporary" work, with its thinness of texture, its lack of complexity, its simplifications and evasions, its indifference to significant form. Spender quotes a spokesman for the other side, Miss Pamela Hansford Johnson:

> The full retreat began in the years between 1922 and 1925, the years that saw *Mrs. Dalloway* and *Ulysses*. It was the retreat into perimetal experiment in verbal and oral techniques: and it pretty well dominated the English novel for the next thirty years. . . . What shrivelled away was any contact between man and society. "Bloomsday" is Bloom's alone, and no one else's. Mrs. Dalloway, if she is anything at all, is merely herself, walking in her own dream of a private world. Everything dropped away from the novel but Manner: all that counted was how the thing was done, and never the thing itself . . . the followers of Virginia Woolf and James Joyce began to lead the novel into sterility. And nobody saw anything wrong in that inexorable process. Why not? Because life was growing too hard for writers to face, and quiet lay in impotency alone.[3]

This passage focuses in a very revealing way the characteristic assumptions which divide the contemporary from the modern. It recapitulates some of the arguments used by Wells against James, and it reverses the attack of Virginia Woolf on Bennett: the assumptions behind Miss Hansford Johnson's remarks are just those which, in Virginia Woolf's view, exerted such a deadening influence on Bennett's work.

The centre of this continuing controversy is the meaning of the word "life." Life, to the contemporary, is what common sense tells us it is, what people *do:* go to school, fall in love, make political choices, get married, have careers, succeed or fail—in Miss Hansford Johnson's words, "man and society." To the modern, Life is something elusive, baffling, multiple, subjective—in Virginia Woolf's famous words, "a luminous halo, a semi-transparent envelope surrounding us from the beginning of consciousness to the end."[4] The contemporary tends to have a fairly simple faith in the competence of ordinary prose discourse to represent "life"; the modern feels the need to employ an elaborate linguistic craft to fix and identify the uniqueness of every individual experience.

The analysis of language is in fact the most precise way of indicating the difference between modern and contemporary writing—and of suggesting the loss involved in shifting from the former to the latter. Let us compare two passages, one from James Joyce's *A Portrait of the Artist as a Young Man* (1916), and the other from John Braine's *Room at the Top* (1957).

> A girl stood before him in midstream, alone and still, gazing out to sea. She seemed like one whom magic had changed into the likeness of a strange and beautiful seabird. Her long slender bare legs were delicate as a crane's and pure save where an emerald trail of seaweed had fashioned itself as a sign upon the flesh. Her thighs, fuller and softhued as ivory, were bared almost to the hips, where the white fringes of her drawers were like feathering of soft white down. Her slateblue skirts were kilted boldly about her waist and dovetailed behind her. Her bosom was as a bird's, soft and slight, slight and soft as the breast of some darkplumaged dove. But her long fair hair was girlish: and girlish, and touched with the wonder of mortal beauty, her face.[5]

> Parked by a solicitor's office opposite the cafe was a green Aston-Martin tourer, low-slung, with cycle-type mudguards. It had the tough, functional smartness of the good British sports car; it's a quality which is difficult to convey without using the terms of the advertising copywriter—made by craftsmen, thoroughbred, and so on—I can only say that it was a beautiful piece of engineering and leave it at that. Pre-war it would have cost as much as three baby saloons; it wasn't the sort of vehicle for business or for family outings, but quite simply a rich man's toy.
>
> As I was admiring it a young man and a girl came out of the solicitor's office. The young man was turning the ignition key when the girl said something to him and after a moment's argument he put up the windscreen. The girl smoothed his hair for him; I found the gesture disturbing in an odd way—it was again as if a barrier had been removed, but this time by an act of reason.
>
> The ownership of the Aston-Martin automatically placed the young man in a social class far above mine; but that ownership was simply a question of money. The girl, with her even suntan and her fair hair cut short in a style too simple to be anything but expensive, was as far beyond my reach as the car. But her ownership, too, was simply a question of money, of the price of the diamond ring on her left hand. This seems all too obvious; but it was the kind of truth which until that moment I'd only grasped theoretically.
>
> The Aston-Martin started with a deep, healthy roar. As it passed the cafe in the direction of St. Clair Road I noticed the young man's olive linen shirt and bright silk neckerchief. The collar of the shirt was tucked inside the jacket; he wore the rather theatrical ensemble with a matter-of-fact nonchalance. Everything about him was easy and loose but not tired or sloppy. He had an undis-

tinguished face with a narrow forehead and mousy hair cut short with no oil on it. It was a rich man's face, smooth with assurance and good living.[6]

Both passages describe a crucial moment of awareness in the life of a young man. For Stephen Dedalus, the young girl is a means of release from the spiritual apathy he finds himself in after the sexual and religious crises of adolescence. The vision of the young girl, arousing neither desire nor disgust, is a symbol of the liberating, recreating power of art, to which he can now dedicate himself with confidence. The language in which the vision is described is intricately wrought, with meticulous attention to sound and cadence, as well as to imagery and diction. The moment is sublime, and the language is correspondingly heightened above the level of ordinary prose by "poetic" devices of repetition and inversion. Running through the passage is imagery of birds ("seabird," "crane," "feathering," "down," "dovetailed," "darkplumaged," "dove"), which is a thematic feature of the whole novel, linked with the myth of Daedalus and Icarus, and the daring, transcending power of art which this myth embodies. The language, here, is in the best sense "artificial," and the vision is in the literary sense "romantic." Yet no falsification or distortion is involved. The girl who wears, for Stephen, such a magical aura, remains a solid figure of flesh and blood. She also wears "drawers": the mundane word is accommodated in the passage without drawing any kind of ribald response. To sum up: Joyce has contrived to select and arrange his words beautifully *and* truthfully.

The passage from *Room at the Top* is longer, but much looser and thinner in texture. The words do not give and receive life and meaning to and from each other. The only metaphors in the passage are the dead metaphors of cliché, like "rich man's toy" and "mousy hair." It must be said, of course, that the author is limited to the kind of vocabulary that can plausibly be put into the mouth of his not particularly sensitive or articulate narrator. But failure in the fundamental literary task of realization in language cannot be justified by an appeal to literary decorum. The narrator's admission that he is using the language of the advertising copy-writer is a revealing one, and he resorts, later, to the same jargon: "The Aston-Martin started with a deep, healthy roar."

The interest of the passage is mainly of a factual or journalistic kind: in many readers it will evoke a mild "thrill of recognition" (it certainly did in my own case, when I first read it), because of its acute observation of physical details which act in our society as an index to class and status. Young men of means in England today *do* dress like that; young men of the narrator's class, on the other hand, put oil on their hair, wear the collars of their open-necked shirts *outside* their jackets, and so on. But perhaps one should use the past tense, for the passage has already dated. And as the significance of such details fades still more, the lack of verbal realization in the passage will become still more evident. For even if some learned scholar of the future devotes a footnote to explaining the significance of a vintage Aston-Martin as a status symbol in the early 1950's, there is little in the text which will assist the reader to see and feel the car in his imagination. The reader must himself have observed an Aston-Martin of the appropriate period in order to compensate for the vagueness of the writer's description.

There are, of course, significant differences between the experiences rendered in these two extracts, as well as between the ways in which they are rendered. Joyce is writing about a rather special young man having a rather special experience. Stephen Dedalus is the artist, whose activity enriches and intensifies experience both for himself and for others, and the passage is itself art in action. Braine's Joe Lampton, as his name aggressively asserts, is a very ordinary young man, having a very ordinary experience: envy. It is easy to identify with him—perhaps too easy. We are invited to indulge ourselves vicariously in a gratifying, but essentially demoralizing emotion. The narrator goes on to recognize and reject his envy, but there is nothing in the *language* which places, defines, and evaluates the emotion, as there would have been, I think, if Joyce had treated the same episode.

I hasten to add that I choose to compare John Braine with Joyce because Braine is a reasonably representative contemporary novelist, and not because he is the best challenger our period can muster. The latter motive would not, however, have seemed quite so bizarre six or seven years ago as it does now; and this reflection leads one to consider the very different problems presented to criticism by the modern and the contemporary writer respectively.

The modern disturbs us with the novelty of his vision and his technique; and since most critics and readers are basically conservative, he tends to be despised or neglected in his youth and maturity, and revered in his old age or when he is dead. The contemporary, on the other hand, is usually much more immediately accessible to the general public. He may attack them, but he does so in terms they understand, in the language they use, appealing to experiences they share. The danger with the contemporary—and it is as much a danger for himself as for the critic—is that, seduced by the superficial thrill of recognition, or by the coincidence of the writer's values with our own, we may overestimate him.

On the other hand it is idle to suppose that we can completely detach a "contemporary" work from its manifold and intricate connections with the culture and society it describes—particularly if that culture and society is our own. The importance of being Amis, for instance, is in a sense greater than the sum of his works, individually considered as autotelic works of art. His novels, stories, poems, reviews, even *obiter dicta* reported in the newspapers, have focused in a very precise way a number of attitudes which a great many middle-class intellectuals of the post-war period find useful for the purposes of self-definition. If I may cite myself as an example, I suppose that, as a Roman Catholic, I could scarcely be more distant from Amis's view of the eternal verities. And yet I constantly experience a strange community of feeling with him, and find that he speaks to me in a way that the great classic novelists do not, in an idiom, a tone of voice, to which I respond with immediate understanding and pleasure and without any conscious exertion of the kind required by critical reading.

Not long ago I was discussing with a friend the unlikelihood of my being able to buy a bigger house. "I haven't got much capital," I explained. "In fact, capital's a rather silly word for what I've got." This second sentence, I realized even while my friend was laughing, was a characteristic Amis locution. His books had taught me that trick of turning a humorous irony simultaneously upon my own pretensions and the pretensions of language itself—in this case the pretensions of commercial language to fit a particular financial situation, my situation.

And here, I think, there is some encouragement for the literary critic. For it suggests that Amis's use of language may be as inextricably part of his importance as Henry James's was of his, or Joyce's was of his. That James and Joyce are vastly *more* important writers need not disturb us. They use language more ambitiously and with more consistent success; Amis less ambitiously and with less consistent success; Braine less and less still. The important thing is that they can all be measured on the same scale—the creative use of language. For ultimately language is the only tangible evidence we have for those vast, vague, unreliable qualities which we bandy about in literary criticism: "truth to life," "moral seriousness," "psychological insight," "social awareness."

The question presents itself: if James's and Joyce's uses of language produce higher works of literary art than Amis's, why doesn't he follow their example? It is a good question, and I shall suggest later that Amis is well aware of its force. The obvious answer—"It's too difficult"—is only partly true. I shall touch on other possible answers later. At this point I wish to emphasize that Miss Hansford Johnson's dissociation of "the way a thing is done" from "the thing itself" is a critical fallacy; that ultimately we can no more dissociate form from content in the work of a "contemporary" than we can in the case of a "modern," temptingly easy though it may appear to do so; that ultimately we are driven back to the critical examination of the verbal structures, large and small, of which a work of literature is composed. It seems to me that Amis is the most interesting and rewarding of our contemporaries just because he accepts this theory of literature, although he remains keenly aware of the circumstances which divide him from those writers—the great moderns—who seem to have put it most whole-heartedly into practice. If this is the case it may be useful to consider *Lucky Jim,* for instance, as a literary artefact rather than as a sociological document, a vehicle of protest or the dossier of a new culture-hero.

Lucky Jim is a comic novel, and Amis is an admirer of Henry Fielding, the first great English comic novelist. It might be profitable therefore to look at Fielding's definition of the function of this form. It deals, he says, in the preface to

Joseph Andrews, with the Ridiculous, and the only source of the true Ridiculous is affectation, which has two aspects: vanity and hypocrisy. Like most comic literature Fielding's comedy is based on contrast, on incongruity: between, for instance, people's actions and their motives. Fielding shows this contrast by commenting on particular situations from his omniscient elevation over the story. The omniscient method, however, is very difficult to employ today, when there are few agreed moral assumptions, and where many people (including Amis) cannot accept the idea of an omniscient God. Although Amis works with contrasts, the consciousness which registers them is not the novelist's, but Jim Dixon's. The mind which sees the incongruity of appearance and reality, of what the Welches and Margaret hypocritically or vainly think themselves to be—sensitive, cultured intellectuals—and what they really are—boring, selfish zombies—this mind is Jim's, and only at a second remove the novelist's. If this were the whole story—if Jim were merely a register of other people's false appearances, Jim might be merely a boorish prig, as many of his literary offspring are; but the saving grace of Amis's novel is that Jim himself is involved in the comedy, he is himself a hypocrite. Temperament and circumstances impel him to present a false appearance to the world: he pretends to be a keen young scholar and university teacher, when in fact he detests his subject and despises his colleagues; he pretends to be sympathetically attracted to Margaret when in fact he finds her plain and tedious. What makes us value Jim above the other shams in the novel is the fact that at least he admits he is a sham, chiefly to himself; and that his deceptions—as in the case of Margaret— can reflect a kind of moral decency as well as a kind of moral cowardice.

The main source of comedy in the novel is therefore the contrast between Jim's outer world and his inner world. While he tries—not very successfully—to show the outer world the image of an industrious, respectable well-mannered young man, his mind seethes with caustic sarcasm directed against himself and others, with fantasies of violence done to enemies, of triumph for himself. So that the characteristic appearance of a page of Amis is an exchange of pedestrian dialogue broken by long paragraphs of densely woven comic and satirical commentary emanating from the hero's consciousness. The first chapter of *Lucky Jim* exhibits this pattern. Jim and his Head of Department, Professor Welch, are strolling through the university grounds, and Welch is describing an amateur concert:

> "There was the most marvellous mix-up in the piece they did just before the interval. The young fellow playing the viola had the misfortune to turn over two pages at once, and the resulting confusion . . . my word. . . ."
>
> Quickly deciding on his own word, Dixon said it to himself and then tried to flail his features into some kind of response to humour. Mentally, however, he was making a different face and promising himself he'd make it actually when next alone. He'd draw his lower lip in under his top teeth and by degrees retract his chin as far as possible, all this while dilating his eyes and nostrils. By these means he would, he was confident, cause a deep dangerous flush to suffuse his face.

> Welch was talking yet again about his concert. How had he become Professor of History, even at a place like this? By published work? No. By extra good teaching? No in italics. Then how? As usual, Dixon shelved this question, telling himself that what mattered was that this man had decisive power over his future, at any rate until the next four or five weeks were up. Until then he must try to make Welch like him, and one way of doing that was, he supposed, to be present and conscious while Welch talked about concerts. But did Welch notice who else was there while he talked, and if he noticed did he remember, and if he remembered would it affect such thoughts as he had already? Then, abruptly, with no warning, the second of Dixon's two predicaments flapped up into consciousness. Shuddering in his efforts to repress a yawn of nervousness, he asked in his flat northern voice: "How's Margaret these days?"
>
> The other's clay-like features changed indefinably as his attention, like a squadron of slow old battleships, began wheeling to face this new phenomenon, and in a moment or two he was able to say: "Margaret."
>
> "Yes; I've not seen her for a week or two." Or three, Dixon added uneasily to himself. (I)[7]

This passage lays down the basic contrast between Jim's inner and outer worlds, and shows Jim aware of the hypocrisy involved in preserving the discrepancy. It also involves him in uncertainty about other people's inner lives, which may well be as secret as his own, an uncertainty reflected in the anxious multiple questions which characterize Jim's thought: "But did Welch notice who else was there while he talked," etc. Welch and Jim fail to connect, not only with each other, but with themselves. Jim has to "flail" himself into an appropriate response, "shudders" in the effort to suppress an inappropriate reflex. Welch's responses are characterized by images of inefficient locomotion—battleships in the quotation above, and shortly afterwards, when his mind has wandered from the subject of Margaret, a motor car: "After no more than a minor swerve the misfiring vehicle of his conversation had been hauled back on to its usual course" (I). (Welch's execrable driving of his awful car is of course an important attribute of his character, and plays a vital part in the plot—his failure to get Christine to her train in time at the end of the novel unites her with Jim.) The rest of this paragraph gives a good illustration of Jim's fantasy-life of violence:

> Dixon gave up, stiffening his legs as they reached, at last, the steps of the main building. He pretended to himself that he'd pick up his professor round the waist, squeeze the furry grey-blue waist-coat against him to expel the breath, run heavily with him up the steps, along the corridor to the Staff Cloakroom, and plunge the too-small feet in their capless shoes into a lavatory basin, pulling the plug once, twice and again, stuffing the mouth with toilet-paper. (I)

Of interest in this passage is the use of the definite article rather than the possessive pronoun—"*the* furry grey-blue waistcoat," "*the* breath," "*the* too-small feet," "*the* mouth." This might be interpreted merely as a means of avoiding grammatical confusion with the possessive pronoun, which refers to Jim, in "*his* professor"; but this could have been avoided equally well by substituting "Welch" for "his professor." The phrasing of the passage has in fact a positively expressive function. "His professor" draws attention to the power-relation existing between Welch and Jim, which the latter seeks to reverse in fantasy. The definite articles have the effect of de-personalizing Welch, so that the violence of Jim's fantasy is comically acceptable; while at the same time they call attention to and render ridiculous and objectionable the particular physical features of Welch's appearance.

One of the characteristic devices by which the inner and outer worlds are linked in the novel is, as the first extract illustrates, the way in which Jim picks up a phrase, usually a cliché—his own or another person's—and mentally subjects it to sceptical scrutiny: " '. . . my word.' . . . Quickly deciding on his own word . . ." " 'I've not seen her for a week or two.' Or three, Dixon added uneasily to himself." One of the most amusing variations on this device is Jim's response to Welch's question about the title of his learned article, where, in a manner that I have already suggested is characteristic of Amis, he turns a withering scorn simultaneously upon his own pretensions and upon the pretensions of scholarly language (and therefore upon the scholars who use it):

> It wasn't the double-exposure effect of the last half-minute's talk that had dumbfounded him, for such incidents formed the staple material of Welch colloquies; it was the prospect of reciting the title of the article he'd written. It was a perfect title, in that it crystallised the article's niggling mindlessness, its funereal parade of yawn-enforcing facts, the pseudo-light it threw upon non-problems. Dixon had read, or begun to read, dozens like it, but his own seemed worse than most in its air of being convinced of its own usefulness and significance. "In considering this strangely neglected topic," it began. This what neglected topic? This strangely what topic? This strangely neglected what? His thinking all this without having defiled and set fire to the typescript only made him appear to himself as more of a hypocrite and fool. "Let's see," he echoed Welch in a pretended effort of memory: "oh yes; *The Economic Influence of the Development in Shipbuilding Techniques, 1450 to 1485*. After all that's what it's . . ." (I)

This conversation takes place in Welch's car, and the continuation illustrates how Amis exploits stylistic incongruity for comic purposes in a very traditional way (it goes back to Fielding and mock-heroic). Here the precise ordering of events, and the cool, measured tone, contrast with the potentially disastrous nature of the situation:

> Unable to finish his sentence, he looked to his left again to find a man's face staring into his own from about nine inches away. The face, which filled with

alarm as he gazed, belonged to the driver of a van which Welch had elected to pass on a sharp bend between two stone walls. A huge bus now swung into view from further round the bend. Welch slowed slightly, thus ensuring that they would still be next to the van when the bus reached them, and said with decision: "Well, that ought to do it nicely, I should say." (I)

Jim is well aware of the way his inner life compensates for the unsatisfactory nature of his outer life. "The one indispensable answer to an environment bristling with people and things one thought were bad was to go on finding out new ways in which one could think they were bad" (XIII). His face-pulling, rude gesturing, and practical joking are only an extension of this strategy—an attempt on Jim's part to give some physical expression to his inner life of protest. After finishing his hated, hypocritical lecture on "Merrie England," for instance:

> With a long, jabbering belch, Dixon got up from the chair where he'd been writing this and did his ape imitation all round the room. With one arm bent at the elbow so that the fingers brushed the armpit, the other crooked in the air so that the inside of the forearm lay across the top of his head, he wove with bent knees and hunched, rocking shoulders across to the bed, upon which he jumped up and down a few times, gibbering to himself. A knock at his door was followed so quickly by the entry of Bertrand that he only had time to stop gibbering and straighten his body. (XX)

For most of the action this kind of behaviour remains secret and furtive, and much comedy derives from Jim's attempts to keep it secret. But as long as he does so, he is involved in evasion, compromise, hypocrisy. The issues of the novel can only be resolved when Jim wills his inner life to coincide with his outer life. The crisis comes when he fights Bertrand and knocks him down:

> After some seconds, Bertrand began moving about on the floor, but made no attempt to get up. It was clear that Dixon had won this round and, it then seemed, the whole Bertrand match. He put his glasses on again, feeling good; Bertrand caught his eye with a look of embarrassed recognition. The bloody old towser-faced boot-faced totem-pole on a crap-reservation, Dixon thought. "You bloody old towser-faced boot-faced totem-pole on a crap reservation," he said. (XX)

At last thought and speech, the inner and the outer worlds coincide. From this point everything starts to go right for Jim. He loses his job, but gets a better one; he loses his girl (Margaret) but gets a nicer one. Jim ceases to be a guilty hypocrite and reaps his reward. We can accept this solution because the comic mode of the novel permits the kind of simplifications that make it possible: that people are as simply nasty as Bertrand, for instance, or that people like Bertrand will fall down when you hit them, or that their falling down will solve problems.

Amis's determination to discard such simplifications in subsequent novels has placed an increasing strain on his literary resources. The language of *That Uncertain Feeling* is unmistakably Amis's, but it has a new sobriety of purpose:

> Feeling a tremendous rakehell, and not liking myself much for it, and feeling rather a good chap for not liking myself much for it, and not liking myself at all for feeling rather a good chap, I got indoors, vigorously rubbing lipstick off my mouth with my handkerchief. (VII)

Like Jim Dixon, John Lewis is trying to reconcile his inner life with his outer life, but in an opposite direction. Whereas Jim struggled to make his outer life realize his inner life of protest and romantic self-fulfilment, John Lewis seeks to discipline his outer life by the moral principles of his inner self. "It wasn't so much doing what you wanted to do that was important, I ruminated, as wanting to do what you did" (VII). Amis doesn't seem to have reckoned with the new technical problems posed by such a radical shift of viewpoint; and those parts of *That Uncertain Feeling* which are most obviously continuous with *Lucky Jim*—such as Lewis's impersonations of a plumber and a Welsh peasant woman—though amusing in themselves, seem least integrated with the total movement of the book. The dilemma of the hero is worked out in terms (his adultery, his repentance, his renunciation of the "fixed" library job, and his flight to the colliery town of his childhood, away from the wicked sophisticated set of Aberdarcy) which make the comic elements in the novel seem mere embellishments, as well as appearing too simply moralistic in themselves. By this latter remark I mean that the assertion of the value of poor but honest provincial domesticity cannot survive the habit of rigorous, sceptical scrutiny generated by Amis's use of language. He has armed us to reveal his own deviations into wishful thinking.

Amis is in fact involved in a kind of philosophic problem concerning ethics; and his language, which makes subtle discriminations in simple and superficially clumsy prose, often reminds one of modern philosophical discourse. Amis's epistemology, as it manifests itself in his novels, is profoundly anti-metaphysical, determinedly positivist, nearly solipsist. "Nice things [are] nicer than nasty things"; and only the individual can decide what is nice and what is nasty for him. The axiom comes from *Lucky Jim* (XIV), but John Lewis endorses it in the cultural and social spheres—preferring *Reveille* to English Literature, for instance, and the new privileged classes to the old privileged classes ("at least this crowd had enough bad taste to drink brandy before 'dinner' ")—though he rejects it in the moral sphere. But if nice things are nicer than nasty things, and there are no sanctions external to oneself, why not indulge in everything nice, "do what one wants to do" and let "wanting to do what one does" follow naturally?

This is the argument of Patrick Standish, the hero of *Take a Girl Like You*. If *Lucky Jim* sends one back to Fielding, the later novel reminds one of

Richardson. It is essentially a modern *Clarissa*. Richardson's novel, it will be remembered, opposes the puritan values of the angelic heroine to the libertinism of the satanic rake, Lovelace, who abducts her and, after a long-drawn-out struggle, rapes her while she is drugged. Amis's Clarissa is Jenny Bunn, who leaves her decent, traditional Northern background to take a job in the decadent pink-gin-and-Jaguar world of Southern England. There, Patrick Standish, the Lovelace of the story, lays prolonged siege to her virginity, and eventually seduces her when she is disarmed by drink. Not only are the plot-lines similar, but both novels feature long debates between the protagonists on the subject of sexual morality, and both are remarkable for their final ambivalence—as if an openness to experience prevented both authors from coming down conclusively on the side they wanted to come down on: Clarissa and renunciation in Richardson's case, Patrick and hedonism in Amis's.

Patrick's strategy is to try and convince Jenny that her belief in pre-marital chastity is an outmoded concept from which the moral and social content has long been hollowed out.

> "It's because you've had the kind of upbringing—very excellent in its way, I'm not saying anything against it—but it's the kind with the old idea of girls being virgins when they get married behind it. Well, that was perfectly sensible in the days when there wasn't any birth control and they thought they could tell when a girl wasn't a virgin. Nowadays they know they can't and so everything's changed. You're not running any risk at all. But you've had that kind of upbringing and that's why you feel like this. Do you see? It's just your training."
> "Maybe it is, but that doesn't make any odds to me. I just don't care why I think what I do, it doesn't change anything. What about why you think what you do? There must be reasons for that too."
> "The difference is that I haven't got my ideas from anyone else, I've thought them out for myself."
> "So have lots of other people who don't think the same as you. Wherever you get your ideas from it doesn't make them any better."
> "At least mine work. Because they fit in with the way life's lived, which is more than yours do."
> "That remains to be seen. And fitting in's not the only thing." (IV)

Jenny can hold her own in this kind of debate about the epistemology of ethics, but she feels the force of Patrick's arguments because she generally shares Patrick's empirical discriminations between the nice and the nasty in life, and because her own faith in marriage as a solution to the sexual problem is disturbed by such portents as the ugly confessions of the drunken sailor beneath her window, the married lives of her friends, and the repulsive appearance of the mothers whose children she teaches. Patrick's position too, however—and this is both the strength and the weakness of the novel—is undermined by experience. His dedication to the physical life is troubled by obsessional fears of impotence, old age, and death, filtered through the characteristic mockery of Amis's slangy but intricate rendering of consciousness, in which the language restlessly coils back upon itself to qualify what has just been asserted, so that the protagonist, instead of progressing confidently, is driven further into doubt:

> All that type of stuff, dying and so on, was a long way off, not such a long way off as it had once been, admitted, and no doubt the time when it wouldn't be such a long way off as all that wasn't such a long way off as all that, but still. Still what? Well in the meantime, this cardiac business of his was obviously psychogenic, or—what the hell was that other—genic one?—neurogenic.... (XXIII)

This particular obsession of Patrick's reaches its climax in the macabre interview with Lord Edgerstoune, who draws an elaborate analogy between the sexual instinct and a battery which eventually runs out. Throughout *Take a Girl Like You* the comedy has a bitter, destructive quality, dissipating Patrick's commitment to the physical life. On the weekend debauch in London, the strip-clubs fail ludicrously to yield their expected gratifications, and the night spent with the demi-mondaine results in humiliation and guilt.

The issues of the novel, like the issues of *Clarissa,* hinge on the seduction of the heroine. In the handling of it one can see Amis twisting and turning in the impasse he has created for himself. The seduction itself, in all its furtive squalor, misery, and remorse, is brilliantly done—so brilliantly that it alienates Patrick from the reader. And yet his argument that it had to happen is in a sense true, because no alternative set of values is established in the novel which would make Jenny's preservation of her virginity meaningful. On the other hand the attempt at the very end to make the *loss* of her virginity meaningful is disastrous:

> She knew more or less what their future would be like, and how different it would be from what she had hoped, but she felt now that there had been something selfish in that hope, that a lot of the time she had been pursuing not what was right but what she wanted. And she could hardly pretend that what she had got was not worth having at all. She must learn to take the rough with the smooth, just like everybody else. (XXVII)

One misses, in the language of this passage, the reflexive, self-scrutinizing element which usually guarantees the sincerity of Amis's characters. If there was something "selfish" in Jenny's former hopes, is there anything selfless in her present position? Is she any nearer to pursuing what is right? Is it, in fact, possible, in the world of the novel, to "want" what is "right"? It seems that it is impossible, in which case Jenny's attempts to cheer herself up seem sentimental and evasive. As if aware of these considerations, Amis closes the novel on a note of helpless regret:

> "Well, those old Bible-class ideas have certainly taken a knocking, haven't they?"
> "They were bound to, you know, darling, with a girl like you. It was inevitable."
> "Oh yes, I expect it was. But I can't help feeling it's rather a pity." (XXVII)

It solves nothing of course, and when comedy raises issues which it cannot resolve, or cannot resolve without strain, it leaves a sour aftertaste, a lingering echo of discords. Such is the effect left on the reader by *Take a Girl Like You.*

Most great classical literature was attached to a metaphysical system of some kind; and the chief problem for writers from the Romantics to the present day has been to find some substitute for a defunct metaphysical orthodoxy. Their solutions are well known: Wordsworth's Nature, Shelley's Neo-platonism, Eliot's Tradition, Yeats's System, Lawrence's Dark gods. But in a sense all these solutions are working hypotheses which do not demand categorical assent from the reader. Transcending these hypotheses in almost every case is a belief in art itself as a substitute for metaphysics, a belief which reached its apex in the great moderns. Such a belief permits a para-metaphysical use of language—the recovery, through such devices as symbolism, irony, ambiguity, and paradox, of areas of experience ruled out by positivism; and such a belief has been associated with the adoption of a certain life-style—the cosmopolitan, the exile, or the Bohemian. Just how much Amis dislikes this kind of life-style and this kind of literary style is clear from his portrait of Gareth Probert, the Dylan Thomas–type playwright, and his verse play, in *That Uncertain Feeling:*

> . . . there were various linguistic clues, and I felt myself on safe ground in inferring that the whole business was rather on the symbolical side. Words like "death" and "life" and "love" and "man" cropped up in every few lines, but were never attached to anything concrete or specific. "Death," for example, wasn't my death or your death, or his death or her death or our death or their death or my Aunt Fanny's death, but just death, and in the same way "love" wasn't my, etc., love and wasn't love of one person for another or love of God or love of blackcurrant purée either, but just love. There were also bits from the Bible turned back to front ("In the word was the beginning" and so on), and bits of daring jargon ("No hawkers, circulars, or saints," "Dai Christ"). Dear, dear, the thing was symbolical all right. (IX)

Certainly the modern mode can produce this kind of nonsense. But if Wittgenstein's dictum, "The limits of my language are the limits of my world," is true, Amis has imposed very restrictive limits upon the world of his books by his rejection of the modern mode. These limits are scarcely felt within the simplified comedy of *Lucky Jim,* but they press hard on the attempt in later novels to incorporate more of the multiplicity of experience. His language, turned back at the metaphysical frontier, returns to sabotage the positivist, common-sense epistemology at the centre of his work, producing that sour, spoiling, comedy which creates such dissonances in *Take a Girl Like You*. The idea of death in that novel, for instance, inhibits the comic impulse towards freedom and happiness, but at the same time is itself deprived of meaning and dignity.

I have treated *Take a Girl Like You* and *That Uncertain Feeling* rather summarily, in order to discuss at some length Amis's third novel *I Like It Here*. On the whole it has been the least regarded, and certainly the most unfavourably criticized of Amis's works. Yet it seems to me that *I Like It Here* is a most interesting example of a special genre, which perhaps begins with *Tristram Shandy,* and which is particularly common in our era. I mean the kind of novel which is not so much turned outwards upon the world as inward upon literary art and upon the literary artist himself. I am thinking of such novels as Evelyn Waugh's *The Ordeal of Gilbert Pinfold* and Nabokov's *Pale Fire*. It is characteristic of such novels that the central figure is himself a writer, often with an autobiographical reference, that there is a lot of parody, many literary jokes, and much discussion of literary questions, and that in this way the author is able to get a surprising distance on his own literary identity.

Garnet Bowen, the central character of *I Like It Here* is a professional writer, and a kind of projection of the most hostile public image of Amis himself, i.e. a man who earns an enviable amount of money from writing, without producing anything of real merit, and without having a very elevated conception of the writer's calling.

> Until a couple of years ago Bowen had been supposed to be a novelist who was keeping himself and his family going on the proceeds of journalism, wireless talks and a bit of lecturing. In the last six months or so he had started being supposed to be a dramatist who was keeping himself and his family going by the same means. He had never really supposed himself to be much more than a journalist, wireless talker and occasional lecturer. (I)

The attitudes of philistinism and vulgar ribaldry which showed signs of becoming unconscious mannerisms in *That Uncertain Feeling,* are here pushed to the extreme of conscious self-parody.

> "Very much the same thing happened in Elgar's career," Bowen blurted out before he could stop himself. He tried to cheapen it with "So a fellow was telling me, anyway," but only succeeded in making himself sound modest. A moral failure on this scale came about through attending too closely to what people were saying. Those perishing vodka martinis at the International Musicians' Club that time must have weakened his protective shell without him noticing. He had thought that the film-producer chap who was buying them all had merely been boring him. And now here was this gross betrayal into non-ironical cultural discussion. (XIII)

Prevented by his wife from using the word "bum," Bowen uses it mentally throughout the novel as a kind of collective noun for things he doesn't like:

> Currency bum, Bowen thought to himself when she had gone. Allowance for self, wife, three children and car bum. Arrangements for drafts on foreign banks bum. Steamer tickets bum. Return vouchers bum. Car documents bum. Redirection of correspondence *by landlord* bum. Permission from Secretary of Extra-Mural Studies to absent self from end-of-session Tutors' and Lecturers' Discussion and Planning Meeting bum. Passport bum. Passport photograph bum. Visa bum. (II)

On embarking for Portugal, he opens a telegram from his mother-in-law: "ALL MY LOVE GOE SWITH YOU MY FARLINGS SEND ALL NEWS AND KEEP PHOTOGRAPHICAL BUM TO SHOW ON RETURN BON VOYAGE + MOTHER. There is a God, Bowen thought" (III).

All through the novel there is this kind of delight in strange locutions, odd pronounciations, verbal errors and unconscious puns. It is indeed a recurrent feature of Amis's work,[8] and the one which brings him closest to the techniques of "modern" fiction. Foreigners "speak funny," not only in the sense that they make mistakes, but that these mistakes have a kind of comic truth—as in the overseas students' pronunciations of English authors and titles: Grim Grin, Ifflen Voff, Zumzit Mum and Shem Shoice, not to mention *Sickies of Sickingdom* by Edge-Crown. "Shem Shoice" is invoked very appropriately here.

The special interest of *I Like It Here* is that it is deeply concerned with the contemporaries-versus-moderns issue. The discussion of it centres round the Wulfstan Strether mystery. "Wulfstan Strether" is the pen-name of a writer of considerable reputation who has kept his true identity from the world, and from his publishers, who assumed that since his last book, in 1946, he had died or given up writing. Now a new book has come from a man in Portugal claiming to be Strether, and the publishers, with whom Bowen hopes to get a job, are not sure whether it is genuine or not. Bowen is asked to make investigations during his trip to Portugal. He is also given the proof of the new book, called *One Word More*.

Strether is, of course, the name of the hero in Henry James's international novel *The Ambassadors*,[9] and the passage from *One Word More* is a very creditable parody of bad James, or of an inferior novelist in the James tradition, says Charles Morgan:

> *It was with a sense of having by now earned the right to attempt penetration of the hard confident sheen that had, since the first morning of his stay, overlaid in her greygreen eyes the smoky tumult he had glimpsed there that spring evening (the strange light all velvet and honey)—it was with such a sense that, presented now with her vigilant yet dreamy profile (it wasn't much good wasting time at* this *stage on speculations about the significance of that comma-shaped mole on the nostril-wing) as they stood at the open-*

> *flung window—before which in the flinty afternoon sun a bourgainvillaea waved—*
> *Frescobaldi brought to utterance: "Do you come here often"*
> *"What a strange question,"—lightly.*
> *Well, he was not to be put off. "You're waiting—"he teased.* (IX)

And so on. Amis-Bowen's objections to this kind of international, aesthetic fiction—they are essentially the same as his objections to Gareth Probert's play—come at the end of the parody, which concludes:

> *But she followed him, her hand lighting upon his arm. She had understood. She, somehow, had seen it too.*
>
> You go out of your way to tell us how, Bowen inwardly recommended, as once to Frank Sinatra in the long ago.[10] He wanted to put the man who had written that in the stocks and stand in front of him with a peck, or better a bushel, of ripe tomatoes and throw one at him for each time he failed to justify any phrase in the Frescobaldi–Yelisaveta scene on grounds of clarity, common-sense, emotional decency and general morality. (IX)

Literary criticism cannot solve the problem of the authenticity of *One Word More* for Bowen. Although he knows the appropriate techniques ("he could turn an honest dollar by getting in first with something he might provisionally entitle 'Full Fathom Five: an examination of light and water imagery in the later work of Wulfstan Strether' "), he is so unsympathetic to the "modern" mode that he cannot distinguish between bad Strether and forged Strether. When Bowen meets the man, who is provisionally called "Buckmaster" until his identity is settled, he gets no nearer to a decision, though he begins to suspect that the man is an imposter. Buckmaster-Strether converses as if reciting *T.L.S.* leaders of thirty years ago.

> Could a man who had really written all those novels really be bounded by James and Conrad and Edith Wharton and Meredith, could he really not have noticed anything that had happened since? (XIII)

Bowen makes up his mind when Buckmaster-Strether takes him to visit Henry Fielding's grave:

> Bowen thought about Fielding. Perhaps it was worth dying in your forties if two hundred years later you were the only non-contemporary novelist who could be read with unaffected and whole-hearted interest, the only one who never had to be apologized for or excused on grounds of changing taste. And how enviable to live in the world of his novels, where duty was plain, evil arose out of malevolence and a starving wayfarer could be invited indoors without hesitation and without fear. Did that make for a simplified world? Perhaps, but that hardly mattered beside the existence of a moral seriousness that could be made apparent without evangelical puffing and blowing. (XV)

Buckmaster pays an efficient tribute to Fielding, and then, as Bowen had feared, opens "the floodgates of English Men of Letters eloquence":

> "But we are surely not to say," it came rolling out, "that the utterances of comedy, whatever their purity or power, can move us as we are moved by the authentic voice of tragedy. That alone can speak to us of the loneliness and the dignity of man. And this, my friend, means that much as I reverence this master of the picaresque, I am unable to consider him my equal. In the field of the novel he is indeed the collossus of the eighteenth century, but I cannot feel that posterity will place him beside . . . will care to place him beside the collossus of the twentieth."
>
> A monosyllable of demented laughter broke from Bowen before he had time to arrange a coughing fit. Too good to be true, eh? And so much too good to be true that Buckmaster must inevitably be able to see it like that as well. Bowen stopped coughing and his eyes went glassy. That was it. Of course. . . . He knew now what Buckmaster was. The evidence might not have convinced others, but it did him. (XV)

Later, Bowen explains to his publisher why he decided Strether must be genuine:

> ". . . given that sort of intelligence he wouldn't have dared to put himself on show as the kind of prancing, posturing phoney who'd say he was better than Fielding. Nothing to be gained by it. And too much danger of affronting my conception of how great writers behave. He'd have been perfectly safe in sticking to humility, reverence and what-have-you. But he didn't. So that meant he couldn't have been putting on an act."
>
> "I think I follow you. But don't you in fact expect great writers to be prancing phoneys or whatever you said?"
>
> "Of course I do, as far as people of the great-writer period are concerned, that is . . . roughly between *Roderick Hudson* and about 1930, death of Lawrence and the next bunch all just starting off—Greene, Waugh, Isherwood, Powell. Or perhaps 1939. But you couldn't expect Buckmaster to know I saw it like that. He'd grown up in that period himself, poor old devil. It couldn't possibly strike him in that way." (XVI)

These passages neatly draw together the threads of the literary debate that runs through the novel. Amis–Bowen's ideal literature is not the tragic, but the comic, not the cosmopolitan post-romantic artistic self-consciousness of the modern "great-writer period," but the sane, morally serious, healthy engagement with life of a Henry Fielding. This might seem a provincial and self-satisfied view if it were not ironically qualified in a number of ways. Fielding's is a "simplified world" and Bowen's is far from simple. And though he is bound to regard moderns, such as Strether, as phonies, he recognizes their integrity within their own system of values, and recognizes too that he is himself a phoney. There are many passages in the novel in which Bowen subjects his own writing to scathing sarcasm. And there is an extremely interesting scene in which he ruefully acknowledges the attraction of the modern mode, and its inaccessibility for himself.

A Portuguese boatman tells him a story about a Finnish ship which is moored in the bay. Apparently its crew, some years before, mutinied and killed the captain. They were subsequently captured and tried. The captain's father came out from Finland to take possession of the ship, but because of its design—unsuited to sardine fishing—he could not sell it. Nor could he raise the money to return to Finland. Thus he is condemned to a life of exile, living alone on the ship and working in the fish market.

> A powerful, useless thrill ran through Bowen. Here was a marvellous story for someone, but not, unfortunately, for him. Only a rather worse or much older writer than himself could tackle it satisfactorily. (XII)

Bowen feels the artist's instinctive relish in the possibilities of this "germ," as James would have called it. But it is not for him. An older writer could have done it; but anyone who tries to do it now would be a worse writer than himself, because, it is implied, he would be working in an obsolete tradition, the "modern" tradition. "W. Somerset Maugham (on grounds of age, not the lack of merit) was the kind of chap." This is a complicated private joke: it was the Somerset Maugham Award which enabled Amis to travel to Portugal and therefore to write *I Like It Here*.

The irony of this situation must have appealed to Amis: that he, a young "contemporary", a reputed Angry Young Man, should have been given an award endowed by a writer of the modern "great-writer period," one moreover who had publicly called the Angry Young Men "scum";[11] and that a condition of the award should be that it must be spent on the activity most characteristic of the modern great writers, and least congenial to the young contemporaries: travel. *I Like It Here* is a gently comic explanation of why travel will not serve the literary purposes it is supposed to serve, of broadening the mind and opening new areas of experience. At the end of the book Bowen tears up his abortive play and resolves to write something "about a man who was forced by circumstances to do the very thing he most disliked the thought of doing and found out afterwards that he was exactly the same man as he was before." That book is of course *I Like It Here*.

To return to the earlier passage, after the reference to Maugham, Bowen considers a Maugham-like or perhaps Conrad-like opening to the Finnish ship story.

> "I have a notion that men are seldom what they seem." Or "Lars Ericssen"—something like that, anyway—"was the skipper of a small Finnish cargo vessel. He was a big bronzed man who never looked you directly in the eye. One hot summer off Tangier. . . ." Hmm. A rather worse or much older writer. Well,

just say a writer, instead of a man who was supposed to be a writer. That would get it. (XII)

I Like It Here is not so much about the importance of being Amis as about the difficulty of being Amis—the difficulty of being committed to aesthetic, philosophical, and moral principles which seem more reliable but drabber than the principles on which most great "modern" art was based. There must be few practicing writers in England today who do not feel the pressure of this situation. Amis's acute awareness of the situation, his sardonic sense of the literary tradition and of the limitations of his own stance towards it, and above all his success in finding a language which articulates very exactly the temper of his generation, make him, I think, a writer of genuine literary "importance."

Notes

1. Frederick R. Karl, *A Reader's Guide to the Contemporary English Novel* (1963), p. 4.
2. Stephen Spender, *The Struggle of the Modern* (1963), pp. 104–5.
3. Pamela Hansford Johnson, "Literature," *The Baldwin Age* ed. John Raymond (1960), p. 182. Quoted by Spender, *op. cit.*, pp. 81–2.
4. Virginia Woolf, "Modern Fiction," *The Common Reader* (Penguin edition, 1938), p. 149.
5. James Joyce, *A Portrait of the Artist as a Young Man* (Travellers' Library edition, 1942), p. 195.
6. John Braine, *Room at the Top* (Penguin edition, 1959), p. 28.
7. Roman numerals refer to chapter numbers in novels.
8. Cf. the occasion in *That Uncertain Feeling* when John Lewis is accosted by two Lascars:

    One . . . seemed to ask me: "Where is pain and bitter laugh?"
    This was just the question for me, but before I could strike my breast and cry "In here, friend" the other little man had said: "My cousin say, we are new in these town and we wish to know where is piano and bit of life, please?" (XI)

9. "Wulfstan" is probably meant to suggest some element of mid-European foreignness—Strether has Conrad as well as James on his bookshelves. But it is not perhaps irrelevant to recall, as well, Bishop Wulfstan, author of the Anglo-Saxon *Sermo Lupi*, which might have been included in that "course of lectures on some piece of orang-outan's toilet requisite from the dawn of England's literary heritage" which Bowen recalls from his days at the university. (VIII)
10. This refers to an earlier scene in which Bowen abruptly turns off the radio: "Sinatra sang. 'When you did that to me I knew somehow th—' You tell us how, a part of Bowen's mind recommended." The Amis-hero is at least consistent in the exercise of his critical faculty. Cf. John Lewis shaking his head over the "maladroit change of image" in the caption to a tabloid's cover-girl. *That Uncertain Feeling*. (VIII)
11. Karl, *op. cit.*, p. 231.

"No, Not Bloomsbury": The Comic Fiction of Kingsley Amis

Malcolm Bradbury

> While he explained, he pronounced the names to himself: Bayswater, Knightsbridge, Notting Hill Gate, Pimlico, Belgrave Square, Wapping, Bloomsbury. No, not Bloomsbury.
>
> Kingsley Amis, *Lucky Jim* (1954)

> "I'd rather go to bed," she said in her habitual monotone.
> "If you're tired some food'll perk you up."
> "I don't mean that. I don't feel tired. I mean sex."
> This was exactly the sort of thing that Ronnie, in his role as a graduate student of Britain's youth, was supposed to know all about. But, for the moment, his reaction was a simple though uncomfortable mixture of lust and alarm, with alarm slightly to the fore. "Fine. Nothing I'd like better, love. We'll grab a taxi and go to my flat." "I can't wait," the girl droned. "I want it *now*." "But you can't have it *now*, for Christ's sake."
>
> —Kingsley Amis, *I Want It Now* (1968)

1

The French have always had a fondness for writers who profess themselves intellectuals, whether they are or not. On the other hand, being different, the British prefer their writers not to be, however philosophical or high-minded they may happen to be in private life. This helps explain something of the difference between most British and most continental fiction; the British have rarely produced the philosophical novel, the serious political novel, or the novel of aesthetic exactitude. What they have produced is the writer of many mediations, the writer who is party to the commonplace and ordinary stuff of life, the realist, the observer, the humorist. Political and social attitudes, even strong ideas, may play a part, but it is best if these are presented as prejudices, instincts or eccentricities rather than theories or ideologies. Indeed, one of the things that has mediated social, political and intellectual life in Britain

---

From *No, Not Bloomsbury* by Malcolm Bradbury. Copyright © 1988 by Columbia University Press. Reprinted with permission of the publisher.

is its capacity for manifest humour. And this may be why one of the triumphs and pleasures of the British fictional tradition is the comic novel. We have a strong comic line in the novel, and it still goes on. But even in this matter the British taste has been generally for the untheoretical. Two lineages started in the early days of fiction, one with Henry Fielding, the voice of good-humoured benevolence, the maker of one of our great-comic heroes, Tom Jones; the other with Laurence Sterne, who invented and abstracted the anti-novel almost before the novel form had begun, and so became one of the great heroes of experimental modernism, as well as the discoverer of comedy as a form of response to pain and mortality.

In general it has been the lineage of Fielding that has prevailed. Jane Austen, commonsensical as well as sharply ironic, familiarises us to the difficult world of social manners. Dickens was a man of exacting social ideas, but a great writer of the familiar and the popular. Joyce is, in *Ulysses,* a most remarkable comic novelist, the supreme parodist of text; but Evelyn Waugh, fiercely and splendidly prejudiced, his social attitudes often dismaying, his compassion nil, is surely the best twentieth-century British comic novelist to date. His fiction is darker and sharper than it often seems, but like much modern comic writing it refuses many of our most serious notions of literature, and is more *against* ideas than for them. Indeed, the ideologically or philosophically obsessed have usually seemed, in British comic fiction, the enemies of reality and the true comic instinct—Thackum and Square in *Tom Jones,* the dreaming transcendentalists in *Martin Chuzzlewit,* and so on to Professor Welch and his Bloomsbury artistic coterie in Kingsley Amis's *Lucky Jim,* a novel that undoubtedly owed as much of its success to maintaining the eighteenth-century fictional tradition as it did to providing a radical view of its own time, the 1950s. This is not the only place where Amis does homage to Fielding, and in British fiction he has been far from alone. *Tom Jones,* said Gibbon, "may be considered the history of human nature," and the comic novel of human nature has long been found the true British way of doing fictional things.

This in turn may explain how we treat our writers, which is not quite as intellectuals but as outrageous observers of our institutions, mores and political practices. Comedy becomes a way of pursuing offence without offence, and to this day we are capable of producing, and thinking very British, authors whose manner is both spikey and clubbable, aggressive and affable, writers who both outrage and delight us while generally refusing to be our leaders of thought, our makers of political judgement, our constructors of philosophy, our severe critics, our metaphysical explorers. Waugh himself is one of the chief modern examples—a writer of distinction and originality, whose irascible disguises served to hide him from readers, strangers and much of the argument of the world, who was able to sustain at the highest level of arrogance a virtually unattainable intellectual and social position, and in general to claim as the very centre of writing the proprietorial, seigneurial rights of the English eccentric, whom it would be quite inappropriate to gainsay or interrupt. As it happens, and as it does often happen, Waugh possessed powerful intellectual qualities—a strong sense of history, which he had manoeuvred into a theory of a decline and fall that had started with the end of Catholic dominance in Britain and was now quite irredeemable; an unusual aesthetic taste, which could be presented as very proper in a gentleman; a great studiousness which he chose to call "a little learning," and presumably hence a dangerous thing, though less dangerous than a lot of it; and above all a compelling sense of style which could appear at once an art form and a normal possession of a man of rank, but never as a modernist novelty.

Thus *A Little Learning* was the appropriate title for his recessive fragment of autobiography: no tale of an intellectual or an artistic upbringing but an account of personal and social relations invested with an apocalyptic sense of faith, a certain sense of acquired position, and a general instinct that the world is a place of follies. We can understand it, therefore, when Sean O'Faolain, in his book *The Vanishing Hero* (1956), chooses to characterise Waugh's work in much the same way, describing Waugh as "a writer of purely brainless genius, which he had amplified by the possession or development of enormous technical skill." This probably pleased Waugh perfectly well, though it happens to be enormously unfair; Waugh at best is a novelist of very considered powers and devastating human judgement. But we can see how it feels true; Edmund Wilson, who had a good deal of Waugh's temper, and admired him greatly until he met him and found himself treated, as an American, with contempt, aptly identified his fictional and social manner with that of Jowett's advice to the gentleman: "Never apologize; never explain." Waugh did not explain, or not in public; the diaries explain, and explain him, a good deal. He invented remarkable new techniques for fiction, but professed dislike for the modernist avant garde—indeed, as time went on, for everything that had happened in his own lifetime, a fact which made him one of the comic historians *of* modernity. His mannered conservatism hid a pessimist's dismay; his late florid face was a facade over pain. He unlocked all this once, in *The Ordeal of Gilbert Pinfold,* hinting at the general human treachery which drove him to take up his mask—a hard facade that in fact had made him one of the greatest stylistic and comic interpreters of his age in the form of the novel.

2

When World War Two ended, Waugh's style, shaken by the experiences of wartime and the coming of the welfare-state world that followed, seemed half-spent. His later fiction reflects a good deal on this break, and the problem of writing the tale of the new age of dishonour. The new generation of the 1950s gradually emerged, their air apparently puritanical and socially of the lower middle class, their tweedy sports jackets hanging badly off their shoulders, their mildly Left-of-centre social principles everywhere being asserted. It was not, it seemed to Waugh, a climate for his kind of writing, and he raged against it. As for the most comically assured of the new writers, Kingsley Amis, whose impact on the 1950s came to rival that of Waugh on the 1920s, he seemed in almost every respect Waugh's antithesis. Waugh had portrayed British society in a state of irremediable historical decadence, a world of social, political and sexual treachery in which a few inheritors from the past hinted at the better, more stable and fixed world that was falling in, like the roofs of some of our best country houses, on top of us; Amis mocked the past and its styles and manners, and spoke straight from the plain and ordinary present. Waugh had found in the Catholic English past an older history to which he could convert and from which he could gain some sustenance; Amis attacked all that was nostalgic and medievalising in the British character, every notion of a Merrie England, and found his sustenance in the commonplace, the provincial, the bottle of beer and the blonde. Waugh had a religious and metaphysical rage with the contemporary world; Amis seemed full of secular delight in its stuff and its ways. Waugh's first hero was the weedy Oxford student Paul Pennyfeather who falls foul of rogues and rascals far more interesting than he; Amis's hero is the anti-scholar who wins out against the flamboyant adversaries and pretenders in the interest of simple honesty.

Waugh and Amis therefore looked like literary opposites, and the distinction applied equally in political matters. Waugh was not simply a writer of conservative instincts; he offered himself as the one true conservative. Amis, on the other hand, appeared part of the New Left that was emerging in postwar Britain, in an era when there was a new appeal for literary commitment. At St John's College, Oxford, in 1941, he had been an undergraduate communist ("the only party I have ever joined"), of course at a time when Britain and Soviet Russia were allies. During the 1950s he was announcing himself a probable lifetime Labour voter, and explored his Fabian allegiances in a pamphlet called *Socialism and the Intellectuals* (1957), a title that was hardly likely to go down well at Combe Florey. Amis was also not just a striking novelist and a fine young poet writing in the way of the "Movement," but also an academic, teaching English at a British "redbrick," Swansea, and writing fine and rather severe critical essays on which the impact of Leavis and the spirit of new critical intensity was apparent. Thereafter, forsaking the "redbrick" world about which he had written, he went to a fellowship at Peterhouse, Cambridge, with every prospect of a career that united the academic and the literary, the critical and the creative functions. None of this was in the Waugh spirit, except as stuff for the making of satirical fiction. But in the event a sharp break came. Cambridge did not suit, whether because of its often backbiting attitude toward those with literary ambitions, or because criticism itself was in any case being pushed heavily toward more theoretical preoccupations, is not quite clear. It is now that Amis entered on the life of the full-time writer, with great success, and indeed he was to pass the gene on to his son Martin, who has done the same.

Even so matters were changing. *Lucky Jim* and the books that immediately followed were enormously successful, and caught the temper of the times, coupling brilliant comic effects with a sharp sense of social process and even social protest. The poetry was admirable in the new, rational-critical, anti-modernist movement way, and displayed comic vision, good feeling, and commonsense, a much needed voice in the era of purity of diction and a strong sense of anti-romanticism. Amis's essays were forceful and accessible pieces of literary criticism, and he was clearly a central figure of the new "Movement" mood. But the manner was shifting, along with the political sympathies and the mode of social exploration in his work. Amis might well protest that it was the world that was changing, he remaining much the same; but the fiction seems to record a different story. At any rate Amis's politics moved toward the Right, and today he defines himself as a non-wet and so presumably Thatcherite Tory "with a few liberal bits," on hanging, homosexuality, abortion. But the "liberal bits" are only occasionally noticeable, and in the history of post-Orwellian liberalism, which has a lot to do with modern fiction, Amis did not continue as a striking example of the cause. The writer who began to write in the spirit of a humanist commonsense in a post-war time (you might say commonsense was to his world view what post-Heideggerian existentialism was to Jean-Paul Sartre's) took on rage and spleen, sometimes invested against morality and the human condition itself, as in *Ending Up* (1974), one of his deepest novels, and sometimes in a latter-day social ire arrayed against the modernity of the modern world. The writer who wrote compassionately in *Take a Girl Like You* (1960) of the change in sexual and emotional manners became in late books like *Jake's Thing* (1978) a notable misogynist in the age of feminism; the critic who had admired the radical impact of American fiction in the 1950s began to rage against the worthlessness of American writing.

In many ways Amis seemed slowly to have inherited the role of the Comic Bad Man of English Letters which Waugh had so powerfully sustained a generation earlier. Now the similarities began to look very evident. Both of them had begun as spectacular Young Turks, writing the novels of their new age in which, as at Waugh's Anchorage House, the topic of the Younger Generation is much discussed, and had turned into Angry Old Men. Both had captured, in subject and style, the manners, moral upsets, cultural dislocations and social instabilities generated by a recent war. Both of them were strictly anti-romantic writers who carried somewhere in their work a secret but gradually more explicit nostalgia. Both revolted against the extremities of experimentalism and the impact and significance of the modern movement. Both darkened deeply with the years, taking on a pervasive awareness both of the absurdity of the social world and the hideous weight of mortality into which human life is born, so that their comedy is touched with pain. Both turned youthful attitudes that seemed fresh and exciting into something crusted with an air of powerful prejudice, and protected those prejudices with an engaging but troubling comic conviction. Both, as they grew into public figures, turned their comic masks into public faces, into a manner that was both clubbable and crusty, amusing and bitter, rotund and misanthropic, a disguise that did not quite seem to disguise everything. Both started with a complex social awareness and an extraordinary cunning of observation, and nurtured it in the direction of an enraged dissent from most of what was observed. And both—this can certainly be said of Waugh, and I think we will say it of Amis—turned, with their virtues and their faults, into major writers whose mixture of basic craft, remarkable social perception, comic vision and gift for rage and outrage managed to construct a lifetime of writing of extraordinary dimensions and decided influence. It has been said that few contemporary comic writers can get free of the intonations of Amis, and the tradition of modern comic fiction in Britain has an inescapable source in Waugh, who will, I think, be seen as one of the great black humorists of the century. Both suggest that the comic is both a stylistic capacity and a form of human pain, and both indicate what I think is a very British way of dealing with it which may have striking limitations and peculiar strengths. And, as a result, both are difficult to write about, provoking both annoyance and respect, a sense of a talent often imperfect yet of an extraordinary force.

3

Literary dates have a calendar of their own, referring not just to the clock but to styles, moods and visions in writing which have their own momentum. Today the literary Fifties seems a distinct period in fiction, drama and poetry, an artistic, intellectual and critical community which still half guides us but also seems remote. Its sensibility, in which Amis himself was central, is marked by a burst of new writing in which a serious progressive severity, a new critical instinct, took hold, and much of that critical instinct was turned to the immediate past. The new tone seems determined to dispense with the experimentalism of the 1920s and 1930s, with the romanticism and apocalypticism of the 1940s (the exemplary figure was Dylan Thomas, still a target in Amis's most recent novel to date, *The Old Devils* (1986)), the Beckettian despairs emanating from Paris, though there is an underlying existentialist influence. Amis's Oxford friend Philip Larkin came in poetry to exemplify the new voice, plain-speaking, exact, observant, pessimistic, anti-romantic; he also helped prepare the way in fiction by publishing his early novel about Oxford life, *Jill* (1946). The connection reaches further, for Larkin is the dedicatee of Amis's first novel *Lucky Jim,* which became a summative work of the new spirit in fiction much as John Osborne's *Look Back In Anger* did in drama. There were other books to reinforce it—from John Wain's earlier *Hurry On Down* to Iris Murdoch's slightly later *Under the Net*—and so to suggest that a meritocratic, critical, comic and youthful voice was sounding across the entire literary scene.

One thing that seemed to feed the new tone was the social background and the education of these newer writers, speaking from a lower-middle-class, and just occasionally a working-class, orientation, though usually with a college education. They looked across a landscape that was deeply changed by the world of the welfare state, was divided by war from the past generation, and was probably more comfortable than the depression age of the 1930s, even though it was pressed by nuclear anxiety. Mores, manners and social accents were changing, in life and fiction, and the writing was amenable, open, speaking plainly, from recognised social positions, in clear rhetorical tones; it had few oblique angles, few signs of avant-garde displacement, and it offered to return the literary arts to the accessible ways that prevailed before the coming of modernism; an artistic spirit, Philip Larkin suggested, that could only interest Americans and had as its two main concerns mystification and outrage. It thus seemed painstakingly British, and it painted British culture in a time of relative liberal recovery, touched by social hope even if at times with a stoical despair. All these elements seemed present in Amis's work, and had much to do with the cultural success of the early novels, in which liking it here and wanting it now were very much the theme and the basis of the amenable vernacular tone. In an age which lacked strongly ideological feelings but had a powerful sense of generational transition, Amis's fiction had a generous comic rapport with the times, an appropriate social feeling, and a distinct moral vitality.

No doubt the success of *Lucky Jim* came largely from these elements, though we should also add that it was and remains one of the funniest modern comic novels. But the success was not entirely simple. The book had been round several publishers before it came out in January 1954, and it took something like another year before it acquired its popular if not mythical status. Nor was it quite what it seemed at the time. When it appeared, in a climate hungry for a postwar fiction, it was largely acknowledged as a work of the New Anger, and read for its social rage and protest. To reread it now does not confirm this, for like many books in the 1950s it seems to have been a reassessment of the 1930s and the shadows left over a world that suddenly seemed very different. Jim Dixon's seemingly dangerous adversaries are largely variants on what Angus Wilson had already named the "darling dodos," those of waning social power who still hung on to the mannerisms of the past. Jim is the traditional innocent comic hero, as well as the man who is pleasantly attuned to the present in its plainest forms. According to a traditional comic plot (the plot, we might say, of *Tom Jones*), he is rewarded by comic good fortune, becomes "lucky" Jim, winning a job in commerce and the prettiest girl in the story, freeing himself of the disguises and moral pressures that have kept him restrained. The plain form of the novel is justified by artistic presumptions developed in the book, as in several more of Amis's novels. For the danger of art is Bertram's danger, mannerist pretension, and that above all is represented by Bloomsbury. The way Jim is pointing is quite clear. "No, not Bloomsbury," he thinks to himself, when the lure of modern London beckons at the end and he searches for his right address.

Lucky Jim declared itself and a mood surrounding itself in a great many ways that took their place in postwar literary style. It had little to do with the aesthetic mannerisms, or indeed the ideological allegiances, of the generation gone just before. It turned from political matters to commonsense moral vision, throwing off not just Bloomsbury but provincial sexual repression, conventional intellectual behaviour, academic respectability and social snobbery. To express all this, it captured (much as in the United States J.D. Salinger captured in *The Catcher in the Rye*) a workable vernacular voice, comic and loosely argued, a voice that did sound like a voice and spoke out against unnecessary complexity, instituted social deceit, disguises and hypocrisies, and detected false intonations. It set the unfaked against the faked, the unphoney against the phoney, the unpretentious against the pretentious, the near-at-hand against the far-away, the allusion to close domestic gods against mystificatory and distant deities. A redbrick university was an ideal location for Jim Dixon's story, since here the manners of other places—the traditions and snobberies of privileged Oxbridge colleges, the mannered eccentricities of upper-middle-class donnish style, the constant appeal beyond the here-and-now to an imaginary Merrie England—prevailed in a world which gave them no support.

The story, however, could easily be shifted elsewhere, to many another department of British social life, and it touched on the nature and spirit of literary life itself, one reason for the unease of many of the critics of the previous generation who attacked the new phenomenon. The vernacular voice of Jim, which is so clearly the deployed voice of the author, speaking the author's own mind, constructing his distinctive world, coercing by a teasing sentence-structure the true way of saying things out of the false way in which they are usually said in writing, can thus become, in Orwellian fashion, the voice of commonsense itself. It is a knowing voice, tugging at sense in order to gain the commonsense, showing itself not so much angered, rather as fundamentally appreciative—of the good simple things that speech and life give us, like girls, money, drink, and a sturdy language that is not laid upon us by our social betters.

Here were the dominant virtues of the book, which have not stopped sounding in Amis's later works, though they sometimes take strange turns. For its language was able to construct a sceptical social and moral realism which found sense, dismissed aesthetic over-formulation, knocked against pretension, and gave to the stuff of ordinary life a comic enjoyment, a reinvigoration of the banal. Amis, indeed, was a moralist inside the moral tradition of the novel, just as the shape of its fiction was the shape of romantic comedy, surrounding the hero—anti-hero, said the reviewers—with the stuff of good fortune won by moral and linguistic persistence and generating an alliance between his simple commonsense and the comic muse. Jim has to live in social disguise for much of the novel, to hold down his intellectual job. When drink releases him from the intellectual convention he is forced to practise, we see this as a satisfying comic explosion of truth, though it could just as well be a naive reaction to ideas or a form of prejudice of its own. As David Lodge once observed, the triumphant moment in the book comes when Jim no longer has to hide his vernacular vision in his thoughts but comes right out and speaks: "The bloody old towser-faced boot-faced totem pole on a crap reservation, Dixon thought. 'You bloody old towser-faced boot-faced totem pole on a crap reservation,' he said." This is classic comic gratification, the victory of the small over the not so very big, the silent over the expressive. But the freedom it expresses is the freedom of the comic spirit itself, at least accounting for its own feelings. In the tradition of the social and moral novel, as in Jane Austen for example, *Lucky Jim* takes the bearers of false and hypocritical sentiment to task and replaces their world with one of true feeling. But it was the old novel in a new form, sounding a fresh, impertinent, culturally active voice and giving it fictional energy.

For several novels thereafter Amis wrote in much the same spirit, good-hearted and morally critical of the pretentious social world. *That Uncertain Feeling* (1955) took on a long-lasting adversary, contemporary Wales, the home of a spirit of bardic pretentiousness epitomised in the work of Dylan Thomas and those who have used it to justify a sentimental and nostalgic Welshness of a kind that still haunts his most recent fiction. Other novels and some short stories caught aspects of a related theme: the shabby gentility and banality of much of wartime and postwar British life, and the way it was lit and excused by false justifications. Certain distinctive gifts became notable, and Amis grew expert in presenting the social character who is just off-key, voicing loud claims and understandings that do not quite sound right, and then playing in the sound that does. The comedy stayed intimate with realism and common life, and grew more observant about manners and mores. Not all previous writers admired the tone, and Somerset Maugham condemned the new writers like Amis as "scum."

It was ironic that Amis should now win the Somerset Maugham Prize for Fiction, even more ironic that the consequence of this travelling prize was travel, and to Abroad, which Amis famously did not like. He chose to spend the booty in Portugal, perhaps because their pillar boxes are like ours; the fruit of the voyage was *I Like It Here* (1958), the story of a writer called Garnet Bowen who suffers the selfsame fate. Another plain-speaking hero constantly caught in what he calls "bum"—bureaucracy, restriction, pretension and formality—Bowen goes off to Portugal to find there an expatriate writer who is the absolute antithesis of himself. This is John Wulfstan Strether, a parodistic figure who clearly owes much to Henry James and something to Bloomsbury, and who suffers from severe logorrhea and high-flown artistic pretensions. Bowen longs for home, the "here" of the title, but finds his reward in discovering in Lisbon the grave of Henry Fielding, the eighteenth-century British novelist who showed us, as the novel puts it, that fiction could express "a moral seriousness that could be made apparent without evangelical puffing and blowing." The homage is clearly that of Amis himself, and is the most interesting thing in a rather loosely constructed book. Like many another postwar British novelist Amis was writing into his contract with the novel a sense of its tradition, and its continuing power. The novel of comic morality, of benevolence, good feeling and good judgement was capable of revival in postwar British circumstances, and Amis's fiction for a time seemed set to confirm this.

Certainly this was appropriate to Amis's next novel, *Take A Girl Like You,* which is one of his best, and seems to mark a decided change in his work. The farcical tone and the comic male hero here give ground, as larger issues, broader social observations and greater moral complications enter the novel. Interestingly the underlying eighteenth-century reference point here is Fielding's adversary and object of parody, Samuel Richardson, and the novels alluded to are *Pamela* and *Clarissa,* while the central theme of the novel is the Richardsonian principle of procrastinated rape. Amis here sees the story largely through the eyes of his heroine, Jenny Bunn, though he complicates matters by acknowledging the need for a stronger male character, Patrick Standish, and hence plays against Richardsonian themes the kind of criticism Fielding made of them. In any case, where Richardson's standpoint is that of a rising merchant class elaborating a controlled economic and sexual morality, a growing Puritanism and Victorianism, Amis is writing of a time when the inherited lower-middle-class standards largely derived from this were giving way to postwar notions of sexual liberation and permissiveness. Amis's aim here is clearly to write a capacious and compassionate novel of contemporary morality and changing sexual roles, about morality as inherited standard and the making of morality for oneself.

Jenny is a contemporary girl who is granted a strong moral sense, and is caught in a familiar crisis about right and wrong, focused on the price, value and meaning of her virginity. The high value she sets on it is contested by her lover-adversary Patrick Standish as the product of a "bloody little small-town conscience." Her friends cannot help her define the prize she seeks to retain: "I thought it was all to do with arranged marriages and betrothals and all that." Amis's writing takes much of its force from his sense of contemporary mores and social detail, and the theme of changing sexual moralities has been crucial to his work since. He creates Jenny's values and ways as a vital and comprehensible compound of juvenile innocence, traditionalism, and a desire not to be exploited or discarded, in a world that, for a girl like you, the girl of the advertisements of the time, is a series of sexual confusions and traps. In this world the men in turn look for immediate sexual pleasure and gratification, and the story of the rape is told as a kind of enforcement of historical necessity. Jenny is left with appropriately ambiguous feelings: "she could hardly pretend that what she had got was not worth having after all," what she gains by her loss of virginity being access to contemporary experience. Patrick, with his own shivers of mortality, becomes an interesting hero, a rake with a strong sense of modernity—and also a precursor of the shit-hero who would figure in several books to come.

Take a Girl Like You is Amis's most balanced book morally, and shows his debt to the literary tradition. But it also opened the way for Amis to take on a new kind of writing, in which the 1960s mood of sexual liberation and then of growing male-female conflict were to be dominant themes. The Amis shit-hero, a kind of echo of Evelyn Waugh's Charles Ryder, becomes a common character in these books. Waugh also seems echoed in the subject of *One Fat Englishman* (1963), in which, like Waugh in *The Loved One,* Amis responds to the image of booming, materialist, liberation-hungry, opportunistic America with a good deal of suspicion. Like Waugh he presents this by having his hero out-exploit the exploiters, and the book, like several of Waugh's later novels, is a conflict of unattractive opposites. The book came from a teaching visit Amis made to Princeton, and this apparently confirmed him in his sense of "Britishness" as a writer. (Some of his work had, strangely, been compared with that of the American "Beat Generation.") Amis evidently did have his roots in the tradition of moral fiction that flourished in the British 1950s. But during the 1960s the liberative mood that had showed in Amis's earlier work was changing, growing more dangerous, and the task of the critical observer and analyst, the interpreter of manners, becoming harder. This showed in part in the change away from moral fiction and towards more open, random and spontaneous forms of writing, what Philip Roth called a "letting go." Amis's writing had depended on a degree of social certainty as well as a gift for capturing the generational mood, and as the new manners seemed to break away from the old morals Amis's 1960s fiction began to show the strain.

4

Liking it here and wanting it now had been very much Amis's theme; but as the moral intonations of the 1950s gave way to the freer, franker, and often more frantic liberationist attitudes of the 1960s (we can see their price paid in the world of punk, money, success and disgust explored by Martin Amis later), his subject seems to have grown more difficult and elusive. The issue is one he confronts directly in *I Want It Now,* the novel he published in the key year of 1968. Here the hero, Ronnie Appleyard, is a television interviewer, a specialist in contemporary mores, and a self-described shit who meets an androgynous boy-girl, Simon Quick, at a party. It is the Sixties, she wants it now, and all that seems needed is to gratify the sensual satisfactions indicated by the title. For this the novel shows much sympathy but also much anxiety; this is Amis, and some moral explorations have to be conducted before gratification comes. So, just as *Take a Girl Like You* depends on the principle of procrastinated rape, *I Want It Now* depends on the notion of deferred orgasm. Simon is frigid, and Ronnie seeks a semi-psychological account of the cause. This, in the end, proves to be an overwhelming mother, a female ogre-figure from the familiar Amis stable. This permits Amis to shift the novel into more usual Amis territory, into the world of the darling dodos, in which Ronnie can administer the usual putdowns and comeuppances. Moral examination can be conducted before we reach a final mood of reform and renewal, which even affects Ronnie himself. "I was a shit when I met you," Appleyard declares at the close. "I still am in lots of ways. But because of you I've had to give up trying to be a dedicated, full-time shit. I couldn't make it, I hadn't the character. Which is a pity in a way, because when you fall back into the ranks of the failed shits or amateur shits or incidental shits you start taking on responsibility for other people."

In short, Amis ends the book the contemporary moralist, as he always was, trying to capture the temper of the times but also trying to relate it to a conception of decency, responsibility and virtue. So, if his heroes were now becoming less bastard-detectors than bastards themselves, they retained a capacity for self-improvement and permitted the story to provide a moral gratifiction. Amis's heroes from the start had been heroes of prejudice, excused because they are attractive, have history and the spirit of change, as well as the muse of comedy, on their side, and possess the gift for exposing bastards far greater than themselves. Thus it was always possible to embody their preferences, instincts and prejudices in the basic linguistic tone of the book, and make them sound like the voice of a truth. But it seems just to suggest that by the later 1960s Amis was finding it harder to construct convincing contemporary heroes, delineate them with cultural precision, and still give them some moral authority. Ronnie is an apt example. It is the shit in him that makes him continue to pursue Simon after their first hopeless lovemaking, because she is an heiress. This brings him into contact with her family, and lets him shine as a bastard-detector among various tattered lords and neo-fascistic American southerners. The trouble was that, in a tale for the times, the boorish rich no longer appeared particularly potent material for satire, and when Ronnie finally lures Simon's mother onto a television programme and gives her her comeuppance in public the result seems slight and trite, a routine and contingent victory, part of Amis's taste for setting up characters in order to knock them down. What is important in the book is that Amis clearly is seeking, generally, to widen the confines of the social and moral novel, and attempt a new range, one that will capture the flavour of contemporary culture in its fashionable, frantic, elusive turnover. The change in sexual mores is an essential concern, as is the new androgyny represented by Simon Quick, and the use of sex as therapy. But the novel ends not on some strong emotional discovery but in accordance with the familiar habits of comedy, as Ronnie defeats the wicked mother, releases the sleeping beauty, loses the base inheritance but acquires a happy romantic relationship in a conclusion of classic comic and moral shape.

5

In the late 1960s and early 1970s it was hard to see what direction Amis's work was taking, some of his novels, like *I Want It Now* and the later *Girl, 20* (1971) being telling reports on contemporary mores, pointing toward a new kind of book about an age of moral nullity and opportunism, and others testing out a playful variety of modes. Amis now tried detective fiction, briefly assumed the mantle of Ian Fleming to write a James Bond adventure (*Colonel Sun,* 1968), and explored another genre that interested him, science fiction, or what he called "future fiction." But there were books of stronger personal feeling and more powerful vision, the most notable of which is *Ending Up,* a work that brought to the centre of his writing a theme that had long belonged to it, that of the pains of ageing and mortality. The sense of mortal sadness in that novel deepened his work, but the pattern of his early success, where the vernacular of the age yields up values sufficient to construct a vision of it, seemed to elude him more and more. This is one part of the disturbance that seems to afflict *Jake's Thing,* the book in which the sexual moral comedy of his earlier work suddenly goes sour on us. An angry mortality had become part of Amis's central theme, and with it goes a deep sense of the failure of the body to provide its appropriate satisfactions, a vision of lost joy that is answered by rage. If the ageing and fading powers of the hero provide part of the story, so does the revolution in sexual relations which has led less to a general emotional liberation than to the rise of feminism and aggressive and hostile male-female relations. After the mechanical libidinousness and polymorphous perversity of the 1960s comes the feminist revolution of the 1970s, abrogating the effective sexual contract, the love-relation, on which so many of his own earlier novels, like so many of the novels of the past, had been based.

Jake's Thing, a painfully miserable book, is a tale of fundamental sexual manipulations and exploitations, written in what seems a masochistic rage. It is a story of an age of fashionable therapies and chic models of interpersonal relations and group dynamics, of sex-therapies, of Masters and Johnson, of women who can do everything without men, and the shit-hero has turned into the shit-heroine. Jake Richardson, sixty years of age, an Oxford don who also happens to live in London, has had a healthy sexual past, of "more than a hundred women." But now he is suffering from a loss of libido, a word he is not even sure how to pronounce (libeedo? libighdo?), and requires treatment. This leads him through the world of the new behaviourism and the fashionable spirit of sexual engineering—the late 1970s waste land. And Jake is notably *not* in tune with his times. "I don't particularly object to oral sex or anal sex or the rest of the boiling, I just don't enjoy that kind of thing as much as the . . . straightforward stuff," he says. His problem comically causes him to stand trouserless in lecture theatres, study pornography, and have measuring devices attached to the once private parts he loves so well. He is the male chauvinist who has turned from hero into victim, and who sees his world in collapse, as his Oxford college starts to admit women, female roles everywhere change round him, and gentrification hideously transforms the surrounding landscape, while even the buses are driven by Asians. The tone of the book, like that of several of Amis's novels, works two ways: it can be seen as a punishment vested on a presumptuous male chauvinist and a hero of prejudice, but also as a reverse satire, assaulting the modernisation of the world all the way from the social landscape to the bedroom, and to this extent a vindication of Jake and his irritation. Jake is an uncomfortable figure, the shit-hero caught in the bitterness of late life, a bundle of savage prejudices and decencies which are virtually impossible to disentangle tonally, for even the decencies are prejudices, as they always have been. But the lesson of the book is clear: Jakes's lost potency comes not simply from his physical ageing but from the intrusive claims and the modern attitudes of the women themselves; and in this novel Amis turns into a striking, disturbing, splenetic novelist of contemporary male sexual pain and persecution.

There is, of course, no reason why he should not. In an age of female and feminist fictions the raging, pained, felt voice of the male should have its place in return. But the form sounds uncomfortable in the work of the writer who had once celebrated women as nicer than men and who had made the commonplace world of sexual relations the basis of a moral feeling. These difficulties return in *Stanley and the Women* (1984), a novel which deals with a sequence of darkly troubling events which suddenly overtake the life of the central character, the obscure Stanley Duke, an advertising manager for a tabloid newspaper, who is confronted with the madness of a teenage son who thinks he is being watched and programmed by strange cosmic powers. Stanley, twice married, but living now in Amis's late-life world where males drink themselves stupefied in order *not* to be sexually possessed by their women, finds himself an accused victim. His son's schizophrenia is first treated by chemo-therapy, but then it passes into the hands of a woman psychologist who treats the family as the cause, and Stanley is placed in the role of the guilty father. The women in Stanley's life all seem to betray him, and appear not as comically incomprehensible figures but an actively malign force. In one passage Stanley turns to a male psychologist for help, asking if all women are mad? No, the psychologist tells him, they are terrifying and logically sane in their use, and misuse, of the male. It is clear from the tone that this is no simple moral comeuppance vested on an old lothario overproud of past sexual victories. Both these books, in their way disturbing in their open truth, are explorations of the dark punishments women eventually impose on male sexuality, as well as on the loss of joy and the emptying of meaning that has come when behaviourism and commercial modernity have come along to displace, and replace, a more deeply felt human culture. Both seem to expose rather than interpret the pain they display, as the moral world seems to dissolve before unreason.

These are powerful books, striking because of their edge of pain and their sense of cultural disorder. Their theme is strong in modern fiction, for instance in Ford Madox Ford's Tietjens tetralogy, where the man of honour from the old world, the man who would not, finds that world corrupted by sexual treachery and brought to collapse. A similar fate befalls Waugh's hero of prejudice and hopeful virtue, Guy Crouchback, who in the *Sword of Honour* trilogy goes off to fight for the chivalric virtues he hopes quixotically to maintain, only to find that the war's purposes are corrupt and women themselves help corrupt it. The image of perverted sexual relations has been a powerful one in modern fiction, a key figure for the way in the modern world the attempt to sustain history as innocence and virtue collapse, virtue grows stained, and moral purpose is defeated. Amis's later fiction thus seems to have taken a familiar if terrible shape, toward a late-life vision of cultural emptiness, sexual corruption, and mortal exposure; the world promised by Jim Dixon, the world of commonsense taking its victory over pretension and hypocrisy, and social clarity over social falsehood, has not done well, and moral competence can no longer be sustained. Yet the naked frankness and force remain, to remind us that Amis is one of our most disturbing contemporary novelists, an explorer of historical pain. In these two novels the pain does not acquire the largeness of a vision, but in *The Old Devils* (1986) the theme is extended, and indeed this novel is surely the best of his late books.

The story of a group of retired middle-class couples living a notably drink-soaked existence amid the pleasant landscapes and modernised miseries of contemporary Wales, *The Old Devils* returns to the more complex feeling of *Ending Up,* and even carries something of the joy of the earlier books, for these are ageing versions of Amis's young characters of the 1950s, a time to which they look back. It is not entirely an easy read, the boredoms of ageing and Wales being heavy, sometimes banal material, which even the famous Amis vernacular cannot always stir into joy. But the writing is spirited, the language attentive, and the subject considerably felt; while the now very familiar Amis tricks—the elaborate putdowns and comeuppances, the large bursts of rhetorical complaint, about the modernness of the modern world and the awful youth of the young—take their place in an inclusive vision. Amis chooses to tell his story not from the standpoint of one single male hero but from several angles, and *The Old Devils* is, perhaps as befits its Welsh setting, unusually choric. This is a tired and contingent world; for the couples, sex has virtually died, marriages are hostile, egotism prevails, the body is a trouble. Drinking starts early, if it ever really ceases; few novels are as washed in wine and spirits. The men gather daily for their "Bible" session at the Bible and Crown, the local pub; the women gather in each other's homes to pull the cork on the first bottle of Soave and begin the day. Drink opens up the voices, which grouse, complain, hold the floor, or otherwise upstage. Their speeches deal with Welsh pretentiousness, the vulgar tastelessness of modern improvement, the ruination of town and landscape, the misbehaviour of the young. Behind all this sounds the chatty Amis vernacular, making the characters sound a communality of voices speaking against the banality of the world, which lies over most things.

The banal, troubled couples are stirred to life by the return of two of their former number—Alun Weaver, a successful media Welshman and a local lothario, and his wife Rhiannon, with whom two of the men have been in love. Between them they stir up the old emotions, past glimpses of joy and error, the remnants of past feeling. All this Amis recreates with loving care and a strong map of emotion, the woman characters as strongly felt as the men. The mannered rage against the modern world is mediated and made part of the sadness of what has been lost, and the present even summons up some striking notes of moral maturity in several of the characters. Wales itself becomes less a comic issue than a state of mind that has to be accepted, and the story comes to a compacted, symbolically appropriate, even hopeful end. This troubling but strong book contains the most painful kind of anger, against the mortal human condition itself, for which none of us has the cure. The Angry Young Man may feel like a Bitter Old One, the moral seriousness of the early novels open to defeat; but his writing can still contain a moral desire, a sharp, self-challenging honesty. Amis remains one of our most troubling comic novelists, still directing his assault on the way we live now, and on the pain, the self-enclosure, but also sometimes the secret joy, of ageing life itself.

The Language of Kingsley Amis

Norman MacLeod

For a wide and loyal following, Kingsley Amis stands now as the most entertaining and readable of present-day novelists—so much so, indeed, that there is likely to be widespread agreement (even if some academic critics may carp) with the claim made by Alan Watkins, that Amis is "the outstanding English novelist of those who began their writing careers after 1945."[1] Such a view is, among those of us who hold it, not only a firm but also a long-standing one, typically espoused from the moment of one's very first delighted encounter with an Amis novel. My own case is exactly like that described by the American literary critic William H. Pritchard, who identifies himself, at the conclusion of an approving review of Amis's *Collected Poems 1944–1979*, as "one for whom since the day I first read *Lucky Jim* back then, Amis has been the most entertaining, the most exhilarating of contemporary writers."[2] Pritchard is reporting an experience probably familiar to many of Amis's readers, just as his closing descriptions point to the fundamental reason for Amis's continuing appeal—the fact that Amis's novels are consistently exhilarating and amusing. Amis has, for more than thirty years now, reliably provided his readers with splendidly readable and entertaining fictions, and it is this consistency which has won for him the kind of solidly based admiration expressed in the unstinting estimate of author-cum-bibliophile Joseph Connolly: "Amis's talent is unique. There is no other writer who can amuse so consistently and yet always be so bloody *good*."[3] Mr Connolly is very clearly a fan, and we can appropriately make him the spokesman for all Amis's fans: Connolly's straightforward and emphatic (and appropriate—that "bloody") expression of enthusiasm captures exactly the sense of ungrudging and grateful admiration that long-standing readers of Amis tend to feel towards their favourite author.

For any writer—but especially, as his own criticism shows, one like Amis—the admiration of a loyal readership, where that admiration is related to the pleasure provided by their reading, must rank highly, probably above any other standard of literary judgement.[4] Following such a criterion it might seem that nothing else needs to be said by way of pressing a case for Amis's standing as a writer. Here, after all, he is, a mature, full-time novelist,

From *Kingsley Amis in Life and Letters,* ed. Dale Salwak (London: Macmillan Press, 1990), 100–129. Reprinted with permission of Macmillan Press, Ltd.

acclaimed winner of the Booker Prize and of other prizes and awards, his popular status enviably secure, now at a late-flourishing peak in a long and fairly prosperous career, throughout which he has produced a distinctive body of work (notable for its contemporary themes and generic range, and for markedly individual and original treatments). Is that not enough (especially by the criterion of literary success that Kingsley Amis himself has sought to have recognised as primary, with his creative work accordingly being seen as a means—as well as a beneficiary—of a re-emergence of critical common sense)? Is there anything more that needs to be said?

Yes there is, and for a number of very good reasons, the most pressing of which is that any shift in literary values, of the kind wished for by Amis, Philip Larkin and others, bringing a restoration of the naturally central significance, in making estimates of a writer, of that writer's being widely and appreciatively read, has not happened; and that (as usual) popular success seems to deflect, or inhibit, any widespread expectation or possibility of serious interest and artistic merit being found in what is also approved by popular taste. Amis is not the only writer to have been affected by this paradox and by the comparative critical inattention (or worse, unjustified but smug dismissal) that it induces, but his case is among the most puzzling for those of us who would want to argue that here is an author in whose work it is possible to establish a clear connection between his success with readers and what he has contributed to the art of the novel—that, indeed, the well-made, sprightly and renowned readability is the consequence of a serious interest in the technical possibilities of prose allied to a considerable linguistic awareness. In fact, the work of Kingsley Amis can be shown to be a test case for the standards of assessment that contemporary critical approaches bring to the art of the novel: failure to see that Amis's work is *seriously* interesting, and that he is a serious and honest artist in fiction, reflects more on the criteria and the concerns of present-day literary analysis than it does on Kingsley Amis's achievement.

Contemporary literary scholarship and criticism are too frequently unaware of the work of literature, and especially the novel, as a linguistic creation—that is, as an artistic and technical exploration of the resources of the writer's language and of the extent to which he controls them. The novel continues stubbornly to be regarded as Henry James's "loose and baggy monster" and a central element of this view is the notion that the language of fiction is a sort of dismissible scaffolding: the novel as a work of art is seen as a reducible object, with its language discounted as not being artistically integral, merely an inert—even accidental or provisional—means. There may be some point in such an attitude from one perspective, that of the ordinary reading experience engaged in unreflectively, since the changeful, transient, volatile, melting grasp we have of a book as we read it can seem to involve the formation of a reductive understanding that holds on to something other than language and wording. But a reductive conception inattentive to linguistic form can promise no headway with understanding the making and construction of the written text of a novel—the stable and finished piece of written language crafted, and given textuality, by the writer. It is here that one finds the true location of the art of the novel, and the novelist's fundamental artistic materials—in language.

Even when criticism does recognise matters of language and technique it is often only because technical features are so obtrusive and deviant that such attention becomes inescapable—as much a challenge to the reader or critic as they are a means of engagement with him. But a writer like Kingsley Amis, whose technical daring and considerable linguistic originality never involve a disturbing or less-than-standard-looking textual surface, tends not to attract this kind of interest, literary analysis not recognising the serious artist and technician who lies behind the openly realist and avowedly traditionally minded popular writer. Indeed, Amis's considerable technical resourcefulness remains so opaque to most contemporary criticism that all one is left with, by way of a positive estimate of his place as a writer, is the fair enough but far from complete view summed up—though not espoused—by Barbara Everett (when she, too, was puzzling over the relative lack of critical interest in Amis's work).

Dr. Everett saw the critical estimate as seeing Amis as "an entertaining comic social reporter who interrupted his development with bewildering excursions into the 'darker' forms of 'genre' or 'romance' fiction."[5] In thus characterising the general view (without, of course, subscribing to it) Barbara Everett also offered a reason for the "rather little critical attention" shown to Amis's work: "a reason is possibly its deficiency in 'seriousness,' as evidenced not only by humour but by lack of aesthetic concentration and intensity."[6] This makes it seem likely that criticism generally, in making a career-wide assessment of Amis's work, is only going to offer a version on the grand scale of the same kind of misunderstanding that, less macroscopically but very tenaciously, attached itself to Amis's first novel, *Lucky Jim*.

Early single-minded estimates of *Lucky Jim* either emphasised its humour (and the situational rather than the verbal side, with much praise for its farcical and slapstick routines), or made it the focus of portentous sociological speculation, or took it unquestioningly as the angry anti-cultural tract of an unappreciative vulgarian. Technique and construction and style went unconsidered, or were not appreciated, as with V. S. Pritchett's pre-publication conclusion that Amis was "writing with his boots."[7] Perhaps only Anthony Powell, in a (very) short notice in *Punch,* glimpsed at the time the literary qualities that more recent and considered estimates have brought to the fore, when he remarked that "*Lucky Jim* is perhaps a shade over-written, but it has energy and form."[8] And it is Powell who, almost thirty years later, sees *Lucky Jim*'s reputation established, not as a "half-educated hooligan['s] . . . professionally philistine book" but as "one that could only come from a writer who had thought a great deal about the arts—notably the art of writing."[9] A similar revaluation, similarly artistic in its emphasis, covering the wider scope of Amis's complete fictional *oeuvre,* is now called for, as a way of recognising the importance of his contribution to the contemporary art of the novel, and adding to the significance already claimed for Amis by critics like David Lodge.

There *is* an artistic case to be made out for Amis's work, and it is one that will be seen more and more to be grounded in matters of language, technique and constructional skill: "more and more" not only in the sense of an increasing awareness and appreciation of Amis's technical resourcefulness and linguistic skill (hardly recognised in any serious way so far), but also in the sense that the significance of this aspect of his work is to be seen as coming more noticeably to the fore as his career has developed. While technical adroitness and distinctive language are both there from the start (indeed, *That Uncertain Feeling* is as linguistically alert as any of the more recent works—and ditto *I Like It Here* in terms of construction),[10] it is also the case that Amis's most technically interesting works belong, first of all, to the middle period of his career from the late sixties to the early seventies—here, particularly, one thinks of *The Green Man, Girl, 20* and *Ending Up*—and then to what some people have seen as the late renaissance of his career—the period of his three masterpieces, *Jake's Thing, Stanley and the Women* and *The Old Devils.* Even though there are arguments of a similar kind to be made for the rest of the *oeuvre,* it has to be recognised that these six novels of Amis's stand out as being the main achievements of his career as a novelist and as the works which are most representative of his mature art, and of the firm grounding of that art in linguistic technique.

Raymond Tallis has acutely identified the most prominent features of Amis's work, listing them as "comic vision, linguistic skill, and mimetic genius."[11] Tallis's concise tripartition exhibits the necessary over-simplification of any critical discussion or analysis with its suggestion that elements involved in a complex and unified relationship can easily or naturally be separated out from each other. It has to be borne in mind (even as one analytically pretends otherwise) that the writer's art blends vision and skill—and that the writer's achievement is defined or measured by the interdependence of imagination, insight and technique.

In Kingsley Amis's case, "mimetic genius," although it goes much beyond how people talk into people's dress and behaviour, is very regularly a matter of splendidly alert and accurate linguistic observation. Similarly with "comic vision": from the very beginning of his career, wording as well as incident has been central to Amis's comedy, his humour being as much one of statement as of situation, indeed one where statement and situation are mutually productive, with imaginative wording enabling the creation of comic incident and fanciful incident calling forth appropriate and delightful wording. In Amis's work, Tallis's three elements—comedy, observation and technique—belong harmoniously together, so that any separate discussion of Amis's language on its own can run the risk of curtailing and limiting adequate coverage of all its significance. Nevertheless, and clearing the ground with such provisos, a closely focused and specifically linguistic discussion has to be undertaken, since ultimately the case for Amis's fictional art rests on an appreciation of his linguistic alertness, his stylistic virtuosity and the cultural role defined by his linguistic temperament.

It was in cultural and literary-historical terms that language was first seen as significant in promoting and establishing Kingsley Amis's importance as a writer. This was in the argument, first advanced by David Lodge, which viewed Amis's work in terms of its relation to recent literary history rather than in the sociological, political or even broadly cultural terms that had been emphasised by the earliest criticism of Amis, and which had associated the concerns of his novels with those of writers like Alan Sillitoe, John Braine and John Osborne. For Lodge—and on this matter he has continued to speak not only with the growing authority of a leading novelist and critic but also as a testifying beneficiary of the linguistic turn that he associates with Amis's work—the importance of Amis has to do with his use of language.[12]

Lodge sees himself as belonging to a generation for whom the possibilities of English fiction were transformed by Amis's early novels. Amis's work defined and established a new tone of voice, and—as Lodge would have it—*Lucky Jim* was a "magic book" because "it established the linguistic register we needed to articulate our sense of social identity, a precarious balance of independence and self-doubt, irony and hope."[13] This development, in Lodge's view, identifies Amis not only as "the most interesting and rewarding of . . . contemporaries" but indeed as "a writer of genuine literary 'importance.'" Amis's achievement in *Lucky Jim* inaugurates for Lodge—or, perhaps more accurately, makes possible—

> a whole new school of British novelists, who refused the mythopoeic streams of consciousness of the great modernists, and the somewhat specialised social and spiritual preoccupations of their successors, like Greene and Waugh, in favour of an observant and irreverent rendering of the texture of ordinary life, especially provincial life, in Britain, as the nation sluggishly tried to free itself from the constraints of the prewar class system.[14]

Lodge also acutely pinpoints the true cultural sources and the real, non-Great Traditional literary antecedents of Amis's innovative "linguistic register" as well as its most prominent technical qualities:

> It was not really anger that fuelled Amis's writing, but rather an acute sense of affectation and hypocrisy in social and personal behaviour. This he was able to convert into farcical comedy and a very distinctive prose style, superficially inelegant, but in fact full of artful and amusing rhetorical device. Kingsley Amis belongs to a very British tradition of novel writing that goes back to Dickens, Smollett, and Fielding, which uses irony and humour to explore serious subjects.[15]

To the socio-cultural and moral concerns of the central stream of the English fictional tradition Kingsley Amis brought, in Malcolm Bradbury's words, a "contemporary tone, expressed in that strongly-voiced, vernacular way of writing that has always been his signature, and which has let him turn particular resentments into comic good sense."[16] Amis was, according to Bradbury, voicing a "virtuous provincialism," expressing a plain-spoken commonsense through "the sound of a lower-middle class voice against upper-middle class language." Similar observations have been made by Neil McEwan, who thinks of language that is "delicate and close to ordinary speech" as Amisian, and who splendidly catches the tone and quality of Amis's language with his observation that "[Amis's] prose has been for many of his readers the language of contemporary common sense."[17]

Throughout the comments of these critics, it is noticeable that the distinctness of Amis's style is identified in dualistic terms, so that it is seen as a merging of normally separate—perhaps incongruous, certainly not coincident—elements: so the style is notable for being "superficially inelegant" but "artful," "upper-middle class language" now heard with a "lower-middle class voice," implying a speech that is "ordinary" but "delicate." The Amisian voice seems to be characterised by an unexpected balance of the natural and the artistic that matches with those other qualities ("independence and self-doubt, irony and hope") by which Lodge defined the mid-century experience that the voice came to express. It is a voice and a style that melds a traditional and confident consideredness with a sense of a pressing, seemingly unreflective spontaneity—a use of language, indeed, that brings close together the different values of the separate modes of speaking and writing. With hardly any other writer does one feel as securely as with Amis the sense of a written prose so idiomatic that it could straightforwardly transpose to unhalting, easy, literate speech, and no one else's writing conveys so clearly an almost audible sense of individually cadenced, directly spoken talk, of a communication shared between listening reader and informally talking author.

There are other qualities, again often recognised dualistically, that typify Amis's prose and that can be corroborated from the observations of other critics and reviewers. David Hughes gives the style its own name—"Amisspeak", a token of its unmistakability—and defines it in terms of paradox as "spiky prose, aimed at both accuracy and funniness."[18] And Martin Cropper, very acutely—and perhaps pinpointing the essence of what he calls an "educated blokeish dialect"—sees that "Amis's funniest sentences have been born of a marriage of two voices, erudite and demotic."[19] In fact, Amis's style (bearing in mind that each new work redefines and extends his range, and that each of his novels needs and finds its own stylistic specifications) is a splendidly individual read-along style, which is—the hallmark of Amis—both demotic and at the same time accurately depictive, managing to be both precise and colloquial, its apparently throw-away surface embracing judgement and consideration.

The Amis style is recognisable without ever becoming distracting. At its most recognisable and characteristic, it is a style that is detailed, informative, confiding, one that lends itself to nominal just as much as to verbal modes of report—that is, it is a style which sometimes prefers noun-centred phrasal statements of nomination, quantification and complex qualification before (though not ever, of course, to the suppression or exclusion of) verb-based clausal statements of predication and association. It is a style where the elements that make up clauses, and of these elements particularly noun phrases, come to the fore and do the kind of work, of relating and associating phenomena, that is usually, or primarily, the preserve of clauses themselves. It is a style where syntax provides modes of extension and linkage usually achieved by lexical means: and where lexical connections can as much depend on repetition as on variation and alternation. Over the piece, order (and directly processable sequence) matters more than—and carries more weight than—the more basic syntactic processes of relation and strong dependence. It is a syntax that allows a more than usual seepage between the categories and structures of distinct constituents, and which can appear loose, virtually unbound, even capricious.

But it is here that we can usefully recall that Amis's prose involves a sprightly and controlled coalition of the written and spoken modes of English, and of the different organisations of these two varieties. This is a complex matter, but Amis's prose mingles the lexical density and variety of written English with lexical habits more characteristic of speech—repetition, non-specificity and reference by nonce phraseological formations; and similarly his syntax blends and mingles characteristics, so that the nominalised and heavily self-embedding phraseological character of writing is supplemented with the elastic and intricate multiple-clause-linking choreography of speech.[20]

The end result is a consistent and recognisable style, notable for a pace-setting fluency that shows considerable idiomatic resourcefulness both in sentence structure and in word choice, but which never threatens to compromise what are clearly strongly held and (largely) well-thought-out puristic attitudes. Canons and conventions are extended or explored to the full, but never infringed, to the extent that Amis's prose can be seen, as by John Vaizey, as our own day's embodiment of the best and most effective written English. Reviewing *Ending Up,* Lord Vaizey observed:

> The book is compulsively readable and beautifully constructed. There is no writer now alive, other than Anthony Powell, who writes such classically pure English which is at the same time accurately and exactly idiomatic. This is a very rare gift that Mr. Amis has cultivated, so that there is nothing he cannot say economically and precisely if he wants to.[21]

The linguistic interest of Amis's writing is not confined to his timely establishment of a voice expressing emergent cultural attitudes, nor to the fact that that voice and style have come to occupy a ranking and even standardising position in the present-day fiction of the English socio-comic and moralist tradition. Amis is also a documentarist and student of the varied language he finds around him, and accurate renderings of contemporary English are often basic to his comedy. As Anthony Burgess has observed, generously and probably correctly, "The future will learn about the state of English today not from the linguists but from the novels of Amis. To say nothing of the customs and morality that go along with the language".[22] It is no wonder that Burgess likes Amis before any other modern English novelist and "read[s] his work with great relish."[23] The documentary naturalism of Amis's recent language must inevitably draw the admiration of Burgess, doubly qualified as both language student and novelist, who correctly saw that *Stanley and the Women* was

> beautifully written, meaning that the dialogue sounds for the most part as though its speakers had never read a book in their lives, and the *récit* is an exact analogue of somehow getting through the day, fuck it. When are critics going to learn that Augustan elegance may be all right for Church Triumphant satire but won't do for genuine fiction?[24]

In similar terms, Burgess found the excellence of the very recent and more typically Amisian *Difficulties with Girls* to be located in "the style of the *récit*, which always catches the torn edges of the strain of getting through the day, and the cunning of the dialogue, which is far more true to life than anything a tape-recorder could pick up."[25] These are generous and serious—and authoritative—claims from the other English novelist of today noted for an informed and observant concern with language. Burgess's testimonials remind us of the much earlier assessment of Amis, made by Professor Wallace Robson, that he is "one of the most skilful novelists now writing," who "has turned what could have been the gifts of a scholarly linguist, with a refined ear for the nuances and 'registers' of speech, to purposes of satirical observation."[26]

Kingsley Amis is *the* novelist of contemporary social and linguistic observation, bringing the skills of a natural mimic to the representation of present-day habits of speech and linguistic behaviour, either because these are noteworthy in their own right, or because the novelist sees an opportunity to add to the realism of a characterisation, or because of the comedy involved in representing something that is not linguistically standard only with the resources of written standard English.

Among many examples, there comes to mind most memorably (one almost writes "memorablam") nasty Bertrand Welch in *Lucky Jim,* turning final open syllables with the high vowel [iː] or [ɪ] into syllables with a more open vowel, perhaps [æ], and with an accompanying marked labial closure giving a simultaneous nasal articulation, so that the syllable is perceived as closed with a nasal consonant. Bertrand is fixed for ever as the type of sneering speaker who haughtily turns *you see* into "you sam", and *hostelry* into "hostelram," and so on. Then, in *Girl, 20,* there are Sir Roy Vandervane's fashionable assimilations, fully in character, giving colloquially slurred forms like "hambag," "scream-play," "firse discovery," "moce grateful" and so on. Then there is Student Mansfield in *I Want It Now,* loud and from the American South (the name Student no doubt patterned on the more familiar Dean), and with utterances like "I'm a-gettin' pissed off" comically transcribed as *Armageddon pier staff,* suggesting the Southern drawling and lengthening of stressed vowels, and such other Southern features as: monophthongal [a:] as the realisation equivalent to /aɪ/; the archaic *a*-prefix accompanying progressive forms of the verb; voicing of intervocalic /t/; [ɪn] for [ŋ]; centralising and "broken" [+ə] for /ɪ/; and back and unrounded [ɑ] in *off.* Best of all is Ernie, the college porter in *Jake's Thing:*

> The head porter Ernie, as fat and yet as pale as ever, stood in his habitual place at the entrance of his lodge. He gave Jake a savage wink that involved the whole of one side of his face and everything but the eye itself on the other.
> "Nice little lot of young gentlewomen come up to our university these days, eh sir?"
> "Wonderful." Jake put down his suitcase and straightened his tie and smoothed his hair.
> "No problem to you though, I'll be baned." Bound was what most men would have said but this one came from Oxfordshire or somewhere.
> "I don't quite see why you . . ." Oh Christ, he had forgotten again.
> The porter chuckled threateningly and wagged a forefinger. "Nay nay, Mr. Richardson, you know what I'm talking abate. Plenty of people remember the way you used to weigh the girls, I can tell you. A ruddy uncraned king you were. You fancied something—pay! you got it. And I bet you still know how to mark 'em dane."

The most distinctive feature of Ernie's accent, from rural Oxfordshire ("or somewhere"—it could be slightly further south in the Central Midlands) is that the diphthong /aʊ/ is realised as [ɛʉ] or even [ɛy], with a fronted and only weakly rounded second element, and so is heard by the literate and RP-speaking Jake as equivalent to his own /eɪ/ (hence the <aCe>, <ei>, <ay>, <ai> and other spellings).

The most recent instance is in *Difficulties with Girls,* where Jenny Bunn—a Northern English speaker—hears an up-to-date-accented Londoner talking confusingly about the "Reds" in the Spanish mountains (sc. "roads"), and revealing the recent tendency of the RP diphthong /ɛʊ/ (from earlier /oʊ/) to lose or unround the very weak second element, being realised as [e+] or [ɛ+], or monophthongal [e].

Keen-eared and comically spelt observations involve not only natural phonetic forms but also extend to the representation of temporary and bizarre qualities of vocal delivery. The best example of all is in *Take a Girl Like You* where Patrick Standish and Julian Ormerod drive up to London, and—one has to presume—have lunch before spending the afternoon drinking, and then apparently go round (so that Patrick can be introduced) to the girl-friends of Julian's with whom they will be spending the weekend. One of the girls is called Joan, a fact Patrick manages to recall when, by this time very drunk, he finds himself in a strange house and comes upon a woman he has never met before. When he gets her attention, Patrick introduces himself:

> "Hullo, I parry stashed a nowhere hermes peck humour speech own," he heard himself say. "June I haggle unction when donned ring gone oh swear."

What Patrick must be hearing, with a tiny and sober but puzzled part of his mind, is a drunkenly slurred attempt at speech, marred by assimilations and smoothings that destroy normally perceivable syllable structures. He is trying to say:

> "Hullo, I'm Patrick Standish. (I) don't know where I am. (I) expect you must be Joan. Julian and I had lunch and went on drinking, God knows where."

Linguistic observations are not confined to the accurate—and, in standard orthography, comic—rendering of non-standard, innovative, or accidental phonetics. Individual styles of speech and conversation, not necessarily peculiar, but always distinctive, are captured in the round in comic setpieces and vignettes. The comedy in such instances does without the aid of any contrivance of representation; natural and exact representation shows the use of language to be comic and revealing on its own: as in, for instance, all the conversations of Jim Dixon and Professor Welch (best of all, outside the university library); the trendy and awful cleric, the Rev. Tom Rodney Sonnenschein, in *The Green Man,* and in *The Green Man* too, the ponderously circumlocutionary and polysyllabic style of the elderly visiting (and ghost-enquiring) American (a distant Welsh-descended cousin of whose turns up in *The Old Devils*); Stanley Duke's mother- and (better still) awful sister-in-law in *Stanley and the Women;* every single character, each of them idiolectally self-revealing, in *Take a Girl Like You,* and all the oldsters in *Ending Up,* each with his or her childish, child-like or non-adult deficiency or incapacity of speech; the pub landlord in *Difficulties With Girls;* the all too unbelievable Eve Greenstreet in *Jake's Thing;* Julian Ormerod in *Take a Girl Like You;* Dr. Nash in *Stanley and the Women;* and so on, and so on.

Not only personal linguistic styles, but also situationally or generically well-defined or restricted uses of language can be the material of splendid parodic set pieces. Again, just a few examples: Jenny Bunn's unpractised letter home (*Take a Girl Like You*); Maurice Allington's Address to a Pimple (*The Green Man*); a Good Food Guide entry (*The Green Man*); Dylan Thomas's poetry (*That Uncertain Feeling*); the narrative summary of the eviction of the "Old Devils" from their local pub done as an English-audience-guiding synopsis of a heavy Germanic opera (*The Old Devils*); Jake's college-meeting statement on the admission of women; and so on.

The linguistic alertness and virtuosity one finds in the way Kingsley Amis uses English creatively are also to be seen in his observant documentation of developments in contemporary English. Various fugitive or controversial developments catch his attention certainly as readily as they do the attention of linguists—and once or twice with more awareness, it seems: thus forms over whose existence linguists have argued, or against whose existence they have legislated, on theoretical or semantic grounds, are shown—when assimilated to a natural setting in the Amis text—to have an idiomatic function that must justify acceptance of the development (although, in Amis's own case, not necessarily approval). Once more, only a few examples: "It hardly notices now" (*Girl, 20*); "Well, according to me a bit does matter" (*That Uncertain Feeling,* but there are several instances in other, including nonfictional, writings); "What did you pay for it you don't mind my asking?" (*Jake's Thing*); "Well, not the sexton is what I'm suggesting" (*Jake's Thing*), "the telephone rang, Brenda went to or across the kitchen to answer it and was hung up on as soon as she spoke" (*Jake's Thing*); "Oh dear, nor I have" (*Difficulties with Girls*); "The wife's been being a little bit provoking" (*Stanley and the Women*); "No, nobody. Just, I have these interviews fixed in Glasgow tomorrow and . . ." (*Stanley and the Women*); " 'Stanley, you know that new girl, the one with the cage? With the what? Is that the same as the one with the rope?' " (*Stanley and the Women*).[27]

Amis's novels reveal original possibilities of the language in their wider characteristics as well as in specific details, and one modern development that some of the most recent ones (such as *Jake's Thing* and *Stanley and the Women*) catch—and indeed, contribute to in an original way—is the close assimilation of patterns once severely and separately characteristic of written and spoken English. In *Jake's Thing* the free indirect narrative of Jake's consciousness, a mingling of narrator and character that is hard ever to prise apart, is done in a complex prose combining the static and unifying quality of writing with the dynamic and projective character of speech. This led one critic (undeservedly leavening total misjudgement with an unrecognised half-insight) to speculate that the novel had been dictated.[28] And even Martin Amis was led to complain that *Jake's Thing* was coarsely or loosely written, not in the sense that its vocabulary was blue or anything like that, but in the sense that it was written in a swirly or underpunctuated prose, so that commas and so on that one might have expected were missing (and not just in naturalism-seeking spoken bits either), or one found commas where one expected semi-colons and so on.[29]

Both the dictation-sniffing critic and Amis *fils* seem to have recognised or felt that Jake's prose is a mingling of the recognisably distinct (but entirely compatible) complexities of writing and speaking. But insofar as this written prose has taken on spoken shapes they were dissatisfied with it.

The short answer to all this is that *Jake's Thing* is written the way it is for good reasons of characterisation, and this was the answer that Amis *père* gave—that all the "swirly" features were connected with the establishment of a particular tone of voice in *Jake's Thing*. The syntax or construction is not carelessly loose, nor thoughtlessly lacking in lucidity, just as an alleged coarseness of vocabulary—"those rude words," as they were called—was not gratuitous but contributed, Amis also argued, to the reader's awareness of Jake's rage and impatience and the weakening of any standardising pride and constraint.

Amis's response did not elaborate on the function of sentence construction in *Jake's Thing* but the answer is, surely, that Jake has such scholarly, bookish, print-habituated mental habits that any largely spoken–vernacular mode for rendering his consciousness is ruled out. (An example of that singular mode, and of the different problems involved in giving it a narrated written shape, is found in the narrative rendering of Ronnie Appleyard's consciousness in *I Want It Now*.) The shape of Jake's thoughts demands a representation transcending the spoken/demotic and written/Attic divide, and incorporating features of both; the free indirect narrative of *Jake's Thing* is designed to meet this requirement, and hence its most prominent constructional characteristics: extensive and complexly structured noun (and other) phrases—a feature of writing—in conjunction with free-flowing, lengthy, multiple, choreographic interrelations of clauses—a feature of speech.

Stanley Duke's first-person narrative in *Stanley and the Women* involves other kinds of mingling of the conventions and characteristics of writing and speaking; or rather, it is a book naturally engaged with by the reader as a piece of writing, to be processed as text-of-a-particular-written-and-literary-genre in the normal way, but which turns out clearly to have been put together by a narrator more at home with the conventions and possibilities of spoken discourse, and who makes little or no bookishly conditioned concessions to the needs and interests of an absent *reader*. Stanley expects us to have or know from the inexplicit printed pages things he has heard or has come to know directly from situated speech.

A different kind of confrontation or coalition of the spoken and the written is found in *The Old Devils,* a technically disconcerting novel, where the very syntax of the Welsh-accented oldsters, standardly Standard English though it is in construction, seems to guarantee that, reading it, the reader hears it, in his mind's ear, like a Welsh accent. (It is no wonder that Alan Watkins—who should know—"can think of no one who has such a good ear for Welsh graduate English—or, for that matter, any other kind of English—as Amis.")[30] While it is hard (or rather, comic) to imagine Bakhtinian doctrines of fictional language (monologic against dialogic discourse, and the heterogeneous oral and written sources of the dialogic) having any specific influence on Amis's work, or being researched by him, many of Amis's recent and most audacious explorations have been across the discursive separation of written and spoken language. Indeed, with a—surely accidental—Bakhtinian appropriacy, *Russian Hide-and-Seek* keeps its reader keenly aware of the different discursive, textual and even other-linguistic modes that dialogically come together in the text.

Evelyn Waugh famously insisted to his *Paris Review* interviewer that he regarded "writing not as an investigation of character, but as an exercise in the use of language, and with this I am obsessed."[31] Waugh and Amis are coming to be seen as having a good deal in common (even though not all the correspondences are convincingly different from coincidence);[32] it is perhaps no surprise to find that they have overlapping views on the art of fiction, and on the importance thereto of language.

Both Amis and Waugh are deeply concerned always to make proper use of the novelist's medium of language. They both place a high value on being readable, and they both seem to write having in mind the ordinary educated reader's linguistic standards and tolerances. Amis clearly shares Waugh's Pinfoldian readiness to be "shocked by . . . a fault in syntax"[33] and, like Waugh, shares the interest voiced by the rhetorician in Waugh's *Helena* (1950) in "the joinery and embellishment of his sentences, in the consciousness of high rare virtue when every word has been issued in its purest and most precise sense, *in the kitten games of syntax and rhetoric*" (italics added).[34] Finally, and—intriguingly—also in answer to an interviewer (Michael Billington, on "Kaleidoscope" on BBC Radio 4 in 1979), there is Amis's own testimony on the artistic priority he accords to formal and linguistic concerns: "more and more, as time goes by, it's a literary exercise—which may sound a complete platitude, but it's much more to do with the arrangements of words than it is with expressing observations about life and, certainly, trying to change society."[35]

The coincident views of Amis and Waugh have a significant verbal echo that suggests a conceptual overlap: "an exercise in the use of language" (Waugh)—"a literary exercise . . . to do with the arrangements of words" (Amis). It seems that they both regard writing as, fundamentally, an undertaking that develops and enriches one's mastery of the language. There is, between Waugh and Amis, another similarity, one made suddenly relevant in the context of their common insistence on the centrality of language. The point can be illustrated from the case of Waugh. Like his own self-revealing creation, Pinfold, Evelyn Waugh disliked every artistic development of his own lifetime, and yet (as Malcolm Bradbury has noted) despite his "professed dislike for the modernist avant-garde" Waugh "invented remarkable new techniques for fiction."[36] Precisely the same paradox is discernible, but perhaps more decisively, in the work of Kingsley Amis.

For all that he is an unrepentant traditionalist who has consistently scorned the overt and obtrusive technical experiments of literary modernism (with this consistency showing further in a Waugh-like rejection of modernism in all its artistic manifestations) Kingsley Amis remains an innovative, skilful, and technically interesting writer: a writer who is important simply because of the new, but legitimate, things he keeps doing with language. No novelist currently writing rivals Amis's rich linguistic awareness, this awareness showing not only (as we have seen) in exact and accurate, and comically profitable, renderings of the more unexpected forms and idioms of standard and colloquial English, but also in his consummate and alert (and increasingly confident) sense of the endless and still unexplored opportunities available to the present-day novelist writing in English—even (or rather especially) one who is also anti-modernist.

Amis's quarrel with modernism is fundamentally over the technical unwarrantedness of the artistic crisis it represents and promotes, and how it hastens towards a foreshortened end the natural extension of the tradition. "What had happened" (Amis recently argued) "was not that the possibilities of the symphony, the sonnet or the easel picture had been used up, but that for the first time their end could be foreseen—like the end of the civilisation that had given them birth."[37] Almost a quarter of a century earlier Amis—reviewing for the *Spectator*—had rejected the more intrusive kinds of fictional experiment precisely for being technically uncalled-for, for taking such an eclipsing stance over a still-valid adventurousness in more recognisably traditional areas: " 'Experiment' in this context boils down pretty regularly to 'obtruded oddity,' whether in construction—multiple viewpoints and such—or in style: it is not felt that adventurousness in subject matter or attitude or tone really counts."[38]

Amis's own testimony is so emphatic that he is seen—inevitably and unquestioningly, but all too simplistically—as an out-and-out traditionalist and realist. His opposition to experiment, of long standing and typically expressed without qualification, has always been so clear and forceful that it has continued to get in the way of the counter-evidence provided by the construction of his own novels. For instance, in a broadcast discussion in 1974 between Kingsley Amis and his novelist son Martin, Martin Amis observed: "I have always thought it remarkable that someone who is as linguistically aware as my father should never have sought to experiment in prose at all, or to have seen any virtue whatever in slightly experimental prose." Kingsley Amis's immediate answer was brief and uncompromising, and must seem unqualifiedly final: "Experimental prose is death."[39] But by 1974 Amis had already written novels like *The Green Man* and *Girl, 20,* both of them mid-career harbingers of the textual and formal adventurousness that has more and more characterised his later work. Can uncompromising precept and arguable practice be reconciled?

There is clearly a sense, and it must always be given priority, in which "experimental prose," is, for Amis, "death"—namely the kind of writing that manneredly exhibits or noisily proclaims its own technical novelty (like a completed building but with scaffolding left up—different, but also distracting and pointless). But if the dread word "experiment" can be allowed to apply to extraordinarily innovative but apparently ordinary-looking writing, then Kingsley Amis is a writer who—especially recently—has been experimenting in subtle and restrained ways. "Experimental," after all, can have the meaning of showing the efficacy of something previously untried (in other words, being adventurous) as well as having the meaning—the more prominent one in criticism—of using or proclaiming new ways, simply because they are not traditional. One is in danger here of quibbling fruitlessly over words but the point needs to be established—Kingsley Amis is not simply the straightforward realist that his anti-experimental protestations (and the traditional look of his texts) so beguilingly suggest.

A phrase of Amis's from a 1955 review ("that blend of answerless riddle, outworn poeticism and careful linguistic folly"—a denunciation of the apocalyptic style, both in prose and verse, of Dylan Thomas) catches exactly his opposition to language used pointlessly and under almost contradictory demands.[40] Linguistic rationality is to be judged on several levels. Language has not only to be put together carefully but must result in something sensible. One is required not only to have something to say but also to make sense to others. Any use of language must be communicative, and must give the reader a chance to be directly involved. Being a novelist or poet is no excuse for not saying things that people generally can understand. Amis's stance against experiment is not a disavowal of the relevance of technique but against its fundamental abuse. Rather than dismissing technical awareness, Amis dismisses only technical experiment that is unmotivated, obtrusive or obscuring. Experiment can have a point, without being noisily proclaimed and without eclipsing tradition.

One area of Kingsley Amis's work in particular has shown a sophisticated commitment to versatility, indeed to an audacity that is not confined by the traditional and the orthodoxly approved. This is in the construction of highly individual, first-person narratives, especially in those two remarkable mid-period novels, *The Green Man* and *Girl, 20,* with their self-revealing (indeed, self-betraying) narrators. The ghost story, *The Green Man,* has an odd first-person narrator, odd not just as a character but as a storyteller. And the narrator of *Girl, 20,* side-lined and alienated though he is, is a more interesting "character" than anyone else in the novel. Seemingly "no-nonsense" and objective, he gets things exactly wrong: and he is so elusive that he recalls other "designing or naïve?" narrators like Fowler (in Greene's *Quiet American*) and Dowell (in Ford's *Good Soldier*).

But the novel I want to deal with in some, albeit far-from-complete, analytic detail in illustration of just one aspect of Kingsley Amis's linguistic skilfulness is *Jake's Thing,* a novel that is perhaps the most fully achieved and technically resourceful in the whole Amis canon. *Jake's Thing* abounds in the most astonishingly complex—but also natural and comic—conversations involving Jake and one or other of those who are a "trial" to him such as

Geoffrey Mabbott or Dr. Rosenberg: the subtle detail of these conversations stands as counter-evidence to the viewpoint of the pressing and Jake-centred subjective narrative, and in the end what is shown by the conversations counts against Jake, against the reliability of his judgements, and against his whole prejudicial and soured outlook.

In the counterpointing of subjective narrative and "objective" dialogue, the text of *Jake's Thing* provides a typically Amisian instance of the other side getting a chance—with the subjective narrative of the misogynist Jake's perspective counterpointed by the subtle evidence of conversational exchanges involving Jake, which show Jake as a manipulator who can only see things the way he sees things, and who always engages in conversation uncooperatively and so as to put the other at a disadvantage. When we see Jake directly for ourselves as we do in conversations, and when we see how others—whom he has prejudged for us—are treated by him in these conversations, we have to see Jake's mind as prejudicial and set, and wrong, in its views, even as these views are coming at us, almost overwhelmingly, in the narrative. In the end, the reader cannot side with Jake's estimates of people like Geoffrey Mabbott or Dr. Rosenberg; nor indeed—in that notorious ending—with Jake's views on women. The considerable art of the novel lies in the extent to which conversations which might appear to make out that Geoffrey and Rosenberg are exactly as Jake sees them, are prejudicially manipulated or construed by Jake and, of course, skilfully constructed—with deep linguistic insight—by Jake's author.

The title of *Jake's Thing* refers, first of all, to Jake Richardson's obsession and complaint about women and about his dealings with them, and then to his complaint in a medical sense (Jake is suffering from loss of libido), and finally to the organ most visibly affected by this complained-of affliction—his, well, his thing. But the title *Jake's Thing* is also appropriate in another, less expected, sense since the book is very much *Jake's* thing, its subjective narrative embodying Jake's particular and very singular point of view. The novel is narrated almost entirely from Jake's perspective and in his tone of voice. It is a particular, instantly identifiable tone of voice, expressing a very individual cast of mind. The tone is educated-slangy, endlessly resourceful in phraseology and construction, but still sounding vernacular and plain speaking; and the attitude expressed is richly observant, and capable of endless discrimination, but still managing to seem convincingly rational and to be speaking (in that distinctively plain or unconsidered way) nothing but good sense. The combination of perception and expression embodied in the narrative stance of *Jake's Thing* is one which even the most judicious reader has to be wary of, and to treat circumspectly: idea and wording go together so well that what they mutually instantiate can begin to seem objective, uncontroversial and irresistible.

The reader of *Jake's Thing* has to keep in mind all the time that everything is told from the point of view of the soured, sated and bitter central character and that what is presented may not accord with what is objectively factual and true, no matter how much it looks as if it does (and works to persuade us that it does). The reader has to realise that the point of view of the narrative is not only not that of the author but also is not necessarily subscribed to by the author, and further, that the reader's judgement of the narrative's view of things (and then of the real-world author's relation to *that*) is not to be confined only to what the almost omnipresent and single-mindedly prejudicial narrative seems to offer. There may be other sources of evidence.

In *Jake's Thing* there *are* other sources of evidence—in the natural-seeming and realistic conversations Jake has with other characters and which are incorporated within the surrounding Jake-centred subjective narrative. This factor gives the novel considerable technical interest, since it involves the reader in judging the attitudes of the narrative against the dramatic evidence of conversations, but with the additional hazard that the conversations, as they come to the reader, are not—for the reader—independent of the narrative viewpoint but are, in fact, broached by the reader with expectations already conditioned or bespoken by the dominating narrative. In fact, if the reader is not alert to various linguistic ploys, conversations that are simply set up, or that are brusquely and tendentiously engaged in by Jake, can seem to corroborate Jake's point of view: but what they really do is expose Jake's conversational trickery, and after that his general unreliability.

The essence of Jake's conversational routines is to make out that all leaden conversational awkwardness, and none of the intellect, belong exclusively to the other side in the conversation. In fact, these appearances are simply the consequence of Jake's being deliberately uncooperative in conversation with others, and of his refusing to make the imaginative and intellectual concessions that any conversational exchange makes necessary.

The working and progress of conversation depend not so much on matters of common or mutual knowledge, but on matters of mutually discernible relevance.[41] One particular factor which demonstrates this is the lack of any need for what is held to be accepted as true during a conversation to be exactly equivalent to what is generally taken as true about the world. Conversation does not depend on there being a world view common to both or all participants and identical in all respects with a general and scientific world view— the world view that one could find in a very up-to-date, totally accurate, and endlessly specific encyclopaedia. What matters in conversation is that participants understand each other and know exactly what is meant, and perhaps how what is meant comes to be. From the principle that no conversationalist can know and believe everything exactly as it is, there follows a necessary corollary, that knowledge of everything exactly as it is is never a criterion for conversational appropriacy or success. In circumstances where the only certainties are that nobody knows everything, and that everybody is ignorant about different things, a criterion based on what is known and believed (and even on what is mutually known and believed) can not be made to work. But the general principles and structure of conversation make a virtue of this: instead of handicapping or inhibiting conversation, the lack of any reliable basis in mutual knowledge or belief is what lies behind the possibility of ordinary conversation, since it forces the development of compensatory principles.

Among the maxims of conversational co-operativeness framed by the philosopher H. P. Grice is the central injunction "Be relevant" (the maxim of relation), supplemented later by Grice in his additional maxim (of tailoring), expressed as "Frame whatever you say in the form most suitable for any reply that would be regarded as appropriate," or "Facilitate in your form of expression the appropriate reply."[42] These are principles concerned with the adequacy, appropriacy, and (above all) the mutually discernible relevance of utterances—these principles enjoining standards (both of performance and interpretation) on all conversational participants. It is how an utterance measures up to such standards (and not whether it would be allowed to stand in some encyclopaedia or whether it mentions something that everyone should know or understand) which finally determines whether an utterance is qualified to stand where it does in the developing conversational exchange.

Kingsley Amis's novels have always reflected an understanding of the nature of ordinary conversation, of how it works, and of how—when it does not work—it can be funny, and of how all this depends on the degree to which conversational partners co-operate by making utterances that show the fullest possible relevance and that are framed so as to facilitate relevant understanding and relevant response. The following conversation from *Girl, 20,* where nothing much is said apart from bits of the same thing being repeatedly exchanged between the speakers, involves failure of understanding—and, for us, comedy—because Kitty and Sir Roy Vandervane, talking about their small son Ashley, have different notions of how much needs to be said for something to be seen as relevant, and for appropriate—and relevant—understanding and response to be facilitated (Yandell is narrating):

> Behind me, I (quite distinctly) heard Kitty say, "Darling, I wonder if you'd have a word with Ashley about the bathroom."
> Roy answered, "Have a word with him about what?"
> "I wondered if you'd have a word with Ashley."
> "That was the bit I heard. Have a word with him about what? I heard the bit about having a word with him."
> "About the *bath* . . . room."
> "What about the bathroom?"
> "Darling." Kitty sounded relaxed to the point of imminent sleep. "Would you have a word with Ashley about it?"
> "I know! I know! I heard the bit about having a word with him about the bathroom. What about the bathroom? Christ—what is it about the bathroom that you want me to have a word with him, Ashley, about?"
> "Really, darling. About *peeing* in the bathroom. That's what I want you to have a word with him about. If you would."

He howled like a wolf, his usual method of indicating belated comprehension, and said, "There at last. You want me to have a word with Ashley about peeing in the bathroom."

"Yes," said Kitty in a voice full of lines of strain and glazed eyes and skin stretched tightly over cheekbones.

There was a pause, during which Roy nodded his head a good deal and I began to wonder, for the first time in my life, whether the experience of listening to the whole of Bruckner's Eighth Symphony might not have something to be said for it after all. Then Roy asked,

"What about it?"

"*Oh!* Tell him *not* to!"

"I've done that and he goes on peeing."

"Use your authority."

"How? What authority? We agreed he's not to be punished and we can't go back on that. I'm not suggesting for a moment we go back on that. But what sort of word can I have with him? I'm not asking rhetorically, I can assure you. I really would like to know."

In Chapter 20 of *Jake's Thing,* a meeting of the Fellows of St. Comyn's College discusses a problem connected with the layout and upkeep of a churchyard at Stanton St. Leonard near Oxford, over which the college has certain (but only partial) rights: the local community has certain rights as well, and the two sets of rights have become confused. Very active in the discussion is the haughty, smooth and very unappealing Senior Tutor, Roger Dollymore, and at one point he is countered by the College's writer in residence, a brusque, unpolished and over-direct individual, the opposite of Dollymore in style and manner and so quite out of place in the college as well as being ignorant of the procedures of its meetings. The outcome of the discussion seems to be agreement on new, perhaps temporary, arrangements over a recently dug grave not properly belonging in the college section of the cemetery. These involve realignments that will avoid disturbing the grave, the latter being the more extreme procedure advocated by Dollymore. Unwilling to let the matter go, Dollymore hints at a difficulty he foresees with the plan that everyone else has at last agreed to:

He said defiantly,

"It'll be all very well until the autumn."

The writer in residence, who had often declared that he had done no writing at all as yet and had no plans for doing any while in residence, and who was wearing a red-and-black upper garment the material of which had been fashioned by human ingenuity, and who had uttered a loud yelp of deprecation on hearing Dollymore's first proposal for the treatment of the offending cadaver, said, "What happens in the autumn then?"

Dollymore said as to an imbecile, "The leaves fall."

"And?"

"And cover the ground."

"So?"
"So somebody has to clear them eh-way."
"Like?"
"Like? Like?"
"I mean who, you know."
"Oh who. Well not the sexton is what I'm suggesting."
"Why not?"
"Because his responsibility is to us, not to Mr. . . . Goodchild or his relations. He must have nothing to do with that grave and it'll be an ugly sight by Christmas."

This conversational vignette, though not involving Jake, shows us, in a brief scope, all that is wrong with conversation engaged in according to Jake's principles. Again, it is a matter of seeing that intelligence and conversational skill do not all belong on one side and that not being able to see the full picture that the other side already sees clearly, since (the other side would say, "even though") it has been implicated only (*viz.,* "sufficiently") by a cryptic (*viz.,* "explicit") remark, is not grounds for equating temporary conversational unawareness or obtuseness with permanent intellectual incapacity.

The writer in residence knows all about leaves falling in autumn and about their having usually to be cleared away, typically by an appropriate person deputed to do so. The one shortcoming in the conversation begins and ends with Dollymore—who does not make sufficiently clear (and has to have it dragged from him bit by bit) exactly what is the relevance of his point about autumn, and the falling leaves, and their having to be cleared up (as well as his pretending not to recognise a widely current contemporary idiom).

The conversation between Dollymore and the writer in residence does not fail because it depends on a person knowing what autumn is, and what happens then: everybody knows that, but at the very most the only people for whom such awareness could be made conscious and relevant in connection with what has been said by Dollymore would be people fully familiar with the college property at Stanton St. Leonard; a temporarily present outsider is at more than a disadvantage contextually—he has no context at all to draw on. Even people thoroughly acculturated to Oxford college and/or rural life, and aware of the likely environs and standards of a village churchyard falling under a college's responsibility, might be a little disconcerted when trying to see the point of Dollymore's inexplicit reference, which is so elliptical that, rather than being informative, it is merely allusive for those already informed, or who are otherwise knowledgeably in the picture. Dollymore's allusive style might be enough for even an atheist who had read some Hardy or Gray, but it is clearly not enough for an uncontextualised, dislocated, and not-yet-oriented visiting writer (what this might tell us about him as a *writer* could be an issue, but it would be another issue).

The writer in residence has none of the relevant background. He is new to the college, and ignorant of its ways. His background is urban, and he seems likely to be socialist, atheist, and unchurchy. He has probably never seen—even heard of—Stanton St. Leonard, and can have only a hazy idea of the college's involvement with it. Everyone else probably has an idea, more than sufficient to be clearly reminded of the problem Dollymore has in mind with his hint of autumnal troubles. But the writer in residence does not know, and cannot really be expected—without further light being thrown on things—to see much further forward from the glimmer provided by Dollymore. It is not that the writer does not know about autumn, and that the leaves fall then, and that, when they do so, they cover the ground, and that if they stay there in a cemetery someone in a position of authority or responsibility will have to clear them away. It is simply that the writer has heard nothing (until he forces it, detail by detail, from Dollymore) that could be expected to make him—from the context he has—bring these points consciously to mind as the relevant context for the little Dollymore said to begin with. Indeed, once these basic points are made explicit, the writer in residence gathers what the central issue has to be—that there is someone in particular whose job it is to sweep the leaves. It is a little surprising, perhaps, that he does not work out that this will be the local sexton, but in his favour should be noticed Dollymore's vagueness ("somebody has to clear them," almost as if Dollymore himself did not know).

The question of who forces Dollymore to become fairly explicit and clear, although with the astonishing claim "not the sexton is what I'm suggesting." Dollymore may be satisfied that his opening remark about autumn was sufficiently indicative of both its context and its point for all the other established members of the college to have seen that he was suggesting something by what he said. But neither what he said to start with, nor that extended by the details he is forced to supply, has been enough for what he has in mind to have been clearly suggested to the writer in residence.

Once the sexton is mentioned the crucial matter (a mixture of fact and Dollymore's attitude and belief) that could not ever become clear without being made explicit is, belatedly but more or less sufficiently, put into words: that the sexton is responsible only to the college (fact) and that, accordingly, he will be neither able nor entitled to look after the offending grave (Dollymore's opinion). Had Dollymore explained all this straightaway at the start, the writer in residence would have been quite clear what the point was and Dollymore would have been seen as a sensitive person taking account of another person's unfamiliarity with local things in explaining things sufficiently to him. And the writer in residence would not have had (with a mixture of patience and stubbornness, but detrimentally to our first-glance view of his intelligence) to drag relevant details—clarifying a point and establishing a context—from the haughty, opportunistic and sneering ("eh-way," "Like? Like?") Dollymore.

In conversation, Jake is just as unhelpful as—and more exploitive than—Dollymore. He makes out various things about people—for instance, that Dr. Rosenberg is an ignoramus, and that Geoffrey Mabbott is hopelessly confused—simply by tendentious manipulation of conversations with these people. Some of these conversations Jake has with Rosenberg and Geoffrey are among the comic high points of the novel, but many of them are too lengthy and complex to be analysed sufficiently in a limited space. One brief, but entirely typical, example of Jake in conversation with the unfortunate Geoffrey Mabbott can usefully illustrate the various levels of claim made here—and especially the claim that Kingsley Amis is acute and adventurous in the use he makes of language in his novels.

Jake takes every opportunity to put Geoffrey at cross-purposes conversationally. Even the briefest of encounters is turned into an exercise in discomfiting and confusing the wretched Geoffrey. As the opening narrative of the following shows, speedy opportunism is central to Jake's tactics:

> This morning he had dressed in the dark as usual: chocolate-brown corduroy trousers, navy-blue cable-stitch pullover, black shoes and the jacket of his dark-grey suit. His manner was friendly but slightly restless, again a familiar combination. Jake lost no time in asking him whether Alcestis was expected to join them.
> "Alcestis?"
> "Yes. Is she joining us?"
> Geoffrey frowned and shook his head. "No," he said with an upward inflection. "Where did you get that idea from?"
> "I didn't get—"
> "I mean why should she be joining us?"
> "Well, Brenda's here and I thought—"
> "I know, Jake, I know Brenda's here, I've just this moment spoken to her," said Geoffrey, gently enough but with some triumph at having so readily diagnosed the acute senile dementia that must have caused Jake to be brought to this place.
> To distract himself from restraining himself from kicking Geoffrey in the balls Jake said,
> "What's whatsisname like, Ed, the fellow who runs these do's?"

Jake's opening question, about whether Alcestis is going to join them, is brought out without any orientating preamble: Jake doesn't tell Geoffrey why he thinks Alcestis might or ought to be there, he doesn't put the question in terms that relate to Geoffrey's observable circumstances by asking if Geoffrey is there on his own or with his wife, he doesn't first explain that his own wife Brenda is there, or anything like that. Jake just puts his brusque question, and so fails to facilitate either Geoffrey's understanding, or his reply. Geoffrey makes no answer to Jake's maladroit opening question, but instead responds with a question echoing the most prominent item of Jake's. This is a mark both of Geoffrey's being disconcerted and yet of his being willing to enter the conversation once he can see a way to do so: his single-word response "Alcestis?" is (or ought) to be interpreted by Jake as signalling his desire to be orientated—to have it explained why he and Jake are talking about Alcestis.

Jake, of course, chooses to misread Geoffrey's signal, taking it as indicating simply that Geoffrey either didn't hear the question or didn't take it all in, and now wants it repeated. So Jake repeats the question ('Is she joining us') while appearing to agree ('Yes') that Geoffrey was at least right to understand that the unheard or uncomprehended question was about Alcestis. Geoffrey's reaction to the question is all that it should be, given that he still has not had it clarified for him why Jake has (twice now) put the question he has: Geoffrey co-operatively answers "No," but at the same time by means of gesture ("frowned and shook his head") and intonation ("with an upward inflection") he registers what his partner should already have seen, and in fact should have been attentive about from the start—that he is answering the question without the benefit of understanding why it has been asked.

As well as answering Jake's question ("No") Geoffrey tries simultaneously to restore some balance to the conversation by asking a question of his own ("Where did you get that idea from?") which, indirectly if not gently, invites Jake to say why *he* should think that Alcestis would be joining them. Such clarification would put both participants, Jake and Geoffrey, in the picture. Geoffrey's signalled assumption is very fair to Jake—that there was a good and relevant reason for Jake asking his question. Jake, of course, cannot explain his real reason for asking the question, so he is forced to launch on the narrowest and least co-operative of responses, a denial ("I didn't get—") of the exact form of words used by Geoffrey. But Geoffrey overrides his reply, not deliberately or maliciously, but in a move that can be understood as an excess of co-operation, since his new utterance ("I mean, why should she be joining us?") is both a gloss upon, and reiteration of, his previous reorientating request. Moreover, this reiteration is signalled as being explanatory ("I mean . . ."), in a way that softens the force of the rest of the utterance, showing that the whole utterance is brought out with the continuing intention of clarifying the relevance of the original question, and as a positive move which could keep the conversation going, or at least get it properly started.

Jake more or less comes clean, lamely offering something ("Well, Brenda's here and I thought—") which, if he had offered it at the very start, and as setting for his question about Alcestis, would have provided a contextual relevance for that question and so prevented the ensuing cross-purposes exchange. But Jake's minor clarification is too late—in two senses: since it is not only out of its proper place but now also disorientating at the point where it does occur. Coming where it belatedly does, Jake's forced response ("Well, Brenda's here and I thought—") proves uninformative for Geoffrey as an answer to the question *he* has asked. There is no need, from Geoffrey's point of view, for him to be told that Brenda is here—because he is now judging that information as something which he has already been in possession of and has had available when he has been seeking clarification of Jake's question. He just did not have it in mind when Jake put the question at the start. And by now it has lost the fleeting quality of being relevant to Jake's question: the point of Jake's question has already been an issue without drawing out at the right time the known fact of Brenda's being here as something salient and relevant. Now it is too late and Geoffrey's reply ("I know, Jake, I know Brenda's here, I've just this moment spoken to her."), delivered triumphantly as it is, discounts Jake's reply as something rather pointlessly stating the obvious. By now, Jake, who set out to make Geoffrey look stupid, is in danger of himself looking stupid, since he finds himself telling Geoffrey something he already knows as if it were something he didn't. For his own good, rather than for any trumped-up reason, Jake completely changes the subject.

With the prejudices of the central consciousness undermined from within the text itself, *Jake's Thing* is to be seen as a book of daring construction, a novel where the writer is not putting one side (his own), but putting—or allowing for—both sides of a complex issue. The author of *Jake's Thing* presents Jake's case but at the same time allows the case *against* him to have a chance, provided we see the flaws undermining Jake's reliability. It would be too simple to read the novel as one where the central character stands as his author's representative, voicing unreconstructed prejudices that are unreflectively and non-ironically subscribed to by the author.

In 1977, in an influential article—his editorial introduction to a collection of essays on contemporary fiction—Malcolm Bradbury argued that "many of the best English writers of the 1950s were not intrinsically anti-experimental" and had only been defined as such by an unreliable critical orthodoxy that did not appreciate the extent to which a traditional realism could coexist with more abstract artistic concerns.[43] As a result, British and American criticism of the English writers of the fifties, attentive only to a documentary involvement in historical reality, grouped "together writers as various as Kingsley Amis, John Wain, John Braine, David Storey, Angus Wilson and Iris Murdoch as "angry young men," novelists of social realism."[44] Lengthier horizons, and their own later careers, lead Bradbury to see this classification as largely false, since some of these writers of social realism also show a less parochial metafictional concern for such matters as the relationship of writer to text, the perplexing status of the text, and other matters of modernist impulse. "Among the most important of these writers" Bradbury identifies "Angus Wilson, Iris Murdoch, Muriel Spark, David Storey, B. S. Johnson and John Fowles." Thus, by tantalising implication, Bradbury seems to leave, as the rump of the liberal realists of the fifties, only three—Wain, Braine and Amis.

Clearly Kingsley Amis could never belong in a grouping with B. S. Johnson and Muriel Spark and some others. But neither does he belong with

Wain and Braine, who really are close to being exemplars of Anthony Burgess's Class 1 novelists, since they are novelists for whom language is unreflectively a medium, inert and transparent and merely serviceable.[45] This is precisely *not* the case with Amis whose very special linguistic concerns seem to leave him—the cliché beckons irresistibly, for once substantially meaningful—in a class of his own, a novelist who is linguistically alert and technically adventurous but whose novels maintain a linguistically ordinary looking surface.[46]

Notes

1. Alan Watkins, "Kingsley Amis," in his *Brief Lives* (London: Hamish Hamilton, 1982) p. 1.
2. William H. Pritchard, "Entertaining Amis," *Essays in Criticism,* xxx (1980) p. 67.
3. Joseph Connolly, *Modern First Editions: Their Value to Collectors* (London: Orbis, 1987) p. 23.
4. I have in mind here Amis's commitment to the view that authors should write in order to win willing readers, and that pleasure and diversion are what most readers may be looking for. This belief has been expressed by Amis, with different kinds of emphasis, throughout his career—for instance, in the preface to his study of Ian Fleming's *Bond* books. Among other reasons for undertaking such a study, Amis explains: "I felt, too . . . that the works of Mr. Fleming deserved a thorough look because of the scale on which they are read. In paperback form, nine of them have now passed the million mark. I was also impressed by the motive for which every one of these readers reads them: pleasure" (Kingsley Amis, *The James Bond Dossier* [London: Jonathan Cape, 1965] p. 9).
5. Barbara Everett, "Philistines," *London Review of Books,* 2 April 1987, p. 5.
6. Ibid.
7. V. S. Pritchett, "First Stop Reading," *New Statesman and Nation,* 3 October 1953, p. 379.
8. Anthony Powell, "Short Notices," *Punch,* 3 February 1954, p. 188.
9. Anthony Powell, *To Keep the Ball Rolling,* vol. IV: *The Strangers All Are Gone* (London: Heinemann, 1982) p. 159.
10. The construction of *I Like It Here* is discussed in my article, "A Trip to Greeneland: The Plagiarizing Narrator of Kingsley Amis's *I Like It Here,*" *Studies in the Novel,* 17 (1985) pp. 203–17.
11. Raymond Tallis, *In Defence of Realism* (London: Edward Arnold, 1988) p. 138. Tallis also mentions, clearly as a negative point, what he calls Amis's "myopic lounge-bar conservatism", but this is a factor that can be discounted as an artistic issue on various grounds: for one thing, the other side always gets some kind of a say in Amis's fiction, so much so that, if ever politics or issues that people want to regard politically come in, what one would expect to be the more favoured side seems to undergo a kind of deconstruction and to come off worse, or at least certainly not any better; furthermore, as distinctive a feature as any other of Amis's "comic vision" is the capacity of that selfsame "comic vision" to extend to seeing—and treating—its own most heartfelt views and prejudices in a sharply ironic way; again, as Amis has consistently pointed out whenever his novels have been taken as embodying firm political or social issues (typically, in recent years, on the recurrent charge of misogyny), it is "not so" that "a generalisation emerging from a book—"Women aren't all they're cracked up to be"—is the author's last word on the subject, his considered unchangeable attitude in his life." And to

make just one more point, again drawing on Amis's own words, criticism that judges fiction in terms of the author's life and opinions seems to be unaware of "what fiction is, and its real complete difference from fact." Both quotations from Kingsley Amis come from an interview with Michael Billington on "Kaleidoscope" on BBC Radio 4: see "Writing and Warning—an Interview with Kingsley Amis," *Listener,* 15 February 1979, pp. 262–3.

12. Lodge first developed this view in his article "The Modern, the Contemporary, and The Importance of Being Amis," reprinted in his *Language of Fiction* (London: Routledge and Kegan Paul; New York: Columbia University Press, 1966) pp. 243–67.

13. David Lodge, *Write On* (London: Chatto and Windus, 1986) p. 64.

14. David Lodge, "Closing Time," *New York Review of Books,* 26 March 1987, p. 15. The two quotations are also from this source.

15. Ibid.

16. Malcolm Bradbury, "Return of the Angry Old Turk," *The Times* (London) 17 May 1984, p. 10.

17. Neil McEwan, *The Survival of the Novel: British Fiction in the Later Twentieth Century* (London: Macmillan, 1981) pp. 43, 78.

18. David Hughes, "Amis Hits the Mark," *Mail on Sunday,* 25 September 1988, p. 28.

19. Martin Cropper, "Babyish Jingles," *Weekend Telegraph,* 24 September 1988, p. ix.

20. On differences between spoken and written English, see: M. A. K. Halliday, *Spoken and Written Language* (Oxford: Oxford University Press, 1989).

21. John Vaizey, "Compliments of the Season," *Listener,* 30 May 1974, p. 703.

22. Anthony Burgess, "Bunn in the Oven," *Observer* (London), 25 September 1988, p. 43.

23. "Atticus," "As Keen as Mustard," *Sunday Times* (London), 7 November 1982, p. 35.

24. Anthony Burgess, "Woman Trouble," *Observer* (London), 20 May 1984, p. 22.

25. Burgess, "Bunn in the Oven," p. 43.

26. Wallace Robson, "Kingsley Amis as a Critic," *Spectator,* 28 November 1970, p. 690. Robson has also praised Amis as "In our time . . . a master of [the] art" of conveying tone to the reader: see W. W. Robson, *The Definition of Literature and Other Essays* (Cambridge and London: Cambridge University Press, 1982), p. 21.

27. It should be noted that contemporary forms involving reductions and elisions, carefully recorded in *Jake's Thing,* have been "corrected" by an over-zealous editor in the Penguin paperback edition. So "What did you pay for it you don't mind my asking?" is "corrected" to ". . . for it if you don't mind my asking?" and so on.

On some of the points exemplified, see: Norman Macleod, "According to Me, Sentences Like This One Are O.K.", *Journal of Pragmatics,* 9 (1985) pp. 331–43; and M. A. K. Halliday, "On Being Teaching" in *Studies in English Linguistics for Randolph Quirk,* eds Sidney Greenbaum, Geoffrey Leech and Jan Svartvik (London: Longman, 1980) pp. 61–4.

28. Francis King, "Passion Spent," *Spectator,* 23 September 1978, p. 81.

29. In a televised discussion between Martin Amis and Kingsley Amis, "Word for Word," BBC2, 25 September 1978.

30. Alan Watkins, "Books of the Year," *Spectator,* 6 December 1986, p. 32.

31. *Writers at Work: The Paris Review Interviews,* 3rd Ser., ed. George Plimpton, Introduced by Alfred Kazin (London: Secker and Warburg, 1968) p. 110.

32. Malcolm Bradbury, " 'No, Not Bloomsbury', the Comic Fiction of Kingsley Amis," in his *No, Not Bloomsbury* (London: André Deutsch, 1987) pp. 201–18.

33. Evelyn Waugh, *The Ordeal of Gilbert Pinfold* (London: Chapman and Hall, 1973) p. 127.

34. Evelyn Waugh, *Helena* (London: Chapman and Hall, 1950) p. 120.

35. "Writing and Warning—An Interview with Kingsley Amis," *Listener,* 15 February 1979, pp. 262–3.

36. Bradbury, *No, Not Bloomsbury,* p. 203.

37. Kingsley Amis (ed.) "Introduction," in *The Golden Age of Science Fiction* (London: Century Hutchinson, 1981) p. 11.

38. Kingsley Amis, "Fresh Winds from the West," *Spectator,* 2 May 1958, p. 565.
39. "The Two Amises," *Listener,* 15 August 1974, pp. 219–20.
40. Kingsley Amis, "Thomas the Rhymer," in his *What Became of Jane Austen? And Other Questions,* p. 56.
41. See Dan Sperber and Deirdre Wilson, *Relevance Communication and Cognition* (Oxford: Basil Blackwell, 1986) and H. P. Grice, "Logic and Conversation," in *Speech Acts (Syntax and Semantics,* vol. 3), eds Peter W. Cole and Jerry Morgan (New York and London: Academic Press, 1975) pp. 41–58.
42. Paul Grice, "Presupposition and Conversational Implicature," *Radical Pragmatics,* ed. Peter W. Cole (New York and London: Academic Press, 1981) p. 189.
43. Malcolm Bradbury, (ed.), "Introduction," in *The Novel Today: Contemporary Writers on Modern Fiction* (London: Fontana Books, 1977) p. 17.
44. Ibid., p. 18.
45. "Interview: Alastair Morgan Talks to Anthony Burgess," *Literary Review,* February 1983, p. 21. Here Burgess discusses the distinction between Class 1 novelists, whose prose is serviceable, and Class 2 novelists, in whose language "You're meant to observe the structure, as well as the message the structure is trying to convey." This distinction was first propounded by Anthony Burgess in his *Joysprick: An Introduction to the Language of James Joyce* (London: André Deutsch, 1973).
46. I first commented on Amis as a writer of audacious narratives, and as a writer who drew on a linguistic resourcefulness rather than modernist experiment, in my entry "Kingsley Amis," in *Writers of the English Language,* vol. 2: *Novelists and Prose Writers,* ed. James Vinson (London: Macmillan, 1979) pp. 39–42. Similar claims have been splendidly argued by Neil McEwan in the chapter "Kingsley Amis" in *The Survival of the Novel: British Fiction in the Later Twentieth Century* (London: Macmillan, 1981) pp. 78–97. A similar view is also indicated in Sebastian Faulks, "The Old Devil Takes the Booker," *Independent,* 23 October 1986, p. 19. Although it is a brief and occasional piece—appearing in the paper the day after Amis's Booker Prize award—Faulks's essay makes a number of perceptive points about Amis's work.

Appreciating Kingsley Amis

William H. Pritchard

Even as, a few years ago, he became Sir Kingsley and settled into the process of surviving his seventies (he is now seventy-three), Kingsley Amis was largely regarded in this country as a relic, an antic reactionary whose work could be taken seriously only by illiberal males predisposed to chauvinism. His detractors might grant that, yes, his first novel, *Lucky Jim,* was highly entertaining and that there were things to praise in some of the work to follow in the 1950s and 1960s. But his alleged misogyny, increasingly retrograde views on education, race, and the Russian Threat—even on alcohol, whose praise he continued to sing as enlightened times frowned—all together conspired to leave him out there alone on his limb. In *Jake's Thing* and *Stanley and the Woman* especially, he was accused of purveying jaundiced attitudes towards human beings that excoriated many of the men but almost all of the women: the all-purpose comedian had become a sharp-fanged, cruelly unfair satirist. Anyway why should Americans take him to their hearts when, in *Difficulties With Girls,* the only thing adulterous Patrick Standish can say to his latest conquest after she has post-coitally observed "The sky is blue, and I feel gay," is "Are you an American?" Currently the other Amis has more of his fiction in print here than does dad, and perhaps this is a payback for dad's inability, so he claims, to read son Martin's works with pleasure. The point is that most American novel readers gave up on Kingsley Amis awhile back.

Thus has injustice been done to this increasingly impressive writer whose forty years' worth of fiction shows no signs of drying up. For Amis is no less than what one of his critics called "a serious comic novelist": and if the comedy has recently been underappreciated, the seriousness has never been properly recognized and valued for what it is—a highly intelligent, absolutely distinctive take on life that instructs through hugely pleasing art. It's therefore a good sign that, though they've attracted little notice from reviewers or academics, some recent books about Amis have been appearing. In 1989 Richard Bradford and John McDermott both produced short, critically perceptive studies of the novels, and in 1990 Dale Salwak edited a lively collection of

From *The Hudson Review* 48 (Spring 1995): 137–44. Reprinted with the permission of *The Hudson Review.*

essays by English and American writers about the man and his work. More recently Mr. Salwak has followed up with a biographical and critical account; Merritt Moseley has surveyed the novels briefly; and, most agreeably, Paul Fussell has written a passionate apologia for Amis as a man of letters.[1] There remain plenty of distinctions to be made about the novels in relation to one another and their collective force as an achievement.

In titling his book *The Anti-Egotist,* Mr. Fussell must have expected that more than one reader, seeing the epithet applied to Kingsley Amis, would respond, "Are you kidding?" For no one ever accused the novelist of undervaluing his own ego. I remember a symposium about something or other, in London twenty years ago, in which Amis, when he was introduced as a participant, stood up and swung his clasped hands above him like a heavyweight acknowledging the crowd. Instead of egotism, Fussell stresses Amis' disinterested devotion to writing, to literary tradition, to language, also his generosity toward his readers. The focus is on Amis' nonfiction and literary learning: "His performance as a critic, a learned anthologist, a memoirist, a teacher, and a poet—in short, a man of letters in the old sense, a writer conspicuous for complex literary knowledge and subtle taste as well as for vigorous views on politics and society." In these terms Amis would take his place as a late example of a tradition in British letters sketched by John Gross in *The Rise and Fall of the Man of Letters.* Predecessors in that tradition include George Saintsbury, who resembles Amis in his devotion to drink as well as to books— the Saintsbury whom Amis once characterized as "debarred by nature from writing anything not worth reading." The comment suits Amis as well, whose literary knowledge is surely not as wide as Saintsbury's (whose is?) but who, unlike Saintsbury, produces novels and poems of his own.

Early in the book it looks as if Fussell's friendship with Amis, which he makes no attempt to conceal, may get in the way of objectivity in this portrait of the artist as anti-egotist. I at least was pulled up short when, by way of arguing for Amis' "generosity" as not just "a literary or abstract value" but a very tangible one, he confides to us that one Christmas, Amis "loaded my young son with wonderful costly gifts, including his first typewriter, because he wanted to augment his self-respect and make him happy." Doubtless the case, but it puts us in a slightly awkward position of having looked in on a private act we really have no business knowing about—this is the risk of Fussell's avowedly personal treatment. As another example of generosity he notes that once Amis, at a lunch party in Wales, gave the waitress an extravagant tip (the equivalent of fifty dollars or so) because he was so struck by her "intelligence, charm, generosity, and humor." I've no doubt she was a splendid person but would be interested to know more about what she looked like, especially whether she was, as the expression goes, full-figured. There are moments, in other words, when Fussell sounds a little too eager to attest to his friend's sterling moral qualities; whereas readers of the novels get used to thinking of him always as a bit of an old devil.

But if in a couple of places claims for Amis' stalwart nature sound a little like a friend's warm recollection of good acts performed, the claims Fussell makes about Amis' contribution as a man of letters are eminently valid and presented with a documentation—admittedly in the brief span of this short book—that strikes me as undeniable. In particular he draws attention to Amis' performance in areas insufficiently remarked, such as his work as an anthologist, his writing about food and drink, his "amateur" comments on classical music, and his poetry. Amis has done a number of anthologies, all of them distinctive and rewarding (though I have not seen his most recent, *The Pleasures of Poetry,* a collection of poems, each accompanied by brief commentary, which appeared over the course of a year in *The Daily Mail*). Of these anthologies, the most autobiographical is *The Amis Anthology* (1988), a gathering of his favorite poems, not the "best" poems in English. He says that a "favorite" poem is attractive to an individual in part for reasons that are unfathomable. A favorite poem must produce "the illusion that it was written specially for me, however well I may know that it was in fact written for the whole nation . . . or for nobody in particular." Of course no one else would title a collection *The Amis Anthology,* and no one but the compiler would include Matthew Arnold's "Rugby Chapel," a surely overlong and rhythmically undistinguished elegy for Arnold's father ("Fifteen years have gone round / Since thou arosest to tread, / In the summer morning, the road / Of death, at a call unforeseen, / Sudden . . ."). But include it Amis does, and in the notes that follow the anthology (37 pages of explanation and comment) Amis says about "Rugby Chapel" that

> It is hard for us today not to feel from time to time, when words, like *arosest* or *beckonedst* come along, that the forms of the second person plural would have been more natural. But to Arnold's readers in the 1850s, in that context, they might very well have seemed intolerably familiar and indecorous. If faced with the counter-argument that a poet should make a point of not catering to his readers' expectations, one could answer in turn that he should not bother with such trivial concerns when writing about something as important as his father's life and death.

This direct appeal to what "we" might feel and what readers in 1850 might be imagined to have felt, is extremely thoughtful in the unobvious point it worries, and could only have come from an editor who can't or won't tell us why "Rugby Chapel" is a favorite, but who protects its manner of address by invoking subject matter rather than technique. This is a small example of how personal choice gets embodied in the selection.

As for food and drink, which Amis has taken pains not to deny himself over the years, his performance as a restaurant critic is memorable for its vigorous response to pretentious language and to restaurants that fail to deliver the goods. Thus the venerable Rules, of London, gets its dues for serving "two of the most disgusting full-dress meals I have ever tried to eat in my life" (details follow). Of a fellow food-reviewer who announces that "A Hong Kong meal ... is a statement to which customers are secondary," Amis replies, "I know that sort of meal and the statement is Fuck You, and you don't have to go to Hong Kong for it. Soho is far enough." As for the drink part, over twenty years ago Amis wrote a masterwork on the subject, *On Drink,* a guide to the pleasures and perils of alcohol that is surprisingly little-known. (I've loaned it to a number of friends and miraculously still retain my copy.) The best parts of *On Drink* aren't the recipes for drinks you've never heard of before and probably won't get around to trying,[2] but rather the section titled "Mean Sod's Guide," a handbook to stinting your male guests "while seeming, at any rate to their wives, to have done them rather well." (The idea is to provoke a quarrel on the way home between the couple in which "she" defends you as sweet and thoughtful, while "he" labels you a drunk.) Out of many tips I select one, the procedure for dealing with the person who refuses to be content with your pre-dinner serving of a punch made with cheap red wine, soda water, and some cooking sherry, to be served in small glasses. A recalcitrant guest who insists, say, on Scotch should receive the following treatment: "Go to your pantry and read the paper for a few minutes before filling the order. Hand the glass over with plenty of emphasis, perhaps bawling as you do so, 'One large Scotch whisky delivered as ordered, *sah!*' "

But the most original part of this wholly original book is its section on dealing with the Hangover. No reader of *Lucky Jim* will be surprised in the least at Amis' mastery of the subject; even so it is with painful pleasure that we follow him through the steps in dealing, first, with the Physical Hangover ("I must assume that you can devote at least a good part of the day to yourself and your condition"), then, more significantly, the Metaphysical Hangover. For the latter Amis prescribes short courses in literature and music, on the principle that you must feel worse emotionally before you can start to feel better, so that a good cry is essential. For the reading course he prescribes the final scene of *Paradise Lost,* or—if you want something less "horribly great"— A.E. Housman's poems. For music, don't set your sights too high by going for Mozart. Pick someone instead who is "merely a towering genius," like Tchaikovsky, preferably the *Pathétique* symphony. Or perhaps Brahms' *Alto Rhapsody* which, especially in the Kathleen Ferrier version, would "fetch tears from a stone."

Mention of these musical treatments for the Metaphysical Hangover is occasion for a word on Amis' interest as, every now and then, a writer about classical music. From Philip Larkin's account of Oxford days we know how much time he and Amis spent listening to American jazz; less well known— especially after letting Jim Dixon refer to "filthy Mozart"—is how much Amis cares about "serious" music and how that caring gets into his writing. At a farcical level it was first evident to me when I realized that, in *Lucky Jim,* the "Welch tune" "featured in the 'rondo' of some boring piano concerto" and which Dixon sings to himself ("You *i*gnorant clod, you *stu*pid old sod, you *ha*vering, *sla*vering get . . . You *wo*rdy old *tur*dy old scum, you *gri*ping old, *pi*ping old bum") is in fact the main theme from the last movement of Beethoven's First. For some years I thought this my private discovery, but Amis has since made it public knowledge in a 1982 piece on the summer Proms concerts at the Albert Hall. Then there is his poem, "A Chromatic Passing-Note," that begins

> "That slimy tune" I said, and got a laugh,
> In the middle of old Franck's D minor thing:
> The dotted-rhythm clarinet motif.

It's a good poem partly because at a certain state of musical "sophistication" one might well be on guard against possibly sentimental tunes like that dotted clarinet motif in Franck's symphony. That Amis (in the same "Proms" piece) refers to the symphony as "miraculous" suggests that his later self has more than come to terms with it. No such accommodation, apparently, has been made with Mahler; at least to the opening of the first movement of his First Symphony. The narrator of *Girl, 20,* hearing the piece rehearsed, reflects that its length was

> a considerable mercy, seeing that it might so easily have been something broad, full, ample, spacious, massive, leisurely and going on for over half an hour from the Second or the Third. Thanks to some paroxysm of curtailment on the composer's part, I was in for little more than fifteen minutes' worth.

You don't have to agree with Douglas Yandell (and I'm pretty sure Amis as well) about Mahler's "enormous talentlessness" to note that the passage—which contains further particulars—could have been written only by someone who's spent time registering the works of "Gus"; while the phrase "paroxysm of curtailment" marks one more in a long list of Amis' fine-tuned surprises. At the end of a piece entitled "Rondo for my Funeral" (1973) he wrote that as a source of pleasure music took precedence for him over literature, but that as an amateur he could never do more than "catch glimpses of the world of mysterious, ideal beauty that music offers." It takes courage to say this, as well as courage to admit that your favorite composer (not the Greatest composer) is Tchaikovsky. I have heard no one but Amis admit this, and it recommends him to me since my favorite composer is Tchaikovsky.

Elsewhere I've expressed my admiration for Amis' poetry, now a thing of his past evidently. That leaves us with the novels, which like Tchaikovsky's music, are pervaded by a melancholy that's grown as Amis has aged. Yet at the root of them is something other than melancholy though not incompatible with it, a comic-satiric energy that carries the novelist again and again into the things in this world which call out to be rendered, sometimes rended. There is a fine moment at the close of Robert Frost's 1960 *Paris Review* interview when he ponders the nature of what young people call poetic "inspiration":

> But I tell them it's just the same as when you feel a joke coming. You see somebody coming down the street that you're accustomed to abuse, and you feel it rising in you, something to say as you pass each other. . . . Something does it to you. It's him coming toward you that gives you the animus, you know. When they want to know about inspiration, I tell them it's mostly animus.

Amis' inspiration is mostly animus and I suppose only readers who delight in this "abuse" will find tonic and indispensable such astringencies. Yet the animus may sound merely windy unless it finds the right words for itself, and no English novelist of the last few decades has paid closer attention to his words—indeed to language itself—than has Amis. Almost thirty years ago, in what was perhaps the first incisive piece of criticism provoked by his early novels, David Lodge declared unequivocally that Amis' use of language was "as inextricably part of his importance as Henry James's was of his or Joyce's was of his." Lodge was countering the tendency to consider those novels as social documents showing off the angry young man at odds with English conventions and society. By way of redirecting readers, Lodge noted Amis' habit of picking up words and subjecting them to sceptical, playful attention, as in Jim Dixon's mockery of the mindless article he's written, "The Economic Influence of the Developments in Shipbuilding Techniques, 1450–1485": " 'In considering this strangely neglected topic,' it began. This what neglected topic? This strangely what topic? This strangely neglected what?" In "superficially clumsy prose," said Lodge, Amis explored and exploited his fastidious contempt for and large pleasure in "strange locutions, odd pronunciations, verbal errors and unconscious puns."

The Russian Girl, his most recent novel published in this country, won't cause anyone to claim that it's his best since *Lucky Jim,* but it's a wholly professional tale about a Russian scholar at a London institute who falls in love with a visiting Russian poet named Anna Danilova. The trouble is that Anna's poetry is dreadful and the scholar, Richard Vaisey, knows it, even as she enlists him in a political cause—the freeing of her brother who's been arrested, with or without justice, back in the motherland. There is much interesting talk about poetry, politics, love and sex, which bears out Fussell's observation of how Amis' novels sometimes resemble "anthologies of opinions" more than they do fictions. But the places where the book comes to its sharpest and funniest pitch are those in which Richard's wife, Cordelia, is on stage, either in her own person or as the subject of others' disbelieving conversation:

> "Cordelia's the sort of woman—"
> "If you mention her again I'm leaving," said Richard quite violently. *"Not another word on that subject while I'm here. And by the way she isn't a* sort *of woman."*
> "And it's even doubtful if she's a sort of *woman,*" said Godfrey.

Her very name inspires another character's awe: "What a *name* for Christ's sake—Cordelia or Nggornndeenlia as I suppose she calls it. What's wrong with Cordy? Or Deely? See you down the boozer, Cordy. She'd vanish in a puff of smoke." ("Old Cordybags" is yet another riff on the name.) When the woman in question is herself on the phone, she provokes a "plebeian-voiced" caller into the following:

> "Paki, are you, love?"
> "I beg your pardon."
> "Well, I beg yours and all, madam. I just thought, the way you talk, ennit. Was it Europe, then? I said was it Europe?"
> "Vug of, uzzhaul," she said in an eerily unchanged voice, cut him off and punched another number.

When Richard leaves his wife for the Russian Girl, Cordelia launches a series of fiendishly successful attacks on his library, unfinished manuscript, car, and credit card account in a dazzling burst of creative malice. The wife who turns out a shrew has been a recurrent feature in Amis' more recent fiction, especially Susan Duke in *Stanley and the Women*. But never before has there been one as magnificently awful as the perfectly misnamed Cordelia. One can argue about whether Amis is misogynist; or one can wonder at the astonishing energy he accords his female targets, thus magnifying rather than diminishing them.

Henry James once provided "a delightful young man from Texas" named Stark Young with two lists of his novels as guidance for reading the Master's work, on both of which lists were *The Wings of the Dove* and *The Golden Bowl*. On the pretense that some similarly delightful person should ask me for similar help with respect to Amis' work, my two lists would both contain *Lucky Jim* and *The Old Devils*. The former, endlessly rereadable, always fresh and newly funny, is the comic masterwork of our century's second half; while the latter, in some ways Amis' most difficult book stylistically, is dense not only with satiric energies but with two scenes between characters that touch the heart. At least they elicited tears from this hard-boiled reader who never expected to shed them over Amis. On at least one of my lists I'd want *Ending Up*, his shortest novel and most ingeniously verbal working out of the end of five octogenarians living together in a small cottage. And I'd hate for any reader to miss *Girl, 20*, in its ironic celebration of Swinging London and the attempts of a classical music conductor, Sir Roy Vandervane, to swing with it.[3] After that the lists would include *Stanley and the Women*, Amis' strongest onslaught on the psychiatric profession; or *I Want It Now*, in which the rich get their comeuppance; or *The Alteration*, a dystopian-futuristic vision of a Roman Catholic world; or *The Riverside Villas Murder*, a delightful visit to the mind of an adolescent youth growing up in the late-1930s and awakening to sex (the murder part is less interesting). And what about *The*

Anti-Death League or *The Green Man* or *Jake's Thing* or *The Folks That Live on the Hill?* Two lists of five aren't big enough, no more than they are with James.[4]

A recent, strikingly candid and unillusioned interview in a London *Times* Saturday Supplement reveals the following about Amis: no, he tells the interviewer, he doesn't suffer from self-disgust exactly (Auberon Waugh had guessed that he did). But maybe a little bit "when you wish you weren't so fat and so old." Self-hatred? "Yes, from time to time." The interviewer is emboldened to ask Amis whether he likes himself: "No, I don't think I do like myself all that much . . . but I don't want to have to think about that." Dale Salwak quotes him as saying that writing is the only meaningful activity he enjoys, the only possible antidote to the "terrible feeling of gloom and panic and Christ knows what that a combination of drink and the aging process seemed to usher in." That out of such feelings the novels still keep coming regularly, each one giving us something a little different from anything given before, each a fresh entry into the English language and English humor, seems grounds for making the strongest insistence on his absolutely unique and irreplaceable contribution to the art of fiction in our time.

Notes

    1.   *Kingsley Amis: Modern Novelist* by Dale Salwak, Barnes & Noble Books. $64.50. *Understanding Kingsley Amis,* by Merritt Moseley. University of South Carolina Press. $29.95. *The Anti-Egotist: Kingsley Amis, Man of Letters*, by Paul Fussell, Oxford University Press. $23.00.

    2.   Such as Queen Victoria's Tipple (½ tumbler red wine, Scotch) or The Lucky Jim (12 to 15 parts vodka, 1 part dry vermouth, 2 parts cucumber juice, cucumber slices, ice cubes). Obviously the cucumber juice makes all the difference to the latter. Or there is the Tigne Rose (1 tot gin, 1 tot whisky, 1 tot rum, 1 tot vodka, 1 tot brandy). That one, says Amis, is "a drink to dream of, not to drink."

    3.   *Girl, 20* contains one of Amis' finest inventions, the "Fuckettes" wielded by Sir Roy Vandervane as "obscenity-savers." They include School of Thought, Christian Gentleman, Puck-Like Theme, and other phrases to be used in moments of stress.

    4.   Since this was written I have read Amis' new novel *You Can't Do Both* (not yet published in this country) and rank it at the top with *Lucky Jim* and *The Old Devils*.

The Anti-Egotist:
Kingsley Amis, Man of Letters

PAUL FUSSELL

In *Double Agent: The Critic and Society* (1992), a book mainly about American critics of the Amis "social" type but dealing also with such British non-academics as Orwell, Cyril Connolly, and John Gross, Morris Dickstein specifies three characteristics of genuine criticism, as opposed to "literary theory":

1. Criticism is *writing,* and writing in language that is itself worth attending to, that itself becomes part of the pleasure of explanation or valuation. "Its first goal is to interest and hold its readers." That is, it is an aesthetic act, like literature, but unlike "scholarship" or the conveyance of information.
2. Criticism is "personal or it is nothing." Which seems to imply the third characteristic,
3. "Like art, it is a social activity." It "seeks subtly to change the world, starting with the mind of the reader."

Those last words suggest that Amis's criticism might be in Dickstein's mind, but Amis, presumably because he's "a novelist," makes no appearance in his book.

Beginning in 1955, Amis was writing criticism for a wide range of London periodicals, including *Encounter,* the *New Statesman,* the *Twentieth Century,* the *Observer,* and pre-eminently, the *Spectator.* It soon became clear to readers that Amis's essays and reviews were something new, if the newness was not yet, perhaps, clearly definable. But journalist Harry Ritchie saw what was unique: "Those reviews for the *Spectator* in the fifties were exceptional for a colloquial tone and a critical rigor far removed from the belletristic approach that still dominated the literary sections of the press." (What critic before Amis dared refer to writers and their readers as *chaps,* or works of literature as *stuff?* What critic before Amis addressed the reader as *mate?*) Soon other critics and commentators were imitating the no-nonsense, can-the-bullshit tone,

From *The Anti-Egotist: Kingsley Amis, Man of Letters* (Oxford UP, 1994): 63–102. Reprinted with the kind permission of Paul Fussell.

with the result that, as Ritchie says, Amis's criticism "had a profound effect on postwar English writing." Amis was re-introducing the archaic critical virtues of skepticism and honesty as a counterweight to publicity, cant, critical affectation, and cultural orthodoxies. He was also bringing to non-academic criticism a refreshing focus on literature itself as the subject of interest—rather than on literature as an auxiliary to politics, ideology, or manners.

While others were requiring of literature some sort of "commitment"—one of the sacred words of the 1950s—Amis was saying, "No 'commitment' for me, except to literature." And now, forty years later, the literary dimension of literature still takes precedence. Amis liked his neighbor Peter Quennell, but got a bit annoyed by Quennell's apparent disinclination to talk about literature instead of something adjacent. In their conversations, Amis reports, "Time and time again I [would] try to keep the focus on, say, *The Village,* and Peter [would] shift it languidly but inexorably to Crabbe's opium addiction." The more one attends to Amis's criticism, the more one agrees with his view that almost no one in the contemporary world, in or out of universities, is really interested in literature, something else always being substituted as a subject more worthy of interest, whether historical data or myth, biography, politics, an author's attitude towards revolution or sex, and the like. In addition, Amis was perhaps the first intelligent British critic to bring his wide command of literature, as well as his wit, to the task of seriously opposing the critical orthodoxy of Modernism. Stuffy critics had been doing this for some time, but Amis was something different, young, clever, militant, funny, non-academic, and supremely forthright and courageous.

What was this literary Modernism that Amis set out to undermine? It was the late nineteenth- and early twentieth-century theoretical war against the received, the bourgeois, the sentimental, the didactic, and the democratic. Those conscious of engaging in the exciting new movement of artistic Modernism were happy to oppose the "realism" of Victorian and Georgian writing and painting. These artifacts were too close to life itself, and since life was not art, art had to be markedly different. It had to advertise its difference by stylization, conspicuous artifice, abstraction, leanings towards the geometrical, and moral uselessness. The Modernist thinker T. E. Hulme stigmatized as the enemy the "vital," that is, the lifelike, literature and art of the nineteenth century, urging its replacement by the geometrical. (The novelty of what was being proposed can be estimated by imagining Blunden's "Lonely Love" rendered in a de-humanized version.)

In addition, there is audible in Modernist literary behavior an undertone of crude anger which is entirely un-Amisian. This is the characteristic note of Modernist artistic manifestoes like Wyndham Lewis's *BLAST:* "BLAST humor—Quack English drug for stupidity and sleepiness." Shrill adversary tonalities echo even in the private letters of committed Modernists, odd because private letters are normally a literary form associated with charm and even courtesy. D. H. Lawrence afire with self-righteousness is a good example of Modernist fury in action. Imagine Amis saying of the residents of Taormina that they are "*Canaille, canaglia, Schweinhunderei,* stink-pots. Pfui!—pish, pshaw, prrr! They all stink in my nostrils." Ezra Pound is another to whom murderous images come easily. "I personally would not feel myself guilty of manslaughter," he says, "if by any miracle I ever had the pleasure of killing [Henry Seidel] Canby [editor of the stick-in-the-mud *Saturday Review of Literature*] or the editor of the *Atlantic Monthly* and their replicas, and of ordering a wholesale death and/or deportation of a great number of affable, suave, moderate men."

As that suggests, there is built into Modernism a hatred—and that is not too strong a word—of ordinary people, and one traditional genre of painting with which Modernism will have no truck is sympathetic portraiture, which is incompatible with the new emphasis on style rather than representation as the essence of art. José Ortega y Gasset, one of Modernism's most intelligent and powerful spokesmen, puts it this way: "Preoccupation with the human content of the work is in principle incompatible with aesthetic enjoyment proper." It used to be different, he admits: "With the things represented on traditional paintings we could have imaginary [sexual] intercourse. Many a young Englishman has fallen in love with [the Mona Lisa]. With the objects of modern pictures no intercourse is possible." Or, to turn from painting to poetry, with which of Eliot's characters could you fall in love, or even admire? Hardly Madame Sosostris, the late-drinking pub wives or the hysterical high-society woman, the damaged, passive Thames maidens, the unfeeling typist, the perverse Mr. Eugenides, or the brutal Sweeney. In the same way, what response except satiric contempt seems called for by Pound's Mr. Nixon or Lady Valentine? It was this general disdain for people, and people of all sorts, that the Assistant Lecturer in English at Swansea increasingly found offensive in Modernist writings, highly touted though they might be and increasingly a solid part of the university English curriculum. One reason Amis likes Auden, Modernist though he can be at times, is that, unlike Eliot, he can write love poems.

Lawrence in particular Amis singles out, in a review of his criticism, as one of the great Modernist haters of "the mass," regarding himself as one of the elect. "And what are we to do, all the rest of us, the mass? Can we become superior too? Hardly, because it's all a matter of feeling, you see. Thinking . . . won't help. It only makes matters worse. Some are born to sweet delight. Very few." What makes much of Lawrence's criticism valueless except to connoisseurs of eccentric and egotistical moments is the constant intrusion of his "private obsession" and his Modernist will to power over others. Those searching for useful sense in Lawrence will find not much more than "egomania, fatuity, and gimcrack theorizing," and plenty of Modernist "bitterness and censoriousness too."

These strictures can be found in *What Became of Jane Austen and Other Questions,* the collection of fifteen years of his critical pieces Amis published in

1970. These essays, dealing with authors from Austen to Philip Roth and Vladimir Nabokov, exhibit precisely the characteristics attributed to Lawrence by his admirers, "utter and transparent honesty, . . . indifference to academic and journalistic procedures, and above all, what Dr. Leavis describes as [Lawrence's] 'power of distinguishing his own feeling and emotions from conventional sentiment.' " That most of the literary essays in this collection began as reviews is not to their discredit: so did, say, Eliot's "The Metaphysical Poets," which powerfully influenced the taste of a generation.

It is in the first essay in the book that the reader finds Amis registering "the power of distinguishing his own feelings and emotions from conventional sentiment." Conventional sentiment, especially among cultish, sentimental Janeites inside and outside of universities, is likely to hold that Jane Austen is as admirable morally as she is artistically. Amis thinks differently, at least about her attitude toward the behavior of her characters in *Mansfield Park*. Amis finds Austen indeed a moralist, but a moralist with socially offensive habits, "a habit of censoriousness where there ought to be indulgence, and indulgence where there ought to be censure." *Mansfield Park* "continually and essentially holds up the vicious as admirable." Austen presents Edmund and Fanny Bertram as not just nice but admirable people. Amis finds them "morally destestable." Austen's not noticing their awfulness "makes *Mansfield Park* an immoral book." The pietistic propriety of the Bertrams is particularly offensive to the attentive reader when Edmund launches puritanical objections to the play *Lovers' Vows,* proposed for a session of private theatricals. He is a pompous prig, and his priggishness Austen approves of. Fanny, on the other hand, is a monster of egotism and self-pity, and worse, she is "disinclined to force herself to be civil to those—a numerous company—whose superior she thinks herself to be." To such emotions as sympathy and pity she is a stranger, and the horror is that Austen's susceptibility to canons of the socially OK has blinded her to Fanny's severe defects. Austen reveals herself to be, in short, a terrible snob, when her reputation is that of a scourge of snobs. What, Amis asks, "became of that Jane Austen (if she ever existed) who set out bravely to correct conventional notions of the desirable and virtuous? From being their critic (if she ever was) she became their slave." Amis grants that there have been "changes in ethical outlook" since her day, but the essential crime of snobbery, despite shifts of costumes and styles, remains an essential crime. Not everyone can see this in Austen, but the boy from Norbury destined to be humiliated at a Cambridge high table can see it clearly. He can see it clearly too because he taught *Mansfield Park* at Swansea, and, as he says, "One never really closes with a work of literature until one has to, e.g., by teaching it, . . . I found out a lot in teaching *Mansfield Park,* but I had concluded that Jane Austen was . . . second rate . . . while still at school." Many of the essays in *What Became of Jane Austen* come equipped with postscripts written in 1970, which sometimes correct and even withdraw Amis's earlier opinions. Not this essay on Austen. It comes close to encapsulating Amis's lifelong views on sympathy for the ordinary person, with its corollary—an author's obligation to anticipate and sympathize with the likely reactions of the reader.

Amis on Keats illustrates another dimension of his courageous willingness to oppose received opinion. Keats's offense, which again only a critic like Amis can see, is bitching about the real world instead of trying to understand it. As he puts it, "If Keats is to be the ideal poet, ideal poetry too readily becomes a tissue of affectionate descriptions of nice things interrupted by occasional complaints that the real world is insufficiently productive of those nice things." There's a problem too with Keats's favorite style. It is the same tired (as well as implicitly snobbish) neo-classic style reprehended by Johnson in his *Life of Gray* almost forty years before Keats. Johnson had ridiculed Gray's dependence on "the puerilities of obsolete mythology," like "Mars's car and Jove's eagle." Amis finds similar "frigidities" in Keats's "Ode to the Nightingale," like "the blushful Hippocrene (seen as a kind of Greek red sparkling Burgundy, and apparently sedimented at that)" as well as "Bacchus and his pards (brought in to effect a translation into poetese of the unpoetical notion of getting drunk)." Many of Keats's faults Amis considers the result of impatience with revision—distinctly a moral defect. "Shoddily worked sonnets would be thrown off and dispatched to friends the same day, to reappear unaltered in print." Keats could deal with the real world, as his letters indicate, but the real world "was not the kind of subject that 'a glorious denizen' of Poesy's wide heaven could undertake." These views Amis entertained in 1957. In a postscript of 1970, without altering his opinions on Keats's technical shortcomings, he does admit that he "neglected earlier to celebrate . . . that tremendous originality and audaciousness which went far beyond any mere 'decorative' quality, and, by making poetry personal, so to speak democratized it." Keats's personal "My heart aches" does something genuinely new, enabling "anybody at all to identify with him in the process of reading the poem." *Anybody at all:* there's the Amis keynote.

The general adulation of the poetry of Dylan Thomas makes Amis, in general, quite ill, but in an early encounter with Thomas's work, Amis found in some of his short prose pieces, stories and sketches of actual Welsh life especially, considerable merit, much "humor and truth to fact." But Thomas's whimsy is not always kept at bay, nor is his all-too-famous "verbal free-for-all in which anything whatever may or may not be mentioned. . . ." Thomas's problem was a twentieth-century extension of Keats's: too high-falutin' an idea of "poetry," too little interest in actualities. These reactions come from Amis's review of Thomas's posthumous volume, *A Prospect of the Sea,* edited by one Dr. Daniel Jones. Amis is hard on Jones because Jones seems lazy, his title "editor" flagrantly unearned. Dr. Jones has not told the reader which of these stories has been published before, and where, nor has he bothered to ascertain the accurate texts or even to read the proof carefully. His main labor "would seem to have been that of tearing the stories" out of Thomas's earlier volumes "and sending them off to the printer." But "perhaps it was the toil of arranging the stories in order that earned Dr. Daniel Jones his place on the title-page. After all, if my maths are correct, there were more than 10^{12} combinations to choose from." Worth noting there is Amis's meticulous attention to what he is saying. When an American acquaintance wrote doubting his mathematics, Amis answered in his usual friendly but teacherly epistolary style:

> Ah, but you overlook those two vital words *"more than."* 10^{12} was a short way of saying one million million: there were I forget how many items in the book, but it was more than 12. I think 18! $> 10^{12}$, and 18 isn't so large a number as to make the statement uninteresting.

The Amis attack on snobbery resumes in his essay on his own *Colonel Sun* and on Ian Fleming's James Bond fictions in general: Fleming may have his defects, but "not once, in the twelve books and eight stories, does Bond or his creator come anywhere near judging a character by his or her social standing." There's generic snobbery too to be guarded against. Many of those who denigrate spy fiction, "thrillers," Westerns, ghost stories, horror tales, whodunnits, and other popular narrative forms, are mere snobs affecting (as if instinctive) a socially advantageous leaning towards "serious fiction" and other manifestations of high culture. But actually, Amis is brave enough to say right out loud, "John D. MacDonald is by any standards a better writer than Saul Bellow."

If that sort of remark is bound to offend certain academics who conceive that any poem by, say, Arthur Hugh Clough is better than any tale by, say, Sir Arthur Conan Doyle, Amis's essay on *Lolita* is bound to offend, as it did offend, almost everyone else. Amis dislikes *Lolita* intensely, and it is by no means its sexiness that bothers him. Indeed, one of its faults is its failure to convey significant details of Humbert's lovemaking and thus gratify a normal reader's curiosity. Thus, "one of the troubles with *Lolita* is that, so far from being too pornographic, it is not pornographic enough." No, what annoys him is not moral but artistic, or if moral, then moral in a way bad art is ipso facto immoral. This wouldn't matter so much if the book had not been heralded as a rare masterpiece, inviting a cascade of honorific critical language from its champions and blurb-writers—*distinguished, brilliant, great, major, masterpiece.* The book has arrived in Britain "preceded by a sort of creeping barrage of critical acclaim," prompting, in Amis, first wonderment, then indignation.

What's immoral about *Lolita* is, first of all, the style, which despite Nabokov's maintaining that it is Humbert's, not his, is by comparison with Nabokov's other writing clearly Nabokov's own. It is a style full of gestures betraying self-concern in the author and a high level of personal vanity. The reader's attention to the human situation is constantly distracted by "the sustained din of pun, allusion, neologism, alliteration, . . . apostrophe, parenthesis, rhetorical question, French, Latin, 'anent,' 'perchance,' 'would fain,' 'for the nonce,'—here is style and no mistake." "This is Nabokov talking," Amis insists, this is "émigré's euphuism." As Amis says elsewhere, "Nabokov, in a way peculiar to foreigners, never stops showing off his mastery of the language; his books are jewels a hundred thousand words long." And he still hasn't managed to avoid solecisms and vulgar errors inappropriate to his pretensions. "Mr. Chamberlain literally bubbled over with gratitude," he will write, and "with his eyes he literally scoured the corners of the cell." If he means *virtually,* why not say so?

But the show-off style is not the only evidence of immorality. Perhaps more telling is the cruelty, not at all essential to the narrative, thrown in, as it were, for pure entertainment. Some of this can be imputed to Humbert, "but the many totally incidental cruelties—the bloody car wreck by the roadside that brings into view the kind of shoe Lolita covets, the wounding of a squirrel, apparently just for fun—bring the author into consideration as well, and I really don't care which of them is being wonderfully mature and devastating when Lolita's mother (recently Humbert's wife) is run over and killed." Here Nabokov goes into a flurry of stylistic exhibitionism as he describes what the dead woman's head looked like: the top of her head was "a porridge of bone, brains, bronze hair and blood." Amis comments: "That's the boy, Humbert/Nabokov: alliterative to the last." The critic speaking there is the author of *The Anti-Death League,* abnormally sensitive to the pain and injustice that rule the world, a fact calling for tears, not displays of wit.

On the other hand, loathsome as elements of *Lolita* are, Amis tries to be fair by honestly registering the effect on him of some very telling descriptive moments constituting "the portrait of Lolita herself." He says, "I have rarely seen the external ambience of a character so marvellously realized, and yet there is seldom more than the necessary undertone of sensuality." But finally the girl Lolita "is a portrait in a very full sense, devotedly watched and listened to but never conversed with, the object of desire but never of curiosity. What did she do in Humbert's presence but play tennis and eat sundaes and go to bed with him? What did they talk about?" To the melodrama and farce of *Lolita* Amis vastly prefers Nabokov's seven-page story "Colette," published in 1948, where "the Biarritz world of pre-1914 is evoked with a tender intensity" absent from *Lolita.* "Colette" is also about a lost love, but there the theme is treated with an appropriate, and human, tenderness, remorse, and subtlety, with no jokes and no hokey alliteration:

> Instantly she was off, tap-tapping her glinting hoop through light and shade, around and around a fountain choked with dead leaves, near which I stood. The leaves mingled in my memory with the leather of her shoes and gloves, and there was, I remember, some detail in her attire (perhaps a ribbon on her Scottish cap, or the pattern of her stockings) that reminded me then of the

rainbow spiral in a glass marble. I still seem to be holding that wisp of iridescence, not knowing exactly where to fit it in, while she runs with her hoop ever faster around me and finally dissolves among the slender shadows cast on the gravelled path by the interlaced arches of its border.

Amis's ability to look at both sides, as when he does not allow himself, in his annoyance, to overlook the delightful, artistically successful bits in *Lolita,* is at work too in his essay on Richard Hoggart's examination of the British working class, *The Uses of Literacy* (1957), where Amis reveals that his knowledge of people of this class is deep, detailed, and sympathetic. Some of Hoggart's portraits of women, "the wife endlessly working to keep the household warm, properly fed and out of debt, the widow struggling to bring up three or four young children"—"and the various evocations of Friday-evening shopping or Sunday-morning leisure, distil a warmth that cannot fail to engage sympathy." But the other side must be looked at, too, a side Hoggart skimps, namely "characteristic proletarian vices." Like "the serene intolerant complacency manifested by many working-class people, especially older women; the skin-tight armor against any unfamiliar idea." And yet, what can one feel but sorrow and anger watching the way these people are treated by officials ("*Want's* your portion!")? Social workers and the like who read Hoggart's book "will find grounds for exercising the utmost kindness and patience in their dealings."

Readers accustomed to Amis's frequent sneers at Americans, especially academics with their ignorance, clumsiness, and illiteracy, may be surprised by his views on Leslie Fiedler and his *Love and Death in the American Novel* (1961). As a literary person to be taken seriously, Fiedler would seem to have, from Amis's view, everything against him. The photograph on the jacket depicts someone very like a superannuated beatnik, facial hair and all, and seems to call for "a background a row of bottles rather than of Oxford texts." But appearance aside, there's something about Fiedler's performance in this book that rapidly wins Amis's admiration. It is Fiedler's energy and brilliance and risk-taking, and Amis is happy to admit that few in England would be original enough to attempt bold and imaginative criticism of this kind. "There is something striking—and American—in the mere readiness to attempt a work of this size and scope on such a high level of scholarship and intelligence." Fiedler's main point is by now too well known to need much elucidation: American fiction, he has noticed, is sadly deficient in works dissecting and interpreting the kind of man-woman love the art of the rest of the world likes to deal with, like Tolstoy, Balzac, Hardy, or Conrad. Classic American fiction (which means fiction largely of the nineteenth century), on the contrary, is rich in "Platonic" love affairs, or quasi-love affairs, or disguised, or aborted love-affairs, between men, or between a man and a boy, or between a "white" man or boy and a "colored" one. Natty Bumppo and Chingachgook, Ishmael and Queequeg, Jim and Huck are Fiedler's main examples, and Amis, immediately taken with the idea, adds the Lone Ranger and Tonto. In contemplating this audacious and brilliant formulation, Amis confesses to being impressed by Fiedler's "tact and seriousness." He is concerned, Amis notes, "not to shock or titillate but to explain." If he does often "go too far," it is frequently in "a new and illuminating direction." Amis is happy to play quite along with Fiedler's evident pleasure in multiplying examples, as when Fiedler focuses on the Gothic impulse in American fiction, with its fixation on horror and fantasy and perverse sensationalism (Poe, Hawthorne, Faulkner), and Amis quickly makes his own contribution, "Alfred Hitchcock's *Psycho,* that incredible salad of demoniacal possession, transvestism, incest, and necrophily, with the obligatory miasmic swamp in the background." *Psycho,* Amis goes on, makes "British-made chillers like *Dracula* seem chronicles of harmless eccentricity." Despite a few moments of wild excess, Fiedler's "witty, exasperating, energetic, penetrating book will prove indispensable" for anyone interested in national characteristics as reflected in art. As well as, Amis implies, setting an example for the British of how absorbing and stimulating literary history and criticism can be in bold and ungenteel hands.

Like *Lolita,* another wildly popular and critically celebrated book which left Amis cold is Philip Roth's *Portnoy's Complaint.* "Jewish jokes are not funny," he begins, and they are not funny because the humor is in collusion with too much melancholy and anger, the result of racial abuse by a world which regards those without social success and even conventional good looks as contemptible. Victimization implies victimizers, victimizers imply cruelty, and cruelty is not to be dealt with by the guffaws occasioned by the comic novel. Roth's book, Amis acknowledges, is "fluent, lively, articulate, vivid, energetic—all that and more; but as the stream of Jewish-joke-type incidents and epigrams and soliloquies thickened, I found myself hankering for some variation, . . . a bit of farce of a comic line at which one was not invited to laugh once and cry twice and gag three times and rage four times." (In a later footnote, he indicates that on second or third thought, he'd like to withdraw all the attractive characteristics of *Portnoy's Complaint* he originally listed except *fluent.*)

And again, as with *Lolita,* it's not the sexual theme and here, the precise sexual detail, that Amis objects to. Indeed, he rather admires Roth's clearly autobiographical honesty as well as his suggestion that such excessive masturbation as Portnoy's may stem from "resentment at continual parental presence" and nosiness. No, Amis's real objection to this novel is that it's not a novel. It's a collection of sketches, clumsily seamed together as if to hoodwink the consumer into thinking that he's reading something else, and something else much harder to do. The book is made of "odd scraps," a point that becomes all too clear when the reader consults the back of the title-page and finds that "Sections of this book have appeared in slightly different form" in several classy periodicals. "The magazine," Amis concludes, "is the enemy of the novel," and this seems especially an American hazard. "We in England are lucky to have no counterparts [of these magazines], no temptations, no arrangements, to send in whatever we are working on as soon as it gets to thirty or forty pages." Regardless of the cause, however, *Portnoy's Complaint* "is not a narrative, not simply in that it is incoherent, but in that the commentary swamps, erodes, and drowns out character and incident." And furthermore, it seems too merely autobiographical—one indication being the disappearance from the plot of Portnoy's woman, "the Monkey," once she's served her largely pornographic purpose. It's all too much about Roth's own life: "Mr. Roth's unconcern to narrate is connected with his unconcern to invent." Amis isn't quite sure that he's right humorlessness. If the phonies used to be on the Right, they are here, that Roth hasn't simply made this all up, but he's willing to risk being wrong. Roth's subsequent production, since 1969, shows how right Amis's instincts were. He sensed not only the truth but hinted at the obsession in Roth that, in the view of many, has restricted his range and even prevented him from growing into the major writer he might have become.

Literal-mindedness and a want of invention pose threats to writing elsewhere. The focus of Amis's essay "Unreal Policemen" is the traditional intellectual attributes of the great detectives in the classic narratives by Conan Doyle, Simenon, Chesterton, Rex Stout, and John Dickson Carr. "All the sleuths we remember and reverence and take into our private pantheon of heroes," he says, "are figures not of realism but of fantasy, great talkers, great eccentrics, men who use inspiration more than hard work, men to whom Venetian old masters mean more than police files and a good bottle of Burgundy more than fingerprints." By their ability to solve riddles and puzzles, these detectives implicitly celebrate "the power of the human mind to observe and to reason." But what's happened? About 1950 this kind of classic detective vanished, and so did "the classical detective story, in which all the clues were scrupulously put before the reader." That intellectual hero has been replaced by the real policeman, as well as the secret agent, the international spy, and the tough operative whose muscle and cynicism make up for his defect of brain. For confirmation, go into any popular bookstore and observe the new classification, True Crime. Who wants fiction and art and mind when actuality is so easily available?

Amis rounds off *What Became of Jane Austen* with an essay on the conventions of horror films, and with some autobiographical pieces later retrieved for the *Memoirs,* together with his attack on the uncritical expansion of the universities in the 1960s. Here, his memorable words "More Will Mean Worse" became notorious, even if true. "University graduates," he explains, and he means real university graduates, not current-events specialists or business-school products, "are like poems or bottles of hock, and unlike cars or tins of salmon, in that you cannot *decide* to have more good ones." The threat to genuine learning is from all sorts of "quantitative thinkers," as well as from those who conceive the function of the university to create not analyzers and critics and doubters but docile members of a society whose greatest cultural invention is advertising. Amis gave further offense to progressives and utilitarians by asserting that the university, like the church, "must shut her mind firmly against the needs of society," and like the church, "this is not only her age-old duty, it is also her only chance of turning out in the end to have served the needs of society."

This is conservative stuff, surely, to be understood in part by the illumination cast by the essay "Why Lucky Jim Turned Right." Why did Amis turn to the Right? Because he's always been uneasy with orthodoxy, as well as with pretension, self-righteousness, and humorlessness. If the phonies used to be on the Right, they are now found largely on the Left, and after Amis had noticed how few on the Left seemed much bothered by the Russian military intervention into Hungarian affairs, he began to see the light. It was authoritarianism in any form that he came to see as the enemy, and it was his devotion to absolute freedom of utterance that made him hate communism and its liberal apologists with a vengeance. His liberation from the orthodoxy of the Left will surprise few familiar with his liberation from the orthodoxy of artistic Modernism. In both, Big Brother tells the ordinary person what he should approve of.

Another orthodoxy is the religious one, and here Amis mounts a thoughtful attack in his final essay, "On Christ's Nature." Christ is an impressive generator of moral paradoxes, all right, and his values—as in the model of the Good Samaritan—are admirable. His selecting as companions and followers men largely from the working class is greatly to his credit. But the problem for a civilized searcher after religious illumination is Christ's proclaimed loyalty to a God Amis finds loathsome in every way. Amis's religious thought is rough and ready, with little tolerance for theological niceties. He declines to be fancy or over-subtle about the problem of evil, and he declines to revere a God who has seen to it that his universe allows the innocent to suffer, merit to go unrewarded, and scourges like cancer and deformity to torment the harmless and the good. Thus, "in rough proportion as he moves away from being divine Jesus invites approval and affection," but "God" is another question altogether. The Russian poet Yevgeny Yevtushenko once asked Amis, "You atheist?" Amis answered, "Well, yes, but it's more that I hate him." And it's not just God's cruelty that bothers Amis. It's his prescriptive authoritarianism, suggestive more of a dotty sadistic commissar than a heavenly father one loves and respects. Given Amis's opposition to coercion, given his ready sympathy with the deprived and unfortunate, his views on God and Christ follow naturally and become an indispensable element in his outlook and his criticism.

In 1990 he published a second gathering of non-fiction pieces, *The Amis Collection,* in which he recovered about half his miscellaneous writings, many from the *Observer* and the *Spectator,* from the previous thirty years. This volume, almost twice as long as *Jane Austen,* contains a greater variety of things: comments about writing in general and advice to beginners; critical assessments of authors; comments on anthologies and suggestions for their proper conduct; essays on society and education; observations on language; and brief treatments of film, travel, and music. And of course a section on "Eating and Drinking."

Literary egotism being one of Amis's special aversions, it's hardly a surprise to find the lead essay in the book returning to what can be called the *Portnoy Fallacy,* whose first practitioner was probably D. H. Lawrence. This is the novelist's erroneous assumption that writing about things that have happened to him and to real people he has known will guarantee greater authenticity and verisimilitude than writing about made-up events and people. But what this practice actually does is to lull the author into complacency about how well he's doing. Because events from his past seem "real" and gripping and fascinating to him, what reason is there to suppose that they're going to work that way with the reader? It's useful here to notice that most writers' first novels are really autobiographies in disguise, and that (as publishers know) they are for that reason very likely to be bad novels. That view is what lies behind Amis's praise of Iris Murdoch's *Under the Net* as a valuable rarity, "a thoroughly accomplished first novel." Focusing on oneself, delightful though that process admittedly is, is an almost sure-fire way to avoid the crucial, perhaps the only literary question, how is this bit of writing going to go down with strangers?

Karl Miller is one who has noticed without much pleasure Amis's habit in his fiction of placing offensive social opinions that are really his own in the mouths of unsavory characters, like Patrick Standish, Roger Micheldene, Ronnie Appleyard, or Alun Weaver. To Miller, this seems like an attempt to have it both ways, to utter nasty views while appearing to disown them. But Amis's interpretation is quite different. The novelist's central characters, he admits, are and are not the novelist, but the intent is less to distance the author, cunningly, from vile opinions he really holds than to engage in an act of self-criticism:

> The novelist's . . . central characters are clearly meant to do more than just go around being close or distant relatives of him. . . . They are vehicles of his self-criticism. . . . By that very act of distancing, by projecting himself into an entity that is part of himself and yet not himself, he may be able to see more clearly, and judge more harshly, his own weaknesses and follies; and, since he must know that no failings are unique, he may be helped to acquire tolerance for them in others. [And] if the novel comes off at all, the reader will perhaps accompany the writer in some parallel process of self-discovery.

Not everyone will be convinced by this: Amis's pleasure in voicing unfashionable offensive views is so evident that the subject of *pleasure,* as well as *moral duty,* deserves a look-in too. Something besides a noble self-flagellation seems to be going on.

In several essays in *The Amis Collection* he considers a recurring topic, the defects of American writing, and concludes that a large part of the problem is the American writers' and critics' "pursuit of the masterpiece." He has kind words for Whitman and the Salinger of *The Catcher in the Rye* ("marvellous"), but observes that America, still anxious for a distinguished culture all her own, "takes her writers too seriously." The result is pretentiousness and an urge to hypertrophy, producing a succession of overweight flops, usually one per season. More modesty is what's wanted, more understanding that the "minor" writer is not for that reason a failure.

To Amis, some Americans, like some academics, are nothing less than awful. The two are handily available for a sound drubbing in the figure of Professor Hugh Kenner, of the Johns Hopkins University. The theme of his book on modern British literary achievement is right there in its title, *The Sinking Island: The Modern English Writers* (1988). Kenner, "a veteran American critic and teacher," is well known as an enthusiastic celebrator of "International Modernism" as illustrated pre-eminently in the works of Pound, Wyndham Lewis, Eliot, and Joyce, on all of whom he's written copiously. The argument of this book is that "Modernism" was brought about largely by the Americans and the Irish, with minimal help, or even understanding, from the English. Fair enough, perhaps, if you think literature and general culture improved by the spirit of "International Modernism." Amis does not, observing that the Modernist movement has alienated the general reader from serious writing and has allowed him, by default, to drift away to the films, the television, and the football stadium. "Dr. Kenner reveals . . . his whole literary position, when he characterizes *The Waste Land* as above all 'the century's most influential poem' and a 'supremely important poem.' If you see literature as a matter of influences and importances *of course* you are going to fall for International Modernism with its innovativeness, experiments, developments and echoes, so much more inviting to lecture on than the intractable, unclassifiable qualities of an actual work of literature. . . . Importance isn't important. Only good writing is." Speaking of which, Amis does not scruple to impugn Kenner's prose as well as his views, imputing to it specifically American academic faults, like careless diction (the result of pretentiousness and the quest for novelty)— for example, Kenner's saying of Aubrey Beardsley's "sense of line and design" that it is *irrefutable,* or finding it *orienting* that Everyman's Library followed the death of Samuel Johnson by only 65 years. Amis the critic speaks in this essay, but audible also is Amis the patriot—with his back up.

Two essays in *The Amis Collection* celebrate the unpretentious virtues of the publisher Victor Gollancz, who issued excellent books from a shabby office devoid of "oak panelling, sporting print and sherry decanter." He was Amis's publisher for five of his novels, from *Lucky Jim* in 1954 to *One Fat Englishman* in 1963. Gollancz was an example of "*unconscious* goodness," and although a "monster of egotism, vanity and self-delusion . . . [he] was also entirely capable of disinterested generosity both moral and monetary, genuine warmth of heart and readiness to go to endless trouble on behalf of those he valued." His nose for the market as well as his sense of quality can be suggested by his publishing Shaw and Orwell, as well as Amis. His Left Book Club enrolled 57,000 subscribers in 1939 and it doubtless assisted the victory of the Labour Party in 1945. He had an extraordinary talent for spotting winners. When he saw R. C. Sherriff's *Journey's End* he indicated at the first intermission that he'd be delighted to publish it. If he hurled himself too uncritically into socialist causes and thought too highly of the USSR, Amis seems ready to forgive him, for he published and encouraged Amis when no one had heard of him.

Almost a third of *The Amis Collection* is devoted to essays on such novelists as Iris Murdoch, Anthony Powell, Orwell, Somerset Maugham, Evelyn Waugh, Angus Wilson, Anthony Burgess, and William Golding, together with such lesser-known Amis favorites as Elizabeth Taylor and William Cooper (*Scenes from Provincial Life,* 1950), and a handful of science-fiction and detective-story worthies. There are also essays on such people of letters as Max Beerbohm, Kipling, Chesterton, Quiller-Couch, C. S. Lewis, William Empson, the boys' writer "Frank Richards," A. Conan Doyle, and Julian Symons. Such Yanks as Poe and Ambrose Bierce are also passed under inspection. He's written here on the lives and works of poets too: Browning, Tennyson, Swinburne, Housman, Wilfred Owen, Robert Graves, Dylan Thomas, and Philip Larkin. And he's talked about the author or authors of *Beowulf,* whoever they may be, candidates for the distinction, together with the perpetrators of *Piers Plowman* and *Sir Gawain and the Green Knight,* of creating the most boring poem in Old, Middle, or Modern English.

Max Beerbohm has been acclaimed so incontinently by such as Lord David Cecil and E. M. Forster that he must be cut down a bit. One reason is that terrible people refer to him as "Max." Indeed, any author known by his or her first name ("Jane," "Emily") is very likely to be admired by people Amis cannot bring himself to like. How did it happen, he wonders, that "it ever got about in the first place that he [Beerbohm] was worth taking seriously?" Actually, he has nothing to say, his whole stock in trade being "style." And as a critic, Beerbohm is habitually ungenerous, hardly ever avoiding "a note of coldness and disparagement." A sort of proto-Cyril Connolly, Beerbohm was obsessed with "failure, with setting one's aim safely low." His parodies of H. G. Wells, Henry James, and Kipling, as well as his cartoons, are lively and funny, but his alleged masterpiece, *Zuleika Dobson,* remains for Amis a silly, camp, self-consciously cute book implicitly recommending everything at Oxford that is superficial, shallow, and stupid. That novel merely prolongs the insidious belief that Oxford is a place less of scholarship than of magic social prestige and general faerie.

That makes Beerbohm sound almost like the aged Evelyn Waugh, glorifying all the repulsive things about the rich and their clubs, including "exclusive" old-fashioned religions and antique military regiments. Amis's fascination with the final perversion of Waugh's career by snobbery is so intense that he devotes more pages to him than to any other writer. And it's not just snobbery. Amis likewise presents Waugh as an example of the way literature can be ruined, or at least badly weakened, by the intrusion of things that are not literature—in Waugh's case, religion, self-righteousness, and irrelevant anger. *Decline and Fall* and *A Handful of Dust* Amis is happy to praise as successful farces on the theme of "the cruelty and arbitrariness at the heart of the universe." Waugh's depression on this score gradually propelled him in the direction of a system offering an explanation, or a palliative, or something like them. He thus embraced Catholicism, but "to his artistic detriment," and what before had been "an enlivening bitterness" came forth now as "defiance and jeering," together with an embarrassing conviction of personal superiority. The sense of humor hardened into a sense of *I* and *Thou,* with the *I* always right and admirable.

The damage, Amis notes, is abundantly available for contemplation in the *Sword of Honor* trilogy, where Waugh seems to have no idea how repulsive he's made the self-righteous Catholic Guy Crouchback. And Waugh's view of army life is also troubling. It is unsatisfyingly ambiguous and at bottom unsatiric, indeed, admiring. "If one is really going to satirize army life," says Amis, "in all its confusion and arbitrariness, then sooner or later one has got to start satirizing the army itself, which contains in its nature confusion and arbitrariness just as much as order and custom." But Waugh can't satirize the army effectively because he really believes in it too much. It would be like satirizing the Catholic Church. He slavers over Crouchback's regiment just as he does over the church, and for similar reasons, its antiquity, oddity, ceremonial obsession, and airs of superiority. Like the regiment, you don't just "join" the church as if it were a mere social organization. You are "received" into it. "Crouchback is really a terrible fellow," Amis concludes, basing much of this view on the scene "where he tries to seduce his ex-wife in the flush of the discovery that theologically he would be committing no sin." Waugh seems less ready than the reader to agree at that point with the wife, who addresses Guy with, as Amis notes, "truth and finality": "You wet, smug, obscene, pompous, sexless lunatic pig."

Waugh seems equally insensitive to a reader's natural response to Crouchback's prolonged search for an army assignment presumably appropriate to his talents, his social standing, and his own opinion of his value. Very early in the war he's to be found nosing around London in search of a job in the service, and of course he must have a commission. He seeks out "powerful friends at Bellamy's" and writes begging letters to "Cabinet ministers' wives." Contemplating this behavior, unrebuked by its creator and delineator, Amis flies into a democratic fury, asking, "What about all those jobs in the ranks. . . ?—Unthinkable, naturally," for someone like Crouchback. After all, what's the use of powerful friends from school and university if they can't get you made a captain even though you have neither knowledge, talent, or training? The terrible truth, and Amis oddly refrains from coming right out with it, is that Crouchback *is* Waugh and is therefore, to his author and admirer, largely beyond criticism. Or even analysis.

But one must go to *Brideshead Revisited,* both the novel and the lush TV enactment, to witness the worst. There, as Amis puts it, "Waugh's snobbery rages unchecked . . . by the habitual austerities of his style." A reader of "this bad book" would be justified in believing that "since about all [Waugh] looked for in his companions was wealth, rank, Roman Catholicism (where possible) and beauty (where appropriate), those same attributes and no more would be sufficient for the central characters in a long novel . . . to establish them as both glamorous and morally significant." Here Waugh treats such characters "with an almost cringing respect," producing a work Amis "would rather expect a conscientious Catholic to find repulsive" for its yoking of the True Faith with unearned money, social privilege, immense, richly furnished premises, and the very best in food, drink, and servants. No one at Brideshead is a better person for being a Catholic. Merely more self-satisfied. As Waugh's biographer Martin Stannard points out, Waugh, annoyed by Amis's views when they appeared in the *Spectator,* wanted to impute Amis's response to his presumed lower-class origins and, as a new aspirant comic novelist, to mere jealousy of Waugh's earlier success in this mode. He of course did not understand the full weight of Amis's moral disapproval, or notice that the essence of Amis's attack involved a compliment, and regret at a terrible loss. What Amis was registering was, as Stannard says, "disappointment . . . at Waugh's continued suppression of 'that farcical vein which founded his reputation'."

Getting in a final lick at Poe ("Before he turned up, there had been plenty of writers who were no good—Herrick, Cowley, Cowper; Poe's distinction is to have been the first who was positively bad"), Amis turns to the poets. He pauses for some time over Tennyson and does what perhaps he does best as a critic. He confronts "a massive prejudice" against a given writer (Kipling, Newbolt, Betjeman) and tries to argue his detractors into a new kind of, if not acceptance, at least reconsideration and tolerance. Amis sees Tennyson as a brilliant, original, instinctive poet when young, but one gradually pre-empted by the more genteel elements of his world "to become in time a figure uncomfortably close to that pensioner of the establishment taken by many . . . to be all he had ever been." In hostile folklore, Tennyson ends reading his works to his Sovereign (Beerbohm's cartoon is unforgettable) and, no doubt in consequence, receiving the Laurel. As a result of his close friend Arthur Henry Hallam's death at the age of twenty-two, Tennyson learned to register sorrow and loss like almost no other writer of his time— until, perhaps, Housman, and later still, perhaps, Amis. And not just sorrow and loss but "the feelings that lie close to it, despondency, ennui, nostalgia, loneliness, despair and the desire for reconciliation and resignation."

After judicious treatment of Housman and Wilfred Owen and Robert Graves, Amis arrives at the task of dealing with three books which invite the sternest moral (and critical) disapproval of Dylan Thomas. The first is Paul Ferris's biography, which specifies that Thomas was "a chronic liar," sponger, and draft-dodger, overflowing with self-pity, a man who apparently conceived that his talent justified his non-payment of bills presented by tradesmen and landlords. He and his wife Caitlin were given to simply showing up at friends' houses at night, bedding down for weeks, and then stealing the silver. He was a monumental drinker, but also liked to lie about the number of drinks he'd put down. Playing the poet, in the adolescent, Romantic sense of that word, was more important to him than producing poems. He knew but did not advertise the fact that after about the age of twenty, he wrote nothing worth reading. Copious evidence of his shortcomings is available also in Ferris's edition of Thomas's *Collected Letters.* He proclaimed his need for utter independence—from, say, a regular job—but ironically fell into greater dependence thereby, since one spends all one's time managing one's mendicancy, composing begging letters, and contriving lies. Thomas's poetic subject was his childhood, and he did quite well there. But once childhood had passed, "he had nothing more to write about because he had noticed nothing since." His letters "show no curiosity about other people or their lives," as well as suggesting that he read little and was not very interested in literature. (He could have stolen books, but apparently didn't care to.) The third book, *Caitlin: Life with Dylan Thomas,* by his wife with the aid of George Tremlett, serves, unwittingly, to blacken her character too. Despite vivid public quarrels, "what held them together was devotion not only to booze but also to petty criminality, minor fraud, stealing from friends, and messing up their houses, cheating, cadging, above all a shared conviction that rich, complacent people, i.e., those living on their own earnings, deserved to have anything movable taken off them by footloose creative souls like Mr. and Mrs. Dylan Thomas."

Philip Larkin's life and works, to which Amis turns now, make a contrast perhaps too melodramatic. Amis notes his admiration and pleasure at encountering the volume *High Windows* for the first time. Larkin finds his perfect reader in Amis, whose taste is sure for what is best in Larkin's work. Of course he admires "To the Sea" and "Show Saturday," not just because they evoke the pleasure ordinary people take in simple, permanent things, but because of their unshowy art, especially the way their rhymes are so exquisitely managed that the reader is likely not to notice that he is reading a rhyming poem until asking, "What's holding this all together?" Here's the way "To the Sea" begins:

> To step over the low wall that divides
> Road from concrete walk above the shore
> Brings sharply back something known long before—
> The miniature gaiety of seasides.
> Everything crowds under the low horizon:
> Steep beach, blue water, towels, red bathing caps,
> The small hushed waves' repeated fresh collapse
> Up the warm yellow sand, and further off
> A white steamer stuck in the afternoon—

> Still going on, all of it, still going on!
> To lie, eat, sleep in hearing of the surf
> (Ears to transistors, that sound tame enough
> Under the sky), or gently up and down
> Lead the uncertain children, frilled in white
> And grasping at enormous air, or wheel
> The rigid old along for them to feel
> A final summer, plainly still occurs
> As half an annual pleasure, half a rite.

The day beginning to end,

>   the first
> Few families start the trek back to the cars.
> The white steamer has gone. Like breathed-on glass
> The sunlight has turned milky. If the worst
> Of flawless weather is our falling short,
> It may be that through habit these do best,
> Coming to water clumsily undressed
> Yearly; teaching their children by a sort
> Of clowning; helping the old, too, as they ought.

That's Betjeman (or even Blunden) raised to the highest power. The same sort of understanding of permanent rituals distinguishes "Show Saturday," about a country fair combining judging of livestock, display of homemade foodstuffs,

>   a beer-marquee
> That half-screens a canvas Gents; a tent selling tweed,
> And another, jackets,

as well as

> Needlework, knitted caps, baskets, all worthy, all well done.

But it has to end, and the fair folds up, the crowds disperse and go home:

> Back now, all of them, to their local lives:
> To names on vans, and business calendars
> Hung up in kitchens; back to loud occasions
> In the Corn exchange, to market days in bars,
>
> To winter coming, as the dismantled Show
> Itself dies back into the area of work.
> Let it stay hidden there like strength, below
> Sale-bills and swindling; something people do,

> Not noticing how time's rolling smithy-smoke
> Shadows much greater gestures; something they share
> That breaks ancestrally each year into
> Regenerate union. Let it always be there.

That helps show why Amis is Larkin's greatest fan and champion, and it illustrates something more. It helps suggest why Modernism has had so much trouble domesticating itself in England, whose possession of that solid, almost unitary, local descriptive, quasi-pastoral vision and technique is firm and satisfying enough for its performers and readers to feel no need for a revolution.

Amis is skilled enough in Larkin's procedures to sense that "At Grass" is the first poem in the mode Larkin made his own. "It seems almost suddenly that he learnt to take his images from the world of reality and show us, in the vividly drawn picture of a pair of old racehorses, the evanescence of glory, of active life and of life itself." Now quite retired and hidden away from crowds and cheering, the two horses

> . . . gallop for what must be joy,
> And not a fieldglass sees them home,
> Or curious stop-watch prophesies:
> Only the groom, and the groom's boy,
> With bridles in the evening come.

There's the elegiac note that seems curiously English and that Amis responds to so readily and so emotionally. Given Larkin's good luck in attracting Amis as a critic, it's tiresome to see quoted, in George Hartley's book of tributes to Larkin and critical essays on his work, silly, pretentious, mechanical workouts like, for example, Steve Clark's. He specializes in clumsy application of irrelevant aperçus of Freud and Derrida to a poetry quite whole and complete without that kind of make-work. As Larkin once said, "There's not much to say about my work. When you've read a poem, that's it, it's all quite clear what it means." And before leaving the topic of Larkin and his frustrated explicators, Amis takes one more swipe at a professor, this one a hapless Canadian (always, it seems, fair game) whose brash misquotations of Larkin's lines screw up the meter and betray the critic's lack of fitness "to write a book on any subject of this sort." A professor of English need not be bright, but he/she should care enough about words to refrain from offering as Milton's the line,

> They serve also who stand and wait.

Ending Up with Amis

Lawrence Graver

When Kingsley Amis died on 22 October 1995, the obituaries in England and America told a cartoonishly familiar story. Although he was memorialized at length and justly described as the leading British comic novelist of his time, the layout and text of most of the notices played up the more stereotypical and sensational aspects of his life story. The irreverent young man from a South London lower-middle-class family who had become famous in 1954 for a radical lampoon of phoney academic/bourgeois values was everywhere reported to have transformed himself over four decades into an irascible, intemperate, exasperating Establishment figure whose politics (according to Mary Braid of the *Independent*) "were somewhere to the right of Attila the Hun's"[1]—antiwomen, antiegalitarian, antimodern, anti-just-about-everything new and different. "A clamorous communist undergraduate" had evolved "into a growling Conservative diehard," said the Associated Press.[2]

While acknowledging that Amis was a prolific, much-honored novelist, poet, critic and essayist, the obituary writers found it impossible not to be diverted by the sideshows of his literary life: the flow of crusty letters to the press; the uproar caused by his *Memoirs;* the buzz stirred by the delayed American publication of *Stanley and the Women* (allegedly the target of a feminist cabal in New York); the dust-up over the Eric Jacobs biography and *The Biographer's Moustache*. Similarly, the reports of Amis's personal life highlighted botched marriages, serial promiscuity, oceans of wine and whiskey, and the final retreat to a bizarre domestic arrangement in which his first wife cooked his meals and her third husband made his bed. At the end, the bloated old buffer was observed, malt in hand, at the bar of the Garrick Club, denouncing fools and bores while praising Mrs. Thatcher.

Some of these sketches of the Angry Young Man who turned out to be Colonel Blimp, scourge of innovation, were accompanied by more thoughtful and deserved tributes. Remembering Amis as the most gifted of the 1950s novelists—the one with the greatest capacity for development—David Lodge nicely captured the originality of his tone and style: "Language, denied the luxury of metaphysical affirmation and romantic afflatus, coils back upon

---

This essay was written specifically for this volume and is published for the first time by permission of the author.

itself, mocking its own pretensions as well as the follies and foibles of human behavior."[3] For Malcolm Bradbury, Amis was one of the four great fiction writers in England in the late twentieth century, "alongside Golding, Burgess and Lessing."[4] Yet, as John Sutherland later observed, the newspaper pieces overall made it hard "to see the face for the warts,"[5] and a general reader might be forgiven for believing that the headstrong Amis had succeeded only too well in becoming one of his own shit-heroes.

Amis's novels ("an account of myself in 20 or more volumes") actually tell a very different story. If the obituaries offer a colorful caricature of the famous man, the novels themselves provide a far more subtly shaded, multifaceted portrait of the artist and moralist. Since obituaries are occasioned by endings, and this essay was prompted by a reading of the obituaries, now seems a good time to reflect on how Amis customarily closes his novels.

Unlike the obituaries, which depict a man of firmly held, assuredly expressed beliefs and opinions (however they may change over time), the endings of the best Amis novels are marked by a keen apprehension of and respect for contending views, alternate possibilities, and their uncertain consequences. The novels spanning the writer's 40-year career demonstrate not egotism and dogma but a respect for the bedeviling, irreconcilable conflicts that govern most human lives.

A typical Amis novel begins to end when the sexual situation on which the plot is based comes to its highest pressure point. In chapter 17 of *That Uncertain Feeling* (1955), the restless John Lewis has just made love for the first time to Elizabeth Gruffydd-Williams, the Aberdarcy socialite who had helped get him the offer of a better job at the town library. Returning to his dreary flat at 1:00 A.M., he finds his wife Jean in her nightgown and Gareth Probert, a poet he dislikes, fully dressed and ill at ease. A hostile exchange with Probert follows. Later, when John tells Jean that he turned down the promotion because of qualms about how he got it, she stingingly rebukes him. Guessing that her husband has just had sex with Elizabeth, Jean is more irate at his rejecting the promotion (which would have served the family) than at his womanizing. The agitated Lewis flees the house but unexpectedly encounters Ken Davies, the soused, beaten-up son of his landlady. Uncharacteristically concerned, Lewis takes the damaged Davies home, a kind act that leads him to modest self-reflection, reconciliation with his wife, and return to steady work at a colliery in his small home town—on its face, a low-keyed happy ending. But much of the realization, reconciliation, and return are deftly qualified by Amis's quiet erosion of certainty. At home after rescuing Davies, Lewis thinks of what he is now going to do.

> Since I seemed to have piloted myself into the position of being immoral and moral at the same time, the thing was to keep trying not to be immoral, and then to keep trying might turn into a habit. I was always, at least until I reached the climacteric, going to get pulled two ways, and keeping the pull

from going the wrong way, or trying to, would have to take the place, for me, of stability and consistency. Not giving up was the important thing.

I poured the milk into two cups, feeling a bit nervous, because this not-giving up business was all very fine and large, but it wouldn't be any good if I tried it on my own, if it only applied to me. That was the one important condition. I took the cup upstairs and into Jean's and my bedroom.[6]

Part of Lewis's appeal here comes from the exact measure he takes of his own weaknesses (susceptibility to seduction, lack of restraint, untrustworthiness) and of his manifest, if dormant, desire to be better. But shortly, his overly elaborate effort to capture the ever-so-fine shades of feeling that he is being "pulled two ways" is comically revealed to be his distinctive, and endearing, form of rationalization. Dedicating oneself assiduously to "this not-giving up business" is exposed as Lewis's own kind of self-indulgent pleading. Yet overall, the passage—oscillating between sympathy and satire—illustrates Amis's definition of a fully developed fictional character: one viewed from all points of the compass, with respect, irony, impatience, and sadness. From the compass point of irony, we respect Lewis for his intelligence and wit, but we feel impatient with his temporizing and sad at his inability to move beyond accommodating his human weaknesses to asking more of his better self.

The novel's last chapter, which immediately follows this wry revelation, depicts Lewis happily back with his family in Fforestfawr. His father volunteers to baby-sit while John and Jean go to a party at the home of "one of the premier hostesses in this part of Wales." At the affair, John is quickly drawn into an intimate conversation with the flirtatious Lisa Watkin, that "very fine little thing" (*Feeling*, 250) whose husband recently insisted she move to Wales from Oxford. As the titillation increases, Lewis abruptly decides to bolt, "to get away from that woman." As he and Jean walk across the town square, colliers leaving work are headed for the pub, and the novel ends with Lewis observing that "to anyone watching it might have looked as if Jean and I, too, were coming off the shift."

The characteristic Amis touch here is the controlled ambiguity of the situation and the last sentence. Having witnessed Lewis's fancy for attractive women from the first page of the novel, a reader suspects a future liaison with the alluring Lisa Watkin and more trouble in the Lewis's marriage. And the "as if" at the close is a giveaway: the couple are not coming off the shift, not fully part of the local scene. The central moral dilemmas of the earlier action—which turned on sexual fidelity, professional integrity, and class—are not resolved but bracketed, deferred, destined to appear again, and probably soon.

They return in even more interesting forms in *Take a Girl like You* (New York: Harcourt, Brace & World, 1960). In this novel, the closing sequence begins late into a party of the demimonde at Julian Ormerod's fancy house, where a few people have paired off, some have fallen tipsily asleep, and others are cavorting noisily outside. A group of women sit talking in a fatigued, cynical way about everyone else's unbuttoned behavior. Jenny Bunn suddenly asks the novel's basic question: "Why do people make a fuss about virginity?"[7] In a conversation punctuated by yawns and vomiting, the women flippantly discuss the topic in general and Jenny's situation with Patrick Standish in particular. One of Patrick's other girlfriends remarks, "Darling, I didn't know they did. Are you sure they do? There was never any fuss about mine. . . . I got rid of it as soon as I could and put it out of my mind" (*Take*, 300). Agreeing that she, too, had no principles, another woman adds that making a fuss about things having to do with sex always makes things worse.

But making a fuss about things having to do with sex is Amis's lifelong subject. For the rest of this novel he records the minute increments of Jenny's emotions. In the aftermath of the conversation about virginity, Jenny's feelings change to bewilderment and increasingly blur. When she tries to think about Patrick, she cannot recover her thoughts about him and no longer knows "what she thought or felt about anything" (*Take*, 304). Asked by a man "to slip upstairs for a bit," she remembers through an alcoholic haze to say "no," because "that was what you said when men asked you to slip upstairs" (*Take*, 304). Soon after she has been put to bed by friends, Patrick comes in and rapes her while she remains in a stupor.

> What he did was off by itself and nothing to do with her. All the same, she wanted him to stop, but her movements were all the wrong ones for that and he was kissing her too much for her to try to tell him. She thought he would stop anyway as soon as he realised how much off on his own he was. But he did not, and did not stop, so she put her arms round him and tried to be with him, only there was no way of doing it and nothing to feel. Then there was another interval, after which he told her he loved her and would never leave her now. She said she loved him too, and asked him if it had been nice. He said it had been wonderful, and went on to talk about France. (*Take*, 306)

A good part of the effect of this sequence comes from Amis's Swift-like use of understatement and calculatingly slack sentence rhythm that painfully expose the cruelty of what Patrick is doing, while simultaneously blocking any simple moral response to Jenny's woozy acquiescence. Clearly, Amis wants the reader to condemn Patrick's actions and be vexed by Jenny's. Up to this point, she has so persuasively voiced reasons for not yielding that her affectionate reactions after the violation are surprising and hard to gauge.

The events that immediately follow clarify and complicate our assessment. Julian enters the bedroom and frostily denounces Patrick for having taken unfair advantage of Jenny, but then quickly drops the subject; Patrick expresses angry self-incrimination, but this too is short-lived. Later, Jenny has some fine moments in which she forcefully condemns Patrick for his selfishness and moral bankruptcy, and breaks off their relationship. But at the close, she ruefully accepts him back.

> "You know, Patrick Standish, I should really never have met you. Or I should have got rid of you while I still had a chance. But I couldn't think how to. And it's a bit late for that now, isn't it. I'll just change my dress. Well, those old Bible-class ideas have certainly taken a knocking, haven't they?"
> "They were bound to, you know, darling, with a girl like you. It was inevitable."
> "Oh yes, I expect it was. But I can't help feeling it's rather a pity" (*Take*, 320).

Amis often insisted that the note he wanted to sound at the close of the novel was elegiac. The last scene, he told Dale Salwak, is "meant to be a very sad moment, because in fact compared to Standish's behavior she's a better person than he is, and the Bible-class ideas are quite better than his, even though they are quite inadequate." This, Amis went on, "is her trouble—she is presented with a great moral imperative or prohibition without being able to understand the reason for it, without being able to work out the reason for it, and without wanting it, without being temperamentally on the side of it."[8]

But Amis doesn't mention here an earlier, often over-looked scene that he placed between the rape and the rueful resolution—a scene that deepens not only the mood but also the ethical implications of his conclusion. When Jenny returns to her flat after Patrick's betrayal, she finds three visitors: Miss Sinclair, headmistress of the school at which she teaches; Elsie Carter, a colleague; and Mr. Whittaker, the father of John, one of her pupils. The night before, the group explains, John was hurt playing in the woods. Another boy, Michael Primrose, one of Jenny's favorites, promised to bring help, left, but failed to return. John, hysterical, was eventually rescued by a neighbor and kept asking to see Miss Bunn. His parents phoned her at Ormerod's house but were put off by the drunken clamor. Now, Miss Sinclair explains, John is still asking to see Jenny, and the trio has turned up at the flat to escort her to the convalescing boy. Mr. Whittaker, however, sees Jenny's dishevelment and begs off, but not before the headmistress has her chance to glare disapprovingly at the humiliated, guilt-stricken girl.

After the group leaves, Jenny stretches out and cries for half an hour. Patrick arrives and tries to salve her feelings about the incident with Miss Sinclair and the rape at the party, but Jenny thinks that she "would never be able to explain to him what it meant to her not to have gone to John Whittaker when he needed her" (*Take*, 319). Realizing that she will continue to see Patrick, she muses on their future and accepts the inevitable disillusionment that it will be very different from what she had hoped. "But she felt now that there had been something selfish in that hope, that a lot of time she had been pursuing not what was right but what she wanted. And she could hardly pretend that what she had got was not worth having at all. She must learn to take the rough with the smooth, just like everybody else."

This chastening is essential not only for the reader's assessment of Jenny but also for an understanding of how Amis wants the reader to respond to the irresolvable contradictions inherent in the resolution itself. Learning to take the rough with the smooth *does* seem like common sense. Yet the severity of Patrick's betrayal and the intensity of Jenny's shame at failing to console her pupil point to a less reassuring moral: To accept conventional wisdom by saying "ah, well" only accentuates the deficiencies of the principle one is trying to affirm.

Jenny's hedged affirmation—her attempt to find positive values in a thicket of dissatisfactions—is one of the most memorable expressions of Amis's characteristic conclusions. Many of his best books over the next 35 years also close with dramatic sequences in which the protagonists talk or think about the dubious moral implications of their actions, try to locate something hopeful in the present, and yet are uncomfortably aware of what their weaknesses and past behavior portend for the future.

I Want It Now (1968), for instance, begins to end when Ronnie Appleyard, the nasty talk-show host, has a mundane but eye-opening revelation. Having botched an effort to elope with the hippie heiress, Simon, for whom he now genuinely cares, the unprincipled Ronnie squirmingly admits what has happened to him.

> He had begun by using niceness, tenderness, what you will, as a specific aid in the Simon situation, as one of the purest means to an end in all history. And then, frighteningly soon, in fact, unknown to himself, he had started enjoying being nice to Simon, started using tenderness as an end in itself, got hooked on the bloody stuff, in fact.[9]

Ronnie's new commitment to decency leads him to accept a rival TV-host's invitation to participate in a panel discussion about "The Rich." Viewed by millions, he denounces the wealthy as power-crazed egotists and tells Simon's mother, Lady Baldock (a fellow panelist), that he wouldn't touch a penny of the family money. Afterward, unhappily reconciling himself to the loss of Simon, Ronnie is dumbfounded when Lord Baldock brings her to him so that they might go off together. On the last page of the novel, the couple discuss their surprising good fortune:

> "Very odd, this whole thing. I was a shit when I met you. I still am in lots of ways. But because of you I've had to give up trying to be a dedicated, full-time shit. I couldn't make it, hadn't the strength of character. Which is a pity in a way, because when you fall back into the ranks of the failed shits or amateur shits or incidental shits you start taking on responsibility for other people."
> "You're not a shit in the least. Well, not now. I've been a terrible fool all my life and I still am. I haven't changed. Well, perhaps a bit."

"A hell of a lot. And nobody could blame you for what you were."
"Oh, I could. I do. No sense at all. Silly all the time. Awful."
"Perhaps we'll have to work on each other."
"Helping each other not to be as bad as we would be on our own."
"That's it."
He picked up the suitcase. They went out and in a diagonal shuffle, arms about shoulders, made their way across the road. (*Now,* 254–255).

In one respect, *I Want It Now* can be read as a piquant fairy tale for the '60s, in which the suspect prince rescues the stoned beauty from her moneyed mother and dastardly suitors. Indeed, it shares with *Lucky Jim* the distinction of being the only other Amis novel that seems at first look to have a classically romantic ending. But in another sense, the unvarnished truth-telling at the close highlights the possibility that the lovers' satisfaction will be temporary. Pledging not to be a shit, when he has worked so long and successfully at refining the role, does not inspire confidence in Ronnie's future behavior. Reviewing the novel in 1968, Anthony Burgess shrewdly praised the description of the couple going off "in a diagonal shuffle" as a disavowal of "any straight progression towards being better."[10] And Amis himself told Clive James: "The threat isn't withdrawn."[11]

Variations of the signature pattern described here can also be found in books as different as *The Anti-Death League* (1966); *Girl, 20* (1971); *Difficulties with Girls* (1988); and *The Folks That Live on the Hill* (1990). Two of the most accomplished works from Amis's last decade illustrate the fresh ways his endings leave the reader not with a feeling of finality but with a desire to reflect on the entire action's implications.

"Malcolm," the concluding chapter of *The Old Devils* (1986), is set just after half a dozen climactic events have occurred and the major strands of the story have been agreeably tied together. The vain, rakish writer and popularizer of "Welsh consciousness" Alun Weaver—whose return to Wales had set the plot in motion—has died of a stroke after gagging on a drink. His admirable widow, Rhiannon, has encouraged old Peter Thomas, with whom she had an affair in their youth, to move in with her. Peter's wife, the icy Muriel, has abandoned him and Wales to go back to her native Yorkshire. The Thomases' son, William, has just married the Weavers' wise daughter, Rosemary; before she leaves to pursue a career as a lawyer, the bride affectionately orders Peter Thomas not to let her mother down. "If you do," she says, "William and I will kill you, okay?"[12]

In the novel's last scene, Malcolm and Gwen Cellan-Davies are precisely where they had been on page 1: at the breakfast table chatting about the goings-on of their friends. Gwen offers a caustic gloss on an upbeat letter from Muriel about her new life in Yorkshire. Malcolm tries weakly to put a more favorable spin on its contents but is no match for his wife's mockery.

Gwen asks (as she has done for 30 years) if he minds her taking "first knock in the bathroom" (*Devil,* 380). He says (as he has 10,000 times) "Go ahead," and when she leaves, he glances at the morning paper and thinks "as strongly as ever before" that the barbed breakfast ritual reminds him of those that took place at 221B Baker Street between Sherlock Holmes and Dr. Watson.

> There, as here, the first party regularly offered well-meaning provisional explanations of bits of human behavior and the second party exposed their naivety, ignorance, over-simplification, non-virtuous unworldliness. But there, unlike here, the exposures were sometimes softened with a favorite-pupil tolerance or even varied with an occasional cry of "Excellent!" or "One for you, Watson!" Nor was it recorded of Holmes that half of what he said came in aural italics or bold sanserif. Had Gwen started piling this on recently? Or had she only started doing it so's-you'd-notice recently? Well, they had been married a long time (*Devils,* 381).

Gwen comes back in; the conversation turns to the subject of Peter moving in with Rhiannon; and Malcolm again wilts in the face of his wife's disdain. She leaves the house and he heads off to the bathroom, where he continues to reflect on the unhappiness of his marriage. Observing that Gwen has not mentioned Alun's name since he died, Malcolm muses on the meaning of her suppression.

> What kind of punishment or self-punishment her silence was meant to inflict he had very little idea, but if she had wanted to remove any doubts he might have been trying to hang on to about whether she had some sort of affair with Alun—well, she had pulled that off in fine style. He had not quite lost the hope that one day a casual pronouncement of the name would touch off an equally casual allusion to that affair, and he could tell her that that was of no consequence and never had been. But he judged it very unlikely. And it was odd how a taboo on a single, less than all-important subject had seemingly turned out to impose a blackout on so much else (*Devil,* 384).

After finishing in the bathroom and puttering about, Malcolm settles down to his work table, hoping to put in an hour or so on his translation of a long poem by Cynddelw Mawr ap Madog Wladaidd (c. 1320–?1388) before he heads off to the pub. He admits, however, that his manuscript is more of an adaptation than a translation, for he has changed the central figure's physical traits to correspond with Rhiannon's. And the narration concludes: "If she had found love with Peter he was glad, because he had nothing to give her himself. But she had given him something. The poem, his poem, was going to be the best tribute he could pay to the only woman who had ever cried for him" (*Devil,* 384).

Although the external action of the last chapter is static and familiar (Gwen always flattens her husband at mealtime), the passages in which Amis invites us into Malcolm's private world open the novel out in surprising and satisfying ways. The melancholy Malcolm has been portrayed throughout as an aging sentimentalist with feeble poetic aspirations, aware of his shortcomings yet long past the time when he might be able to do anything about them. But Amis shows us here, more graphically than before, the man's wisdom and moral maturity.

Malcolm's amusing comparison of his breakfast table ritual to that of Holmes and Watson not only displays the rich imagination of a retentive reader and a connoisseur of expressive typefaces but also the sensitivity of a man who recognizes that everyone needs encouragement and support, not least of all "non-virtuous" unworldly people like himself. The mix of pathos and humor in his reflection shows his typical way of dealing with defeat: he retreats to an enclosed inner world where his wit and emotionalism allow him to savor victories and deal with despair. His reflection on Gwen's silence reveals how little he understands his wife's motives and feelings but how much he cares, and how much they both have paid for their inability to communicate. Yet his conjectures expose a generosity that has rarely been given adequate opportunity for expression.

And, finally, his thoughts turn to Rhiannon. Malcolm remembers an afternoon outing some weeks earlier when he drove her to a romantic abandoned church and asked if she recalled having been there with him more than 30 years before. Her whispered "yes" moved him to say what he believes he said to her when they were young: "And I said, I know I'll never mean as much to you as you mean to me, anywhere near, and I'm not complaining, I said, but I want to tell you nobody will ever mean as much to me as you do, and I want you to remember that, I said. And you said you would, and I think perhaps you have, haven't you?" (*Devils*, 224) Rhiannon's nod of assent provided Malcolm with a moment of bliss, but suddenly it dawned on him that he was confusing different occasions and that her concurrence was a well-meaning lie. Perceiving that she remembered little or nothing, Rhiannon hid her face, turned aside, and cried.

Now, at his writing table, Malcolm gratefully accepts her tears as a substitute for the love she never felt for him, and correctly (if ironically) assesses his modest translation of an obscure medieval Welsh poem as the best tribute he could muster. This shivery, elegiac moment expresses a depth of sympathy not only for Malcolm and Rhiannon but for all the other "sadly comic and comically sad" Old Devils.[13]

In *You Can't Do Both,* published just a year before he died, Amis provides an ending that combines the melancholy wisdom of *The Old Devils,* the irreverent comedy of his earliest fiction, and some discomforting opinions from the books in between. The final effect, however, is different.

The last chapter of *You Can't Do Both* opens in *Lucky Jim* territory. Thirty-five-year-old Robin Davies, an affable, well-off reader in classics at a university in the English midlands, sits alone in his office making funny faces and obscene gestures to convince himself that "he has not yet sunk in complacency."[14] Lecturing on Pindar, he surveys the breasts of the girls (ranked as "low" and "high" security risks). Afterward he attends to correspondence related to his off-campus life as a womanizer. At lunch with his wife and daughters, he is perturbed to hear that an odd woman had phoned in his absence. He lies about knowing who she is. A week later, he heads off to a London hotel for "a nice spot of adultery" with his cousin Dilys, deciding (as he has often before) not to let "a bagatelle like a hurried marriage interfere with what he had always done or at least wanted to do" (*Both,* 298).

Soon after the cousins have eagerly bedded down for the night, Robin's wife Nancy, having been tipped off by the detective she hired to follow him, phones from the same hotel and orders her husband downstairs to talk. In the strong scene that follows, Nancy shifts from the pleasure of discovery to anger, and then to derisive condemnation, cool analysis, tears, and finally violence, as she tells her husband precisely what she thinks (and has long thought) of his actions. Still caring for him, she indicts Robin not only for a failure of trust and love but also for a fundamental moral nullity: an inability to take seriously anything other than his own incorrigible promiscuity, his feeble strategies of concealment, and his self-exculpatory logic.

"When did you stop loving me?" Robin asks; and Nancy turns on him furiously: "Believe me, chum, there's nothing I'd like better than to be able to tell you I don't love you, and mean it. Do you think if I hadn't been I'd have come any of the way with you at all? You don't stop loving someone just because you find out they're not worth it" (*Both,* 304). Sighing and swallowing her pride, she offers him another chance with different rules: "If I ever stop being sure you're not trying to get away with something then I'm off for good with Margaret and Tilly, all right? You can have the three of us, or you can have everyone else. Not both." Then she suddenly swings round and lands an enormous backhanded blow on his cheek. "That was just to be going on with," she says, and walks from the room (*Both,* 305). Alone, the ruffled Robin can think only about his blackeye and his thirst for another drink. Ordering a whiskey and a sandwich, he telephones his brother, George, who had helped Nancy engage the detective and who, in her words, "is very fond of you, he just doesn't think much of you. Rather like me in a way" (*Both,* 300).

Much of the force of this closing sequence comes from a new proportion of sympathy and judgment. Although the scene is reminiscent of the scenes at the end of *Take a Girl like You* and *Difficulties with Girls,* in which the moral Jenny Bunn talks with the rakish Patrick Standish, this encounter is more unrelentingly bitter than bittersweet. Amis is far harsher toward Robin's contrary instincts and irreconcilable inclinations, far sadder about Nancy's disillusionment and inability to break away, than he ever was toward Patrick's waywardness or Jenny's disenchantment.

Yet even so, the ending has its own surprises. As Philip Roth put in another context, the burden of life is not really either/or, "consciously chosen from possibilities equally difficult or regrettable. It's and/and/and/and/and as well. Life is and.... This times this times this....."[15] Although Robin Davies has twice confronted the truism that "you can't do both" (once from his father as a boy and now from his wife), he will not likely choose either/or in the future. Amis's ending does not endorse either/or and certainly no prospect of synthesis. Rather he endorses an unstable accommodation between contentious desires that promises inevitable dissatisfactions and uncounted costs. Reading the autobiographical *You Can't Do Both* as addressed to Amis's first wife, Hilly, Eric Jacobs has called it "an apology, a message of love and regret."[16] One might also describe it as another refutation of the portrait of the artist that was presented in the periodical obituaries.

Notes

Unless otherwise noted, all essays cited in this essay appear in this volume.
1. Mary Braid, "Obituary," *Independent,* 23 October 1995, p. 1.
2. "Obituary," *Boston Globe,* 23 October 1995, p. 17.
3. David Lodge, "Obituary," *Independent,* 23 October 1995, p. 16.
4. Malcolm Bradbury, "Obituary," *Independent,* 23 October 1995, p. 1.
5. John Sutherland, "Obituary," *Sunday Times,* 27 October 1995, sect. 7, p. 11.
6. Kingsley Amis, *That Uncertain Feeling* (London: Penguin Books, 1985), 239–40. Hereafter referred to as *Feeling*.
7. ———, Take a Girl like You (New York: Harcourt, Brace & World, 1960), p. 132. Hereafter referred to as *Take*.
8. Dale Salwak, "An Interview with Kingsley Amis," in this volume.
9. Amis, *I Want It Now* (London: Penguin Books, 1988), 225. Hereafter referred to as *Now*.
10. Anthony Burgess, *Listener,* 10 October 1968, p. 475.
11. Clive James, "Profile 4: Kingsley Amis," *New Review* (July 1974):27.
12. Amis, *The Old Devils* (London: Penguin Books, 1987), 378. Hereafter referred to as *Devils*.
13. Burgess, *Observer,* 30 November 1986, p. 21.
14. Amis, *You Can't Do Both* (London: Flamingo, 1996), 290. Hereafter referred to as *Both*.
15. Philip Roth, *The Counterlife* (New York: Farrar Straus Giroux, 1986), 306.
16. Eric Jacobs, *Kingsley Amis* (London: Hodder and Stoughton, 1996), 359.

Seriocomic Amis and True Comic Edge: *Lucky Jim* and *You Can't Do Both*

Robert H. Bell

> As often in life, what had seemed nothing but a jest became a glimpse of a large and painful truth the second time round.
>
> —*You Can't Do Both*

Rarely does comic fiction provide probing moral inquiry or compelling psychological realism. Critics like F. R. Leavis, primarily concerned with these qualities, deny masterpieces like *Tom Jones* and *Tristram Shandy* status in the Great Tradition,[1] and gifted writers like Kingsley Amis are disparaged by John Updike as "winsomely trivial . . . in thrall to the weary concept of the 'comic novel,' " without "true comic edge."[2] Though I would dearly like to repudiate Updike's position, I can only take issue with it. After 30 years of enjoying and admiring Amis during a career of explicating and justifying comic writing, I must reluctantly concede the partial validity of Updike's criticism. What I can dispute and eagerly argue is that Jim Dixon is a comic hero with some unexpected (and, all right, strangely neglected) intricacy; for a remarkably long time we cannot know what will become of him, nor are we ever entirely sure how to assess him. The result is an engagingly problematic comic novel, with moments of uproarious farce, that precipitates a measure of thoughtful laughter and reflective scrutiny. But *Lucky Jim,* animated by comic impulses and faithful to comic imperatives, has limited depth, especially compared with Amis's more rigorously seriocomic late novel *You Can't Do Both*.[3] Ultimately, one of the most telling and impressive of Amis's achievements is his successful conversion of humor's limits into a subject, an issue, and a resource.

Our initial responses to James Dixon are not particularly complicated: we share his point of view and generally sympathize with him. He's a beleaguered young man in danger of losing his job, compelled to please Professor

---

This essay was written specifically for this volume and is published for the first time by permission of the author.

Welch, who is insufferably boring, inhumanly obtuse, and prone to addressing Jim by the name of his predecessor in the History Department. Jim is likable because he is without pretense or self-delusion. He'd be the first to admit he's unheroic and all too human. Jim modestly considers that he had been "drawn into the Margaret business by a combination of virtues he hadn't known he'd possessed: politeness, friendly interest, ordinary concern, a good-natured willingness to be imposed upon, a desire for unequivocal friendship."[4] Jim wins our sympathy not by his impressive character or conduct but simply because he is better than the fools and phonies whose follies he mocks. Jim protects himself and amuses us with satiric wit and comic defiance. He correctly describes himself as "quick off the mark" (133). He's a great mimic, an inventive actor, a master impersonator, and a well of outrageous vitality. Jim is the only live sensibility in a mausoleum of death—the incarnation of Bergson's *élan vital,* the life force pitted against stultifying authorities and mechanical inhumanity as embodied by Professor Welch. At one point, enjoying his plot against Bertrand, he "threw back his head and gave a long trombone-laugh of anarchistic laughter" (103). Jim's "anarchistic laughter," mocking conventional morality and decorum, is the stock-in-trade of comedy. Set the Marx Brothers loose in an opera house, or the brothers of *Animal House* amid a civic parade, and welcome Topsy-Turvy: exuberant youth discombobulates venerable authority. "The pure sense of life," says Suzanne K. Langer, is "the underlying feeling of comedy."[5] Such comic energy is amusing but often excessive and infantile (Updike's phrase is "unabashedly sophomoric"), as when Jim writes "Ned Welch is a Soppy Fool with a Face like a Pig's Bum" on Welch's steamy bathroom mirror, or when he imagines devoting the next 10 years to "working his way to a position as art critic on purpose to review Bertrand's work unfavorably" (50).

While laughter is crucial to Jim's survival and sanity, it contains more "anarchic fury" than he realizes or controls. Here, psychological intensity with significant implications creates a discrepancy between Jim's self-awareness and our reaction to him. To Amis a fully defined character is perceived "from all points on the compass, with respect, irony, impatience, and sadness." The narrative point of view in *Lucky Jim* is stable and reliable, or at least stably and reliably the hero's. But the viewpoint provides more: it is just over Jim's shoulder, and it dramatizes Jim thinking and feeling—thus enabling us to regard Jim with more ironic detachment and critical skepticism than Jim himself would or could muster. The aggression we see so often is a far more dangerous quality than, say, the high spirits or amorous inclinations of Jim's comic ancestors, Joseph Andrews and Tom Jones. Jim can barely suppress the impulse to attack Professor Welch or Bertrand.

His favorite means of purging rage or containing loathing is to enact that dazzling repertory of faces; my favorite is Jim's "Sex Life in Ancient Rome" face, suggesting the saturnalian spirit he represents. Jim acknowledges that his imitations "frightened him." He is less aware of how much self-hatred he has: his aggression, deflected from its exterior objects, boomerangs. Some of his capers, like stealing the cab from his senior colleague at the dance, are reckless kamikaze gestures, represented by Amis (but not Jim) as self-destructive. So often is he enacting roles, performing mimicry, and making faces that it must confuse Jim himself or distract him from the burden of introspection and self-awareness. He's certainly lax and unskilled at self-examination; he seems happiest pretending to be someone else, impersonating people on the telephone or forging letters. This hero, with conflicts and tensions beyond his own comprehension, sustains a high-wire act that keeps his audience, including readers, off balance; his volatile energies are very funny and quite desperate.

Such anarchic qualities, by definition unpredictable, are inherently amoral. Jim rarely stands *for* anything: he defines himself mainly by what he despises. He is a contemporary descendent of the picaro, attractive but fundamentally mischievous and self-seeking, a rogue or what Amis would term a bit of a bastard. We indulge the rascal, perhaps, to the extent that we recognize our own infantile, libidinal, unsocialized impulses. Yet under scrutiny his character is bound to cause confusion and consternation. He is ludicrous and likable, so smart and such a smart-ass, objectionable yet admirable, heedless yet life-affirming. Marvelously protean, he is elusively ambiguous. Consider again Jim's meditations on the "Margaret business." Jim's catalog of qualities that got him into the relationship is accurate but incomplete. It omits rather less appealing qualities one might just as readily attribute to Jim, such as cowardice, passivity, timidity. He often behaves unscrupulously, in ways that provoke both amusement and impatience, one of the key points on Amis's narrative compass.

Even Jim's ironic self-appraisal, normally a winning trait, is highly disorienting, as when he considers the title of his article: "It was the perfect title, in that it crystallized the article's niggling mindlessness, its funereal parade of yawn-enforcing facts, the pseudo-light it threw upon non-problems" (16). For living without illusion, Jim surely gets full marks, but he veers beyond candor and humor toward self-abuse. His assault upon sham and pretense includes self-loathing and Philistinism, what we might term the "filthy Mozart factor" to commemorate the moment Jim hears somebody in the bath singing "some skein of untiring facetiousness by filthy Mozart" (66). Jim's impertinence and his antipathy to culture illustrate the way his satiric assaults rebound upon himself.

However, Jim is not merely the center of value and the voice of the satirist but also the object of humorous and substantial evaluation. Here, for example, he fends off his ardent student Michie, the veteran intrigued by scholasticism.

> Clearly, the more students, within reason, Dixon could get "interested" in his subject, the better for him; equally clearly, too large a number of "interested"

students would mean that the number studying Welch's own special subject would fall to a degree that Welch might be expected to resent. With an honours class of nineteen and a department of six, three students seemed a safe number to try for. So far Dixon's efforts on behalf of his special subject, apart from thinking how much he hated it, had been confined to aiming to secure for it the three prettiest girls in the class, one of whom was Michie's girl, while excluding from it Michie himself. Added to Dixon's dislike of thinking about work at all, the necessity of keeping Michie at arms length went far to explain his present discomfort (30).

Delineating Jim's comic discomfort, as in many other moments of half-probing introspection, the narrator says nothing, strictly speaking, that Jim doesn't know and wouldn't admit. Yet even while adhering rigorously to Jim's perspective, the narrative viewpoint implicitly demands critical response. Through such revelations, Amis exposes the hero as expedient, cynical, manipulative, and lazy. Jim's moral nature is not merely "winsomely trivial" but deeply equivocal. He is part victim but not necessarily more sinned against than sinning, for he is also and often the maker of his own muddles. The pattern is established early in the novel when Jim regrets the "bad impression" he'd first made at the university by "his having inflicted a superficial wound on the professor of English in the first week. This man ... had been standing on the front steps when Dixon, coming round the corner from the library, had kicked violently at a small round stone lying on the macadam.... [It] had struck the other just below the left kneecap" (18). Characteristically, Jim's violent, vague hostility backfires; he partly invites or precipitates his troubles. He was drafted to sing madrigals at the Welch's party and was mortified because he lied when he said he could "read music 'after a fashion' " (38). Jim is stuck in the wrong role without the courage to repudiate it or the dignity to transcend it. "He'd never be able to tell Welch what he wanted to tell him, any more than he'd ever be able to do the same with Margaret" (86).

There is psychological intensity, or "true comic edge," in the serious nature of Jim's fears: because his psyche is crippled and vulnerable, we know we cannot rely upon a happy ending. As his plight is problematic, his progress is genuinely suspenseful, replete with real perils, so that we hang upon events, hopeful but doubtful.

Amis concocts comedy from traditional ingredients in a modern mix. In *Joseph Andrews,* Fielding plays with the possibility of disaster when, for example, he addresses the anxieties the reader "must have felt on the account of poor Fanny, whom we left in so deplorable a condition ... wondering what happened to that beautiful and innocent virgin, after she fell into the wicked hands of the captain."[6] Even describing the imminent peril of rape, Fielding's tone reassures us that the danger is exaggerated, the virgin inviolate, protected (in a phrase he uses elsewhere) "by the deity who presides over chaste love." Fielding, of course, is that benevolent deity, maintaining providential design and comic suspense. His blend of cheer and fright is beautifully counterpointed but always inclined toward humor because the dangers are treated melodramatically and with cavalier insouciance. We do not read far in Fielding without realizing that he always guarantees virtue and never irreparably harms his favorites. We learn to anticipate a pattern of apparent catastrophes and hairbreadth escapes, to recognize hyperbolic fears or parodies of danger as comic analogs of fear. Above all, we can trust our omnipotent, ubiquitous narrator; the suspense is ultimately not *if* but *how* Fielding will bring his beloved hero and innocent heroine through the storms to the happy shore.

Lucky Jim contrives a similar but distinct synthesis, a modern version of Fielding's melodramatic perils. As Amis alternates reassurance or equanimity with dread or suspense, we are far less certain of deliverance than Fielding's reader was. Unlike Fielding, Amis does not flaunt his power, enter the stage directly, and show off. He is more like the tactfully withdrawn narrator of modernist fiction, in the Flaubertian phrase of Stephen Daedalus, aloof, absent, paring his fingernails. Relatively abandoned or bereft of avuncular narrative protection, Jim Dixon appears to be the prey of fickle fortune, not the favorite of comic destiny. The third-person limited point of view gives us Jim's plucky pessimism and no warrant for believing he is lucky at all; given his confused travail, Jim would be surprised to learn the title of his adventures. Cued by the title, the reader suspects that Jim will survive and prosper. Yet as a result of the narrative reticence and authorial deftness, the providential tendency of Amis's comedy is barely discernible as it subtly steers the hero toward more luck than he can imagine.

The open-ended uncertainty of the romantic triangle illustrates the deft comic plotting. Until remarkably late in the novel, the limited omniscience of the narrative viewpoint and Jim's exaggerated sense of his hopelessness give us little authoritative assurance that Jim will get rid of the wrong girl and get hold of the right one. Amis conveys the grand illusion that events are determined by character rather than designed as we like. It is another mask—apparent contingency disguising ultimate design. Jim is initially and apparently endlessly involved in a bloodless liaison to which he musters only intermittent passive resistance: "Suddenly he'd become the man who was 'going round' with Margaret, and somehow competing with" (12) a rival named Catchpole. Margaret, recovering from a half-baked suicide attempt, is just plausible and pathetic enough to command Jim's attentions. Yet his feelings toward her are thoroughly vague and utterly confused: compassion, irritation, evasiveness, little desire. Plain and priggish, she addresses Jim as "Poor James." His drunken advances, at first zealously reciprocated, are abruptly rebuffed, an indication that her feelings are as tepid or ambivalent as his. The next morning, feeling resentful, her response to Jim ruining the bedspread with his cigarette is sternly censorious, the voice of an aunt or librarian, not a sweetheart. Her reproaches resonate and precipitate two familiar feelings in Jim: panic and guilt. Yet somehow Jim, under a kind of wicked spell, is drawn further into bondage to Margaret, manipulated into escorting her to the dance.

Though Jim's escape sparks a frightful row with Margaret, he still cannot bail out. Arguing furiously, she reveals her true colors: "You don't think Christine would have you, do you? A shabby little provincial bore like you!" (158). She falls into hysterics and Jim, realizing that Margaret can still exploit his decency and weakness, sinks into bleak depression. He perceives but can't address a flaw in his character, passive acquiescence to manipulators like Margaret and Professor Welch (who are of course warm friends). It takes Jim an inordinately long time to realize that he is "well schooled in giving apologies at the very times he ought to be demanding them" (174); in this important regard, Jim resembles his literary cousin Robin Davies in *You Can't Do Both*. Jim remains something of a schlemiel, fearful, estranged, terrified that he won't know what to do in the company of quality. Like the classic picaro, he is the perpetual outsider or marginal figure, but without the traditional rogue's poised mastery.

So not simply his situation but also his limitations make Jim an unlikely hero, romantic or otherwise. His first meeting with Christine is unpromising: she appears as Bertrand's companion at the Welch's arty weekend and arouses powerful, contrary responses in Jim: desire, alarm, and anger that he can't have such attractive women. When he dances with Christine at the ball, he is nearly unmanned by apprehension: "He found it hard to believe that she was really going to let him touch her, or that the men near them wouldn't spontaneously intervene to prevent them" (117). Yet ever since they met, there have been dimly perceptible omens, such as Christine's grinning in comic complicity with Jim when they both remake his bed with the ruined spread. Again what the narrator withholds is crucial, for without an omniscient Fielding to guide us the signals remain wonderfully mixed. Since the characters don't know what they want or should do, we can't guess what will happen. In one breath Christine praises Jim's impersonation of a reporter, in which he gulls Bertrand, as "brilliantly funny," then regrets seeming to be in a "conspiracy to get the better of Bertrand" (119). As in classical comedies like *Tom Jones, A Midsummer Night's Dream* or *Pride and Prejudice,* the characters unwittingly form discernible dance-like patterns.

Hope and dread remain finely balanced until quite late in the novel. Given Jim's malaise and uncertainty, failure seems more likely than success. He drifts back to Margaret, "directed by something outside of himself . . . not out of any willing on his part" (186). He and Christine meet, each prepared to renounce the other. As late as chapter 19, four-fifths of the way through the novel, Jim's dreams remain far-fetched if not inconceivable. His only solace is a gradual clarification of his own weaknesses: "I'm sticking to Margaret," he tells Christine, "because I haven't the guts to turn her loose. . . . So I do that instead of doing what I want to do, because I'm afraid to" (201).

As late as Jim's tour de farce, the Merry England lecture, his prospects with Christine remain highly dubious. He helplessly watches Bertrand "with his hand on Christine's arm, confident, proprietary, victorious" (219). The reader has no way of knowing what's in Christine's mind and can only pity "Poor James," whose "spirits were so low that he wanted to lie down and pant like a dog: jobless, Christineless, and now grand-slammed in the Margaret game" (220). Not until the very last scene, improbable but plausible, can we perceive that comic destiny has, all along, been disguised as fickle fortune. As Carol Goldsmith says, in another context, "It's all connected, all connected" (125). Even the Professor's notoriously terrible driving, which early in the novel puts Jim at real risk, enables the comic and romantic denouement.

Another way Amis makes Jim's ultimate good luck utterly unexpected yet realistically acceptable is by deploying Gore-Urquhart as the comic deus ex machina. Notice that even in the crucial phone call, when Gore-Urquhart offers Jim the coveted job, we do not lose sight of the hero's unimposing stature: "It's not that you've got the qualification for this or any work. . . . You haven't the disqualifications, though, and that's much rarer" (234). As Gore-Urquhart humorously underscores, Jim only more or less deserves such good fortune—yet comic destiny has decreed that our hero, bad as he is, shall live happily ever after. Like Tom Jones or Joseph Andrews along the way to the promised land, Jim makes unremarkable, indeed quite slight, progress. Like most comedy, *Lucky Jim* depends upon a series of recognitions rather than dramatic revelations. These recognitions fall into two categories: facts and self-discoveries.

The recognition of facts, or a more lucid apprehension of the way things are, comes gradually but regularly to Jim's consciousness. Some of these facts are crucial to his understanding other characters, such as his discovery of Bertrand and Carol Goldsmith in a compromising situation. This of course makes it ethically easier for us to applaud Jim's efforts to steal Christine from Bertand, exposed as a two-timing hypocrite as well as a pompous ass. Another important fact is Carol's speculation, later corroborated, that Christine hasn't yet been abed with Bertrand: like Fielding's Fanny and Sophia, she is inviolate, innocent, and pure for the hero.

Another fact in the cascade of comic recognitions, as crucial as the glad tidings of the Pedlar in *Joseph Andrews* or the Lawyer Dowling in *Tom Jones,* is Catchpole's testimony regarding Margaret's sham suicide. The revelation of her deep neuroses liberates Jim from the strictures of his conscience and the bondage of their relationship. "Don't try to help her any more," says Catchpole, more helpfully than he could know, "It's too dangerous for you. I know what I'm talking about. She doesn't need any help either, you know, really. The best of luck to you" (242). Helpful, hopeful, it's virtually a benediction. An opposite possibility, almost equally strong, illustrates the continuing complexity. One might conclude that a staged suicide indicates profound problems that deserve sympathy, respect, and patience rather than impatience, irony, and self-protection.

The second category of recognitions in comedy, self-discovery, is considerably murkier than the discovery of plain truths. Compared to Tom Jones and Joseph Andrews, Jim is much more self-aware and complicated; he is too reflective, pained, and internal to be described as a flat comic character. Yet like Tom and Joseph, Jim's character remains relatively fixed, incapable of radical transformation. He experiences a modicum of self-discovery, a gradually enhanced comprehension of himself and his world. Marking his limited progress is his final gesture, a "howl of laughter" at the Welch family, for the things he has learned delight but don't instruct all that much; they won't take him beyond gleeful victory into what Yeats termed the "abyss of self." Jim remains for better and for worse a comic hero in a comic novel, with keener perceptions and vague development. He has understood the need to leave Margaret and abandon academics; neither act will prove painful. Jim has learned that he needn't be so timid, so afraid to approach a girl like Christine just because "she's a bit out of my class" (128).

A conversation with Carol Goldsmith at the dance illustrates the fundamentally comic qualities and limits of Jim's growth. When he confesses his fear of approaching Christine, she tells him to grow up, stop apologizing, and seize the day. Wiser and more cynical, Carol gives Jim's mission half-facetious, half-serious sanction: "You've got a moral duty to perform" (129,130). For once Jim is invited to do something he wants to do and to feel *good* about it, which is a comic if not often realistic opportunity, a pleasant development not to be confused with "moral duty." Jim is stunned to hear that Carol had informed her husband about her affair with Bertrand, and reflects "that he knew absolutely nothing whatsoever about other people or their lives" (123).[7] Thus our hero remains in need of rather basic lessons fundamental to fiction and life. He has become luckier and a bit less pathetic and callow without becoming much more mature or even much less naive.

By the end of the story, Jim has not developed far enough, strictly speaking, to merit his cornucopia of luck. The book knows this and contains more comic wisdom than the hero attains: Jim's experience illustrates two of his favorite, vitally comic, and only modestly penetrating credos: "Nice things are nicer than nasty ones," and "Doing what you want to do is the only training for doing more of what you want to do." The comic closure of *Lucky Jim* fulfills wishes but does not measure merit. The discovery of some facts and simple truths brings fantasy and reality closer, as when Jim thinks and says out loud the same insult, terming Bertrand a "bloody old towser-faced bootfaced totem-pole on a crap reservation" (214). As David Lodge observes, from this instant when "thought and speech, the inner and outer world coincide," things "start to go right for Jim."[8] Language has amazing capacity: recognizing and designating the truth miraculously transforms self and world into something better.

In the world of *Lucky Jim,* overseen by an invisible but benevolent deity whose requirements are lenient and standards generous, such divinations are perhaps sufficient. Jim remains relatively superficial in his ethical growth, even though his character is far from simple. And though *Lucky Jim* is hardly trivial in its psychological intensity, the novel does not test its protagonist deeply but rewards him in accordance with more purely comic imperatives. The denouement is a pleasing gesture toward comic justice, but it rewards Jim for comic energy and resilience rather than for any more profoundly ethical attributes.

Tempted as he must have been to repeat the winning ways of *Lucky Jim,* Amis never exactly rebottled its champagne mirth, which he found inadequate for the kinds of investigations he wished to pursue. Many of his best novels have sharper edges and deeper stakes, without "evangelical huffing and puffing"[9] but with more sustained exploration of ethics and of comedy's limited ability to treat the problems. By the end of his career, when he wrote *You Can't Do Both,* Amis had mastered seriocomic inquiry significantly like and unlike *Lucky Jim.* Robin Davies, the protagonist of *You Can't Do Both,* resembles Jim Dixon yet becomes a more complicated character with a curious fate. As the story begins, the 14-year-old Robin lives in a modest South London suburb, excels at school, and copes gamely with his father's policy of "round-the-clock chaperonage."[10] Any mild transgression provokes paternal ire and a stern reprimand. Robin regularly accepts blame and apologizes grudgingly. Deflated, bullied into outward submission, he invents interior monologues where he triumphs or at least vents his anger. As with *Lucky Jim,* we are situated inside or just above the consciousness of a hero whose plucky wit and vital energies enable his encounters with objectionable authorities. Both novels compel sympathy for a restless, put-upon hero with exceptionally sensitive, accurate boredom and BS detectors yet invite more critical assessment of only partially "authorized" figures. If Jim Dixon is a lovable rascal who gets his just desserts with an extra helping, Robin Davies is an appealing, engaging youth who always wants to have his cake and eat it too. Yet Robin is regarded by nearly everyone as a self-seeking egoist and is treated rather less tenderly than Jim Dixon by providential design. *Lucky Jim* rewards comic values and scarcely considers the limits of comedy; *You Can't Do Both* tests comic values and becomes a compelling seriocomedy. Initially Robin seems unexceptionable—like Jim, he is the source rather than the object of critical inquiry. He is highly intelligent with normal adolescent yearnings and resentments—a hard-up hero facing various obstacles, some reasonable, some arbitrary. This conventionally comic situation produces increasingly somber developments. The hero's wants, needs, and conduct are examined much more rigorously than they were in *Lucky Jim,* and evaluation becomes more intriguingly problematic, most conspicuously in the sexual sphere.

For a long while, Robin appears blameless, exploring, experimenting, and blundering, guilty of nothing more than ordinary horniness and callowness. We enjoy the comedy of Eros, as when Robin contemplates a female Oxford student, "half-way up Category 2, that comprising girls it would be jolly nice/perfectly all right to find yourself in bed with but not worth serious trouble to get them there" (81). Indicating availability, she catapults to Category 1. Yet in Robin's more interior, conflictive personality, sex causes disturbances and precipitates reflections that cut deeper than in Jim Dixon's amusing yearnings. Pondering sex, Robin's language becomes more sinewy, a convoluted sin-tax, doubling back upon itself, conveying ambivalence and confusion. Robin's introspection causes us simultaneously to like and to distrust him, and gradually to assess him more critically. Like Jim Dixon, Robin has appealing comic bravado and carefree self-regard, but what was disconcerting in Jim becomes more worrisome in Robin. When Robin meets Nancy Bennett, for example, he instantly categorizes her (I-B, beautiful complexion and a perfectly adequate though not quite distinguished bosom): "Robin hoped very much to get into a position soon where a decent chap would have to keep reminding himself that, hang it all, the girl was still not yet eighteen years old" (96).

You Can't Do Both challenges Robin's humorously self-indulgent point of view through several sterner commentators. His old mate Embleton lectures Robin: "A piece of you agrees with me that Nancy isn't the right sort of girl for you to persuade to follow your confounded intentions or whatever they are. What I've been saying is designed to strengthen that piece and do some damage to the other piece, the one that says it's all right to go after something you want if you really want it" (97–98). Embleton's cautionary note sounds valid: maybe it's *not* always all right to go after something you want simply because you really want it. We're prodded into regarding the hero as more than merely a comic rascal with a license to fool, for the hero of *You Can't Do Both* lives where his conduct has substantial implications, some more nasty than nice.

Nancy is quite obviously a nice girl, the kind to marry. Her blushing sincerity fills Robin with "transient compunction" (wonderful phrase) and makes him "slightly uneasy" (127). With such a heroine, the male penile project, generally condoned if not sanctioned in comedy, gives pause. Unlike the girls in *Lucky Jim,* Nancy has a family history and concerned parents. Her dad is another Welshman of the old school with decided views, self-dramatizing rhetoric, and the traditional, unenviable role of a blocking force frustrating the hero's amorous pleasures: "If I find you've trifled with her affections, to use a pompous but expressive phrase, I shall be greatly upset and also very cross with you indeed" (104).

Even more difficult to dismiss or mock is the anguished Mrs. Bennett, who informs Robin that Nancy's older sister Megan has an illegitimate child. But Robin, intent on his pursuit, only considers how this "would affect him" and entertains a fleeting fantasy of contacting fallen sister Meagan, "who sounded more and more like the very thing he was looking for" (107). Though Robin is not a heartless cad, he stirs himself to combat with rakish aphorisms: "For every second not spent in driving or dragging a given female towards bed, you were going to have to put in an extra minute later on" (100), and "Liking them got in the way" (101).

It is easier in *You Can't Do Both* than in *Lucky Jim* to respect the voices of authority. Here is an exchange between Robin and Mr. Davies:

> "Is it your intention to marry little Miss Nancy—is it Bennett?"
> "Yes, meaning yes it is Bennett. As regards the rest of it, isn't it a bit early in the game to start talking about my intentions?"
> "Robin, please, it is no game."
> "I only mean. . . ."
> "If you treat it as a game it's my duty to inform you that you're in for a rude awakening, my lad."
> "Sorry, Dad, I expressed myself badly. I assure you I regard it as a very serious matter indeed" (117).

We should not be distracted by the old duffer's archaic idiom or his incessant insistence that this matter, whatever it is, "deserves to be treated rather more seriously than you show signs of doing" (122). Like Nancy's dad, Robin's dad is tiresome but not foolish and should be heeded: "Nancy is a *good . . . girl, and I suggest to you it's in your own interest that you pay due heed to that fact,* which in my view it is."

One must continually distinguish Robin's viewpoint from that of the narrator and regularly contemplate the adequacy of all perspectives—bumptious hero, blocking forces, and elusive narrator: "Again, Robin thought himself equal to paying heed to things unaided, but this time he said as if he meant it, 'I promise you that's something I'll never be fool enough to let myself forget' " (119). Much virtue in an *if.* Some, at least—but not enough, for Robin proves unequal to the task and foolishly (his word) forgets his promise and violates his responsibility. Responsibility is man's estate, as it was not in *Lucky Jim,* where we excuse Jim for concluding that "nice things are nicer than nasty ones" and "doing what you want to do is the only training for doing more of what you want to do."

Though Jim Dixon's comic credos don't survive the more demanding climate of *You Can't Do Both,* the results are oddly seriocomic, more disorienting than the relatively straightforward *Lucky Jim.* We would be mistaken, I think, to judge too quickly or harshly Robin's unwillingness to pay more heed. In virtually every way, as a son, friend, and student, Robin is truly a good lad, with sensitivity and mostly decent motives; he's far more likely than Jim Dixon to repudiate his own gestures and sentiments as "false, insincere" (120). He recognizes Nancy's admirable unsuitability for a sexual fling. "It could not be, he was sure, that he regarded her physically with less than irreproachable carnality, most of the time at least. But a certain other times . . ." (109). The thrust and retreat of the language, the note of male dominance ("irreproachable carnality"), and the ultimate ellipsis indicate both the extent and the limits of Robin's introspection.

It's only in the romantic arena that his self-assertion requires correction. Robin's inner jests are jarring, as when Nancy apologies for talking about her parents: "Robin would sooner have heard about Nancy's detailed plans for a career in indecent films.... These family chronicles ... seemed to lead further away from the life of inventive fornication his fantasies designed for her" (129). Our laughter is uneasy or guilty because we are made more mindful that getting what you want isn't an innocent enterprise. Soon enough, Robin makes the most of an unexpected break from parental presence, only to be confronted, unmanned, and coerced into confession and of course apology by his father, who is heavy-handed but not altogether preposterous in underscoring "the question of [Robin's] responsibility in this mess" (137). Robin's vision is inadequate, blinkered.

In this comedy manqué, the blocking forces are not straw men, like Professor Welch or Fielding's Squire Western, but substantial, with serious purpose, imploring Robin to take intimacy seriously. What's fascinating is how *You Can't Do Both* never simplifies but repeatedly complicates our perceptions. Robin's older brother George is another reasonably reliable figure, challenging Robin's motives yet open to challenge himself. Many voices are enabled, none is sanctioned. "Whereas," George says, "your intention at this stage of your life is to engage in an indefinite series of fornications and you'll think about the next stage in your life when you come to it" (147).

> "It's just, well, you can understand, George, I want to keep my options open as long as I—."

Robin's "attempt at self-justification was misguided," says the narrator, but it's unclear whether that means wrong or merely unsuccessful. "George said with renewed annoyance, 'Yeah, you've always been a great one for keeping those buggers open. I can remember when you were about twelve, not saying whether you were coming to the pictures or not till the last moment in case you got a more attractive offer from somewhere. Good old O. O. Davies Dad used to call you, standing for 'Options Open'" (220). People Robin encounters and trusts continually express irritation with his self-seeking, sometimes with more chagrin than seems warranted, except in the vexed area of sexual relations. Certainly we never saw young Robin behaving as frivolously as George remembers and can hardly imagine that boy crossing his dad.

As in *Lucky Jim,* but with richer complexity and more confusion, there is tension between comic license and ethical compunctions. It is never easy to determine how severely to judge Robin, nor to calculate how bad he should feel. More so than in *Lucky Jim* evaluation is irresistible but tricky and troublesome. Robin exists around the muddy middle, neither one of Amis's bastard-heroes nor simply an appealing young man. He fights a losing battle with desire, that least vicious of sins, but still one of the seven deadly: "He deeply wanted not to be the sort of man who, when just getting into his stride with a satisfactory love-affair, nevertheless seriously contemplates getting started on another," he meditates. "Unfortunately, at other times or even at the same time, that was just the sort of man he at least as deeply wanted to be. It had even occurred to him that sticking firmly to one girl could be unethically used to obtain exemption from the sometimes grueling task of promiscuity" (149). Here Robin, humorously playing a shell game with ethical concerns and humorous needs, caps a sentence with seeming sanction that ricochets out of his control and beyond his ken.

The first two sections of *You Can't Do Both* sympathetically depict Robin at 14 and at 19. The third section dramatizes Robin five years later, near the end of World War II. Robin has served in the armed forces, refuses to exaggerate his travail as a POW, indeed continues to be perfectly agreeable: a good mate, kind to his super mum, dutiful to his duty-minded dad, and still intimately linked to Nancy. Now, though, his romantic activities are evaluated more often and more stringently than ever. Jeremy Carpenter, the gay friend who had seemed so glamorous, sounds older and wiser. He's been incarcerated for refusing military service and again for some homosexual encounter. Now Jeremy views his youthful ideology of liberation, "all that sacredness of desire stuff," as shallow propaganda, "though it might have encouraged you to do what you felt like doing and to hell with other people, that's if," he adds tellingly, "you needed encouragement" (159). Subdued by suffering, Jeremy now questions "wanting something that by definition it's impossible to have" (284), sarcastically termed "Good advice for eleven-year-olds, do what you want" (289).

Robin's main problem remains effectively his only problem: he wants sexual adventure *and* emotional security, but as he has long been told and as adults are supposed to know, you can't have both. In pure comedy, such fun and games take place far from the law courts and church bells; in *You Can't Do Both* such antics are not licensed freedom. More like Pip in *Great Expectations* than like Tom Jones, Robin is highly sensitive to criticism, especially from family, and excessively guilt-ridden, increasingly living not in the house of mirth but in the house of sorrow, where mortals sicken and suffer, stumble and fall.

Robin continues to be a much more sensitive, solicitous son than lover. Brother George again berates him for failing to marry Nancy, to which he reacts with fluent self-justification. When Nancy becomes pregnant, Robin reassures Nancy that he won't let her down "ever." The narrative commentary is crucial: "Robin had meant everything he had said in his promise to Nancy. He was greatly encouraged by the readiness with which she had believed him, thinking it went to show that when he was being honest his honesty shone through" (199). But then comes the Robin Davies's two-step, simultaneously winning regard for Robin's candor and exposing his continuing callowness: "It was only later that he saw the force of the rider to that proposition, namely that when he was being dishonest his dishonesty must shine through as pellucidly." And a not quite saving grace: "Not that he could at the moment foresee any need for successful dishonesty, he just knew enough about life or about himself by this time to be reasonably sure one would be along soon" (199).

A bit of fun comes along soon enough at Dad's cremation, in the cheering presence of Cousin Dilys, who is married, in London, and still eager for some dilly-dally. Robin's "spark of irresponsibility" (210), charming but disquieting in a youth, is more ominous and egregious in an adult. Like a resilient, supple, and irresponsible comic hero, Robin absorbs shocks that in more serious characters might catalyze change and growth. Instead, he carries on, with no signs of pleasure or indications of sadness. He hears but shakes off George's reproaches, just as he is sensitive enough to be staggered by a vision of "something sharp cutting through Nancy's flesh" (231), "but only for a short time."

In the long night before Nancy's operation, Robin, considering his two possibilities to marry or abandon her, thinks "the second was not unthinkable in the least, it was as thinkable as anything he had ever thought, but that was as far as it went" (245). Robin's persistent irresponsibility seems triumphant, greased by self-sophistry: as "everybody else would fervently have agreed, he was almost an ideal non-husband for Nancy, being selfish, self-indulgent, lazy, arrogant, and above all inextinguishably promiscuous by nature" (245). But some self-reproach is also self-evasion. Robin's key concern is that marriage and children "would be no fun for anybody" (245), certainly not Options Open Davies.

Nancy's anguish just before the surgical abortion provokes a jumble of feelings, "some he knew now he had been trying with fair success not to acknowledge, others of whose existence he had been altogether unaware" (250). He decides to rescue her. Robin is neither romantic hero nor dastardly bastard. Despite the hairbreadth scape, *You Can't Do Both* doesn't conclude with romantic/comic redemption. The champagne they drink to celebrate their engagement is cheap station stuff, while Robin's "cheerio" toast is even flatter. "There," Robin comments. "What more can I say," to which Nancy replies forlornly, "Nothing I suppose" (254).

Neither Robin's brother nor mother can be simply celebratory. Mum confesses that she is "a wee bit disappointed" (261) that Robin didn't manage affairs better. The Bennetts are disappointed that their daughter is marrying a boy who turns out to be "nothing but a common seducer" (262), "the kind of man who thinks only of his own pleasure" (265). Robin is not, as he protests, a "libertine like in Restoration comedy" (265)—but neither is he particularly admirable. Smart enough to know that he's "missed something indefinably important through lack of curiosity, lack of attention" (263), he's not wise enough to identify what he lacks nor quite sure what it means to have it.

We get a sharper image of what Robin is missing when George's wife berates him for failing to tell Nancy he loves her: "You stupid *bugger*" (269). Robin's response is classic Amis humor, which helps us see more clearly how

You Can't Do Both differs from *Lucky Jim:* "It occurred to Robin . . . that all talk of a male militia, of men spontaneously uniting in defence of their interests against the encroaching female, misrepresented the situation. Men operated something like a confused, poorly armed guerrilla-type rabble; women, in comparison, ran a highly trained, superbly equipped SS panzer corps complete with parachute brigade and grenadier back-up." The zest, the rich detail, the energy, so reminiscent of *Lucky Jim,* are nearly irresistible, so hilariously cocksure that we might almost overlook the aptness of the sister-in-law's reproach.

In *You Can't Do Both,* witty formulations don't compensate for shallow emotions. Robin hasn't troubled himself with Nancy's parents, who "had never been much fun" (272), which is true but irrelevant. He could happily do without them forever, "But then of course there were Nancy's feelings to be considered. Rather dully, but not unwillingly, he tried to imagine a future state of consciousness in which someone else's feelings, in this case his wife's, would seem to him as important and immediate as his own" (273). He tries sometimes, half-heartedly but dully, to imagine a feeling that comes more naturally to some husbands. Indeed, Mum's most effective point, trying to persuade the Bennetts to attend their daughter's wedding, is to lay all blame squarely on her boy. "Look after number one, that's all you can trust him to do" (275). Later Robin remarks that he knows she didn't mean all those terrible things. "I didn't say I didn't mean it, dear, I said I was sorry I had to say it. You must know yourself it was true" (276). It's as though Mum sadly agrees with George that Robin hasn't bloody well grown up and damn well should. Though he marries Nancy and even remembers to tell her he loves her, "he soon stopped focusing on the two of them and went back to the one of him" (277). Pondering the many reasons for sticking to Nancy and putting her first always, he also remembers "the million or so bad reasons for not doing so all the time" (278), the girls with whom he might have lots more fun.

You Can't Do Both becomes progressively grittier and grimmer. Life is evidently no laughing matter. Robin's Mum drops dead, and though the doctor assures Robin that he has no need to reproach himself, he feels otherwise: he "would never be free of that shadow of guilt" (281). Why might Robin feel guilty? Only, I think, if he is displacing the guilt he should feel about Nancy toward Mum. He's disappointed his parents not by being an unkind or unruly son but by being an unreliable person and an unfaithful husband.

Comedies often end before or at the wedding because a humorously carefree existence is difficult to sustain after marriage and children. A coda to Robin's saga, set nine years later, illuminates the quality of Robin's marriage, but the resolution is far from the comforting comic closure of *Lucky Jim.* Robin is now 35, a successful classics don with hopes of an Oxford fellowship, married to Nancy, and the father of two daughters. Eyeing his students' "tits," as he says, he sounds unrepentantly adolescent. Home life is interrupted by a phonecall from a mysterious lady, whom Robin parries with phone antics worthy of Jim Dixon. More than casually, Robin resembles Jim, especially enacting "a vigorous silent routine of obscene gestures involving most of the top half of his body and accompanied by the pulling of hideous faces. This sequence he performed every morning in term-time or nearly" (290). Like Jim, Robin overflows with anxieties and animosities; but unlike Jim, Robin is a middle-aged man with a successful career and a family and without constant humiliation to fuel and justify his aggression.

We learn without too much surprise that Robin leads a busy secret life. That mysterious caller is a sexual liaison gone sour, now "an unacceptable security risk. Over the years," Robin "had got quite good at applying the closure" (295). Nancy doesn't know that Robin regularly pursues "his former naughty life" (297), "screwing around whenever an opportunity came along provided it had good tits, goodish anyway, and a face to match. Meaning no known case of anything that could have been called self-restraint on his part" (297). Amis's precision is devastating: "provided it had" and "no known case" telling us all we need to know about Robin's sexual egotism.

Robin sees himself through a glass, darkly, without introspecting deeply or progressing substantially. He will not agonize for long "over what was no more than a few harmless bits of fun" but proceeds with a "grim determination not to let a bagatelle like a hurried marriage interfere with what he had always done or at least wanted to do" (298). Thus Robin visits London for a nice spot of adultery with dear old Cousin Dilys, good fun for a bit, but then hard cheese on Robin. Nancy finally catches Robin virtually *in flagrante delicto*. Robin's tears are, for what it's worth, sincere. "I'm sorry," he says yet again, "no excuses, just me being a shit" (303). The problem remains that we can't know what his tears are worth, and apparently neither does he. Yet Robin finds a convincing or at least efficacious way to say he is sorry and seems to mean it: "For a moment he was afraid that he really would die, and then he wondered whether that might not be best after all" (305). Nancy consents to try again under different rules, one we know from the title page. He can have his family, or he can pursue other women. "Not both" (305). He accepts her terms, and instead of kissing him, Nancy punches him, leaving Robin with a black eye, a whiskey and soda, and altered plans, if not a changed heart.

It's a distinctly discomfiting conclusion, suggesting a continuing competition between apologia and confession, and indicating the tendencies, reach, and restrictions of Amis's art. We never see the effects of Robin's philandering: the awkward lies, the lonely wife, the needy children, the messy, transient, and loveless liaisons. Robin has behaved callously and heedlessly without apparent consequence or cost until—finally—he is exposed and revealed for what he really is. Yet Nancy forgives him, with scant reason to believe any reformation is likely and plenty of reason to suspect that he will always be as he has always been. We're troubled not by the mere absence of blustering, or huffing and puffing, but by the narrowness of what Amis makes real, substantial, and significant. In muffling the impact of Robin's faithlessness and crediting the sincerity of his regrets, the novel avoids not only judgment of his misconduct but also serious consideration of its meaning. We've seen that *You Can't Do Both* does not treat Robin's "harmless bits of fun" as merely humorous hey-nonny-nonny, so the denouement is bound to be ambiguous and disturbing. Whether we feel that Nancy treats Robin appropriately or too leniently, we're forced to regard the problem as more serious than comic, more so than anything in *Lucky Jim*, yet insufficiently resolved. I'm not satisfied that the ending of *You Can't Do Both* does justice—imaginative or ethical—to the conflicts the novel raises and Amis has long contemplated. For all his subtlety, sophistication, and craft, Amis never convincingly portrays crucial realms of human experience; that these passions, longings, and sufferings are inhospitable to the comic muse makes his effort to describe them all the more admirable and poignant.

Notes

1. Most notably by F. R. Leavis, who wrote that "life isn't long enough to permit one's giving much time to Fielding," and who dismissed *Tristram Shandy* as "irresponsible (and nasty) trifling." See *The Great Tradition: George Eliot, Henry James, Joseph Conrad* (N.Y.: G.W. Steward, 1948).
2. John Updike, "Jake and Lolly Opt Out," in this collection.
3. In an interview with Dale Salwak, in this volume, Amis used the term "seriocomic" to characterize his fiction.
4. Kingsley Amis, *Lucky Jim* (New York: Viking Compass, 1958), 10. All subsequent citations identified by parenthetical numerals.
5. Suzanne K. Langer, *Feeling and Form: A Theory of Art* (New York: Charles Scribner's Sons, 1953), 327.
6. Henry Fielding, *Joseph Andrews,* ed. Martin Battestin (Boston: Houghton Mifflin, 1961), 227.
7. Compare Robin Davies's realization that he doesn't understand anything about marriage.
8. David Lodge first made this point, and it is subsequently made by almost everybody discussing *Lucky Jim*. See Lodge's essay "The Modern, The Contemporary, and the Importance of Being Amis" in this collection.
9. Garnet Bowen's phrase in *I Like It Here* for what Henry Fielding happily withholds.
10. Kingsley Amis, *You Can't Do Both* (London: Hutchinson, 1994). All subsequent references are to this edition.

Traditional Comedy and the Comic Mask in Kingsley Amis's *Lucky Jim*

BRUCE STOVEL

Readers of all sorts continue to find *Lucky Jim* exhilarating. Anyone who has taught Amis's novel recently to North American undergraduates knows that it still has a unique energy and immediacy, though the social controversies which swirled around it in the years following its publication in 1954 are now history. Yet there have been few attempts to account for the intensity of laughter *Lucky Jim* produces. The prevailing view is that "Amis's humor is mainly satirical."[1] An alternative is to acknowledge gratefully that Amis's funny business is very funny indeed and leave the matter at that: "Have we forgotten how to take humor straight? Unable to exit laughing, the contemporary reader looks over his shoulder for Something More. The trouble is that by now he knows how to find it. So Amis's prodigious gifts were regarded from the start as instrumental, a kit for exploring social problems, and fairly restricted social problems at that."[2] I would like to outline here a third position: *Lucky Jim* is neither satire nor high-spirited farce (nor a uniquely adroit fusion of the two[3]), but, like its eighteenth-century progenitor, *Tom Jones*, absorbs satire and farce into a broader comic structure and vision. David Lodge, in his penetrating chapter on Amis in *The Language of Fiction*, approaches the novel in just these terms; but because Lodge's subject is the creative use of language in English fiction, he concentrates, as do several other critics, on the wordplay so evident in the texture of Amis's novels.[4]

Lucky Jim, then, has itself become a strangely neglected topic. In all that has been written on the novel, for instance, nobody has observed that its title alludes to its comic structure and perspective as surely as do, say, *Much Ado About Nothing* and *Pride and Prejudice*. Similarly, Jim's face-making, the funniest single device in the novel and the one which stays in the reader's mind as its great comic invention, gets very little critical attention.[5] I will argue here that Jim's faces function as a modern version of the comic mask: they create the holiday world of comedy, just as the masquerade—the donning of masks—does in traditional comedy.

From *English Studies in Canada* IV (Spring 1978): 69–80. Reprinted with permission of *English Studies in Canada.*

First, though, we should note how artfully Amis has recreated in narrative form the conflicts, patterns, devices, and vision of traditional stage comedy, just as his literary hero, Henry Fielding, had done two centuries earlier in *Tom Jones*.[6] Both novels have a fast-paced, external action: scenes succeed each other with accelerating speed as the comic hero hurtles toward a disaster which he miraculously—luckily—escapes at the last minute. Both have the age-old plot of young lovers rebelling against an obstructing society of foolish elders which has power—in *Lucky Jim,* both psychological and social power—over each of the lovers. The lovers are ideal in their very normality; Jim is a comic everyman (as Tom Jones is by his very name) and wins his job at the end, not because he is qualified for it, but because he is told, "You haven't got the disqualifications, though, and that's much rarer."[7] The spontaneous desire of Jim and Christine, the healthy young lovers, is strong enough to impose a happy ending on the story, overcoming not only the drab logic of reality, but, as well, their own considered objections to their union.

My point is that our laughter is not so much at individual moments in *Lucky Jim* as at the conflicts and movement of the whole action. Suzanne Langer argues that comedy presents the rhythm of life overcoming obstacles and renewing itself; since laughter itself, according to Langer, is a surge of vital feeling, our laughter while reading or seeing a comedy is the crest of a wave of intensified vitality, the rising to a breaking-point of our response to the work as a whole.[8] This notion allows us to understand Jim's luck. It is not, in fact, chance or coincidence, but the providence that rules in comedy, where the predictable happy ending is heightened and enriched by the playfully unpredictable quirks of circumstance which produce that ending. If the dammed-up energy and high spirits in Jim bring him horrendously bad luck from the first stone he kicks as Welch's subordinate, the same energies finally bring him, as a counterbalance, astonishingly good luck. Furthermore, Jim's comic providence, like that of Tom Jones, is voluntarist, not predestinarian: luck will save Jim, but only if and when "for once in his life Dixon resolved to bet on his luck" (136).

The external source of Jim's luck, Gore-Urquhart, is frequently criticised as a gratuitous character imported from the realms of romance. But such a character is the traditional agent of fortune in comedy, the genial older man whose authority overrules the obstructing society (Jonson's Lovewit, Sheridan's Uncle Oliver). Northrop Frye considers such a figure inherent in the three-phase movement of comedy, where "we have a stable and harmonious order disrupted by folly, obsession, forgetfulness, 'pride and prejudice,' or events not understood by the characters themselves, and then restored."[9]

The action of the novel, then, is the essential comic one: the struggle of two social orders. Professor Welch is not merely a classic instance of Bergson's mechanical man, solemn, unaware of himself, slow-witted, absent-minded ("Faulkner"!), unable to use rudimentary social conventions like syntax, and predictable in all these traits; the professor is also the centre of power in his own constricted, absurd, and life-stifling society. His vague invitations to tea or dinner, and his wife's more pointed threats, have an absolute power over Jim. Allied with the Welches are those they sponsor among the younger people, Bertrand and Margaret. These would-be lovers, another comic convention, are also mechanical: their manipulative behaviour is as predictable as their mannerisms—Margaret's laugh as of tiny silver bells, Bertrand's "you sam" and hackneyed witticisms.

Set against the Welches and their spy, Johns, is a comically diverse group: Jim, Christine, Carol, Gore-Urquhart, Atkinson. The characters are grouped symmetrically, as in traditional comedy: for every Margaret, there is a Bertrand, for every Atkinson, a Johns. Jim tells Christine on the way home from the dance that she and Bertrand represent "the two great classes of mankind, people I like and people I don't" (143). Those whom Jim likes share Christine's "more normal, i.e. less unworkable, character" (242); Margaret and Bertrand, Jim realizes, are radically different, and, unlike them, Jim has "no desire to range himself with children, neurotics, and invalids by thus specialising his needs" (141).

Another important comic convention in the novel grows out of the struggle of social orders: the double plot. Bertrand, like Blifil or Congreve's Fainall, is the hero's rival both for the girl he loves and for a higher place in society. This double struggle anchors the comic action in the world of actual satisfactions; more importantly, it creates an intricate, rapid train of events which can finally be resolved into a complex and balanced harmony. This counterpointed plotting forces comic detachment on us, as we must stand back to grasp the multiplying complexities and the patterns that emerge through them. For instance, a reflective reader notices that Gore-Urquhart is a comic *deus ex machina* in both plots, not only offering Jim a new job, but also freeing Carol to tell Christine about her secret relationship with Bertrand.

As in traditional comedy, the characters without realizing it trace a symmetrical, dance-like pattern. Just as we see Sophia pursue Tom Jones to Upton, and then emerge, hurt and indignant, with Tom in pursuit of her, so Jim's eager compliance with Christine's message that she will be at the railway station if he cares to join her is the exact counterpart of her acceptance, halfway through the novel, of his offer to wait outside the dance for twenty minutes if she cares to join him. The book begins with Welch adding to Jim's trials by confusing an appointment; it ends with Welch saving Jim by confusing train departures. Just as Christine surprises Margaret and Jim at Margaret's door as he is being indignantly bundled out, so Margaret surprises Christine and Jim laughing together outside the same door the next morning. Only we can see how apt Carol's reply to Jim on the dance floor is; as he tries to understand why she is angry, why she wants him to pursue Christine, why she attacks Margaret's hold over him, Carol says, "it's all connected, all connected" (121). The union of Carol and Gore-Urquhart, implied in the final pages, is an important part of this comic design.

This conception of *Lucky Jim* as a comedy has been far from obvious to critics of the novel.[10] It seems, then, an idea worth pursuing in further detail, and I would like to do so by looking in turn at four characteristics of traditional comedy which figure centrally in *Lucky Jim:* the happy ending, the use of festivity, the mood of play, and the pervasive comic irony.

The end of comedy, both its goal and its conclusion, is the achievement of what might be called a morality of desire. That is, what the central characters want to do coincides in the end with what they ought to do. Fielding makes this the theme as well as the pattern of *Tom Jones:* Tom's impulses lead him inevitably into foolish errors, but they are also a necessary part of the beneficent pattern of growth into maturity. Comedy presents a conflict of morality and desire, but resolves that conflict into a larger harmony. Jim's desire for Christine is "as natural to him, as unimportant and unobjectionable, as reaching out to take a large ripe peach from a fruit dish" (73). By the same token, Jim's conscience eventually leads him to, not away from, Christine: Carol repeatedly tells him, "you've got a moral duty to perform. Get that girl away from Bertrand" (125). Jim's truth is more than a truism when he affirms "his theory that nice things are nicer than nasty ones" (140).

The happy ending of traditional comedy usually results from immersion in a festive, carnival world: the characters, freed from everyday constraints, sort themselves out into new and truer relationships. *Lucky Jim* concentrates its action in and through three scenes of spurious festivity which Jim turns into genuine saturnalia. These scenes, the arty weekend, the midsummer ball, and the Merrie England lecture, take up about half the novel's length. In the first and last, Jim gets wildly drunk; at the ball, he drinks freely and enthusiastically. In all, he experiences a violent, child-like desire that the adult world should be more as he wants it to be. The important point is that Jim's saturnalia grow increasingly communal, marking his progress from misfit and secret rebel in one society to central figure in another, fitter one. Jim's carnival is, at first, private: the "festive, Yule-tide pop" of the Welch port bottle makes him alone feel splendid (59), even if his drunkenness does clarify his relations with Margaret (not to mention Mrs. Welch) and set in motion a new relationship with the "dignant" Christine. Jim is one of six lovers at the ball, which tries out all possible pairings and sorts the lovers into proper partnerships as surely as a Shakespearean revel. By the Merrie England lecture, Jim is the Lord of Misrule, turning a pious tribute to folk custom into a living celebration of merry-making. Fittingly, Jim's final face, the farewell to face-making he uses to celebrate happiness, is his "Sex Life in Ancient Rome face" (250). This pattern is amplified by Jim's growing participation in another, more mundane festivity, laughter. Bergson points out that laughter expresses and demands shared delight, complicity: we are uncomfortable laughing alone. Thus the action of comedy—the creation of a new community—is a formal counterpart of the communal impulse in laughter. Surprisingly, right up until Christine's laughter over his bed forces Jim to laugh with her, we have never seen Jim laugh, and even then it is "not because he was much amused but because he felt grateful to her for her laughter" (73). But his subsequent explanations to Margaret finally allow him to reach a comic detachment: "As he talked, his incendiarism and the counter-measures adopted struck him for the first time as funny" (74). From this point on, Jim and Christine are brought together again and again by her healthy and contagious laughter.

The ending and the festive scenes are structural features; equally important, perhaps, in creating traditional comedy is the comic mood. Unlike modern comedy, in which no person or act can be merely or finally ridiculous, the traditional sort assumes, like children at play, that there is a larger realm of serious reality which, in turn, allows the creation of a special, holiday world of mock-seriousness.[11] The very title-page establishes this mood: there we find the epigraph-cum-title of serious works of fiction like *The Sun Also Rises* or *The Sound and the Fury* or *Tender is the Night,* but we are directed for metaphorical significance, not to the Bible or Shakespeare or Keats, but to an unknown and suspiciously appropriate OLD SONG. And Amis keeps us aware from the start (for instance, by Jim's memories and dreams of London) that there is a larger frame of reality, in relation to which the university world is a separate mock-world with its own arbitrary rules. Jim at least knows that he is playing games, unlike Welch, Bertrand, and (particularly) Margaret: even when his fortunes are lowest, he knows that he is "jobless, Christineless, and now grand-slammed in the Margaret game" (220). Comedy maintains this playful mood by assuring us implicitly throughout that good will eventually triumph. Just as no sensible reader doubts whether Tom Jones will win his Sophia or be hanged, no matter how much artful suspense accumulates, so we are assured that Jim will triumph by the good luck which, symmetrically and emblematically, consoles him and us for every stroke of bad luck. If he is acutely uncomfortable opening and closing his mouth in silence while madrigals are sung, Bertrand and Christine arrive just in time to prevent his exposure (38); if Welch makes a particularly irritating demand on his "time and integrity" by asking Jim to do his busy-work, luck throws Jim the vignette, emblematic in itself, of Welch struggling to enter a revolving door the wrong way: Jim "felt it was things like this that kept him going" (174). In such a play world, there can be no real or lasting suffering: Margaret's neuroticism is so melodramatic and widely advertised as to seem unreal, while Jim's humiliation at his lecture is the means to his final reward. Similarly, evil is ultimately powerless: the Don Johns and Blifils can be laughed off or even forgiven. Jim comes to see that Welch is actually decent enough, for all his self-absorbed stupidity: Jim regrets, once he has been fired, "having spent so much of his time and energy in hating Welch" (229).

It is worth pausing over my final characteristic, irony, since it plays such a central, yet subtle role in *Lucky Jim.* Irony is inherently comic. Not only does the shock of ironic awareness always engender detachment; the movement of traditional comedy is itself an ironic process. Irony exists when there is a clash of ostensible and real meanings in a speech or situation; traditional comedy dramatizes the clash between fossilized forms and energies hidden within or beneath those forms. Consequently, the movement of a comedy like *Lucky Jim* is ironic, since we can see the familiar comic action fulfilling itself, without the knowledge and even against the will of the main actors in it. Jim, like the heroes and heroines of Shakespeare or Congreve or Jane Austen, unconsciously resents the power over him of his need for Christine: when he taunts Bertrand into personal combat over her, he *thinks* he does so solely for the pleasure of giving Bertrand what he deserves. Furthermore, the narrative method is ironic. Jim is himself an ironist: the contrast between his public mask—conventional, mild, subservient—and the violent energies within is Amis's chief ironic, and so comic, device. Confronted with Margaret's avowals at the ball, Jim manages "a remark both honest and acceptable: 'You mustn't say things like that' " (111). The novel itself is told not simply from Jim's point of view, but in a concise, understated style which corresponds exactly to Jim's own ironic way of communicating. For instance, we last see Welch's car "parked slightly nearer one kerb than the other" (250).

This ironic vision becomes richest when it is trained upon Jim himself, something that Jim is unable to do, since Jim is as self-deceived as the other major characters. Critics think of Jim—just as he thinks of himself—as a clear-sighted penetrator of other people's folly; but, as Anthony Burgess points out, "although we are meant to be on Dixon's side, we are also intended to laugh at him, to pity his ignorance."[12] Jim's ignorance is mainly of himself: if he is unwilling to admit to his love for Christine, his feelings about Margaret are even more tangled and obscure. Margaret has Jim hoodwinked, though he thinks he is in control of the Margaret game. Note, for instance, how Jim refuses to acknowledge to himself Margaret's brazen desertion of him for Gore-Urquhart at the ball. After Jim and Margaret agree to call off everything between them, "he thought of his appointment with Christine the next day but one, and regarded it entirely without pleasure. Some part of what had happened in the last half hour had spoilt all that, although he didn't know which part. Somewhere his path to Christine was blocked; it was all going to go wrong in some way he couldn't foresee" (164). It is part of himself that spoils the break with Margaret, the part that welcomes humiliation and enjoys grievances, the part that Margaret, and Margaret alone, knows and addresses as "James." Jim is like Beatrice and Benedick, or Elizabeth Bennet and Emma Woodhouse, in that the obstacles between him and his love are internal, mental blocks rather than simply blocking characters. We may suspect that more than nobility lies behind Jim's refusal to tell Christine of Bertrand's affair with Carol: Jim confesses as much to Christine at the novel's end.

Jim's conscience is a source of irony. It is both his scourge and his salvation: "He'd been drawn into the Margaret business by a combination of virtues he hadn't known he'd possessed" (10), yet his conscience is also Margaret's ally and the source of her power. Again and again, Jim tries chivalrously not to notice her manipulating poses and blames himself when he does. His conscience is always telling him he must try harder, be more understanding: he mustn't "allow his irritation with some things about her to do what it always did, to obscure what was most important: that she was a neurotic who'd recently taken a bad beating" (77). Jim's patronizing concern allows him to remain independent and invulnerable. After inviting Christine to join him outside the dance, Jim thinks, "She wouldn't come of course, but at any rate he'd made his gesture. In other words, he'd thought of a way of hurting himself more severely than usual, and in public" (128). The note of self-pity is typical: if Margaret holds Jim by "pity's adhesive plaster" (243), that pity is partly self-pity for his own constant sacrifices. We see the pattern at the ball when Margaret addresses Jim as "Poor James." Jim bristles inwardly, but then goes through the familiar cycle of guilt for his resentment, self-castigation for his callousness and neglect, and renewed pity for her loneliness. Within ten lines he is thinking, "Poor old Margaret . . . He must try harder" (111). Just as Christine is, ironically, a mirror image of Jim's split nature, so Margaret and Jim echo each other. She secretly despises Jim; the mask falls for a moment the day after the ball when she bursts out with, "You don't think she'd have you, do you? A shabby little provincial bore like you?" (158).

Analysis of the psychological ironies is misleading. Comedy has no time for such introspection: inner conflicts and changes are conveyed in extroverted form (Tom wins his Sophia, Jim leaves Margaret for Christine). But the conflicts and changes are none the less there. Jim's comic liberation is finally the freeing of himself from himself. His anxiety throughout over his job is more complex than it seems: he does not really want the post (or, more precisely, the success by Welch standards necessary to win it).[13] His nervousness as the lecture approaches is partly nervousness lest he should be able to go through with such a complete prostitution of his talents as this exercise in ventriloquism clearly is (see the three snippets from it: 166, 195, 205). Jim's split response to both Christine and Margaret is similarly, if much more subtly, ironic. Certainly Jim's real luck is Catchpole's sudden reappearance, though Jim begins to feel that he needs even more than Catchpole's evidence: "Failing some other purgative agent than facts, he could foresee himself coming to disbelieve this lot altogether" (238). That agent immediately appears when Jim learns of Christine's offer to meet him halfway, so to speak, at the station. Jim's own acts, culminating in his lecture, win him Gore-Urquhart's favour and Christine's love, but only comic providence can extricate him from Margaret.

This context of traditional comedy enables us to understand more precisely how Jim's fantasies, and particularly his secret faces, work within the novel. Jim's faces have two functions: they establish him as the comic hero, bursting with frustrated and misdirected vitality; they also create an inward version of the masquerade, the carnival interregnum, of comedy. If we look at any one of Jim's faces, we see it creates sympathy with him, yet keeps that sympathy detached and comic. When Jim makes his shot-in-the-back face on being hailed by Michie (27), or his lemon-sucking face in the darkness on hearing Christine express Bertrand's philosophy that artists are special (141), the image allows us to experience from within Jim's inner repudiation. At the same time, we join in transforming his life into the "intensified, speeded-up, exaggerated" world of comic types described by Langer (p 135). Yet Jim must outgrow his secret and self-pitying faces by sharing them, by communicating his vital powers.[14]

Jim's face-making, more than anything else, conveys to us these heroic powers. Jim's public mask, the one he wears in hopes of succeeding in Welch society, is completely untrue to his inner nature. He must "flail his features into some sort of response to Welch's humour" (8); though he struggles to complete his lecture by the evening of delivery, he must pretend to Welch that he has long since finished it (172) and that "I guarantee I could read that script blindfold, I've been through it so many times" (212). Jim compensates for his hypocrisy by an ever-erupting volcano of inner revolt. Face-making is merely his main outlet: his hands surreptitiously form fists and he makes mocking, obscene gestures (12, 194, 175, 241); he mumbles a long string of swear words to himself (81) and hums his derisive Welch music (87, 147, 174); he imagines abusive analogies, seeing Welch as "an African savage being shown a simple conjuring trick" (12), a broken robot (79), "some obsolete howitzer" (84), possessed of a "sexual maniac's smile" (175), and, as the moment of judgment nears, "an old boxer, given to a bit of poaching now and then, standing with his ex-kitchenmaid wife" (220). And every reader must be struck by Jim's fantasies of attacking the Welches. Each instance of dithering absurdity or affectation ignites a precise fantasy of physical revenge. Jim not only sees through the Welch crowd—he also rebels against them violently, if secretly, with dammed-up moral, emotional, and imaginative energy. Jim is, after all, a rough and ready poet of the moral life. His faces are metaphors: his Edith Sitwell face, for example, concretizes his triumphant disdain after the disguised telephone interview with Bertrand (102).

It is worth remarking that Jim's face-making draws its power from a condition in everyday life. Faces are, by far, the most expressive part of our bodies—so expressive, in fact, that we are trained not to allow this expressiveness its free play. Ernst Kris argues that laughter is so satisfying a release because it is the one time in social intercourse that adults allow their faces their natural expressiveness.[15] The physical constraints, like the moral ones Freud stressed in his discussions of humour, no longer rule. George Santayana's reflections on the comic mask, which he considers the primitive spirit of comedy, offer a suggestive parallel: "Objections to the comic mask—to the irresponsible, complete, extreme expression of each moment—cut at the roots of all expression. Pursue this path, and at once you do away with gesture: we must not point, we must not pout, we must not cry, we must not laugh aloud; we must not only avoid attracting attention, but our attention must not be obviously attracted; it is silly to gaze, says the nursery-governess, and rude to stare."[16] Jim and his creator are both keenly aware of the sensitive, magnifying power of facial features. Jim not only makes faces to himself, but he exuberantly transforms the face on the cover of Johns's magazine with a few pencil strokes. Welch's small eyes and "large, open-pored tetrahedron" of a nose (86), Margaret's removing her glasses, Bertrand's flattened eyeballs, all convey dramatic meaning. Jim even sees that Christine's face "touched upon other sorts of faces by a sort of physiognomic allusion"—but, unlike Margaret, whose face reminds him of a man he once knew, Christine's facial analogues are all female (154). Welch's face, like his personality, is to Jim a mechanism running on without human intervention: "Welch went on talking, his own face the perfect audience for his talk, laughing at its jokes, reflecting its puzzlement or earnestness, responding with tightened lips and narrowed eyes to its more important points" (178).

Jim's faces are, by contrast, "the irresponsible, complete, extreme expression of each moment"; they have the power to, and eventually do, create a joyous carnival, just as Santayana says the comic mask does. We can describe the action of traditional comedy—of Shakespearean comedy, for example—as a masquerade, a playful, fantasticated donning of masks, which leads to a final clarification or restoration of true identity. The comedy ends when masks no longer need be worn. Yet here the masks are internalized; they can only create festivity when Jim shares them, and so the action of the novel traces Jim's gradual freeing of his inner resources in overt, communal action. Leslie Fiedler has claimed that Jim's faces are more significant than the plot of the novel;[17] the truth is that the faces reflect, and create, the curve of Jim's movement from isolation to community.

Jim's faces are, at first, a venting of his concealed antagonism. When making his Sex Life in Ancient Rome face at the end, he reflects, "what a pity it was that all his faces were designed to express rage or loathing" (250). But once he leads Christine onto the dance floor, he feels a positive counterpart to his usual face-making: "Dixon felt like a special agent, a picaroon, a Chicago war-lord, a hidalgo, an oil baron, a mohock" (113). No longer is Jim secretly a crazy peasant, a consumptive, a tragic mask, or a Martian invader. Christine draws Jim into public, rather than merely private, independence, into offensive and not simply defensive maneuvers, into war against Bertrand rather than mere rebellion.

It is Jim's physical triumph over Bertrand, in fact, that sets in motion, as if magically, the upward swing of his fortunes—and it is in this scene that his faces are first made for others. Until now, Jim has never made his faces publicly, just as he has never declared openly his own feelings (his "Well, hard luck" to Margaret is a momentary dropping of his public mask which he quickly repairs [158]). Only once, two days before the lecture (and the fight), have others seen one of his faces: his grimace at his ripped pants is inadvertently witnessed by Christine, Bertrand, Mrs. Welch, and Margaret (179). Now, though, his faces come into the open. Bertrand enters in the middle of Jim's cathartic ape-imitation and takes it as a personal affront. Jim makes their fight inevitable when he shrieks, "I'm not Sam, you fool," at once exposing Bertrand's mask and revealing his own secret mockery: "This was the worst taunt of all." And, after the battle, Jim finally utters what is inside him, in ritual manner, over the prostrate Bertrand: "The bloody old towser-faced boot-faced totem-pole on a crap reservation, Dixon thought. 'You bloody old towser-faced boot-faced totem-pole on a crap reservation,' he said" (209). Michie immediately knocks on Jim's door "as if discreetly applauding this terminology" and quickly enters.[18]

From this point on, Jim's comic masks are more and more openly, and more and more publicly, displayed. He puts on, and speaks through, the mask of American mobster with Christine and Bertrand at the sherry party: "Better do as he says, lady, otherwise he's liable to kick your teeth in" (216). Jim is surprised in the washroom by Gore-Urquhart while making a more savage version of his Evelyn Waugh face; Gore-Urquhart sympathizes and helps create Jim's carnival by plying him with whisky (220–21).

The lecture shows Jim's comic invention, as well as the novelist's, at its most brilliant. Jim creates a carnival by putting on a medley of funny faces. At first, his masks are unconscious imitations of Welch and the principal, but they soon turn to voluntary assertions. Jim decides to go down fighting, if go down he must: "He'd do some good, however small, to those present, however few. No more imitations, they frightened him too much, but he could suggest by his intonation, very subtly of course, what he thought of his subject and the worth of the statements he was making" (225). Jim finally shares his face-making genius: "Within quite a short time he was contriving to sound like an unusually fanatical Nazi trooper in charge of a book-burning reading out to the crowd excerpts from a pamphlet written by a pacifist, Jewish, literate Communist" (226). Jim completes the lecture by dropping his masks entirely: he comes around to the front of the lectern and denounces Merrie England and Merrie Englanders *in propria persona.*

Jim's faces keep their comic functions until the very end. On the one hand, his expressiveness is his distinctive power as a comic hero: he catches the crucial bus by winning over the bus conductor with "the best-known obscene gesture" (241). At the same time, now that he can make his faces publicly, Jim releases his dammed-up energies and no longer needs his faces. When he discovers that Caton has stolen his article, "at a loss for faces, he drew in his breath to swear, then cackled hysterically instead" (229).

The final tableau summarizes both the comic action and Jim's changing use of his faces. Structurally, Jim, with Christine on his arm, stands in the centre of this little dumb-show, laughing with manic energy at the Welches, revealed for what they are—waxwork dummies. Jim's face is at the centre of this scene: he first puts on "a fruity comic-butler voice" and nods indulgently to Mrs. Welch, since "he remembered something in a book about success making people humble, tolerant, and kind." But this mask is soon replaced by simple, total, open delight: "With Christine tugging at his arm he halted in the middle of the group, slowly doubling up like a man with the stitch, his spectacles misting over with the exertion of it, his mouth stuck ajar in a rictus of agony. 'You're . . .' he said. 'He's . . .'" (251). Northrop Frye suggests that the three-phase action of comedy is "like the removal of a neurosis or blocking point and the restoring of an unbroken current of energy and memory" (p 171). The action of *Lucky Jim* is not simply like such a removal—it *is* that removal.

Notes

1. Rubin Rabinovitz, *The Reaction Against Experiment in the English Novel, 1950–1960* (New York 1967), p 59.
2. Ralph Caplan, "Kingsley Amis," in *Contemporary British Novelists,* ed Charles Shapiro (Carbondale 1965), p 4.
3. See R.B. Parker's "Farce and Society: The Range of Kingsley Amis," *Wisconsin Studies in Contemporary Literature,* 2 (Fall 1961), 27–38.
4. *The Language of Fiction: Essays in Criticism and Verbal Analysis of the English Novel* (New York 1966), pp 243–67. Some brief but illuminating comments on *Lucky Jim* as comedy occur in Gerard Strauch, "Calendar, Construction, and Character in Kingsley Amis's *Lucky Jim,*" *Recherches Anglaises et Americaines,* 3 (1970), 57–66. Several critics have stressed Amis's wordplay; James Gindin, for instance, in *Postwar British Fiction: New Accents and Attitudes* (Berkeley 1963), speaks of his "quick verbal incongruities" (p 38).
5. Lodge is a notable exception (see pp 254–55). Two sober existentialist interpretations of Jim's faces are: Ted E. Boyle and Terence Brown, "The Serious Side of *Lucky Jim,*" *Critique,* 9 (1966), 100–7; Naomi Lebowitz, "Kingsley Amis: The Penitent Hero," *Perspective,* 10 (1958), 129–36.
6. During the fifties Amis frequently proclaimed his admiration for Fielding. The most striking instances are the tribute paid in the climactic scene of Amis's third novel, *I Like It Here* (London 1958), and Amis's essay, "Laughter's to be Taken Seriously," *New York Times Book Review,* 7 July 1957, pp 1, 13.
7. *Lucky Jim* (London 1961), p 234. Subsequent citations from this edition are given in the text.
8. "The Rhythm of Comedy" in *Comedy: Meaning and Form,* ed Robert W. Corrigan (San Francisco 1965), pp 119–40 (esp pp 131–36). The essay first appeared in *Feeling and Form* (New York 1953), pp 326–50.
9. *Anatomy of Criticism: Four Essays* (Princeton 1957), p 171. Frye's views have influenced my discussion of comedy throughout this essay.
10. For instance, Amis is alternately taken to task by F.R. Karl (in *A Reader's Guide to the Contemporary English Novel* [New York 1962], p 224) and praised by James Gindin (in "The Reassertion of the Personal," *Texas Quarterly,* 1 [Winter 1958] 128) for lacking an artful structure in *Lucky Jim.*
11. Elder Olson makes a relaxation of seriousness essential to comedy in his *The Theory of Comedy* (Bloomington 1968), esp pp 16, 36. Corrigan has some suggestive remarks in "Com-

edy and the Comic Spirit," Corrigan, pp 4–7. Both develop the implications of Aristotle's definition of the ludicrous (*Poetics,* ch v).

12. *The Novel Now: A Student's Guide to Contemporary Fiction* (London 1967), p 142.

13. John Hurrell, in "Class and Conscience in John Wain and Kingsley Amis," *Critique,* 2 (1958), 19–53, argues that Jim is trying subconsciously throughout to get himself fired.

14. This point is made in rather different terms by Alan Kennedy in *The Protean Self: Dramatic Action in Contemporary Fiction* (New York 1974), pp 272–73.

15. *Psychoanalytic Explorations in Art* (New York 1952), pp 217–39.

16. "The Comic Mask," Corrigan, p 75. This essay and a companion piece, "Carnival," are reprinted from *Soliloquies in England and Later Soliloquies* (New York 1922).

17. "The Class War in British Literature," *The Collected Essays of Leslie Fiedler* (New York 1971), 1, 420.

18. Lodge discusses the fight scene in similar terms: "The issues of the novel can only be resolved when Jim wills his inner life to coincide with his outer life" (p 255). Jim's declamation finally expresses his initial response to Bertrand: "He thought of a sentence in a book he'd once read: 'And with that he picked up the bloody old towser by the scruff of the neck, and, by Jesus, he near throttled him' " (50). Amusingly, Jim's sentence is from the Cyclops episode of Joyce's *Ulysses.*

What Are Little Girls Made Of?

JEREMY TREGLOWN

Who wrote these exchanges?

"Another thing I was thinking this morning," she went on, speaking less quickly now, "was that I could leave everything else like a shot if I could just keep you. I saw a play once where you spent all your time in a room with three other people and that was meant to be hell—you know, real hell, instead of flames. Well, if it was just you and me there I wouldn't mind it at all. Even if they arranged it so we couldn't make love. I wouldn't mind never going out and seeing the sun and the flowers and things, or reading a book or anything. That was what I thought, anyway. It was ridiculous really, I suppose. In a hundred years we'd run out of things to say."
"We wouldn't."

"It would be quite ludicrous for me to try to tell you not to worry about this," she said. "But there is one part to do with it where you can feel absolutely safe and secure, and that's anything involving me in any way. I'll do whatever I can and whatever you want me to. I may not always know what that is and whenever you see I don't you're to tell me straight away without thinking. What I mean is, it doesn't matter if it seems a lot to ask, or even too trivial to ask—you tell me and I'll do it. Now have you got that, darling?"
"Yeah. Thank you, love," I said. . . .

"Please don't ask me to guess, I couldn't bear to get it wrong."
"Oh, I'd never do that. What it is, I'm going to have a baby."
He put his glass down on the kitchen table.
"I got the result of the conclusive test just this morning but I think I'd known some time before then. I asked the doctor if he thought it would stay, you know, after what happened before, and he said there was nothing to show I was any more likely to lose it than any other mother. But don't go falling down any stairs, he said."
Patrick's face was covered with tears. He came over and put his arms round her and just squeezed, and they both stayed like that for some time.
"How wonderful," he said. "For us both. I'd stopped hoping or imagining. You clever little thing. . . ."

From *Grand Street* 9 (Autumn 1989), ed. by Ben Sonnenberg. Reprinted by permission.

There are some clues: the determinedly unpretentious monosyllables; all those stiff upper lips (the first main speaker has cancer, the second is consoling a man whose son has suddenly gone mad, "what happened before" to the third was of course a miscarriage); especially the glass Patrick has to dispose of before embracing his wife. Taken on their own, it's unexpected that all three are by that satirical old woman-hating curmudgeonly comedian, Kingsley Amis. But in their bleak contexts of fear and inadequacy they are as clearly signed by him as anything more obviously extractable: hangover descriptions, farcical bedroom set pieces, cameos of dull, selfish men who don't buy their round or affected, rapacious and unpredictable women. Like the eighteenth-century English novelists he has admired and has often been compared with, Amis is clever with sentiment: generosity, kindness, loyalty are the domestic-scale measures by which most of his main characters are nonetheless found wanting; marital concord is the end to which, against all warnings, the narrative still makes his readers hope the hero and heroine will be drawn; romance may be romance, but is usually something either funnier or more painful, or both.

The third quotation comes from the end of Amis's latest novel, *Difficulties with Girls* (Summit Books; the others are from *The Anti-Death League,* 1966, and *Stanley and the Women,* 1984). Patrick is Patrick Standish, the schoolmaster-rake of *Take a Girl Like You* (1960), now, eight fictional years on, working as a publisher and still just about married to the Girl mainly in question, "little" Jenny Bunn. Jenny's bun—the one Patrick, in the then phrase, put in her oven at the end of the first book—didn't cook, so the new story can once more use a pregnancy for an equivocal tying-up. Amis quickly disabused reviewers who read this ending as happy: certainly nothing either here or anywhere else in his work should make one think that any change in any marriage will alter the underlying situation much, and Patrick's own chances of serious reform are no higher now than they ever were. The sequel is morally tougher on him, in fact, than the first story, where, even so (as Malcolm Bradbury noted), the hero as detractor-of-bastards has become a bastard himself. Apart from the perennial Amis-hero qualities of wit and a hatred of cant, the new, late-1960s Patrick hasn't many redeeming features. A contemptuous philanderer well on the way to becoming a drunk, he is only saved from helping along the destruction of a professional colleague by the honesty of a shrewd old authoress, and from (less credibly) setting up Jenny with an old friend, by her so far incorruptible fidelity.

In his well-judged, if a shade prim, critical study, *Kingsley Amis: An English Moralist* (Macmillan, 1989), John McDermott gives a good analysis of how Amis pins down hypocritical hedonistic self-extenuation, quoting a passage of John Lewis's from *That Uncertain Feeling:* "feeling a tremendous rake-hell, and not much liking myself for it, and feeling rather a good chap for not liking myself for it, and not liking myself for feeling rather a good chap, I got indoors." McDermott says:

the humour of its self-regarding convolutions distracts us, and, more importantly, Lewis into losing sight of the moral culpability that was the sentence's starting-point, so that he goes indoors feeling guilty, certainly, but only on a lesser charge.

If he had been able to take in *Difficulties with Girls,* McDermott might have been interesting, too, on Patrick's similar scaling down of his guilt about having an affair with their new neighbor, Mrs. Porter-King, to guilt about losing Jenny's cat. (There are other ways in which McDermott's book would have been better for having at least anticipated the possibility of Amis novels yet to come. He writes unnervingly as though the author were dead, the works complete.) But if the cat is a deft touch, Amis now seems unusually keen to make sure we don't miss it, or others like it. Patrick, the story tells us, is "too frivolous and impatient to put in the mental reconnaissance necessary for effective deceit." Again, "One of his great characteristics had always been the ability to come round fast and completely from his own troubles and crises. Only a mean person would have suggested that perhaps he had not had all that far to come." The non-mean person through whose thoughts this non-suggestion is firmly suggested, is Jenny: and if here she, and her author, are still pretending to be oblique, she doesn't fail elsewhere to have her northernly direct say.

Anthony Burgess claimed in his review that "The point of the novel is that Jenny Standish's sexual morality is right, as is most of her thinking." This makes Amis a less interesting novelist than he is. Karl Miller came closer in saying that while the novel wants to make us respect Jenny's Victorian values, Amis is "less inward, less collusive, with her than he is with her husband," working her views too hard "as a purchase on wrong thinking." But "collusive" still seems to miss something, given those almost George Eliot-like asperities about Patrick. And if there is a problem involving "inwardness," it affects him at least as much as Jenny, though for a different reason. Amis invented both characters in the late 1950s. He has chosen not only to pick them up again from a distance of thirty years, but to put them into yet another now-remote period, 1967. It's true that Jenny's Priestleyesque homespun wisdom sometimes reads awry, but so does Patrick's often unreconstructed late-Amis idiolect. There's too much old-chapping, to my ear, for a young 1960s publisher, and generally it's hard to hear Patrick as a person distinct from Amis—for example in this anecdote of his, early in the novel, about his boss Simon Giles (whose meanness fills the gap left by Jenny's landlord, Dick, in *Take a Girl Like You*):

> Not long ago he gave a bottle-party at his place, an antiquated institution anyway these days, you might have thought, but one with a great sentimental attraction for your man Giles. It seems he put away a bottle, put away in a cupboard a bottle of goodish claret brought by some cunt, sorry darling, by some booby he'd decided it was too good for the likes of.

"Your man"? "goodish claret"? "some booby"? It sounds less south-of-the-river, 1967, than Garrick Club, 1988. If this is what Miller means by "collusive," fair enough.

The novel's questions about right thinking, and Jenny's position in relation to them, are I think subtler and more ambiguous than they have been taken for. *Difficulties with Girls* seems to have been hard for reviewers to read without bringing to it an unusual number of prejudices and expectations of their own. Michael Wood, for example, in what was (with one other exception) a characteristically subtle and just review, protested that "All the women here but one are bitchy, selfish, vain, sex-starved and entirely unreasonable." Yet, Jenny apart, there are two extremely sensible, practical, kind and otherwise unobjectionable women, in my reading: the elderly Irish novelist Deirdre, whom Patrick (mainly because she is those things) detests the idea of so violently that Wood seems to have accepted his verdict—though Deirdre gets Patrick's measure quicker than anyone else, and acts skillfully and decisively to save him from damaging his colleague, her editor; and Ann Wolstenholme, sister of the mysterious Tim, who has been led to believe he is homosexual. (Of these two, more later.) Still, for Michael Wood, Jenny is Amis's "redeeming female figure"; as for Anthony Burgess and the more circumspect Karl Miller, she is in some ways his spokeswoman. Yet none of these sophisticated critics would normally expect a good novelist to supply such a character, and Amis himself has often deprecated the idea that an imaginative writer is a paraphrasable commentator on life, rather than someone (as Shakespeare is seen in another of the novels) "content just to describe it.... No theories or interpretation."

Setting aside what Jenny (or Patrick or Deirdre or Ann or anyone else in the book) says and thinks, the tale tells something else again. Here is a clever, selfish, funny, randy and feckless man married to an attractive, far from stupid or weak, but shy, secluded and surely over-indulged "little" woman. She has given up her teaching job, believing that a woman's role is to run her husband's home—in their case, a small flat containing a cat and numerous plants. Childless (the early miscarriage), she does a little voluntary work with children at the local hospital, a task she is unable to make sound interesting in their new world of literary parties. (It doesn't help that she doesn't drink.) Socially nervous, made wretched by Patrick's infidelities, she now has to confront the 1960s in the form of various kinds of sexual license, not least homosexuality, the more repressive British laws about which are repealed during the course of the story. Jenny doesn't know what homosexuals do to each other, and is ill at ease in their company.

However much we may sympathize with these and other aspects of her predicament, Jenny is tiresomely priggish. Almost any man she would like would get bored by her, and Patrick is pathologically prone to boredom. ("Yes," he answers one of her more naïvely censorious comments, "life's full of little bits that aren't what we'd, well, you know, if it was up to us, et cetera, as many have remarked. Let's get a drink.") The fact that he's too loyal, or perhaps just too guilty, to think some of the fault in the situation may be hers, doesn't alter what the book shows: that the couple is sadly but all too understandably doomed. As for Jenny's plucky and quite moving resolve, the shrewd (and, she admits to herself, scared) toughness which helps her make less of a fuss, but more effectively, about Patrick's latest affair—we have seen such heart-warming behavior go bad in Kingsley Amis's fiction before. That very touching avowal by Stanley's wife, promising him he can feel absolutely safe and secure about anything involving her, doesn't stop her deserting him later. Difficulties with girls are, in Amis's books, as much reason's common theme as death of fathers in Shakespeare.

But would the novel be changed by being called *Trouble with Men?* Not a lot. Certainly, Jenny's problems with Patrick, Deirdre's with her publishers, Tim's family's with his misguided antics, are as fully part of the story as the other way around. Even the homosexual marriage, in which Eric's relations with Stevie explicitly and funnily parallel what goes on between the most nightmarish of heterosexual couples ("Some sort of row, I presume?" asks Patrick, finding Eric locked out. "I presume too," he says), requires our sympathy on both sides: when Stevie's moods become too much, after all, Eric sticks a knife in "her" neck. Patrick's apart, though, the main difficulties as far as real girls are concerned are those of the improbable Tim, whose marital restlessness, and confession of various straight male vagaries like promiscuity, and losing interest in women after sex, have led a psychiatrist to persuade him he is homosexual.

This isn't the best aspect of the book. As an Amis "character," Tim is below par: his sneezing and yawning, and his general hopeless confessional hanging around, seem rather perfunctory gags, and although Patrick and Jenny, particularly Patrick, are very anxious to stop him thinking he's gay, it doesn't much matter to the reader—partly because we've seen nothing of his earlier life, but mainly because he's so obviously straight (as well as romantically well-endowed with wealth, class, physical courage, good clothes, etc.) that there's no doubt he'll get himself right sooner or later. Besides, the perverse shrink has become a somewhat predictable type in Amis's books. Out of this side of the story, though, comes a reinforcement of what could be taken as a main theme: the destructive effect not, as Amis himself said in an interview, of too much sexual freedom, but of too little concealment. The worst thing anyone can do in this book is to come out. Jenny doesn't want Patrick confessing to her; Stevie and, especially, Eric (with his double-double life, not only at the Admiralty but in a heterosexual drinking club in Soho) will be worse off now their relationship is notorious; and their small tragedy is largely caused by Tim's deluded self-revelations. If anyone sums all this up, it is not Jenny, but Tim's sister:

> Bring the whole business out in the open, he [a friend of Tim's] said, or words to that effect. Isn't that the most half-witted, irresponsible advice you can

imagine? In my experience if a thing's been hidden away for a long time and kept quiet about, then there's a jolly good case for leaving it there. Of course, I realise people think they know better these days.

No one has managed to miss the fact that *Difficulties with Girls* is an attack of the 1960s, though few have said that even if the period were well realized by Amis, it isn't a very original target at the end of the 1980s. There's a twinge in finding the old taboo-buster so integrated with the moral majority. Admirers of Shaw must have felt similarly when welfare socialism grew up around him, but at least that was a decent status quo to have helped bring into being. Fortunately, Amis is—*pace* John McDermott—a better novelist than moralist; *pace* Michael Wood, too, who has disparaged him (would he make this criticism of Juvenal, or Pope?) for the sense his books give "of a strong intelligence working itself into a nasty corner." Sexual relations can be a nasty corner, and when they are (as well as when they aren't), Amis's romantic moments help light it up, so that it can be seen better. Karl Miller is right that "It isn't every comic genius who would undertake to send his talent into such painful places." But if I understand him, Miller thinks that in the main plot, those places are only made by Patrick's behavior.

Here are the very last words of an ending no reviewer I've read has understood. Tears, remember, cover Patrick's face:

... He kissed her hands. "You've done it. Changed everything. You've saved us."

Jenny was happy. She was going to have him all to herself for at least three years, probably more like five, and a part of him for ever, and now she could put it all out of her mind.

"Him" can only be how Jenny is thinking of her future child, now, not Patrick, who would make the thought nonsense. The wretched remorseful husband is no more than the "it all" she has instantly put out of her mind. It's an ingeniously sour twist to a mixed book.

Perhaps there is a hint of a third installment. Jenny, having ejected the yet again unfaithful Patrick and won a punitive maintenance order, will stay on in the flat with her child (a girl, after all), the cat and the house plants. After a while she lets Tim move in as a nanny and odd-job man. In the early 1970s, she writes a feminist version of all this, lightly disguised as a novel and very successfully published by Simon Giles (for whom Patrick no longer works), under the title *What Are Little Girls Made Of?* Except that one of Kingsley Amis's best qualities as a novelist is that you can never predict what turn his next books will take.

When the Curse Begins to Hurt: Kingsley Amis and Satiric Confrontation

D. R. WILMES

Satire is confrontational in at least two senses: the reader sees evil, and he is entangled in a struggle with it. As a response to the threat of evil, the satiric impulse is revelatory and aggressive. The threat is extraliterary—evil threatens the values and beliefs of the satirist; something, the *writer* feels, must be done. Thus a satiric David is sent to battle Goliath, St. George again swings a sword at the dragon. But the giant, or evil dragon in Philip Pinkus's metaphor, eventually wins, for it is at this point that satire parts company from the rest of literature.[1] The confrontation will end badly for the satirist. He must at last be content with revelation: the reader will have at least seen evil's scaly face. Perceptual confrontation is in fact implicit to a satirist's intention. His very sensitivity to evil forces him to recognize the odds against St. George; satirists tend to be painfully realistic. But there remains the hope of perception, and its consequences. Perhaps, having seen the face of evil, we'll bring heavier artillery to the next battle, some assistance for the necessary yet rusty and antiquated weaponry of ethics, morality, and human goodness or decency. It's a thin hope at best. Satire, particularly modern satire, is often a pessimistic art, quite separate from comedy, with which it is often linked. Kingsley Amis, who has long tried to reconcile the two—writing with a fine comic talent and a conflicting satiric impulse—embodies tensions that may again remind us of the terrible power of satiric action, its hopelessness and its hope.

Amis may be best known for his first novel, *Lucky Jim* (1953). Most readers would agree that Jim Dixon is an inept, even antiheroic St. George, while Professor Welch—or his son Bertrand—are equally inept dragons. Dixon, an ultimately fortunate *picaro,* struggles with a world of folly and evil that impedes his progress toward freedom, comfort, and Christine Callaghan. His weapons are a curse and a snicker, but he avoids confrontation. His "shot-in-the-back face" is turned toward the wall; penciled graffiti must be hurriedly sketched on the cover of an enemy's favorite magazine before the

From *Studies in Contemporary Satire* v (1978): 9–22. Reprinted with the permission of *Studies in Contemporary Satire.*

enemy arrives. The battle is real and earnest, but no blood is shed. All ends happily for Dixon, if not for the world he escapes *via* the eight-seventeen to London. Even these pitiful dragons win, but the reader is hardly prepared or armed for a new confrontation.

Yet there are other battles in Amis's novels, where terrible wounds are inflicted. Somewhere along the road to *Ending Up* (1974) and beyond, the curse has begun to hurt the reader if not the satirist. For satire, as opposed to comedy, can hurt, most painfully when the reader sees that he may have been cheering not for the knight, but for the dragon. Could any reasonable man resist an Irish baby? At the conclusion of *Ending Up,* there is no train to London. The reader is left facing a corpse, wondering which accepted premise of the novel has condemned him finally to be abandoned in the presence of death and evil. Amis himself acknowledges a change: "There's been an increase in the dim view which is taken of life, and the element of horseplay and high spirits decreases."[2] Amis speaks—cogently, I believe—of continuities, variations within a constant line of development. As "a writer of serio-comedies" (S, 7), his work has always involved more than a laugh and a chuckle. It is the tortuous line of seriousness in Amis's work that I wish to examine here, a line that is neither comic nor tragic, which is in fact deeply influenced by the demands of satiric confrontation.

This is not to say that Amis has been a satirist in a consistent or unambiguous manner. His chosen forms are consciously varied. In a new form, a different genre or subgenre, he seeks a hedge against the fear of having "nothing left to say" (S, 17). Yet there is in his writing, and indeed in his self-conception, a strong satiric impulse. It can be seen in his definition of his role as a "British writer," whose job is "to write about human nature, the permanent things in human nature. I could reel you off a list as long as your arm, beginning with ambition, sexual desire, vainglory, foolishness...." (S, 4). Amis has the satirist's essential Juvenalian surprise at evil, the emotional inability to accept evil or avoid its prominence in human nature: "What extraordinary things [people] do and say when they are very hypocritical, when they're very respectable, and when they're very mean" (S, 5). Concomitantly, he has the satirist's urge to reveal evil through a confrontation that is also a battle, an attempt to expose: "It's essential from my point of view that the bad people should be ridiculous as well as bad" (S, 5). That Amis's use of "ridiculous" here has more to do with satiric reductionism than comic play is suggested by his moral insistence and his belief that he is somewhat isolated in that moral concern: "In my novels there are good people and bad people, which is very rare these days" (S, 5). He is not the first satirist to have felt alone in his perception.

In the later novels, this moral concern becomes more evident and insistent, and is more harshly dramatized. In *Girl, 20* (1971), for example, Sir Roy Vandervane betrays his own identity as a serious musical artist by composing and performing a piece for violin and rock band. The performance of *Eleva-*

tions 9 by Vandervane and the "Pigs Out" is a failure to the popular critics and audience and to Douglas Yandell, classical music critic and narrator. Yandell arbitrates between the authentic and corrupt in Vandervane, seeing evidence of Vandervane's true identity only in the virtuosity of his performance: "Oh God, I thought, how could he not know that this lot positively disliked the idea of the difficult being made to seem easy, seem anything at all, exist in any form—that what they liked was the easy seeming easy?"[3] The "dislike" culminates in the destruction of Vandervane's Stradivarius by some young thugs, as moral transgression and consequence are juxtaposed. Vandervane pays for his misperception of reality and value; more crucially, perhaps, the world itself pays: there is one less Stradivarius.

In *Girl, 20,* as in some of his other novels, Amis has located a normative value in culture and art.[4] The substance and tone of Yandell's judgment is basically conservative. Privileged knowledge and vision confront the barbarians. Yet Amis's swing to the right in the years since *Lucky Jim* has not violently shifted his moral stance. The concern with moral issues, particularly as dramatized through the struggles of the conscience, was an important theme in *Lucky Jim,* and remains so in the best of the later novels.[5] We can see, then, that Amis's writing is influenced by a fairly traditional satiric impulse to expose recognized evil and aggressively defend a normative moral stance. Despite his determined shape-shifting, Amis has traveled a single path as a novelist.

As I have been suggesting, it is the changing nature of the satiric focus in Amis's art, the evolving quality of Amis's literary reaction to evil, which more particularly directs the line of advance in his career. We can detect an enormous evolutionary range in Amis's satire. Given his engagement with satiric confrontation and his commitment to variation in his choice of subgenres, we could hardly expect otherwise. In fact, the theoretical considerations here are basic to satire, since the satiric mode is historically the result of a grafting of an impulse to confront evil with a variety of literary forms that were originally nonsatiric. Mode and genre have not blended simply or easily. In the course of evolving from the purest and most direct form of verbal aggression, the curse, satire has acquired a variety of indirect qualities and tactics, in response to the varying demands of *literary* forms.[6] Thus in distinguishing between the curse and satire, we are speaking of indirection and its attendant complexities. James W. Nichols's definition recognizes this basic denotation: " 'Satire' . . . is a certain kind of aggression, oblique or indirect."[7] In tracing the angles and means of satiric focus—figures of indirection—in Amis's satire, we are examining the varying ways in which his satiric impulse has interacted with his more general novelistic intention "to write about human nature" in the context of the modern world.

Amis's first three novels, *Lucky Jim, That Uncertain Feeling* (1955), and *I Like It Here* (1958), have much in common. The protagonists have satiric possibilities; they are, for example, in confrontation with cultural and intellectual hypocrisy and pretension. In *Lucky Jim,* the best novel of the three, Dixon plays the role of the satirist, with a minimum of indirection, but the *reader's* involvement is not fully satiric. An attack on the intellectual mediocrity and mendacity of academia, *Lucky Jim* presents a truncated confrontation: we see that Professor Welch is one of Amis's 'bad' people, but we don't struggle with his badness. Welch is a clown, defeated by his own farcical ineptitude, not by the reader's recognition and rejection of him. Welch, attempting to leave the library by turning a revolving door the wrong way, is a fool. There is no significant involvement, no struggle, between him and the satirist, who maintains a passive stance: "Dixon stood and watched, allowing his mandrill face full play."[8] Even Bertrand Welch, a potentially more threatening character than his father, is too much the fool to be the object of a fully satiric action.

The complexity of *Lucky Jim* is inward looking: will Dixon find a role, a self-conception, which is moral and humane? The satiric weakness of the novel is contingent upon the weakness of Professor Welch. We, as readers, allow him no active social power; yet, paradoxically, he wins, maintaining his position and driving Dixon off to London and a no doubt better world. But neither the better world nor the face of evil is quite real for the reader. As John D. Hurrell asks, "What is so wrong with society that Jim cannot cope with it without making a fool of himself."[9] There is a real satiric confrontation in *Lucky Jim,* but its active force—as opposed to its weak perceptual component—is completely bled off in most cases by the novelist's strongly comic intention. Dixon is limited by the comic face of the dragon and restricted by the direct, explicit nature of his cursing response. Amis, in this novel, can forgive; he draws Dixon's sword back before it touches. Yet there is an occasional sense of manic energy in Dixon's disgust with the Welchean world, a direct, cursing focus, the tongue stuck out at the enemy when he isn't looking. Amis recognizes the primitive power of invective, but the design of his novel hides the curse behind the protagonist's comic situation: "Mentally [Dixon] was making a different face and promising himself he'd make it actually when next alone" (*LJ,* p. 10).

In *That Uncertain Feeling,* John Lewis' distaste for hypocrisy or cultural fakery is similarly bundled up in comedy and farce, or channeled into invective: "If stuff like *The Martyr* represented Welsh culture, then the sooner it shut up the better."[10] This novel, and *I Like It Here,* continue to reveal Amis's concern with moral issues (Should Lewis reject a job he needs to support his family for ethical reasons? Should Garnet Bowen advance his career by spying on a man who accepts him as a friend?), a concern that fully controls Amis's novelistic intentions—and overcomes his satiric impulse—in *Take a Girl Like You* (1960). Despite its involvement with "good" and "bad" people, *Take a Girl* is not in the mainstream of Amis's development. Amis employs a shifting point of view; no character is in a position to be a satirist, while the author's interest is concentrated on the comic, social, and moral dimensions of the central conflict between Jenny Bunn and Patrick Standish: Patrick "was in too much of a situation with her—adult, real, mutual, involving conscience, choice, action—for his mind to treat her as it liked. And a good thing too, eh? Hell, who said he had to feel all right, anyway?"[11]

However, in his fifth novel—*One Fat Englishman* (1963)—Amis developed a mode of indirect confrontation with the face of evil that was to remain central to his art for at least eight years. His problem was to find a satiric voice equal to the complexity of evil in the modern world, for despite his simplification of the problem of evil in the Salwak interview, Amis's definition of evil has grown steadily more complex.[12] The outline of his solution is to be seen in Jim Dixon's outward readiness to curse and play the fool, and his inward lack of assurance concerning his own role and place in the moral world. In brief, Amis designed a protagonist aggressively willing to confront evil, a figure equipped with a variety of indirect satiric weapons and not limited to the directness of the curse or the "mandrill face." The jokester and curser also become the satirist, but more importantly, the inward ambivalence toward the self and the self's relation to the outer world is correspondingly allowed greater orders of complexity. The satirist's own identity is involved in the satire; the misanthrope becomes a type of the satirist satirized. In *One Fat Englishman,* an English Thersites travels to America, hurling the expressions of his foolishness and his anger about for all to hear.[13]

Roger Micheldene, the protagonist of *One Fat Englishman,* is an archetypal and liberating character in the progress of Amis's career. Amis's own unrepentant sardonic and satiric vision is allowed full play within the form of a character toward whom the reader will have an oblique and uneasy relation.[14] Micheldene is demonstrably and seriously unpleasant. He himself can joyfully dance with the dragon, caught in the coils of his aggressive instincts and lust: "Never call a Jew a Jew unless you can be sure of making him lose his temper by doing so—a sound rule which the memory of Helene had flustered him into breaking."[15] Yet there is no alternative to Micheldene. The reader must finally accept his satiric attack on the American context, participate in his Gulliver's journey through American life and academia. There is no other guide, a fact which many reviewers had trouble accepting. As Edward Kelly points out, "that Roger himself is an immoral glutton does not exonerate the host of Americans . . . who are as bad or worse. Besides Roger knows he is immoral and likes it, while most of his American tools are confused about what to like or dislike."[16] The reader's ambivalence toward the outer Micheldene (chauvinist, lecher, and glutton) cannot reach a final judgment. We must finally accept Micheldene's ethic as an authentic if not true position, because he has established an inner sense of honesty. In a chaotic and unfair world, he knows who he is—the first requirement for any satirist. His prayers, for example, accept his own dilemma:

> Now look, this isn't good enough. You know what I'm like and yet you keep on at me. All those people—you know as well as I do they're the type I can't

stand. Why do you keep sending along bastards like Atkins and Macher and bloody fools like that Pargeter creature if you don't want me to be angry? (*OFE,* pp. 39–40)

Roger Micheldene, like Jim Dixon, is terribly angry, but Micheldene knows precisely why. His relation with society, with the world itself, is kinked; it is perhaps God Himself who put in the twist. Sensing the possibility of this final irony, Micheldene's curse at Father Colgate is voiced, not turned to the wall or repressed as Dixon's curse had been: "I'll confuse you, you bead-telling toad. I wouldn't take your absolution if you begged me. Try absolving yourself from the disgrace of abetting a disgrace. And stop telling me what to do, you silly little man" (*OFE,* p. 117). No one else can, finally, tell Micheldene what to do; we must allow him—perhaps with horror and certainly with some sense of distaste—the right to his own satire.

In Micheldene, Amis established the model of a suitably ambivalent and tarnished St. George, a figure who will trade unpleasantries with the dragon rather than hoping to kill it, yet is not perceived as evil himself. Confrontation is enough: one may be, in the end, both moral and rather nasty. The right to moral judgment, in Amis's estimation, is not earned through any necessary absolute rectitude, but by taking the dragon seriously and doing one's imperfect best. Amis argues that his stance as a moralist "doesn't mean of course that I behave any better than anybody else. If I weren't a moralist I might behave even worse than I do in ordinary life" (S, 6). The novelist—or satirist—does what he can. With the passing of romance, St. George has become only relatively good. The modern satirist *knows* he won't win.

In the series of novels ending with *Girl, 20* in 1971, Amis used the Micheldene model—the ambivalent protagonist, the satirized satirist—to confront a variety of modern evils. Only in *The Anti-Death League* (1966) did he fail to use this device, returning to the figure in designing *The Green Man* (1969) and *Girl, 20.* Yet, *The Anti-Death League* is a significant variation, since the novel's leading character, James Churchill, is defeated because he tries to be a pure, idealistic knight in a fully modern world. Amis's chosen subgenre here is the spy novel, a fruitful territory for a study in the defeat of idealism, as Eric Ambler and his successors have shown. Rather than slinging the muck of the modern world back at it—the Micheldene tactic—Churchill opts out of the confrontation, overcome by what he is facing. Confronting a political horror (his belief that he is being trained to conduct bacteriological warfare) and a series of personal horrors (the deaths of a number of acquaintances, culminating in the discovery that the woman he loves has cancer), Churchill retreats: he literally will not get out of bed or speak. His idealistic vision has traced the pattern of evil; he rejects the possibility of relativity or chance:

"I'm not creating a pattern, I'm recognizing a pattern that's been there all along. The over-all pattern. It's an evil one. It's got death in it, you see."

"You mustn't talk like that. The whole thing is totally random. All chance. Nothing and nobody behind it or in it or anywhere at all."

"I know there's nobody there. But there are such things as patterns, even when we know nobody willed them. Runs of bad luck, as I said. And a system that runs itself is still a system."[17]

Churchill, ironically, has drawn a metaphor from the terminology of megadeath in discovering this pattern. The pattern is one of "nodes" of evil—of death: "Well, we're in a lethal node now, only it's one that works in time instead of space. A bit of life it's death to enter" (*ADL,* p. 201). Once he believes in the absolutism of the pattern (believes that the metaphorical concept, the idea, is real), its very range and magnitude, founded on the shape of modern evil, will destroy any possibility of struggle. The theological dimensions of Churchill's perception of evil, his recognition that the concept of God is untenable since He would then be responsible for evil and death, is an extension of Micheldene's suspicion of a sense of perversity in the Deity. But again Churchill reaches an absolute conclusion: only those "with no sense of right and wrong" could believe in God (*ADL,* p. 236). Naidu, a minor character, suggests the formulation Amis will settle for:

> Death is not your enemy. Death's nobody's enemy. Your enemy's the same as everybody else's. Your enemy is fear, plus ill feelings, bad feelings of all descriptions. Such as selfishness, and not wanting to be deprived of what comforts you, and greed, and arrogance, and above all belief in your own uniqueness and your own importance (*ADL,* p. 278).

The example of Churchill is an argument for a moralist with an eye for relative goodness and badness. Amis returned to the type in *The Green Man.* The real dragon, in Amis's view, feeds on selfishness, greed, and the like—these failings Micheldene, or Maurice Allington of *The Green Man,* know only too well.

Allington, Ronnie Appleyard (*I Want It Now,* 1968), and Douglas Yandell (*Girl, 20*) are modifications of the Micheldene type, illustrating a gradual refinement of the self-satiric method of *One Fat Englishman.* Micheldene's relation to the original curser, Jim Dixon, is quite explicit, once one recognizes the extent to which comic intention had affected the design of the Dixon character. Micheldene is the uncomical curser, the railer become satirist. However, in his development of this character-type, Amis begins to move away from the directness of the curser. Increasingly, the satiric weaknesses of the central character become matters of serious moral concern in themselves. The characters remain the central dramatic judges of good and bad, better than anyone else in their worlds, but the onus of satiric attack falls increasingly on the authorial voice and the self-revelations of the other satiric victims. Roger Micheldene, at the conclusion of *One Fat Englishman,* is condemned only to continue in his anger, as he discovers that the insufferable

Strode Atkins will be travelling to England on the same ship. But the later characters are seriously chastened and punished for their failures. They are less and less able aggressively to confront the evils they perceive. As the author begins to take over the role of satirist from his characters, there is a corresponding increase in the darkness of the satirically envisioned, corrupt worlds pictured in the novels.

Roger Micheldene, for example, had blasted Father Colgate with the explosive energy of his own anger at easy answers; Colgate is actually an unexceptionable if rather fatuous character. But the corresponding figure in *The Green Man,* The Reverend Tom Rodney Sonnenschein, is outrageously and completely corrupt, and is shown to be so by the author, not by anything Maurice Allington says or does. "You know," Sonnenschein remarks, "this whole immortality bit's been pretty well done to death. One's got to take the historical angle. Immortality's just a passing phase."[18] By the time Joyce, Allington's wife, begins to ask the obvious questions of Sonnenschein, the satiric attack has already been pressed fully home: "What-. . . 's-the-point of somebody like you being a parson when you say you don't care about things like duty and people's souls and sin? Isn't that just exactly what parsons are supposed to care about?" (*GM,* pp. 174–75). It's left to Allington, "a hardened unbeliever" (*GM,* p. 169), to confront the devil (in the person of Dr. Thomas Underhill's ghost) and God, who appears as a well-dressed young man and reveals that he is merely someone who has been given a "game" to play (*GM,* p. 194). Allington comes to accept his own failings, as Micheldene had, but there is no bouyant anger in his acceptance, no curse for anyone but himself:

> Death was my only means of getting away for good from this body and all its pseudo-symptoms of disease and fear, from the constant awareness of this body, from this person, with his ruthlessness and sentimentality and ineffective, insincere, impracticable notions of behaving better, from attending to my own thoughts and from counting in thousands to smother them and from my face in the glass. . . . I put on my dinner jacket . . . and went downstairs to begin the evening round (*GM,* p. 242).

Allington will live with his self-knowledge, but there's little hope for the future in his moral awareness.

Similarly, in *Girl, 20,* Yandell is condemned to be both a judge and an accomplice of the book's principal satiric target, Sir Roy Vandervane. All Yandell's attempts to confront Vandervane fail. Vandervane wastes his art and identity in the pursuit of youthful pseudo-art and girls 20 and younger. Yandell, for all his perceptiveness, is manipulated by the deluded waster: "My job here, and perhaps not only here, was to dish out his medicine and watch him taking it like a man. He had planned to be helped to feel how deeply he was affected by the case against what he wanted to do before going off and doing it anyway" (*Girl,* p. 136). Amis launches satiric attacks left and right against

Vandervane and the youth-cult, his more general target. Yandell, for example, is shown considering what to wear at a pub that caters to the young: "All things considered, the ideal outfit would have been a leather jacket that became the top half of a dinner-suit when turned inside out, a denim dickey over an evening bow, steel-tipped patent-leather pumps, and so on . . ." (*Girl,* pp. 83–84). But Amis's characters are less and less able to injure or to survive the evil he attacks. Having failed with Vandervane, Yandell hopes to save Penny, Vandervane's daughter, from corruption. Again, he fails. She becomes a heroin addict, wishing to escape "that awful business of getting married and having children and being responsible" (*Girl,* p. 245). Penny has the last word in the novel, the final black joke: "We're all free now," she says.

It is the grotesque, the perversion of humor, which begins to triumph in Amis's novels after *Girl, 20.* The tension of his satiric anger and his comic talent pushes his art toward the absurd and nihilism. There are suggestions of this in the earlier novels: Ayscue, the chaplain in *The Anti-Death League,* is finally able to believe in "God's glory." Immediately after his recognition, as if in answer to the exaltation of his insight, Ayscue's beloved dog Nancy is run over by a truck (*ADL,* pp. 314–15). Commenting on the theological theme in this book, Amis remarks in the Salwak interview that "God is showing his malicious, malevolent side" (S, 16). But Amis's excursion into the black humor of a responsible God in a world of evil in *One Fat Englishman, The Anti-Death League,* and *The Green Man* does not deeply move either Amis or the reader. Amis always returns to the human face of the dragon. This he does with a vengeance in his latest novel, *Ending Up.*

The thesis of *Ending Up* is quite simple. Amis presents, in "Tuppeny-hapenny Cottage," a closed world, a perversely envisioned English country setting, where in happier days Agatha Christie might have set one of her bloodless murders. Five old, decrepit, and quite unpleasant people live in this cottage, thrown together by the accidents of their lives (that Adela and Bernard happen to be brother and sister, that Marigold happens to have become Adela's friend in the past). Now, in old age, they have come thoroughly to dislike each other and the disheartening weaknesses and habits that age has brought to each of them. Each begins to feel that life would be more pleasant without the others, and in varying ways they seek to inflict pain on those who have particularly irritated them. Marigold, noticing the dog's ball lying on the stairs, leaves it there, "saying to herself idly that it would do one or the other of those two no harm to tread on it and take a bit of a toss."[19] Retired Brigadier Bernard Bastable concocts elaborate plans to convince Shorty, his servant and onetime homosexual lover, that Shorty's drinking has begun to affect his bodily functions. Bernard thus launches Operations Stink and Incontinence, the latter consisting of heating a can of urine, so as not to disturb his victim's sleep, and pouring it on him. These operations involve a high order of humor and farce, as Bernard, for example, attempts to heat the urine in the kitchen and get the container upstairs to Shorty's room. Adela arrives and begins one of her typically empty conversations. "How much longer was he to go on chatting away with a can of piss about his person?" (*EU,* p. 147). Disaster threatens; Adela begins to notice something:

> "Funny smell, isn't there?"
> "I haven't noticed anything."
> "Perhaps one of the animals . . ."
> "Very likely" (*EU,* p. 148).

But Bernard succeeds in getting to Shorty's room and accomplishing his purpose, although not with the desired result of destroying Shorty's self-confidence: "Bernard put the blankets back and stared down at the sleeper. 'If you'll pardon the intrusion, Shorty, I think that's very funny,' he said, and left the room" (*EU,* p. 149).

The problem is that the reader is allowed little alternative but to think, in some ambivalent and blackly humorous way, that it *is* "funny." The author draws us deeper and deeper into the world of Bernard and his compatriots; we laugh at them, and begin to participate in what we take to be an essentially comic action. But in the penultimate chapter, all five characters die, killed by their own unpleasantries. Bernard, embarked on a new operation, falls off a ladder while trying to cut the phone line into the cottage: "He had broken something, something large. There was also a lot of what must be blood. Crying out with pain now, he crawled a little way. . . ." (*EU,* pp. 173–74). Marigold slips on the ball herself. "Shorty had fallen off the w.c. seat and was lying in a considerable pool of brownish water with long streaks of dark blood in it" (*EU,* p. 175).

The moral failure, the failure of compassion or goodness that Maurice Allington, for example, is able to live with through his own accepting self-perception, is the reader's own failure here. Yet *Ending Up,* with the essential unfairness of satire, assures that the reader will fail. We could say that the satiric target of the book is modern society's attitude toward the aged, its condemnation of them to the roles of the senile and the childish. But the solution is unsatisfying. We've been made to laugh, then made to realize that we've laughed with and at the dragon, who really isn't very funny. In this latest formulation of Amis's art, the curse is directed at us, and it hurts.

The reader departs from the experience of *Lucky Jim* poorly armed for confrontation with the evil of his own world. The same could not be said of *Ending Up.* There we are painfully warned that evil must be carefully and perceptively confronted, that our true and only useful weapon against evil may be our own compassion and humanity. We learn that modern dragons don't spit fire or allow their scaly armor to shine in the sun. Amis is a highly skilled novelist and possesses a truly comic talent. But he is also a satirist. He can not deny the power of human evil; he must warn his readers not to put away their swords, yet he is pessimistically sure that they will always wish to do so.

Notes

1. Philip Pinkus, "Satire and St. George," *Queen's Quarterly,* 70 (1963), 30–49.
2. Dale Salwak, "An Interview with Kingsley Amis," *Contemporary Literature,* 16 (1975), 7. Hereafter identified as S. This interview was conducted in January, 1973, when Amis had completed *The Riverside Villas Murder* and was working on *Ending Up.*
3. Kingsley Amis, *Girl, 20* (New York: Ballantine Books, 1973), pp. 217–18. Hereafter identified as *Girl.*
4. Edward Kelly, in "Satire and Word Games in Amis's *Englishman,*" *Satire Newsletter,* 9 (1972), 132–38, demonstrates that Amis uses language to fix his satiric targets in *One Fat Englishman,* providing a basis for his literary satire in that novel (the attack on Irving Macher and his novel, for example). Artistic and cultural values have always been important in Amis's work, even in the early novels. Richard J. Voorhees discusses this point in "Kingsley Amis: Three Hurrahs and a Reservation," *Queen's Quarterly,* 79 (1972), 42–44.
5. See John D. Hurrell, "Class and Conscience in John Braine and Kingsley Amis," *Critique,* 2 (1958), 39–53.
6. See Robert C. Elliott, *The Power of Satire: Magic, Ritual, Art* (Princeton: Princeton University Press, 1960) and Alvin B. Kernan, "Aggression and Satire: Art Considered as a Form of Biological Adaptation," in Frank Brady, John Palmer, and Martin Price, eds., *Literary Theory and Structure: Essays in Honor of William K. Wimsatt* (New Haven: Yale University Press, 1973), pp. 115–29.
7. James W. Nichols, *Insinuation: The Tactics of English Satire* (The Hague: Mouton, 1971), p. 14.
8. Kingsley Amis, *Lucky Jim* (New York: Viking, 1958), p. 179. Hereafter identified as *LJ.*
9. Hurrell, "Class and Conscience," 43.
10. Kingsley Amis, *That Uncertain Feeling* (New York: Harcourt, Brace and Company, 1955), p. 105.
11. Kingsley Amis, *Take a Girl Like You* (New York: New American Library Signet, 1963), p. 184.
12. In several of the later novels, for example, Amis examines the theological implications of evil. John Pazereskis briefly discusses this theme in "Kingsley Amis—The Dark Side," *Studies in Contemporary Satire,* 4 (1977), 28–33.
13. Elliott analyzes the history and nature of this satiric character-type in *The Power of Satire,* pp. 130–222.
14. *Englishman* may be compared with Amis's essay, "Who Needs No Introduction," in John Fischer and Robert B. Silvers, eds., *Writing in America* (New Brunswick, N.J.: Rutgers University Press, 1960), pp. 73–77. Amis's essay deals with lecturing in America in general, and in particular, with an occasion when he shared the stage with Jack Kerouac. Amis's tone is very close to the tone he created in the novel; Kerouac, for example, is shown responding to the audience's applause "with more weaves, bobs, and a chimpanzee-shuffle or two" (p. 76). The theft of Amis's lecture script at a fraternity house party is clearly the source of a similar incident in the novel (p. 75).
15. Kingsley Amis, *One Fat Englishman* (New York: New American Library—Signet, 1965), p. 71. Hereafter identified as *OFE.*
16. Kelly, "Satire and Word Games," 137. See Kelly's survey of the reviews of *OFE,* 138n.
17. Kingsley Amis, *The Anti-Death League* (New York: Ballantine Books, 1967), p. 214. Hereafter identified as *ADL.*
18. Kingsley Amis, *The Green Man* (New York: Ballantine Books, 1971), p. 169. Hereafter identified as *GM.*
19. Kingsley Amis, *Ending Up* (New York: Harcourt Brace Jovanovich, 1974), p. 173. Hereafter identified as *EU.*

Looking Back on *Lucky Jim*

David Lodge

First published in 1954, *Lucky Jim* quickly established itself as a classic comic novel, a seminal campus novel, and a novel which seized and expressed the mood of those who came of age in the 1950s. That reputation is deserved, but each aspect of it now invites some qualification.

Lucky Jim is still a very funny novel, but not as continuously funny as one remembers it being, or as its legend might lead new readers to expect. There are many passages in it where we are not invited to chuckle, or even smile; passages, usually to do with the hero's sentimental education, that are surprisingly serious in tone and import. More about this in a moment. First, let us pay due tribute to its comedy, which derives from Amis's flawless sense of timing: the way he controls the development of an action, or a sentence, to create that combination of surprise and logicality that is the heart of comedy. Comedy of situation is exemplified by such memorable scenes as Jim's accident with the bedclothing at the Welches' and his efforts to conceal the damage, his hijacking of the Barclays' taxi after the College Ball, and his drunken lecture on Merrie England. All these episodes involve the violation of a polite code of manners and contain an element of farce; they belong to a tradition of British comic writing which goes back through Waugh, Wodehouse, Dickens and Fielding to Restoration and Elizabethan comedy.

The comedy generated by Amis's style was more original, and introduced a distinctively new tone into English fiction. The style is scrupulously precise, but eschews traditional "elegance." It is educated but classless. While deploying a wide vocabulary it avoids all the traditional devices of humorous literary prose—jocular periphrasis, mock-heroic literary allusion, urbane detachment. It owes something to the "ordinary language" philosophy that dominated Oxford when Amis was a student there. It is a style continually challenged and qualified by its own honesty, full of unexpected reversals and underminings of stock phrases and stock responses. This, for example, is Jim's private interrogation of the scholarly article on whose publication his professional future depends:

> "In considering this strangely neglected topic," it began. This what neglected topic? This strangely what topic? This strangely neglected what? His thinking

From *The Spectator* 268 (18 April, 1992): 32–34. Reprinted by permission of *The Spectator*.

all this without having defiled and set fire to the typescript only made him appear to himself as more of a hypocrite and fool.

Lucky Jim was the first English "campus novel," to which all subsequent practitioners, including myself, are deeply indebted. According to Amis's *Memoirs,* the original inspiration was a glimpse of the Senior Common Room at what was then University College Leicester in 1948, when he was visiting Philip Larkin, who was a librarian there:

> I looked around a couple of times and said to myself, "Christ, somebody ought to do something with this." Not that it was awful—well, only a bit; it was strange and sort of *developed,* a whole mode of existence no one had got on to from outside.

Jim Dixon's anxiety about his professional future, his dependence on the patronage of a senior colleague whom he despises, are recurrent features of the genre, and in Professor Welch ("No other professor in Great Britain, he thought, set such store by being called Professor") Amis drew an immortal portrait of the absent-mindedness, vanity, eccentricity, and practical incompetence that academic institutions seem to tolerate and even to encourage in their senior staff (or at least did before the buzz-word "Management" began to echo through the groves oacademe in the 1980s). But academic politics in the broader sense, taboo sexual relations between staff and students, and the social and educational dynamics of the seminar and tutorial; which are the stuff of most campus novels, British and American have little or no place in *Lucky Jim.* Its university setting functions primarily as the epitome of a stuffy, provincial bourgeois world into which the hero is promoted by education, and against whose values and codes he rebels, at first inwardly and at last outwardly.

In the Fifties *Lucky Jim* was perceived as part of a new literary phenomenon known as "The Angry Young Men." This term, originally put into circulation by a leading article in *The Spectator,* and echoing the title of John Osborne's *Look Back in Anger,* grouped together a number of writers, and/or their fictional heroes, who were vigorously expressing their discontent with life in contemporary Britain. Amis himself repudiated the label of Angry Young Man, but it stuck to him as such things tend to do.

Although these writers "arrived" in the Fifties, their education and careers had in many cases been delayed or interrupted by the second world war, and their formative years were really the 1940s. If one looks carefully at the text of *Lucky Jim* it becomes clear that it is a novel *about* the 1940s, and distinctly under the shadow of the War. Jim's oppressively keen student Michie is an ex-serviceman "who'd commanded a tank troop at Anzio when Dixon was an RAF corporal in Western Scotland." Jim keeps his lecture notes in an old RAF file, and visualises the streets and squares of London by "remembering a weekend leave during the war." Even Welch, in an unwonted display of compassion, remarks that "it's only to be expected, after a war" that young men should find it difficult to settle into a job.

No dates are specifically mentioned in the text. It cannot be set later than 1951, since a Labour Government is in power: Bertrand Welch's remark about their inability to "pour water on troubled oil" may be a reference to the Persian oil crisis of that year. By the time *Lucky Jim* was published, the Tory Government elected in October 1951 was well into its stride, encouraging consumerism and free enterprise, but the atmosphere of the novel itself is clearly that of socialist, "austerity" Britain in the 1940s, when a young university lecturer might plausibly possess only three pairs of trousers, live in a lodging house, surrendering his ration book to his landlady, not even dream of owning a car, and keep anxious count of his cigarette consumption, not on health grounds but financial ones.

By the same token, the life-style of the Welches has a quality of the pre-war bourgeoisie. They live in a house that boasts a *music-room,* and have *maid-servants.* The two Welch sons, the "bearded pacifist painting" Bertrand and the "effeminate writing" Michael, seem in many ways hangovers from pre-war Bohemia. Indeed Bertrand's pacifism is hardly consistent with the Tory-ism he expounds in his political arguments with Jim. For his part, Jim's socialism is not ideologically sophisticated:

> If one man's got ten buns and another's got two, and a bun has got to be given up by one of them, then surely you take it from the man with ten buns.

It is not entirely surprising that once progressive politics became trendy, as they did in the 1960s, Kingsley Amis and his heroes turned against them (see his 1967 essay, "Why Lucky Jim Turned Right").

The received wisdom of the 1940s was that World War II, "the People's War," the landslide victory of the Labour Party in the general election of 1945, and the establishment of the Welfare State, had genuinely democratised British society, and got rid of its class divisions and inequalities for good. But to many young people who grew up in the post-war period, and benefited from the 1944 Education Act, it seemed that the old pre-war upper classes still maintained their privileged position because they commanded the social and cultural high ground. For myself and many others, it was doing National Service in the peacetime army that opened one's eyes to this fact. For Jim Dixon, it was taking up a university post at a time when provincial universities were all mini-Oxbridges, aping, and largely staffed from, the ancient universities.

Jim is ill at ease and out of place in this milieu, preferring pop music to Mozart, pubs to drawing-rooms, non-academic company to academic. He feels a fraud as a teacher. His students "waste my time and I waste theirs." Why did he take up this uncongenial profession in the first place? He gives a revealing answer when his friend Beesley asks him this very question: "Feeling I'd be no use in a school and so on." When he loses his university job, however, Jim resignedly prepares to take up school-teaching. A huge proportion of first-generation humanities graduates in the Forties and Fifties went into educational careers not because they had a vocational call, but because entry to the other liberal professions—administrative civil service, the foreign service, law, publishing, etc., was still controlled by the public-school-Oxbridge-old-boy network. They were the ideal readers of *Lucky Jim*.

Nowhere is Jim's scorn for the protocol and pieties of the academic life expressed more pungently than in his private commentary on his unpublished article, already quoted. The note of self-accusation in that passage is crucially important. For most of the novel's action, Jim's rebellion against bourgeois values and institutions is purely mental, or physically expressed only through the pulling of grotesque faces when he thinks he is unobserved. His desire to take violent action against those who oppress him is discharged in harmless, private fantasies of a childish nature (though no less funny for that)—plunging Welch feet-first into a toilet bowl, beating him about the head and shoulders with a bottle, pushing a bead up Margaret's nose, etc. The first occasion on which Jim's inner and outer speech exactly coincide comes after he fights Bertrand and succeeds in knocking him down.

> The bloody old towser-faced boot-faced totem-pole on a crap reservation, Dixon thought. "You bloody old towser-faced boot-faced totem-pole on a crap reservation," he said.

After this, Jim's fortunes begin to improve, in spite of deceptive appearances to the contrary, and he is rewarded with the job, and the girl, of his dreams.

Several critics have observed that there is a fairy-tale buried in the deep structure of *Lucky Jim,* in which Jim is the Frog Prince, Christine the Princess, Gore-Urquhart the Fairy Godmother, and Margaret the Witch. But Jim's relationship with the two women is more subtle and complex than that analogy suggests. It is the most serious strand in the novel, and is pursued with particular attention in the chapters leading up to Jim's fight with Bertrand. The character of Christine, admittedly, rarely rises above her archetype, the blonde, beautiful, virginal yet voluptuous object of male desire, and the conversations between her and Jim are often embarrassingly banal. The dark, skinny, neurotic Margaret is much more interesting. Just as Jim goes through the motions of being a university teacher, knowing he is in bad faith but unable to do anything about it, so he feels bound to go through the motions of being Margaret's partner, even though he has no desire, and hardly any affection, for her. When he finally brings himself to tell her this, candidly, in Chapter 16, she throws a fit of hysterics, then apologises: "You were absolutely right, saying what you did. Much better to clear the air like that."

This would seem to release Jim honourably from any further responsibility for Margaret, freeing him to pursue the promising intimacy he has established with Christine. Yet he remains perversely in Margaret's thrall.

> He looked at Margaret and an intolerable weight fell upon him.... He remembered a character in a modern novel Beesley had lent him who was always feeling pity moving in him like sickness, or some such jargon. The parallel was apt: he felt very ill.

It is part of Jim's loathing for all high-cultural affectation that he will never admit, even to himself, to remembering the names of the books and authors he has read. But there is little doubt that he is recalling here Graham Greene's *The Heart of the Matter* (1948) whose hero, Scobie, is dominated and finally destroyed by the emotion of pity. The word "pity" occurs scores of times in the text, often in similes like the one half-remembered by Jim Dixon (e.g. "Pity smouldered like decay at his heart.") When he was B. Litt student at Oxford, between 1947 and 1949, Amis was commissioned, rather improbably, by an Argentinian university to write a book on Graham Greene. The project came to nothing, and one may infer Amis's opinion of his potential publisher by the fact that the academic charlatan, "L. S. Caton," who plagiarises Jim's article, disappears to a chair in Argentina. But it is certain that Amis would have been reading extensively in Greene, and would have read *The Heart of the Matter* on its publication with particular attention, when his own first novel was in gestation.

Lucky Jim is a comic inversion of Greene's tragic (and highly acclaimed) novel: the typical act of a young writer wanting to challenge the literary values of a previous generation. Many phrases describing Scobie's feelings towards his shrewish wife would apply equally well to Jim's feelings towards Margaret, e.g.: "pity and responsibility reached the intensity of a passion"; "he was bound by the pathos of her unattractiveness." Even that quintessentially Greeneian sentence, "He felt the loyalty we all have to unhappiness, the feeling that this is where we really belong," seems applicable to Jim, as he resumes his joyless association with Margaret. Jim, however, is freed from his self-imposed loyalty to unhappiness by two developments in the plot. First, he is liberated from an unsatisfying career in education by Gore-Urquhart's offer of a job as his private secretary—a post doubly desirable because it entails living in London, where Jim longs to be, and because it is coveted by Bertrand. Secondly, he is redeemed from his emotional thraldom to Margaret by discovering that she faked the suicide attempt that originally bound him to her. He determines to back his luck—and Christine's.

> Christine was still nicer and prettier than Margaret, and all the deductions that could be drawn from that fact should be drawn: there was no end to the ways in which nice things are nicer than nasty ones.

Is this contrast drawn between the two women sexist? Of course it is! So was most fiction written by men in the 1950s, or indeed at any other time, judged by 1990s standards of what is Politically Correct. The real objection to the characterisation of Margaret is not that she is portrayed as hysterical, deceitful, and sexually frigid, for it would be absurd to pretend that such women have never existed, but that the behaviour in which she manifests these traits is in one important respect rather implausible. I refer to her double deception of Jim and Catchpole over her faked suicide attempt, entailing the forging of a doctor's prescription. Like the sudden intervention of Gore-Urquhart with his job offer, this works in narrative terms only because it occurs in a comic novel, because we want to believe in it, because we want the hero to be released from his enchantment and find happiness. Margaret's story is potentially tragic, but it is not told here (it was to be told many times, and powerfully, by women novelists).

Perhaps the ethical pragmatism finally embraced by Jim Dixon can only be sustained if the subject enjoys good luck. "Nice things are nicer than nasty ones" is not much of a consolation for or defence against disease, madness, addiction, depression and death. As Kingsley Amis allowed these nasty things to impinge more and more on the world of his later novels they became progressively darker, to the disappointment of many readers of *Lucky Jim,* but also deeper.

Jim, Jake and the Years Between: The Will to Stasis in the Contemporary British Novel

KEITH WILSON

Kingsley Amis's thirteenth novel, *Jake's Thing,* appeared by a convenient symmetry almost exactly twenty-five years after the publication of *Lucky Jim,* the first novel that shot him to immediate fame and itself to cult status.[1] That fact, seemingly at first of no more than passing interest—the kind of interest possessed by the unsettling photograph of a jowled, late-middle-aged face staring from the dustjacket of *Jake's Thing*—becomes on closer examination worth attention. *Lucky Jim* was unequivocally a young man's book, its ultimately affirmative disrespect calculated, and still able, to fill an undergraduate audience with a surprisingly creative joy.[2] *Jake's Thing,* by painful contrast, proclaims in every embittered chapter that a glory has passed away from Amis some time between Suez and Vietnam, and we have long since grown accustomed to the inevitable but inaccurate view of him as the angry socialist young man who became the petulant Tory old one—"a difficult old sod"[3] as a recent interviewer, smarting from a harrowing lunch, proclaimed him. The tenor of *Jake's Thing,* then, surprises no-one. But the extent of its similarities to *Lucky Jim,* the strong feeling that in Jake Richardson goes, but for the grace of Gore-Urquhart and Christine, Jim Dixon, is of considerably more than nugatory interest. In situation and rhetoric the two novels have many links; in mood and resolution, they could not be more different. That distinction not only illuminates some of the things that twenty-five years have done to Amis and his work but also reflects the quiet desperations that have typified a large number of recent British novels. What distinguishes Jake from Jim is a self-willed stasis that helps to define a national mood that the contemporary British novel has begun to suggest.

Amis created in Jim Dixon, as surely as John Osborne was to do in Jimmy Porter, a period archetype. The young university lecturer, contemptuous of the phoney academic world in which he expends a great deal of opportunistic energy trying to guarantee himself a permanent place, seemed a type almost before Amis so supremely typified him.[4] His eventual escape from

From *Ariel* 13 (Jan 1982): 55–69. With permission of *Ariel,* Copyright © 1982 The Board of Governors, The University of Calgary.

provincial academic atrophy into the metropolitan sophistications that come from being secretary to a public figure and having a woman like Christine Callaghan is fair reward for such an inspiring piece of iconoclasm as the Merric England lecture. Jim was a hero who vindicated us all, all we right thinkers that is,[5] by getting, as Philip Larkin (to whom *Lucky Jim* is dedicated) has the speaker in his poem "Toads" fantasize, "the fame and the girl and the money / All at one sitting."[6]

In Jake Richardson (the "son of Dick" and therefore etymological descendant of Dixon), sixty-year-old Reader in Mediterranean History at Comyns College, Oxford, Amis creates a Dixon thirty years on, transposed from his provincial redbrick but carrying with him many of his youthful alter ego's characteristics. Like Jim, Jake is contemptuous of most of his colleagues and anxious to reduce his own engagement with anything academic to the minimum that is reconcilable with professional survival: he lives in London, commuting to Oxford for a three day working week. Like Jim, with his self-parodying disdain for the one ill-starred article he has managed to produce,[7] Jake has a dispassionate awareness of the value of his own scholarly achievements.[8] Like Jim, Jake has a residual integrity that costs him professional advancement, "condemning him, with some assistance from laziness, to the non-attainment of a professorial chair" (p. 136). Like Jim, Jake's intellectual honesty makes him challengingly parade the enjoyment he derives from "low-brow" pursuits, in his case television serials and mystery novels. Like Jim, Jake suffers from the unwanted attentions of a neurotic woman who stages a fake suicide attempt. And, like Jim, Jake eventually, also aided by drink, manages to reconcile inner thoughts and outer statements in a swingeing denunciation of a cause he is supposed to be espousing—the admission of women to the male preserve of Comyns College. In his Prufrockish self-mockery, his dislike of pretension and unwarranted self-esteem, his suspicion of intellectual posturing and consequent retreat into an aggressively anti-academic stance, and his hatred of the trendy and superficially cosmopolitan, the aging Jake is the logical extension of the young Jim.

But it is precisely in the adjectives that the primary distinction lies. Jim is still a young man, young enough to escape from an early unwise choice, made through drift and lethargy, into a braveish new world of post post-war austerity in London. His horizons are expanding, circumscribed only by the magical London names that he lovingly savours on his provincial tongue: "Bayswater, Knightsbridge, Notting Hill Gate, Pimlico, Belgrave Square, Wapping, Chelsea."[9] Jake, by contrast, is undeniably aging; indeed, the central plot of the novel is concerned with his once libidinous body telling him so. The sexual ennui that Jake faces after a lifetime of very successful womanizing—"well over a hundred" (p. 43) as he proudly tells his apparently adolescent therapist—is not, however, his basic problem but merely the most obvious indication of the general world-weariness from which he suffers. In searching, via the latest psycho-medical faddery, for a cure for his loss of interest in sex, Jake is constantly forced into recognizing the extent of his deliberate disengagement from the contemporary world. He eventually accepts that disengagement as a refuge, rejecting the physical treatment that will revitalize his moribund libido and retreating into absolute solitude. His basic difficulty is not that he has become a misogynist, but rather a misanthropist.

If the end of *Lucky Jim* was a triumphant opening up of the future as Jim and Christine headed to London and success, the end of *Jake's Thing* is a jaded closing down, a closeted spurning of a world for which Jake can have, at best, only indifference—a retreat into TV dinners and TV movies. O tempora, o mores.

The differences are embodied in the ways that Jim and Jake respond to their immediate environment. One of the main indices of Jim's developing capacities is his increasing ability to control his life, in however piecemeal a way, by controlling those who would take his fate out of his own hands. Those memorable moments of mock-epic contortion in which Jim improvises his way to salvation are stages in the process that will eventually allow him this control. When he escorts Christine home from the Summer Ball, having appropriated someone else's taxi and browbeaten a churlish driver into submission, the cavalier command of situation is a key to his development, and Amis makes the transition explicit:

> More than ever he felt secure: here he was, quite able to fulfil his role, and, as with other roles, the longer you played it the better chance you had of playing it again. Doing what you wanted to do was the only training, and the only preliminary, needed for doing more of what you wanted to do. (p. 149)

Jake's Thing has its own echo of Jim's insight, but with a significant modification. Jake is discussing his therapist, to whom he has thus far shown an absurd deference:

> ... my "therapist" works on the principle that the way of getting to want to do something you don't want to do is to keep doing it. Which seems to me to be a handy route from not ... pause ... wanting to do it to not-wanting, wanting not, to do it. But I am paying him to know best. (p. 227)

Once one has worked out the syntactical riddle, one recognizes the willed stasis in Jake's response. The verbal game, by introducing and playing on a negative, turns Jim's affirmation into Jake's denial. Jake has arrived by the end of the novel at a stage of "not-wanting" everything, the novel closing with a final denial: " 'No thanks,' he said" (p. 285).

Jake always finds himself confronted by negatives in his dealings with others. Like Jim, he encounters class-churlishness but, unlike Jim, he emerges the loser. At the beginning of the novel he makes a purchase at a liquor store, lured in by a notice advertising a discount:

"Er, the. . . . You've charged the full price for the chocolates."
"Right."
"But your notice says 10p in the pound off everything."
"Everything bar chocolates and smokes."
"But it says everything."
"It means everything bar chocolates and smokes."
"But. . . ."
"You want them, do you, squire?"
". . . Yes."
"Right."
After a short pause, during which he took a blow on the kneecap from the corner of a wire basket in the hand of a man in a blue boiler-suit, Jake paid, picked up his goods and left, remembering he should have said Cheers just as the exit door swung shut after him. (pp. 13–14)

His failure, not only to carry his point but also to establish linguistically his membership in the new classless Britain by use of the ubiquitous and equalizing "cheers," establishes him as an outsider by the end of the first chapter. The extent of his alienation is revealed in almost all his subsequent dealings with the various sections of society that he encounters.

Like Burgess's Enderby, who over the three volumes devoted to him fleshes out more expansively the failure of an artist and individualist to adapt successfully to the ad-mass world that he is forced to inhabit, Jake is an elitist, a traditionalist, and an individualist who values his privacy. His misfortune is to live in a rapidly changing world which is egalitarian, liberal, and communal. His alienation is inevitable and, since it is in part caused by people like those who are trying to cure him, untreatable. What he faces as soon as he leaves his home, which is why he does so increasingly reluctantly, is an accelerating process of change to which he has neither the desire nor the ability to adapt, that very ability which allowed Jim Dixon to emerge triumphant. In throwaway comments that litter the developing narrative, Amis establishes Jake's distance from the England of the seventies, a distance that makes him, in effect, a stateless person.

The examples are legion, the following a representative cross-section that establishes Jake's distance from what was once his own familiar territory, England. His Harley Street doctor cuts short a consultation in order to see another patient, an Arab sheikh; Jake decides against taking a taxi since "No sooner had one black, brown or yellow person, or group of such, been set down on the pavement than Americans, Germans, Spaniards were taken up and vice versa" (p. 12); he has difficulty in negotiating his way through the endless streams of traffic in the centre of London; a dirty overalled customer in the off-licence talks nonsense about wine, communicates in formula phrases, and peels off twenty pound notes while Jake wonders if he can afford one bottle; his is the only house in the neighbourhood that has not been trendied up by new young owners; his train-fare to Oxford is outrageously high; English place-names have been changed and are unfamiliar to him; the telephone refuses to work. The list is virtually inexhaustible, a litany of day-by-day stimuli that constantly grate on Jake's nerves and compel further and further withdrawal until the final statement of denial: "No thanks." Like the solitary player in Beckett's *Act Without Words* who, having failed to order his small world at all, sits in solitude on an empty stage looking at his hands, Jake refuses any longer to respond and retires permanently into his television room.

If the surrounding stimuli are increasingly foreign, the elements of his own private and professional life offer no sanctuary. He is led into humiliating public exercises in consciousness-raising by a therapist who turns out not to know where Freud did his major work and has no idea what happened in Europe in 1848; his wife, who can no longer tolerate his lack of interest, deserts him; his college is about to admit the women whose minds he despises, and his existing students are illiterate. Even the areas that were most particularly his, college and home, are selling out to the opposition, forcing on Jake the isolation that he will eventually, willingly, take on. While Jim Dixon had a world that he could move into in triumph, Jake Richardson has only one from which he is being gradually dismissed in ignominy. His need to look back, if not in anger then in petulant irritation, is far more stultifying than Jimmy Porter's, for at least the young man can look forward too, if only with the anticipatory pleasure of seeing the upper-middle classes inevitably evaporate.

The distinction between the backward and the forward look is the basic distinction not only between *Lucky Jim* and *Jake's Thing* but between the British novel of the early 1950's and the British novel of the late 1970's. *Lucky Jim* pictures a world of constant process, a world subject to rapid change, but change for the better, change from post-war grey and the last restraints of pre-war class constipation to post-Festival of Britain release and the quick ten year run to the Britain that had never had it so good. The Welch family attempts to hold on to the cultural privileges that are the obvious hallmark of their class position and Jim Dixon, having discovered that he really doesn't have to pretend to be able to read music and glorify the past to survive, leaves them to it. He is off to a new medialand non-job—"meeting people or telling people I can't meet them" (p. 238)—which will have him strategically placed for when London starts swinging in the sixties. Within a few years of the publication of *Lucky Jim,* the British novel became dominated for a while by the work of regional naturalists like Barstow, Braine, Sillitoe or Storey, all writing of a working class that, within whatever limits, was on the move; even those not upwardly mobile were becoming financially powerful and threateningly articulate. If Jim Dixon was an imaginative "type" of the early fifties, John Braine's Joe Lampton from *Room at the Top* (who would rather join the middle-classes than beat them) and Alan Sillitoe's Arthur Seaton from *Saturday Night and Sunday Morning* (who would rather beat them than join them) are corresponding types from the early sixties. The degree of their success is evidenced in the alienation of a Jake Richardson, for whose generation and class in the England of 1979, the mood has to be at best elegiac, at worst stagnant.

Were Amis alone in this rendering of a mood of defeat and confusion the phenomenon would be worthy of note as a significant development in an important novelist, but nothing out of the ordinary in one who has himself gone from relative youth to late middle-age in those years. But far from being alone, Amis synthesizes in the single character of Jake a variety of confusions that have become evident in a wide range of recent British novels. One can of course say that most novelists of established reputation will be of a certain age, and therefore more susceptible to bouts of jaundice that will yellow their environment. But that elementary possibility is insufficient to account for Margaret Drabble, a writer who is nearly twenty years Amis's junior, producing in *The Ice Age* (1977) a "state-of-England" novel that pictures an England "sliding, sinking, shabby, dirty, lazy, inefficient, dangerous, in its death throes, worn out, clapped out, occasionally lashing out."[10] Nor does it account for John Fowles, whose *Daniel Martin* (1977) says things as interesting about England as about his eponymous hero, providing as an epigraph an extract from Antonio Gramsci's *Prison Notebooks* which reads: "The crisis consists precisely in the fact that the old is dying and the new cannot be born; in this interregnum, a great variety of morbid symptoms appears."[11] Nor does it account for William Golding, after many years of silence, producing a book in which the texture of contemporary England is an important part of the moral complexities with which he is dealing and which bears as title the threatening Miltonic paradox (in its original incarnation a reference to hell) *Darkness Visible* (1979).[12] Indeed, the Miltonic context is powerfully suggestive:

> A dungeon horrible, on all sides round
> As one great furnace flamed, yet from those flames
> No light, but rather darkness visible
> Served only to discover sights of woe,
> Regions of sorrow, doleful shades, where peace
> And rest can never dwell, hope never comes
> That comes to all; but torture without end
> Still urges, and a fiery deluge, fed
> With ever burning sulphur unconsumed.[13]

Not since Eliot's epigraph from Petronius's Satyricon, standing on bleak guard at the entrance to *The Waste Land,* have we seen such weighted associative couplings in a major work of British literature.

Since the process I am charting is one that we are still in the midst of, the map cannot be definitive. But for the purposes of suggesting certainly the literary, and perhaps the national, mood that subsequent commentators may well see dominating the Britain of the late seventies and early eighties, Drabble's *The Ice*

Age is the most telling accompaniment to discussion of *Jake's Thing,* and this despite the fact that the two novels are radically different in style, subject-matter, and even "political" viewpoint. *The Ice Age* begins with an extended image that sums up the mood of what I have called the will to stasis very economically:

> On a Wednesday in the second half of November, a pheasant, flying over Anthony Keating's pond, died of a heart attack. . . . Anthony Keating, who had not died of his heart attack, stared at the dead bird, first with surprise . . . and then with sympathy, as he guessed the cause of its death. There it floated, its fine winter plumage still iridescent, not unlike a duck's in brilliance but, nevertheless, unlike a duck's, quite out of place in the water. It gave rise to some solemn reflections, as most objects, with less cause, seemed to do, these solitary and inactive days. . . . It was large, exotic, and dead, a member of a species artificially preserved. It had the pleasure, at least, of dying a natural death. (p. 9)

The attributes of the bird—its stature, its artificial preservation, its death against an alien background—image the solitude and inactivity of the displaced Keating. The subsequent narrative records not only Keating's displacement but that of nearly all his contemporaries, struggling as they are with various aspects of a collapsing and increasingly foreign Britain. What they encounter are changes that are similar to those that infuriate and baffle Jake Richardson. The first character to appear after Keating, Kitty Friedmann, has just sent him a letter whose opening words are "These are terrible times we live in" (p. 10), a judgment she is particularly qualified to make since her foot has just been blown off by the same terrorist bomb that has killed her husband. The novel develops, via a broad panorama of characters, into a state-of-the-nation lament that ranges over the property development that renders the environment unfamiliar, the misplaced egalitarianism that apparently destroys the educational structure, the sexual anarchy that ensures impermanence in relationships, the youthful unenlightened self-interest that casts even darker shadows over the future—in short, becomes a parade of disasters, both personal and public, physical and psychic, that makes the crazed comment of an aging prison inmate a central touchstone: "Something has gone wrong . . . with the laws of chance" (p. 169). At times, Drabble assumes a Dickensian narrative distance that allows her to indulge in expansive assessment:

> Not everybody in Britain on that night in November was alone, incapacitated or in jail. Nevertheless, over the country depression lay like a fog, which was just about all that was missing to lower spirits even further, and there was even a little of that in East Anglia. All over the nation, families who had listened to the news looked at one another and said "Goodness me" or "Whatever next" or "I give up" or "Well, fuck that," before embarking on an evening's viewing of colour television, or a large hot meal, or a trip to the pub, or a choral society evening. All over the country people blamed other people for all the things

that were going wrong—the trades unions, the present government, the miners, the car workers, the seamen, the Arabs, the Irish, their own husbands, their own wives, their own idle good-for-nothing off-spring, comprehensive education. Nobody knew whose fault it really was, but most people managed to complain fairly forcefully about somebody: only a few were stunned into honourable silence.... A huge icy fist, with large cold fingers, was squeezing and chilling the people of Britain, that great and puissant nation, slowing down their blood, locking them into immobility, fixing them in a solid stasis, like fish in a frozen river: there they all were in their large houses and their small houses, with their first mortgages and second mortgages, in their rented flats and council flats and basement bedsits and their caravans: stuck, congealed, amongst possessions, in attitudes, in achievements they had hoped next month to shed, and with which they were now condemned to live. The flow had ceased to flow: the ball had stopped rolling: the game of musical chairs was over. *Rien ne va plus,* the croupier had shouted. (pp. 64–65)

For those who stay in Britain, like Anthony Keating's mistress Alison, watching over a daughter who suffers from cerebral palsy, there seems no likelihood of escape. Keating himself, who ends up in an Eastern European prison camp, escapes into an inner world of spiritual contentment which may eventually find external expression in the book he is writing on "the nature of God and the possibility of religious faith" (p. 295). But if Britain is to escape from its ice age, with its population fixed in a "solid stasis,"—a possibility which is suggested somewhat dutifully in the novel's last sentence—it is presumably only Anthony Keating's newly rediscovered God who knows how. The fragments he has shored against *his* ruins are clearly supporting an exceptionally fragile structure.

In the light of "Jake's Thing," a minor character in *The Ice Age* becomes especially relevant. Linton Hancox is a classics don at Oxford, prepared by upbringing and native bent for conspicuous academic success. His failure to realize his potential becomes apparent "in the late sixties, when everyone else was beginning to do better," and the dissatisfactions from which that failure derives are identical to some of Jake's:

> His sourness took a common ... course: he began to complain about falling standards in education, about the menace of trendy schoolteachers who couldn't even teach children to read, about the dangers of assuming that all learning could and should be fun.... These remarks about education were paralleled by remarks about the state of poetry. Linton's own poetry was, naturally, academic, intelligent, structured, delicate, evasive, perceptive, full of verbal ambiguities and traditional qualifications: his reaction to the wave of beat poets, Liverpool poets, pub poets, popular poets, was one of amusement, then of hostility, then of contempt tinged with fear. (p. 73)

Drabble's analysis of the withdrawal and alienation that Hancox endures centres on his total rejection of the contemporary world and his retreat into the misanthropy of the impotent. The decline of Hancox's chosen academic discipline, and the comfortably enclosed world that fostered it, causes him, like Jake, to reject *in toto* what could be salvageable in part:

> A pond, out of which the water had slowly drained, leaving Linton stranded, beached, useless. Unable to adapt, unable to learn new skills, obstinately committed to justifying the old ones—and alas, as so often happens, ruining quite unnecessary and disconnected parts of himself in his willed, forced, unnatural, retrogressive justification. For there was no reason in nature why Linton should not teach classics to a lot of second-rate students, and yet continue to write first-rate poetry. Why should the whole man grow sour, because one part of him was no longer vital? . . . It was as though Linton, in his rejection of the modern world in education, had resolved to reject the modern world altogether, and his poetry too had become sour, petty, carping, reactionary, lightened only by the odd flash of fairly useless and despicable nostalgia. . . . (p. 77)

The image of himself as a stranded whale, like that of the dead pheasant at the novel's beginning, gives graphic visual embodiment to Hancox's suicidal retreat from action, expressing more assertively the automatic glibness of the fish-out-of-water simile. In the new ice age, no-one is more decisively beached than the educator.

If *Jake's Thing* and *The Ice Age* can offer only visions of contemporary decline and willed retreat, a late-seventies stasis that is given visual rendering in the dustjacket illustration for *The Ice Age* that shows tortured eyes staring out from the blue depths of a cube of ice, Anthony Burgess's *1985* (1978) apocalyptically projects his version into the future in an uncertain attempt to redefine Orwell. Again Arabs and Trade Unions loom large, uniting to become the main cause of the moral and social petrifaction that have overtaken the country. Burgess has working for him the inherent overstatement that the anti-Utopian conventions he is using allow, although they are conventions that easily allow propaganda to take the place of imagination. Just as the distance between Jake's attitudes and Amis's own seems short, so the responses of Bev Jones, the central character in *1985,* clearly reflect some of Burgess's own irritations, and they are surprisingly close to Amis's. In *1985,* inflation gallops, England is ruled by Arabs and trade unionists, language is the standardized and corrupt "Worker's English"—in fact, England has become the stuff of which Jake Richardson's wildest nightmares might be made. While Jake watches what he sees as a prostitution of education that makes his own profession increasingly untenable, Bev lives in an England in which educators have become outlaws, and in which youth gangs yearn for the education of which they have been deprived:

> "We go to school, we lot, till we're sixteen. That's the law. Okay, we go and we don't listen to the crap they call sociology and Worker's English. We sit at the back and read Latin."

> "Who teaches you Latin?"
> "There are these antistate teachers about. You a teacher?"
> "History. Very useless."
> "Okay, there are these thrown out of schools for not wanting to teach the crap they're supposed to, right? They wander, like you're wandering. We give them the odd wad like we're doing to you. Then they give us a bit of education in return. Real education, not State school crap."
> "You want something now?"
> "One thing. . . . How did we get into this mess?"[14]

Anything approximating to education becomes the preserve of the social outcast, and it is never able to withstand the pressures of the automatized society against which it rebels. Bev, imprisoned for life as a hopeless recalcitrant who refuses to adapt or keep quiet, commits suicide by pressing his body against the electrified fence that encloses him, "puzzling an instant about why you had to resign from the union of the living in order to join the strike of the dead" (p. 219). His only resource is the ultimate retreat, the ultimate act of stasis—self-destruction. His final verbal defiance could have come from Jake Richardson's lips:

> "Look, I can't see where I've gone wrong. I was brought up under a system of government that was regarded as the triumph of centuries of instinctual sanity. I see the world changed. Am I obliged to change with it? . . . It won't do, it won't, it won't, it won't." And then: "Forget it. It's like addressing a couple of brick walls. Do what has to be done. I'm in your hands." (pp. 214–15)

There is no need in the present context to go beyond Burgess's imagined *1985,* although Kingsley Amis's new novel, *Russian Hide and Seek* (1980) does precisely that, looking forward to a twenty-first-century England that has been taken over not by Arabs and unionists but by Russians, who inherit the disaffection.[15] We are concerned with the past and the present, which have created the will to stasis in the contemporary British novel, rather than the future. That the mood is there in the literature, a reading of almost any significant novel published in England in the last five years will establish. That it is there in the nation will take longer to establish, although the anecdotal usually contains a sufficient germ of truth to give pause for thought. In 1971, much was made of the identity crisis that the British passed through with the introduction of that most alien intruder, decimal currency. One of the much reported stories was of the old age pensioner who, having ordered a pint of beer at his local, was quoted the price in the new currency. He pulled out a handful of coins, looked at them in a mood that passed from confusion to irritation to rage and, throwing them at the barman, shouted "There you are; take the bloody lot," walking out of the pub sans both beer and money. That gesture of impotence, puzzlement, anger and eventual retreat, from that bastion of comfort and custom, the English local, is one that Jake Richardson and his literary peers would well understand.

Notes

1. The extent of the cult can easily be forgotten. *Lucky Jim* was first published in January 1954. By February 1956 it was into its sixteenth impression, a success story rarely equalled in contemporary fiction.

2. The appeal of *Lucky Jim* to North American undergraduates has frequently provoked comment, most recently in Bruce Stovel, "Traditional Comedy and the Comic Mask in Kingsley Amis's *Lucky Jim*," *English Studies in Canada*, 4 (1978), 69–80.

3. "Pendennis," "A difficult old sod," *Observer* London, 3 Feb. 1980, p. 44.

4. *Lucky Jim* was the first significant post-war "campus" novel in Britain, and the founder of a substantial line of which the most successful have been Malcolm Bradbury's *Eating People is Wrong* (1959) and David Lodge's *Changing Places* (1975).

5. The appeal to unaffected good sense and intellectual honesty is a crucial part of Jim Dixon's popularity and Amis's own assumed popularist mask. In a 1973 interview, Amis defended this stance: "Jim and I have taken a lot of stick and badmouthing for being Philistine, aggressively Philistine, and saying, 'Well, as long as I've got me blonde and me pint of beer and me packet of fags and me seat at the cinema, I'm all right.' I don't think either of us would say that. It's nice to have a pretty girl with large breasts rather than some fearful woman who's going to talk to you about Ezra Pound and hasn't got large breasts and probably doesn't wash much. And better to have a pint of beer than to have to talk to your host about the burgundy you're drinking. And better to go to the pictures than go to see nonsensical art exhibitions that nobody's really going to enjoy. So it's appealing to common sense if you like, and it's a way of trying to denounce affectation." Dale Salwak, "An Interview with Kingsley Amis," *Contemporary Literature*, 16 (1975), 8. The extent to which for Amis this *is* a mask is made apparent when one considers that the year before he gave this interview, he published *On Drink*, which spends some considerable time discussing wine, including burgundy.

6. Philip Larkin, "Toads," *The Less Deceived* (London: Marvell Press, 1955).

7. Jim's article ("The Economic Influence of the Developments in Shipbuilding Techniques, 1450 to 1485") has a disconcerting air of authenticity about it. In his *Anatomy of Britain Today*, Anthony Sampson lists "the first four entries . . . for the degree of Bachelor of Letters in Modern History at Oxford in 1961"; they read:
    A study of the "Narratio de Fundatione" of Fountains Abbey.
    The rise and influence of the House of Luxemburg-Ligny from 1371.
    A bibliography of Henry St. John, Viscount Bolingbroke.
    The Archiepiscopate of William de Corbeil 1123–36.
Anthony Sampson, *Anatomy of Britain Today*, 2nd ed. (1965; New York, Harper Colophon, 1966), p. 228.

8. "Books? Don't make him laugh: apart from the juvenile one about the sods in Asia Minor there had been three others, all solidly 'researched,' all well received in the places that received them, all quite likely to be on the shelves of the sort of library concerned, all combined still bringing in enough cash to keep him in bus fares. Three or, in the eye of charity, four books were probably enough to justify Dr Jaques ('Jake') Richardson's life. They were bloody well going to have to." Kingsley Amis, *Jake's Thing* (London: Hutchinson, 1978), p. 100. All subsequent references will be to this edition and cited in the text.

9. Kingsley Amis, *Lucky Jim* (London: Victor Gollancz, 1954), p. 225. All subsequent references will be to this edition and cited in the text.

10. Margaret Drabble, *The Ice Age* (London: Weidenfeld and Nicolson, 1977), p. 97. All subsequent references will be to this edition and cited in the text.

11. John Fowles, *Daniel Martin* (Toronto: Collins, 1977), p. iii.

12. William Golding, *Darkness Visible* (London: Faber and Faber, 1979).

13. John Milton, *Paradise Lost* I, II. 61–69.

14. Anthony Burgess, *1985* (London: Hutchinson, 1978), pp. 134–35. All subsequent references will be to this edition and cited in the text.

15. Kingsley Amis, *Russian Hide and Seek* (London: Hutchinson, 1980).

Kingsley Amis

Patrick Swinden

Near the middle of Kingsley Amis's second novel, *That Uncertain Feeling,* there is a very funny scene in which John Lewis and Elizabeth Gruffyd-Williams are almost discovered making love in the lounge of Vernon Gruffyd-Williams's house. Lewis, escaping into the hall, avoids bumping into Gruffyd-Williams and his guests by concealing himself in a cloakroom under the stairs. The whole of the next chapter (10) is given over to a farcical account of Lewis's travels around the house, part of the time disguised as a plumber, part of the time as a Welshwoman; and his escape in the Welshwoman's clothes out of the house, onto a bus, and, finally, through the streets of the town to his own front door. Though it is a not untypical Amis situation, its general aspect, and some particular incidents, recall scenes from Whitehall farces of the forties and fifties, or from Ealing films of about the same period. Indeed, it provided one of the high spots of the film *Only Two Can Play,* a free adaptation of this novel which, though released in 1962, employed the services of several of the old Ealing hands of the 1950s.

Other features of the episode, however, are typical Amis. None more so than the display of motive, or rather lack of it, for Lewis's extraordinary behaviour. For Amis deliberately removes Lewis's most obvious reason for behaving as he does (i.e. to conceal from Gruffyd-Williams the fact of his presence in the house) by having Elizabeth get up and dress quickly enough to go and tell her husband that Lewis is visiting them—in entirely uncompromising circumstances. So Lewis has no good reason to leave the house at all, certainly not to go to great lengths to escape from it unseen. Having decided that that is what he *will* do, he has no reason to prolong the plumbing charade for as long as he does, and none at all, so far as I can see, for disguising himself in the Welshwoman's dress. Later this dressing up is interpreted as an act of therapy to enable Lewis to face the outside world again. But, by the time he leaves, the disguise has become a mere encumbrance. Just beforehand he had promised himself that he would "soon have these farcical garments off," and would have had them off if a couple of Gruffyd-Williams's guests had not entered the room and been about to draw back the curtain of the

From *The English Novel in History and Society, 1940–1980* (New York, St. Martin's Press, 1984):180–209. Reprinted with permission of St. Martin's Press and Macmillan Press Ltd.

205

window-seat in which he was hiding. Lewis's behaviour in the Gruffyd-Williams house is psychologically quite implausible. Amis has made it so deliberately. He has gone out of his way to divert our attention from Lewis as a comprehensible, motive-driven human being, to the sequence of events into which he has been precipitated by the controlling whim of his creator.

What does this incident tell us about the kind of novelist Amis is—beyond the fact that he is an accomplished writer of comedy which usually has broad farcical overtones? I think, first of all, there are a number of things it tells us about the kind of novelist he is *not,* but that many critics have assumed he resembles much more closely than in fact he does. I am referring to two, related traditions of English writing with which Amis has been associated: the tradition of the Edwardian novel of social comedy, as represented by Wells in such novels as *Kipps* and *Mr. Polly;* and the "tradition" (hardly established by 1954, when Amis published his first novel) of the post-war novel of revolt against middle-class *mores* and middle-class literary, as well as social, assumptions. This latter tradition is represented by "working-class" novelists of the fifties such as Alan Sillitoe, David Storey and Keith Waterhouse; and it has had lumped with it, by association of a rather facile kind, the picaresque early fiction of John Wain and Iris Murdoch.

The Wellsian aspects of Amis's work have been discovered in his "realistic" presentation of lower-middle-class heroes in situations that dramatise movements among different social groups within the same waveband of the English class system. But, whatever the reality of Amis's interest in a similar area of the English social structure half a century after Wells, his method of dealing with it is totally different. In any case, movements across the classes during those fifty years have been so rapid, so perplexing, that it cannot ever be said that Amis is describing the same social groups that Wells described. Other novelists, such as Thomas Hinde and V. S. Pritchett, have come much closer than Amis has to emulating Wells—as even a cursory reading of *Mr. Nicholas* or, especially, *Mr. Beluncle* will make abundantly clear.

Pritchett's description of how Beluncle's house is furnished, for example, with its emphasis on the impermanence of chairs, tables, even carpets that are "on loan" from the directors of the business ("Be careful with it. It may have to go back"), is both funny and informative about Beluncle's character. He is a queer mixture of obstinacy and diffidence, of overbearing pomposity in no way mitigated by a disturbing undercurrent of financial worry. All of this is vividly suggested by Pritchett's description of the rooms he occupies. Amis's writing has something of the ebullience of Pritchett's, but little of its capacity to bring to life that area of a character's personality which lies half-way between the sort of person he really is and the effect he makes on other people. The description of Patrick Standish's room (*Take a Girl Like You,* ch. 4), for example, in the "row of Auntie Minnie houses" where he rents a flat, is serviceable, in so far as it establishes the physical location of Patrick's attempts to seduce Jenny Bunn and Sheila Torkington. Its *décor* of books and gramophone records also tells us something of Patrick's tastes and outlook. But it goes no farther than that. The success of Amis's descriptions of what happens in the room has more to do with the play of Standish's mind over and beyond the objects in it than with any imaginative interaction between the room and its owner. When Amis does make an imaginative observation about some aspect of his hero's environment, it is likely to be of a less personal and more generally characteristic kind. His description of the bar at the Queen's Head (in *That Uncertain Feeling*), for example, establishes the pretentiousness of the place, and of all such places, with its list of warming-pans, soup ladles, candle-snuffers hung around the walls, "and a thing that would have come in handy for getting fried ostrich eggs off a frying pan." The uselessness, silliness and typicality of this last object, which we have all seen at some local Queen's Head, are brilliantly caught in the reference to ostrich eggs. But beyond adding to the impression we have already received, that pretentious people patronise pretentious pubs, the description tells us nothing.

Externals have a way of remaining external in Amis, while even in an extravert novelist such as Wells or Pritchett they tend to enliven our appreciation of the characters' minds at, it is only fair to say, a relatively unintrospective level of activity. Pritchett handles those elements of a situation that lie both on its surface and just a little below it in brief, almost aphoristic passages that would not have discredited Dickens. In *Mr. Beluncle* "Miss More did not know how to leave; she knew only how to be replaced"; "Mr. Chilly watched his restless hands, surprised they had remembered to come with him"; and Mr. Beluncle's meetings with Mrs. Robinson at Lippard's tea-rooms "were a kind of suicide pact in which their voices and their autobiographies died together over the counter twice a week." There is none of this affectionate curiosity about people in Amis. His characters' negotiations with the world around them is consequently embattled and irritable, lacking authorial intervention by recourse to which the one might have been explained by reference to the other.

Though Amis's heroes share something of the awkwardness and social inexperience of their Edwardian predecessors, as mediated through the work of Pritchett and Hinde, their place in the world is more exposed than Kipps's, or Beluncle's, or Mr. Nicholas's. This is because their author's prose has the effect of detaching them from the things that are in the world—things that in Wells and Pritchett are also devices for "colouring" their characters, and giving them a purchase on life in linguistic terms even when their purchase on the life of society remains precarious.

Amis's lack of common ground with the "angry" novelists of the fifties is much easier to show than his separation from the Edwardian tradition, mainly because it is much more complete. Beyond a rather cavalier treatment of plot, there is nothing much in Amis to compare with Sillitoe or Waterhouse. Not only is the class background of his heroes completely different from theirs (if his characters are a class above Wells's and Pritchett's, they are as much as two classes above Sillitoe's); the form their rebellion against society takes is also strikingly at variance with that represented by Arthur Seaton in *Saturday Night and Sunday Morning,* or the anonymous Borstal boy of "The Loneliness of the Long Distance Runner." Seaton and the boy are possessed by a nihilistic destructive energy. But their urge to destroy is revealed mainly in their detestation of people who occupy superior positions to their own in the social hierarchy, people who are placed in positions of authority over them, such as the works manager or the governor of the Borstal. Although it may seem unfocused and hysterical much of the time, Sillitoe's anger is directed at what he seems to agree with his characters is a large-scale social abuse, a fundamental defect in the system. In spite of his early leftward leanings, nothing could be more different from Amis's own very real anger, and its relation to the view of society that emerges from a reading of his novels.

For Amis's anger is anger at the human condition. That sounds a portentous way of describing the achievement of a popular comic novelist, but I believe it is true all the same. Anger—apparently aroused by the pretensions and hypocrisies of society, actually by something having little to do with real social abuses—is the characteristic response of the Amis hero to his situation. Before we go on to look at how that anger is expressed, and how it is related to other emotional traits—lust, boredom, irritability and panic—we need to trace its origins to a deeper stratum of the English literary tradition, the eighteenth-century picaresque novel. Here is a form and an expression of attitudes more closely resembling what Amis is trying to achieve than was present in either of the two more recent fictional analogues I have been looking at. Reference to the eighteenth century might also help to explain the peculiar nature of farce in Amis, to which I referred *à propos* of the passage from *That Uncertain Feeling* with which this chapter began.

Amis's admiration of the eighteenth-century novelists is no secret. The most categorical statement of it is made by Garnet Bowen, the publisher hero of *I Like It Here,* whose views on Fielding closely parallel Amis's own:

> Bowen thought about Fielding. Perhaps it was worth dying in your forties if two hundred years later you were the only non-contemporary novelist who could be read with unaffected and whole-hearted interest, the only one who never had to be apologised for or excused on the grounds of changing taste. And how sensible to live in the world of fear. Did that make it a simplified world? Perhaps, but that hardly mattered beside the existence of a moral seriousness that could be made apparent without the aid of evangelical puffing and blowing.

Before we look at this more closely it might be a good idea to throw into the melting-pot two other, less well-known passages on the same subject. The first of them is spoken by Roger Micheldene, the hero of *One Fat Englishman,* and suggests an evaluation of Samuel Richardson almost as high as the one

Bowen offered of Fielding. Micheldene claims that "Even before *Clarissa* there had only been a few touches in Aphra Behn and Defoe (*Colonel Jack,* of course, not *Crusoe* or *Moll Flanders*), and what was there since?" Precious little, according to Maurice Allington, landlord of the "Green Man," who, though unamiable, like Micheldene, nevertheless, also like Micheldene, shows good taste in his choice of reading. Allington has no novels in his library. He finds the art of the novelist "puny and piffling,"

> one that, even at its best, can render truthfully no more than a few minor parts of the total world it pretends to take as its field of reference. A man has only to feel some emotion, anything differentiated at all, and spend a minute speculating how this would be rendered in a novel . . . to grasp the pitiful inadequacy of all prose fiction to the task it sets itself.

Of course, we shall be reminded, Micheldene, Allington *et alia* are characters in a novel, not Amis speaking *in propria persona.* I hope I shall be able to expose the fallacy of looking at Amis's principal characters in this way (a fallacy so far as anything critically useful can be extruded from it) at a subsequent stage of my argument. However, it is true that, some one hundred pages after Allington has expressed the views quoted above, he does make at least one literary judgement with which we might expect Amis to disagree. Stopping by a supermarket in Cambridge, Allington (who is speaking) "went in and bought something I had never heard of by a writer whose first book, a satire on provincial life, I remembered had been commended at the time . . . I got through about forty minutes' worth of this . . . before going out and dropping it into a rubbish basket." It looks as if *Lucky Jim* is to be included in the list of post-Smollett novels Bowen, Micheldene and Allington can't bring themselves to read.

Two features of Bowen's confession, and one of Allington's, strike me as being of more than passing significance. Bowen acknowledges that Fielding's is a "simplified world." Nevertheless it is one in which moral seriousness, divorced from a too explicit advertisement of didactic aims, is plainly at work. The more recent novelists to whom Allington refers—Stendhal and Proust—are dismissed because they are unable to render in their chosen form any kind of emotion, or indeed "anything differentiated at all." Taken together these comments suggest something about Amis's ambitions as a novelist, and about his achievement too. He has created a flattened-out world in which, or on the surface of which (it is *all* surface), the complexities and subtleties of human feeling have been deliberately excluded. Poetry, even Lord de Tabley's poetry according to Maurice Allington, can do that kind of thing much better. The novelist's job, in Amis's view, is different. His seriousness will show itself in the way he handles characters and situations that have been simplified in the interests of moral clarity. As in Fielding, this leads in the direction of the picaresque. Even more than in Fielding, it leads in the direction of farce.

It also leads to parody—not just within the novels (though there is plenty of that too, of which more later) but also in their overall structure. After all, Fielding began his career as a novelist with a parody of Richardson's *Pamela*. So why shouldn't Amis make his fourth novel (*Take a Girl Like You*) into a parody of *Clarissa?* That is what we get when Patrick Standish, the Lovelace of the story, spends his time in the novel trying to seduce pretty, little Jenny Bunn (also pursued by the odious Dick Thompson—i.e. Soames in a fifties semi), and rapes her whilst she is unconscious at the end. *That Uncertain Feeling* is probably a parody of Fielding, John Lewis being pursued by aristocratic Elizabeth Gruffyd-Williams just as Tom Jones was pursued by Lady Bellaston—although nice ordinary Jean, like Sophia Western, is the girl he really loves. Late novels such as *The Anti-Death League* and *The Green Man* make their moral point to a large extent by parodying more contemporary fictional genres—the Le Carré–Deighton spy thriller, and the later nineteenth- and early twentieth-century ghost story respectively. There are pronounced hints of parody too (coming closer to home) in such novels as *I Want It Now* and *Girl, 20*. I hasten to add that these are affectionate parodies, not vicious lampoons. Amis delights in mimicking the novels he admires, and clearly feels that the plots and situations deployed in them contain much that can still be made morally persuasive.

It is possible to agree, I think, that Amis has succeeded in his ambition to simplify his material, at the same time as denying that he has got away from the expression of emotion. But the emotion belongs to him, the author. It is a prominent feature of his moral awareness, and through him it infiltrates a sizeable percentage of his characters. These characters are not free inhabitants of a world Amis has created for them to live in. They are expressions of his own temperament, usually in a very direct way. That is to say, in a quite simple sense they tend to "stand for" him; they have been constructed so as to enable him to speak from them in his own tone of voice, often, but not always, expressing his own opinions. Other characters are set up as targets against which this tone of voice and set of attitudes is encouraged to expend itself. Ieuan Johns, Professor Welch and Bertrand in *Lucky Jim,* Gareth Probert and Bill Evans in *That Uncertain Feeling,* Dick Thompson, F. B. Charlton and Charlie Crosland in *Take a Girl Like You* are examples of such characters. Almost everybody except Micheldene in *One Fat Englishman* is one of them.

Women usually don't qualify, Amis being on the whole too idealistic or too chivalrous (more eighteenth-century virtues?) to insult them in the downright way he goes about insulting the men. This is usually bad for the women, because, not having been allowed to exist as free characters, they are not being allowed to exist as comic stooges either ("stooge" is in any case a word that they use about men, never about other women—see Jenny Bunn in *Take a Girl Like You*). That leaves them in a sort of limbo from which only one or two of the minor characters (such as Lewis's landlady and his colleague

Jenkins's wife) and perhaps one of the major ones (Margaret Peel in *Lucky Jim*) escape into some semblance of life. The others, even girls such as Jenny on whose behalf Amis has put in a great deal of work, are inert. Their behaviour is either discontinuous and therefore baffling (thus Jean Lewis: who could believe that she would in any circumstances enter into a clandestine affair with Gareth Probert?) or utterly hazy in a mannishly idealising sort of way (see Catherine Casement in *The Anti-Death League*). I think the trouble is that, since none of these women can be allowed to be exposed to the full brunt of Amis's comedy, and they can't become like some of the men and act as substitutes for Amis's own presence in the novel, they have no alternative open to them but to become characters—separate and discrete—and Amis can't manage characters of this sort, as Bowen's comments on Fielding make clear. Therefore they end up as nothing much at all, except fixed points in the plot towards which the men can advance or from which they can retreat, as the situation requires.

I made the point that many of Amis's male characters speak in his tone of voice though they might not invariably express his own opinions. Ever since Jim Dixon resented Professor Welch's singing "filthy Mozart" in his bath on the night of the burnt sheets (*Lucky Jim*, ch. 6) most if not all of Amis's most sympathetic, or at any rate centrally positioned, characters have given expression to opinions that we know, from other, non-fictional sources, Amis doesn't hold, indeed positively detests. Jim's hatred of Mozart is just one early example of this. Standish's dismissal of the Latin authors (he teaches Classics at a public school—and incidentally also hates Beethoven) is another. But the most atrocious unAmisian opinions are ventilated by two characters—Micheldene in *One Fat Englishman* and Sir Roger Vandervane in *Girl, 20*—who at other times speak a lot of sense where we would usually expect to hear humbug. And they do this in a rude and forthright vein characteristic of their author. With his usual strokes of broad comedy Amis has established Micheldene as an appalling snob, snuff-taker and Americaphobe, and Vandervane as an aging Humbert Humbert who goes into youth culture and the pop scene in a big way. We have to pay attention to the nonsense they speak about all these things at the same time as we have to admire their welcome dismissal of other forms of cant—such as the rubbish that is represented by Irving Macher's novel, *Blinkie Heaven,* in *One Fat Englishman;* or the politics of envy and meanness Vandervane keeps brushing up against in *Girl, 20*.

The most reliable guide to Amis's approval or otherwise of his male characters is their attitude towards women. If they show due appreciation of women as sex objects, then they can invariably be counted on to be "above the line." This is the one consistent area of comparison between Jim Dixon, John Lewis, Roger Micheldene, Maurice Allington, James Churchill, and so on. This, of course, is bad news for the women, not only because they might prefer to be thought of as something more elevating than sex toys, but also because they can't very well go about making passes at each other, because then they'd be lesbians, and nowhere in his novels before *The Anti-Death League* (with the sympathetic portrait of Max Hunter; Joyce Allington and Diana Maybury in *The Green Man* show a great deal of physical interest in each other too) does Amis display any enthusiasm for homosexual practices. However, this lowest common denominator does help us to separate one goat from another, even if it leaves us nowhere so far as the sheep are concerned. So long as the sex thing is all right no amount of twaddle about drink, snuff, books, music or Americans will finally bring the hero down—even if he is fat, filthy or, like Graham McClintoch in *Take a Girl Like You,* a "stooge."

The description of Amis's novels I am skirting is one that sees them as comic, satirical and irresponsible. Comic I have already discussed, and I shall go into the detail of the comedy in due course. But satirical *and* irresponsible? Here again I am bearing in mind Amis's tastes in eighteenth-century fiction, and the most recent exemplars of what it was that he found to admire in that fiction. I am thinking of Swift and Evelyn Waugh in particular. We know that Amis admires Waugh's novels (see his essay "My Kind of Comedy," *Twentieth Century,* July 1961), and an article he wrote for the *New York Review of Books* (7 July 1957) strongly suggests that, when he thinks about satire, Swift is the satirist who is most likely to spring to mind. "A society such as ours," he writes, "in which the forms of power are changing and multiplying, needs above all the restraining influences of savage laughter. Even if that influence at times seems negligible, the satirist's laughter is valid as a gesture—a gesture on the side of reason." "Savage laughter"; *"saeva indignatio."* This is the laughter of Swift at the end of *Gulliver's Travels,* where Gulliver, returned from the land of the Houyhnhnms and the Yahoos, is the ridiculous mouthpiece of his author's despair at the fact that he would have men behave reasonably, if it were a reasonable thing to expect men so to do.

Amis would have men behave reasonably. But he would have them behave lecherously too. The illogical compatibility between reason and lust, both of them distractions from what otherwise would be the unbearable boredom and futility of life, is what Amis wants to show us. Even though it makes you look ridiculous, the portraits of Standish, Micheldene *et alia* are telling us, it is possible to be intelligently civilised and downright randy at the same time. Just as the author of *Gulliver* can approve and detest his character's behaviour at the end of the *Travels;* and just as, two hundred years later, Evelyn Waugh can admire and despair of Sebastian Flyte's views on contemporary life and manners, so Amis can invite us to judge Micheldene's behaviour commendable and ridiculous. That is what I meant when I used the phrase "satirical and irresponsible." Something in the nature of life makes our best judgements about it perversely inappropriate. To be most aware of how far existence falls short of what we are inclined to suppose are legitimate claims on it, to realise how deficient and unsatisfactory it is, is to be most dangerously and comically exposed to the consequences of that deficiency, that unsatisfactory quality of being. Such a perception about life underlines whatever else Amis's most "sympathetic" characters say and do. It is what makes them so ridiculous and so right, so misanthropic at one moment and so exuberantly involved with life at another, so alternately admirable and off-putting. It is, in fact, what makes them so much like Kingsley Amis himself.

The difference between the kind of novelist many people think Amis is and the kind of novelist I am arguing he is can be highlighted if we put side by side with his work the work of another gifted and very funny writer several years his junior, Malcolm Bradbury. It so happens that they both began their adult lives as university teachers of English (Bradbury still is one) and both of their first novels were set in provincial universities rather like the ones in which they taught. But "rather like" in a different sense, depending on which author is being discussed. Because, although Amis and Bradbury are both comic novelists, and being a comic novelist involves some degree of stylisation of reality, nevertheless there are discriminations to be made. Bradbury's university in *Eating People Is Wrong* is much more realistically presented than Amis's is in *Lucky Jim*. No professor in Bradbury is quite so monstrously caricatured as Amis's Neddy Welch. Indeed his sympathetic central character, Stuart Treece, *is* a professor—not a junior lecturer like Jim Dixon. Also there is no occasion, like Dixon's lecture on "Merrie England," that so patently belongs to a never-never land in which the most humble functionary in a university department is chosen to deliver a set-piece lecture on the occasion of the university's open day. In any case nobody in a university history department in 1954, the date of the novel's first appearance, could have imagined for one moment that he could get away with a lecture on this subject, which was as clearly understood then as it is now to be a fiction of one of the more trivial aspects of the Victorian Gothic revival. All of Bradbury's situations in *Eating People Is Wrong* are plausible. Something like them could have happened—even Mr. Eborebelosa getting stuck in the lavatory. Many of the incidents in *Lucky Jim* couldn't have happened at all. They are conventional exaggerations of what university life is supposed to be like, further exaggerated in the service of Amis's farcical requirements.

More important, Amis's novel is not in any serious way interested in the role the university should play in contemporary society. How can it be, when the people who inhabit it are so grotesquely unrepresentative of the people who teach and learn in such places? Dixon hates the very thought of books, libraries, history, the Middle Ages, anything that could conceivably be expected to interest a university lecturer in Medieval History—which, of course, Dixon knows nothing at all about. Treece, on the other hand, knows a fair bit about English poetry. He is interested in Proust, enjoys conversation with members of the Sociology department, and spends a lot of his time, when he is not failing his driving-test, brooding on the place of the academic intelligence in modern life. He is outraged when he finds that someone in the university has been pulling pages out of the current edition of *Essays in Criti-*

cism and argues, passionately as well as amusingly, about the changing function of the intelligentsia and the effect this change is likely to produce on liberal values in society at large. What follows is a transcription of Treece's thoughts as he reflects on the violation of *Essays in Criticism:*

> The ordinary laws of sound human conduct were slipping; and the people who were selling out were those within the citadel—one's own friends, people one invited to one's home, people who did not destroy aimlessly but with a philosophy of life that comprehended destruction. To Treece, the existence of people, of liberal intellectuals, like himself was infinitely precious. . . . But those who live by the liberalism shall perish by the liberalism. Their own lack of intransigence, their inevitable effeteness, betrayed them. Already liberal intellects like his own found themselves on the periphery. The end was coming, as people like him had less and less of a social function, and were driven out into an effete and separate world of their own, to the far edge of alienation. It was on communication that they depended, and the channels were being closed from the other side; and in the tearing up of *Essays in Criticism* Treece saw the end of the liberal tradition.

This is what *Eating People Is Wrong* is about: a serious issue, not, as in *Lucky Jim,* a farcical transformation of reality into fantasy. Earlier, Treece had described himself as a liberal humanist who believes in original sin. Here he examines the consequences of being that sort of person. Of course there is a comic discrepancy between the nature of the offence Treece is contemplating, and the tone of outrage it has elicited from him. That is funny. But what he is saying, funny in the circumstances, may also be true. The trivial event might be a sign of something altogether more important, something that might assume very much more serious forms in the future. In *Eating People Is Wrong,* for the most part it doesn't. The emphasis falls instead on the discrepancy, to which Treece testifies here, between his sense of the importance of his liberal beliefs and the peripheral position he occupies in society. There is a further discrepancy between Treece's theoretical convictions about liberalism (and the value they attribute to personal relationships), and the difficulties he experiences in forming satisfactory personal relationships with almost everyone in the novel, from Mr. Eborebelosa, the African visiting student, to Emma Fielding and Louis Bates. The comedy arises out of Treece's failure to make very much, or anything at all, of these relationships. It arises out of the mismatching of his genuinely humble appreciation of other people and his pompous supposition that, even when the way he treats them is causing irritation or dismay, his view of life makes him responsible for them. The humour arises directly out of the moral concern Bradbury shares with Treece. It is not the anarchic farce of Amis. It stands in an altogether different relation to reality.

In his "Afterword" to *Eating People Is Wrong,* accompanying the 1979 reprint, Bradbury claims that "the liberalism that makes Treece virtuous also makes him inert." Treece represents "both the absurdity and the virtue of liberalism . . . engaging with its own inconsistency and anticipating its own destruction." This is fair comment, though, as Bradbury would admit, in the novel itself the date at which liberalism is doomed to destruction seems very far away. That is why its tone is so effervescent, its treatment of the humanist dilemma so untouched by anxiety. Until the end, that is to say, when Treece's fortunes take a sudden turn for the worse. We leave him in a hospital ward also occupied by Bates, who has tried to commit suicide after being told by Emma that she has been having an affair with Treece. This is a gratuitously dark note to close on, and one that doesn't indicate very clearly the way in which Bradbury's comic talent was to develop over the next twenty years. More to the point are references in the "Afterword" to a change in cultural circumstances that has taken place since *Eating People Is Wrong* was first published. It seems we no longer share "a sense of possessing a common . . . reality, as I think the fifties did." The destruction of liberalism is well under way, at the hands of the "stern historicism" and the "collectivist passions" of the sixties. This, and the "contradiction between our humanist expectations and our sense of ourselves as exposed historical performers," also referred to in the "Afterword," are what darken the foreground of the very different comedy of Bradbury's most recent novel.

The events described in *The History Man* take place in 1967–8. People like Stuart Treece have little or no place in the University of Watermouth, where Howard Kirk, senior lecturer in Sociology, dominates the scene. He and his wife Barbara have manufactured out of an "interpretation" of their own lives a critique of the liberal cultural values which are collapsing all around them. The ineffectuality of liberal attitudes is demonstrated by the conduct of Annie Callender, a young lecturer in the English department, and Henry Beamish, a renegade from the collectivist passions that Howard exploits with totalitarian rigour and Marxist–Freudian illogic. For Howard, human beings are not the unpredictable, free and opaque individuals who puzzled Stuart Treece in *Eating People Is Wrong*. They are predictable, determined and transparent. Especially transparent. They can be explained completely, explained away one might almost say, in a "socio-psychological context." As a result, human nature has become "a particular type of relation to the temporal and historical process, culturally conditioned and afforded." It is "a particular performance within the available rôle sets." The only way anyone can develop is by "innovating" through "manipulating options among the rôle sets." At first Barbara shared Howard's views about human nature. She even conspired with him to publicise his views about the determination and innovation of social roles. But, when Howard makes a career out of the publicity and leaves Barbara holding the (inevitable) baby, she begins to change her mind. She wonders "what it's got to do with real people." She accuses him of being "a kind of self-made fictional character who's got the whole story on his side, just because he happens to be writing it." That is exactly what Howard does. He confuses history, or at any rate his little bit of history, with a programme of self-advancement, and identifies necessity with the quest for self-satisfaction. This produces one kind of comedy, expressed through the plot of the novel. Something rather like it, but not quite the same, produces another kind of comedy, which has very little to do with the plot, much more to do with Bradbury's manipulation of sociological jargon. I find the second kind of comedy more subtle and more satirically exposing than the first.

I think this is because the plot of the novel cheats Howard of the little that is his due. He is an arrogant but confused person, much more at the mercy of his own self-justifying ideas about history and social determinism than he would need to have been to have perpetrated the moral outrage upon which the plot of the novel turns. For at the very end of the novel Howard more or less agrees with Miss Callender that he organised the scandal of George Carmody's grades so that he could make use of him and Felicity Phee to worm his way into Annie's bed. " 'But what was it for?' asks Annie. 'I wanted you,' says Howard, 'I just had to find a way to you.' " This seems to me to show a calculating selfishness on Howard's part, a willingness to damage two other people's lives in the service of entirely trivial schemes of self-advancement, which is inconsistent with his identification with the historical process that lies at the root of the comedy. Isn't the point Bradbury is making in *The History Man* that Howard Kirk is a stupid, not a vicious man? His relationships with his wife, his children, his colleagues, lack seriousness. He simply doesn't understand them. His materialist beliefs about progress and privacy and history fail to provide him with a moral vocabulary, or even more beliefs, which might enable him to make sense of himself and the world he lives in.

To claim that Howard lacks seriousness, or anything more than a rudimentary moral sense, is not to imply that he lacks idealism. It is to suggest that his ideals are completely identified with history, and that the only way he can develop consistently is to "innovate" by "manipulating options among the rôle sets." But the impression has not been given that the "rôle sets" include unscrupulously plotting his own self-gratification by devising a play and forcing everybody else to accept rôles in it—rôles of which they themselves are quite unaware. Or has it? Is Kirk in fact endowed with a sort of Leninist intelligence, making use of events whilst pretending to be controlled by them? That is what the plot tells us. The breathless present-tense narrative, showing Howard as totally wrapped up in the present, oblivious to the realities of past and future, seems to be implying the opposite. So does the way he tends to disappear under the levelling barrage of sociological jargon he is made to speak every time he opens his mouth, or his book. The plot seems to be pulling in the opposite direction to the dialogue, and to other ways in which the prose underlines Bradbury's attitudes. But either way the comedy is making a serious moral point about contemporary life and thought. It is a technique for dramatising and making comprehensible those "collectivist passions" of the sixties to which Bradbury referred in his "Afterword" to *Eating People Is Wrong*.

Compare this with what happens in *Lucky Jim*. Dixon has nothing of the morally representative existence Treece shares with Howard Kirk. His presence on the teaching-staff of a university is in any but a superficial sense an irrelevance. That is where his author was at the time, and to put him there too was a matter of convenience rather than strategy. Intelligent conversation is non-existent; students, even, are non-existent (with the exception of Michie, who makes no contribution to the plot, but appears occasionally to remind us that students do crop up from time to time in universities). Dixon has colleagues, such as Goldsmith and Johns; but Goldsmith says nothing about history, and Johns's position on the administrative staff is made use of only in so far as it allows Dixon to flush a sample of his insurance policies down the lavatory. I have already discussed the fantasy figure that is Professor Welch, and the fantasy occasion that is Dixon's lecture. Clearly the university is nothing but a geographical location, a building with people rushing about inside it for Dixon to bump into or avoid as the progress of the plot dictates.

Dixon's revolt isn't a revolt against anything that can be described as academic values, liberal or otherwise. Such values do not exist in *Lucky Jim*. Several instances of pretentiousness, hypocrisy, pomposity and humbug exist, but these qualities are merely personal. They don't establish a moral or cultural context to be investigated and ridiculed. That is why F. R. Karl, in his otherwise intelligent account of what he thinks is an Amis–Wain–Sillitoe axis in contemporary English fiction, is mistaken when he takes Amis to task for "nowhere making it clear that Jim's level of revolt is not also his."[1] But Jim's level of revolt *is* Amis's. Jim is one of those characters I discussed above, who are mouthpieces for the expression of Amis's own dissatisfaction and annoyance with the world. To have subjected him to the ironic treatment Karl thinks is appropriate would have been to convert him into a free character of a kind I have suggested Amis takes no interest in. Of course Amis wants to outrage the reader by emphasising the philistinism and sheer rudeness that accompany Dixon's hatred of cant. He also makes Jim physically unprepossessing in order to put some superficial distance between his character and himself. But, in all the important senses, Jim acts on Amis's behalf—pulling his faces, enacting his fantasies, perpetrating his jokes. In this respect Amis is not a bit like Fielding. The irony has to be missing where the Fielding-*like* comic incidents are being used to display a temperament rather than to create a world.

In so far as anything morally interesting is going on at all in *Lucky Jim,* it has to do with Dixon's decision to sever his relationship with Margaret Peel and run away with Christine Callaghan. Although Jim's scenes with Margaret allow her to let off a little psychological steam (Margaret's success as a character anticipates Amis's other successes with temperamentally "difficult" wives and girlfriends—Martha Thompson, for example, in *Take a Girl Like You,* or Adela Bastable in *Ending Up*), they are on the whole rather tedious; as are Jim's reflections on his guilt, or unwillingness to accept his guilt, over the way he has treated her. "Whatever passably decent treatment Margaret had had from him," he supposes, "was the result of a temporary victory of fear over irritation and/or pity over boredom." The irritation and boredom come over very well. It is the fear and the pity which remain mere words, and rather too many of them. In any case, Dixon is let off the hook with Margaret when Catchpole, her previous "lover," tells him the truth about the overdose of sleeping-pills she took the night Dixon was expected to call at her flat. This has always struck me as a reason for Dixon to stay with Margaret rather than to leave her. Her phoney suicide attempt was clearly an act of desperation. Although Dixon might well take the view that he owes her rather less in the emotional sense than she has led him to believe he does, he surely can't think that her behaviour in this matter provides him with a *carte blanche* to forget about her altogether and run off with Christine. In spite of the moral fuss Dixon makes about Margaret, his preference for Christine is really no more than a consequence of his frequently articulated conviction that "nice things are nicer than nasty things," and that Christine's character is "workable," while Margaret's is not. That doesn't seem like a very profound solution to Dixon's dilemma. He has simply substituted pragmatic for moral reasons for behaving as he does. The inconsequentiality of this form of moralising by a character is demonstrated even more graphically in *Take a Girl Like You* when Standish subjects Sheila Torkington to an earnest, carefully considered, ever-so-closely-reasoned lecture on why it would be wrong for him to enter into an affair with the seventeen-year-old daughter of his headmaster, and then goes on to say "However, since you've taken the trouble to turn up . . ." and seduces her. Standish is one of Amis's most admired male leads. I suppose we must interpret his behaviour here as just another of those occasions when nice things are nicer than nasty ones, even when the nice thing in this instance has a long chin and turns out to be two months pregnant.

At the end of *Lucky Jim* Dixon doesn't only get the girl, he gets the money too. More precisely, he gets the job in London, as Julius Gore-Urquart's secretary, that Bertrand Welch was fishing for at the university dance. Bertrand obviously doesn't deserve the job. He is a talentless nincompoop with genteel *fin de siècle* views about art, which Dixon quite properly ridicules. Besides, he is Neddy Welch's son. But does Dixon deserve it? Gore-Urquart's opinion is that, although he hasn't got the qualifications for the work, "or any other work," he hasn't got the disqualifications either. What are the disqualifications Dixon hasn't got? No doubt being a conceited bore and pretentious twit like Bertrand is one of them. But aren't knowing nothing about art, and not having a clue about how to make oneself socially acceptable to people rather massive disqualifications too, for the private secretary to a "rich devotee of the arts" who intends to use him for "meeting people or telling people I can't meet them"? This is not the real world of art and patronage, any more than the university was a real place where people taught things and learned things. It is a world in which farcical vitality and advanced powers of ridicule are rewarded by material success, as a gesture in the direction of comic justice. Just as the funnier the things are that John Lewis does in his effort to escape from Gruffyd-Williams's house, the better time he deserves to have with Elizabeth on the beach, and the greater success he deserves to have at his interview with the library committee (later cancelled in favour of renewed marital harmony and a decent job with the coal board); so Dixon's reward is a reward he earns through his contribution to the farce rather than any sterling moral qualities he has displayed. Although there is more than enough moral fussing in *Lucky Jim,* there is hardly any moral content, in the sense of a correspondence between the moral complexion of what any of the characters *do* and the way the reader is invited to pass judgements on the kinds of people any of them *are.*

One other "moral" aspect *Lucky Jim* shares with many of Amis's later novels is the reappearance of the eighteenth- (and nineteenth-) century novel's dependence on rich benefactors, who are there to impress the hero with their admirable styles of life, and often to provide him with a route to salvation through a lavish display of financial patronage. Gore-Urquart is the first of such figures in Amis's work—as free with his whisky bottle as he is with his sinecures. Gruffyd-Williams plays the part in *That Uncertain Feeling.* Although at first he seems a dull stick, later it transpires that he is a sensitive soul and a handy *deus ex machina* to have about when Lewis and Elizabeth are involved in a car accident. He turns up again in a different guise in *Take a Girl Like You* as Julian Ormerod—treading a delicate balance between the predatory sexuality, and the decent respect for other people (note his attitude over the rape of Jenny Bunn), that Amis admires. Evidently the stream of seemingly inexhaustible financial benevolence shamelessly admired in characters ranging from Fielding's Squire Allworthy to Dickens's John Jarndyce, has not been dammed up by the welfare state. John Wain's Joe Lumley also benefits from such liberal patronage, in his employment as Mr. Bracewright's chauffeur in *Hurry on Down.* None of these notably angry novelists is in the slightest degree angry about Mr. Bracewright and his ilk. But I don't think this is immoral. It is just another piece of evidence that their characters don't live in anything resembling the real world. They are all creatures of fantasy, metaphors of the author's imagination kept busy by being projected onto the accidental twists and turns of an eighteenth-century picaresque narrative.

"Lumley is characteristic . . . of most of the Angry protagonists. They rebel and then find some niche for themselves that fails to accommodate their former intention. The honesty of the intention becomes transformed into the expedience of reality" (Karl). Well, Lumley is characteristic in this way. So are Dixon, Standish, Douglas Yandell (the narrator of *Girl, 20)* and others. But what Karl calls "the expedience of reality" has more in common with those merely literary rewards and punishments that eighteenth-century and Dickensian heroes have handed out to them in the final chapters of the novels they belong to. Amis isn't saying, "Look, Jim, everything you've done proves that you're a fundamentally good and decent fellow, just the right chap for the job Gore-Urquart wants to offer you, and the right chap for that nice girl Christine too." He is saying something much more like, "Well done, Jim, very funny performance. Off you go now and collect your money and give Christine Callaghan an extra one for me." The one interpretation is consistent with reading the book as if it were a basically serious, though comic, commentary on aspects of modern life and society. The other implies that the book is nothing of the kind, but a device for allowing Amis to let off steam about some of his favourite likes and dislikes by matching a persistent mood of exasperation with the kind of story that usually serves the purpose Karl believes this one does. I can understand why he thinks so: there is a fair amount of "evangelical puffing and blowing" in some of the "dead" scenes from the book. But these are superorogatory. On the other hand Amis does claim that he admires "moral seriousness" in novels, and we shall have to inquire as to how he gets this over in his own fiction. First, however, more needs to be said about the comic devices by means of which he conveys his exasperation, irritability and general dissatisfaction with the world, the foundation on which his novels are built.

Abasing himself before Margaret Peel after she has discovered his preference for Christine Callaghan over herself, Jim Dixon finds himself saying things about how he should stick by her, do the decent thing, not throw her over just because he finds another woman more attractive than he finds her. A minute or more passes by, and then Dixon realises that it wasn't really himself speaking. He wasn't really there at all, except as a sort of ventriloquist's dummy manipulated by someone else from outside:

> Dixon felt that his role in this conversation, as indeed in the whole of his relations with Margaret, had been directed by something outside himself and yet not directly present in her. He felt more than ever before that what he said and did arose not out of any willing on his part, nor even out of boredom, but out of a sense of situation. And where did that sense come from if, as it seemed, he took no share in willing it.

There is an obvious answer to that last question. It came from Kingsley Amis. After all, Dixon is only one of Amis's characters. Amis is doing all the thinking and talking, really. But that is not the point he wants to make here. Amis is not one of those novelists, who think it is enormously helpful to let their characters know that they are living in a book, not in a world jointly populated by themselves and their readers. On the other hand I have claimed that they don't seem to live very much in a world at all, if by a "world" we mean, as we usually do when we are discussing novels, a dense network of experiences, memories, places and relationships. I have also claimed that they are very much the expressions or objects of their author's sense of the absurdity of the world, and of his anger, irritation, and so forth, that that is what the world is like. So Dixon's awareness that his behaviour is automatic, and doesn't seem to issue from anything that could be described as his own motives or intentions or requirements is probably related to the way he is being manipulated by an author who is using him to say things and do things over which he himself has no control whatsoever.

Dixon's "automatic" behaviour in this scene with Margaret Peel is not an isolated occurrence. Over and over again in the novels, characters feel either that, like Dixon, they are not responsible for themselves, that they are doing things and saying things that have nothing to do with them and don't concern them; or that they have split personalities, in which what they are doing and what they are thinking are so far apart from each other that there is no logically explicable relation between them. Another good example of this is the episode, also in *Lucky Jim* (ch. 7), in which Dixon cannot rid himself of the notion that both he and Margaret are figures on celluloid, acting in a film that Margaret has scripted. She is acting much better than he is because he can't ignore the triteness of the dialogue, and speaks his lines with increasing exaggeration and insincerity. Examples of what I call the schizophrenic syndrome abound, increasing significantly in number and severity the closer the hero gets to sexual intercourse. Sexual contact is an almost sure-fire precipitant of this curious mental disturbance. Take Maurice Allington, for example, in *The Green Man*. Screwing Diana Maybury, his imaginative lucubrations revolve around performing a piano sonata at the same time as he is lunching off a plate of sandwiches (not altogether off the beam if we remember that he fills in much of the rest of the time counting to himself in units of thousands, with the object of calculating the time "to an accuracy of within two seconds per timed minute"). Or Patrick Standish with "Joan" in *Take a Girl Like You*. He divides his mind between declining the Latin *Dies* in the singular Common, and working out a chess problem involving the move (1) P–K4. The sexual operation itself is described in terms of mains-frequency fluctuation attendant on playing a gramophone record at $16^2/_3$ r.p.m. There are plenty of other such hiatuses between mind and body during the sexual act. For example, instead of declining Latin nouns, Micheldene quotes chunks of the *Aeneid* to himself, followed by a clutch of Greek irregulars, thence to Chaucer, and on to plushy Victorian fourteeners, his mind working "like a motor" until he withdraws into sheer inanition—"One of the really good ones, he thought."

Even allowing for a brake on premature ejaculation, this is an odd way of having sex. But, as I have implied, it is only the intensification of a discordance between thought and action that is widespread in Amis's fiction. At other times it almost takes on a metaphysical rather than a psychological colouring. For example, in *Lucky Jim* (ch. 18) Dixon looks out of the window of Professor Welch's car as it slows at a road junction. On one side he catches sight of his barber, eyeing two pretty girls who have stopped at a pillar box a few yards away. On the other side he sees a batsman being hit in the stomach by a cricket ball. Dixon's response is to wonder "whether this pair of *vignettes* was designed to illustrate the swiftness of divine retribution or its tendency to mistake its target." It seems as if the world at large manifests a lack of connection between thought and action (theologically speaking) or cause and effect (speaking in merely physical terms).

Description of such elaborate mental operations is almost invariably funny. And it combines with other features of Amis's comic method which depend for their effect on disjunctions of one kind or another: between what a character is thinking and what he is doing; or between what he is thinking and what Amis is doing with his thoughts—especially when he gets involved in the mechanics of transcribing actual events into written ones. In these latter cases there is once again a discrepancy between what the prose is telling us and what it sounds like when it is performing that function. The most obvious way the prose draws attention to itself is through the transcription of sounds which either do mean or seem to mean something as sounds, but which mean something entirely different, or nothing at all, when they are written down. In *Lucky Jim* this is happening all the time with Bertrand's habit of adding the suffix "am" to words ending with a long vowel: "Christine is my girl and stays my girl, got mam." In chapter 11 the words of a popular song are set down exactly as they sound, with ridiculous effect:

> Ah'll be parp tar gat you in a taxi, honny,
> Ya'd batter be raddy 'bout a parp-parp eight;
> Ahr, baby, dawn't be late,
> Ah'm gonna parp parp parp whan the band starts playeeng.

Just what you do when you "parp" leaves the mind in a state of pleasurable disbelief, in the same way as we shall never hear Nat King Cole quite as we used to after Amis's transcription of two immortal lines as "Dorling—it's increddabull—that you should be so—unforgeddabull" (*Take a Girl Like You*, ch. 8). Writing it down, in both cases, subtly yet outrageously changes the whole ambience of the song, and with it the human emotions it strives to express through *sound*.

This is not far away from verbal parody of a more conventional kind, and there is a great deal of this too in Amis, often very funny. Examples taken almost at random are the Dylan Thomas-ish lines of Gareth Probert's play *The Martyr* (*That Uncertain Feeling*, ch. 9); the blurb beneath the pin-up girl in John Lewis's magazine (the "Jolly Skipper") a double parody, this, both of that kind of blurb and of Amis's own poem "A Note on Wyatt" (though without the mixed metaphors in the latter case: *That Uncertain Feeling*, ch. 8); Mr.

Bunn's transformation of commonplace Anglo-Saxon surnames into their presumed Yiddish originals (*Take a Girl Like You,* ch. 15); the notes for Fr. Ayscue's sermon (*The Anti-Death League,* pt II); the extract from *The Good Food Guide* about Allington's pub at the beginning of *The Green Man,* plus the brilliant parodies of the eighteenth-century diarists in the same novel; and, perhaps most brilliant of all, the expression of George Zeyer's nominal aphasia in *Ending Up.* The effectiveness of some of these parodies also depends on our recognition of the sounds of the words, before they are written down, and then our surprise at the odd things that happen to them when they are written down. Here again we are being amused by the way things we expect to coalesce, to settle comfortably into position in a single word actually do the opposite: i.e. pull apart from each other, exposing the absurdity of a world that has all the appearance of being a vacuum mechanically inserted between linguistic signs that are performing no useful linguistic function.

Words behave strangely when their sound and grammatical function are isolated from their sense. Combinations of words also behave strangely. Sentences are forced to extend themselves, under the pressure of the anxiety, curiosity or ill temper of whoever has stuck them together, into ever more complex (though they are intended to become ever more accurate) descriptions of what that person wanted to say. Hence planning or forethought or considered deliberation of any kind on the part of Amis is likely to produce almost incredible contortions of syntax. Making arrangements to seduce pretty women almost always bring into being such "multi-sequiturs" as this:

> In the last five seconds it had become almost overwhelmingly unlikely that she would meet me the following afternoon, because she was now in the uncommonly rewarding position of being able to stand me up without having incurred the odium of having actually broken an arrangement. On the other hand, she was very much capable of following this line of argument and so going along to the agreed corner to find me not there, which would shove me back to the wrong side of square one, not to speak of the questions about why I was so changeable and so selfish, and did I think it was because I was so insecure that I would have to sweat through a part of the shoving. And, being Diana, to have got that far would mean she would know, without having to think about it, that I would have got as far as it too. So I would have to turn up anyway. But I had been going to do that all along.

The curious spiralling effect of language is not merely the product of an aberration in Allington's mind. Patrick Standish finds language and logic spinning away from him in ever-increasing circles in just such a way when he is shaving in the bathroom after an early-morning bout with "Joan":

> While he shaved, Patrick thought about that smile. The addition of a lack of sweetness to a look of intellect and to beauty was overwhelming. "*What Lola wants,*" he sang to himself, "*Lola gets.*" It made no difference to point out that

the sweetness was as adventitious as the intellect, because the beauty was not. Beauty was not of an order of being in which it made sense to talk of adventitiousness. *"What Lola goes through the motions of wanting and oughtn't to have, Lola all too often gets."* You could not have beauty that had a look of sourness or stupidity; we didn't call that beauty. Beauty without *real* sweetness or *real* mind was as beautiful as beauty with. It was only when it came to dealing with the two sorts that you saw a difference. Did you? Did he? In two or three years would there be much to choose between his relations with Joan if he were Mr. Joan and with Jenny if he were Mr. Jenny? *"What Lola imagines she might be thought original and interesting if she pretended to want, Lola will use her sex on some poor bloody fool to see that she gets."*

Amis is partial to linguistic puzzles of this kind. His poem "The Voice of Authority" makes its point through a similar kind of linguistic joke to the ones Maurice Allington and Patrick Standish play on themselves, or have played on them (the words and the thoughts both seem to have got completely out of their control) in these two passages.

The comic violence that Amis's novels are full of is another manifestation of the hiatus between thought and action, between the world as a character might actually experience it and the world as Amis makes him reconstruct it in his own imagination. Jim Dixon beats Neddy Welch's head in with a bottle; he shoves beads up Margaret Peel's nose. John Lewis dashes the bodies of the book-borrowers at Aberdarcy library onto the stone floor of his coal cupboard. Patrick Standish and Graham McClintoch hunt Dick Thompson with long-range syringes filled with acid or a solution of itching-powder. The common factor of all these happenings is that they are entirely imaginary. They depend on the existence of a hypothetical twin for each of the characters concerned, a twin who inhabits the purely mental world of the hero, for purposes of humiliation, violence, the infliction of pain. The twins live in completely separate worlds. Often there is no justification, beyond plain dislike, for the extremity of one character's sadistic treatment of the imaginary clone he has created from another.

How are we to explain these peculiarities, shared by so many of Amis's heroes: the mechanistic behaviour, the schizophrenia, the separation of word and thing, the uncontrollable spirals of logic, and the comic violence perpetrated on the unwitting clones? What moral statement is Amis trying to make by recourse to this wild comedy? Or is it just comedy for its own sake, a totally irresponsible playing with words and worlds? We need to trace these peculiar habits of mind to the emotional attitudes they express; and then back to the likeable—detestable heroes in whom they are incorporated. When we have done that we might be able to understand the basic preoccupations Amis has always shared with these characters, and be able to relate them to whatever there is of 'moral seriousness' in the novels he has written.

The most immediately noticeable characteristic of Amis man is his manic irritability. None of the heroes of any of these novels possesses an ounce of composure. The smallest inconvenience is likely to get him to run up a fever of sullenness, petulance or rage. This can happen quite out of the blue, with nothing at all to explain it. It is experienced in a mild, not very advanced form by John Lewis when his wife has left the house for a few hours to meet a friend. He is left with time on his hands:

> How, then, was I going to spend the next hour. . . ? In defending myself, presumably, against a certain feeling. Such defence was never easy, because of its habit of confusing itself with the feeling. How to define this feeling? Depression? Not a bad shot. Boredom? Oh yes. A slight tinge, too, eh, of uneasiness and inert, generalized lust. Yes, indeed. The centre of it might be called boredom, but . . . restless.

Lewis gets rid of the feeling by poring over a photograph of a pin-up girl in a magazine, and then having a blazing row with his landlady. Otherwise the feeling of restless boredom, depression, uneasiness and what he calls "inert generalized lust," it is suggested, would have ended either in the release of auto-eroticism, or prolonged irritability leading to petulance and anger. All the feelings, that is to say, that beset so many of Amis's other characters. Their oscillation between egotism and unrest accounts in large part for our inability to like them, but our inclination to admire them all the same, because they are intelligent and witty and sexually voracious.

By the time we have reached Amis's fourth novel, *Take a Girl Like You,* this feeling of dissatisfaction, of vague uneasiness, has changed to something more definite; though it still breaks in on the hero without warning, and for no apparent reason. Patrick Standish, waiting for Jenny Bunn to come and make love with him at his flat, has been passing the time inventing a list of Twelve Bad Men, a trivial doodling exercise not calculated to stimulate the mind to feats of metaphysical speculation. Then, suddenly, he feels "a sharp uneasiness" start up inside him. As with Lewis, sex has something, but by no means everything, to do with it. "His breathing quickened and deepened as at the onset of sexual excitement, but this was not his condition." Descriptions of various discomforts follow, but, we are told, "Nothing in his thoughts or his situation accounted for these symptoms which, the accompaniments of terror, stirred in him more than one kind of terror, as they had recently been doing every other night or so while he lay awake in bed." What Patrick is experiencing is a disturbing physical manifestation of the fear of death, the terrified thought that one day, perhaps sooner rather than later, he will be part of what he mockingly calls "Charon's quota." It has happened before, in equally inconsequential circumstances. For example, after he had been speaking to one of his pupils about the school play: "his heart vibrated in the way it had recently started to do and he had the familiar but never at other times imaginable, feeling of being outside himself, as if his brain had suddenly frozen and become a fixed camera, while his body continued to breathe and walk and turn its head about in a simulacrum of attention."

Standish's experience is repeated by nearly all the heroes of the later books. Micheldene, Churchill, Hunter, Allington, Bastable all experience in a very physical way the panic that follows on an awareness of the imminence of death. It is interesting that, in the account of Standish's experience, the separation of the mind from the body discussed earlier in relation to Amis's farcical manoeuvres, has become a metaphor suggesting what a person's state of mind might be like at the moment of death. Elsewhere, when Amis's characters brood on death, or are put into a panic by some such physical sensation as Standish feels here, they tend to associate their experience with the workings of a mechanical device. The brain clicks away like a camera at the automaton the body has become. Life itself becomes a mechanism when viewed from the vantage point of death. Looking at things in this way, Maurice Allington comes to realise "we're all on conveyer-belts" that represent the process of dying; and we stay on them "from the moment we're born." All adult human beings, in Allington's view, have experienced life as a mindless machine hurtling towards destruction. Therefore, he claims, it is difficult to understand why they don't spend the whole of their lives thinking about it. These are almost his exact words. And it occurs to me that that is what most of Kingsley Amis's heroes have been trying to avoid doing ever since John Lewis's "uncertain feeling" defined itself more clearly as a fear of death. By the time Amis wrote *The Anti-Death League,* in 1972, the subject had become obsessional. All his best books since that time—*The Green Man* and *Ending Up*—have taken death as their unmistakable central theme.

One would suppose that only a person for whom life is something enormously to be enjoyed would inflate the fear of death to such grotesquely obsessive proportions. In both *The Anti-Death League* and *The Green Man* Amis tries to convince us that, in spite of all the ills that flesh is heir to, this is so. James Churchill has his idyllic love for Catherine Casement, Maurice Allington his affection for his father and love of his daughter Amy. But at the heart of these desirable relationships there is also horror, the intimations of mortality. Catherine develops cancer of the breast and has to be surgically mutilated. Old Mr. Allington dies. And Amy is almost raped and murdered, because her father's selfish lust has drawn the ghost of Thomas Underhill and the green man to his house. In *The Anti-Death League* Churchill and Hunter are employed in a sinister secret army unit which plans to decimate millions of Chinese by infecting them with a terrible plague (or so they suppose). At the end of the last chapter the chaplain's little dog is pointlessly run over by a lorry: in the village church nearby, his master has just presided over the singing of the anthem "Lord, Protect Thou Thy Servants." The League itself has been invented to expose the immorality of worshipping a God who lets the innocent die and arbitrarily kills and maims women and children. As a result the chapter entitled "The Founding of the League" reads at times like a sort of rehash of the scene of Ivan Karamazov's argument with Alyosha in *The Brothers Karamazov.* It comes to the conclusion that to return the ticket is not enough; you have to kill the conductor too.

However, because life is shot through with reminders of death, whether one is considering the deliberate extermination of millions of Chinese, or the accidental destruction of a pet dog crossing the road, it hardly seems worth living after all. Even if your own girl hasn't got cancer, so many other fellows' have. And then there are all those newspaper reports about people swallowing raw potatoes and dying of asphyxiation; jumping from burning buildings and being smashed on the pavements below; gaining their sight one day, after fifteen years of blindness, and dying of a virus infection the next. There is a strong and passionate feeling in *The Anti-Death League* that death has rendered life unendurable, and that, in spite of alternative persuasions from Willie Ayscue and Catherine Casement, it is Churchill and Hunter who represent Amis's own point of view. That is one of sheer despair. In a covert way it has crept into Amis's novels from the beginning. After all, many of even his early poems are about death (for instance, "The Real Earth"). And the first of his (later) "Three Scenarios" is directly comparable with Max Hunter's verses "For a Baby Born without Limbs." In both of the last-mentioned poems Amis's sense of outrage against the existence of deformity and disease is very strongly conveyed. No wonder he wants to return the ticket. But in a post-Christian, irreligious world, the question has to be posed: to whom?

Amis's horror of death, accompanied by a keen sense of the absurdity of lives that are little more than frenetic preparations for it, accounts in large part for the farcical treatment of character, event and language in all of his novels—even those early ones where the obsession went undisclosed. Farce is one way of expressing one's sense of the futility of life. To convert men into machines, and events into a sort of electric current that galvanises them into furious but aimless activity; to play with the words they speak, and that they write down, as if they were basically meaningless coincidences of sounds and ciphers; to invent people all over again and subject them to therapeutic, though imaginary, tortures and humiliations—these are the consequences of not being able to see why one shouldn't spend the whole of one's life thinking about death, or trying to stop oneself thinking about death.

There is a haunting line in one of Philip Larkin's poems about "the costly aversion of the eyes from death." It explains a lot about Amis. His novels show that there is both a pay-off and a price to pay for this. The price is his inability to construct a world that possesses any meaning at all, a world that might encourage one to attend seriously to questions of human motive and intention, and their relation to effects and consequences. The pay-off is his freedom to play with the world as he finds it in as irresponsible a way as God, if he had existed, must be presumed to have played when he first created it.

To do that in literary terms is to create farce. To do it in reality is, of course, to produce quite another thing: tragedy, melodrama, absurdity—or Christianity.

I mention Christianity because that is the soft underbelly of Amis's own culture which seeks to justify a world he thinks is unjustifiable. The God of Christianity actually makes an appearance at Maurice Allington's pub near the end of *The Green Man*. Allington puts the question to him: why did he make that other, more highly publicised visit 1969 years before? "Mmm. I must have been bored," he says. "I thought, why not? Then I thought I was heading straight for disaster. I needn't have worried, need I? He [Christ] hasn't made much difference to anything." Whatever moral seriousness Amis's novels possess has to do with this point of view. For good and ill, it makes it impossible for him ever to be serious about anything else.

Notes

1. Frederick R. Karl, *A Reader's Guide to the Contemporary English Novel* (New York, 1959; London, 1965).

Entertaining Amis

William H. Pritchard

Kingsley Amis's poems have always made critics a trifle nervous, partly because he is such a re-readable novelist that it seems hardly fair he should perform so well in verse. Then there is the presence of Larkin over his shoulder, a writer whose poems take on depths of gloomy richness that Amis, wisely I think, doesn't attempt to match. Speaking as an American, it's my impression that news of Amis the poet has barely reached these shores; in college classrooms at least, Larkin is read and admired while Amis gets there, when he does, as the author of *Lucky Jim*. This is fair enough, but makes it harder for the poems to receive their due. He has been referred to as a "non-Commissioned Larkin," also fair enough if we remember that the NCO's have their own club at which Amis's poetic act is one of the best things currently viewable. At any rate, as someone who for years has been sending people copies of "Lovely" ("Look thy last on all things lovely/Every hour, an old shag said"), I should like to suggest why his poetry is a civilised resource, the sort of thing you want to read aloud to another person.

What the *Collected Poems* reveal is Amis's development into one of the best English writers of light verse in this century (the book is dedicated to John Betjeman, master of such activity). Reviewers of his poems in the past have sometimes disagreed over whether they qualified for the "light" label or were of a higher (or heavier) nature. *À propos* of this question, his Introduction to the *New Oxford Book of English Light Verse* provides a useful gloss on his own work:

> I described *vers de société* earlier as in some degree a continuation of satire. This move can be seen as already in progress by the time of Swift, who was certainly not writing satire in the normal sense of the term, as his avoidance of the heroic couplet would be enough to suggest. . . . We are dealing with a kind of realistic verse that is close to some of the interests of the novel: men and women among their fellows, seen as members of a group or class in a way that emphasises manners, social forms, amusements, fashion (from millinery to philosophy), topicality, even gossip, all these treated in a bright, perspicuous style.

From *Kingsley Amis In Life and Letters* (London: Macmillan, 1990) 173–182. With permission of Macmillan Ltd.

These perspicuous sentences about one kind of light verse are so, partly because they have roots in Amis's own poetry and suggest the way in which, like Swift, he is not writing "satire in the normal sense."

Yet in the earliest poems from the *Collected Poems* (the first six of them were originally published in *Bright November,* Fortune Press, 1947) there is little of the flexibility needed for writing *vers de société.* The portentous style is more contrived than "bright," and contrived in the manner of Auden—in the first poem, "Letter to Elisabeth," even down to the off-rhymed couplets, a practice which seems to be of dubious value in both Auden and Amis:

> In public rooms we guessed at silence, and
> Discussed the end of what has had no end.
> Where none would pause we found an hour to wait
> And clung together when the streets were wet.
> Now in a parted meanwhile rings the beat
> Of married hearts; my scene has shifted, but
> Still flows your northern river like a pulse,
> Carrying blood to bodies at the poles.

There are also Audenesque "fumbling gestures," and resolutions to "speak straight" and "walk without a strut." John Bayley has said of Larkin's first book of poems, *The North Ship,* that "there is a high degree of competence and of effective Yeatsian usage, but no Larkin at all." A similar judgement might be passed on the presence of Auden in Amis's early poems.

Audenesque was not a plausible style for Amis because Amis's poems, unlike Auden's early ones, do not tease us with an unexpected or inexpressive content, a "secret" behind the words.

> That horse whose rider fears to jump will fall,
> Riflemen miss if orders sound unsure;
> They only are secure who seem secure;
> Who lose their voice, lose all.

"Masters" produces further examples of this principle, then turns round to describe by contrast some unmasterful "losings":

> The eyes that will not look, the twitching cheek . . .
> Only these make us known, and we are known
> Only as we are weak.

It concludes as sententiously as it began:

> By yielding mastery the will is freed,
> For it is by surrender that we live,
> And we are taken if we wish to give,
> Are needed if we need.

This is apt, a sympathetic statement of the "liberal" point of view (surely E. M. Forster would sympathise with its message); yet it also feels like an exercise, the style carefully excluding any personal idiosyncracy in favour of sanity and objectivity. When listening to Amis read *A Case of Samples* on the Marvell Press recording, one is surprised to note how little expression gets into his voice, and, as compared with Larkin's recordings, how chaste and impersonal is his delivery. Indeed one wishes for a bit more flare.

The flare of a more personal voice is there, though, in "A Dream of Fair Women," which like Amis's other poems has a principled point to make, but on the way to making it provides us with something other than a dispassionate presentation—as when, in the dream, a bevy of females exercises its varied charms on the narrator:

> Speech fails them, amorous, but each one's look,
> Endorsed in other ways, begs me to sign
>   Her body's autograph-book;
> "Me first, Kingsley; I'm cleverest" each declares.

Here the "bright, perspicuous style" emerges, as it does in "A Bookshop Idyll" when, after the narrator (may we call him Amis?) finds that gents and ladies tend to title their volumes of poetry in discernibly different ways, he finds also that "a moral beckons":

> Should poets bicycle-pump the human heart
>   Or squash it flat?
> Man's love is for man's life a thing apart;
>   Girls aren't like that.

It was very bright of him to bring in the Byron line here (Senator Sam Ervin also quoted it, during the Watergate hearings, in the presence I believe of John Ehrlichman), to reduce the female sex to "girls," and to squash the last line as flat as he managed to do. Generally the poem's daringness seems more pronounced now than it did twenty-five years ago: "Women are really much nicer than men:/No wonder we like them." Name two other English or American poets who would dare to say such a thing in 1979. One hears the chorus of protest, and certainly it takes a really disinterested female reader, blessed with the humorous sense, to like Amis's work.

By not reading his poems or novels very carefully, one could assume that he is simply a professional squasher of the human heart, that he merely delights in letting the hot air out of pumped-up dreams and visions. It is useful then to consider "Romance," the concluding poem in *A Case of Samples,* to suggest how disturbed and moved he has been by this whole matter of romantic inflation:

> The sound of saxophones, like farmhouse cream,
> And long skirts and fair heads in a soft gleam,
> Both scale and are the forest-fence of dream.

> Picture a youngster in the lonely night
> Who finds a stepping-stone from dark to bright,
> An undrawn curtain and an arm of light.
>
> Here was an image nothing could dispel:
> Adulthood's high romantic citadel,
> The Tudor Ballroom of the Grand Hotel.
>
> Those other dreams, those freedoms lost their charm,
> Those twilight lakes reflecting pine or palm,
> Those skies were merely large and wrongly calm.
>
> What then but weakness turns the heart again
> Out in that lonely night beyond the pane
> With images and truths of wind and rain?

This lovely and delicate poem does something interesting with the Yeatsian motto "In dreams begins responsibility," by rewriting it more ruefully and disillusionedly: in dreams begins disappointment or weakness—the heart turned out and away, unable for more than a moment to scale the "forest-fence," to capture or to live in that "high romantic citadel" where you must be as glamorous and undaunted as the others. It is Amis's Fitzgerald poem, as written by a Nick Carraway who had read Empson.

> Was it really he who had spent a whole string of autumn evenings fifteen or sixteen years ago in the front room just off the London–Croydon road, playing his Debussy and Delius records by the open windows, in the hope that the girl who lived at the end of the street, and whom he never dared speak to, would pass by, hear the music, look in and see him? Well, it was a good thing, and impressive too, that he could still feel a twinge of that uncomplicated and ignorant melancholy. (*Take a Girl Like You* (1960))

One notes also that it is a "youngster" who is allowed both to experience the dream and to suffer its consequences. Amis has always held on hard to the images and truths of youthful—one could say boyish—perception (his imagining of the youth, Peter, in *The Riverside Villas Murder* is finely done), which is perhaps why in his poems from the last fifteen or so years, the oldster speaking them is scornful and sad. "A Chromatic Passing-Note," from *A Look Round the Estate* (1967) begins with an oldster talking this way:

> "That slimy tune" I said, and got a laugh,
> In the middle of old Franck's D minor thing:
> The dotted-rhythm clarinet motif.

Amis invariably does something fresh with his musical references, classical or jazz. Here it would be a mistake to remember "filthy Mozart" and presume that a Lucky Jim is up again to his old debunking tricks. The poem goes on to point out, quite didactically, that the tune wasn't "slimy" when the speaker was fifteen, but showed rather "that real love was found/At the far end of the right country lane." Now, having learned different, " 'Slimy' was a snarl of disappointment." What saves the "A Chromatic Passing-Note" from abstractedness and mere lesson-teaching is that there *is* such a clarinet motif in the second movement of the Franck symphony; that one loves it when young and (in my experience) eventually turns on it or away from it as too insistent, too importunate. (Thanks to Amis's poem I've now come to happy terms not only with the clarinet motif but with the whole splendid symphony.)

From here it is but a step, and with hindsight a predictable one, to "The Evans Country." "Adulthood's high romantic citadel" has been too pricey a dream, the human heart too weak to engage it for long. So Amis imagines, with fierce satisfaction, the unromantic architecture against which Evans's courting takes place:

> By the new Boots, a tool-chest with flagpoles
> Glued on, and flanges, and a dirty great
> Baronial doorway, and things like portholes,
> Evans met Mrs. Rhys on their first date.

Here we have moved completely and successfully into the "manners, social forms, amusements, fashion (from millinery to philosophy)" which distinguish *vers de société,* Amis's brand of light verse. The "bright, perspicuous style" continues to engage us as further items of "romance" are catalogued "the time they slunk/Back from that lousy week-end in Porthcawl"; then the poem reaches its conclusion in a strongly assured and compelling rhythm:

> The journal of some bunch of architects
> Named this the worst town centre they could find;
> But how disparage what so well reflects
> Permanent tendencies of heart and mind?
>
> All love demands a witness: something "there"
> Which it yet makes part of itself. These two
> Might find Carlton House Terrace, St. Mark's Square,
> A bit on the grand side. What about you?

Eh, *hypocrite lecteur?* In *The Waste Land* Eliot is also supposed to have squashed flat the human heart; but if one feels, as I do, that the encounter between the typist and her young man carbuncular ("Flushed and decided he assaults at once") has been bicycle-pumped by language into a great caricature that is beautiful (Eliot's language about Ben Jonson), then one can also be truly moved by this moment in the Amis poem:

> But how disparage what so well reflects
> Permanent tendencies of heart and mind?

The question can be asked only when the poet moves beyond the complacencies of more ordinary "satire" ("poking fun", as the undergraduates say) and acts instead as a true witness to love, even Evans's love, by measuring, thus celebrating it in verse.

By the time we reach the end of the final poem in "The Evans Country" ("Aberdarcy: The Chaucer Road") the poet-as-commentator has disappeared. On his way to a quick one with "Mrs. No-holds-barred," Evans reflects on "How much in life he's never going to know:/All it must mean to really love a woman." Yet, the poem suggests, there are compensations, as after the event Evans returns home for a quiet evening:

> "Hallo now, Megan.
> No worse than usual, love. You been all right?
> Well, this looks good. And there's a lot on later;
> Don't think I'll bother with the club tonight."
>
> Nice bit of haddock with poached egg, Dundee cake,
> Buckets of tea, then a light ale or two,
> And "Gunsmoke," "Danger Man," the Late Night Movie—
> Who's doing better, then? What about you?

It is a marvellous stroke to take us, by the flash and movement of the catalogue of anticipated delights, inside Evans country to the extent that the final question totally disarms us. And the tendencies of Evan's heart and mind have been permanently etched.

One might say the same about Amis, after reading through the eighteen poems, some of them very short, which follow "The Evans Country" and make up his published output of post-Evans verse. Often they are recited (Amis edited *The Faber Popular Reciter*—"poems that sound well and go well when spoken in a declamatory style") by the radical–reactionary controversialist we've become familiar with from various letters and columns in newspapers and weeklies since the later sixties. Ageing and rigidifying, he salutes himself on his fiftieth birthday in "Ode to Me" for having at least lived through *those* fifty years rather than the fifty to come:

> After a whole generation
> Of phasing out education,
> Throwing the past away,
> Letting the language decay,
> And expanding the general mind
> Till it bursts.
>
> He at least was born with a
>
>   chance of happiness,
> Before unchangeable crappiness
> Spreads over all the land.

The crappiness is succinctly noted in some lines from "Shitty" (but why in the collection does this poem not come after, rather than before, the poem to which it seems an afterthought, "Lovely"?):

> Look thy last on all things shitty
>   While thou'rt at it: soccer stars,
> Soccer crowds, bedizened bushheads
>   Jerking over their guitars,
> German tourists, plastic roses,
>   Face of Mao and face of Ché,
> Women wearing curtains, blankets,
>   Beckett at the ICA.

The crappiness has spread to Salisbury, where St. Edmund's Church is to be turned into a modern hotel, a prospect particularly apt to produce images of things shitty:

> Fancies of Japanese, back from Stonehenge,
> Quaffing keg bitter by the pulpit stair,
> Swedes booking coach-tours in the chancel.
>   ("Festival Notebook")

Those Swedes were originally at their deadly work in Oxford too, but in putting "Their Oxford" into the collection Amis (to be fair no doubt) replaced them with other foreigners, engaged in lousing up the "old hotel/Now newly faced." Thirty years ago the hotel was a slow, safe boring place; today

> You have to do yourself well as you may
> In the dimmed bar, where fifty Finns arrive
>
> Just before you, and budding businessmen,
> Though dressed like actors, call at bruisers' pitch
> For Highland malt with stacks of ice.

It's possible that a truly decent liberal democrat might find all this unamusing, even repellent. Since such a reader has also taken many courses in anthropology and sociology at his university he would be similarly unappreciative of the poem's ending, when Amis invokes the lostness, the pastness of "that Oxford that I hardly knew": the Oxford of privilege, of "Champagne breakfasts (or were they mythical?)", or the perhaps equally mythical one of "giant" teachers like Bowra and Lewis ("Men big enough to be worth laughing at"). He disapproved of much at the Oxford he attended, but now, when nobody "except the old" cares how it "used to be," does it make any sense for him to disapprove?

> What seemed to me so various is all one,
> A block of time, which like its likenesses

> Looks better now the next such has begun;
> Looks, and in this case maybe really is.

The fine last line gives a slight but lethal kick in the head to the relativist's wisdom about how nothing really changes, about how "you just *think* things were better back then." Maybe they really were, and it is the poem's art to make one entertain that possibility.

Robert Frost used to say that rather than entertaining ideas he liked to try them out to see whether they entertained him. Amis's poems, especially the recent ones, work this way by invoking contemporary crappiness so magnificently and expertly that—like the poet, and perhaps the man himself—we are positively exhilarated by the awful spectacle. The next-to-last poem in the book, "Farewell Blues" uses Hardy's "Friends Beyond" (the Mellstock Churchyard poem) to eulogise dead jazz musicians, much of whose music moulders in the vaults of dead 1930s record companies. What is alive, alas, is music made by 'Bongo, sitar, 'cello, flute, electric piano, bass guitar' that sounds like this:

> Trumpets gelded, drums contingent, saxophones that bleat or bawl,
> Keyless, barless, poor-man's Boulez, improvising on fuck-all,
> Far beyond what feeling, reason, even mother wit allow,
> While Muggsy Spanier, Floyd O'Brien, Sterling Bose and Henry Allen lie in
>   Decca churchyard now.

In the immortal language of one of Larkin's uncollected poems, the contemporary improvisor is "A nitwit not fit to shift shit." But the final stanza of "Farewell Blues" brings together much of what makes up Amis's version of things: contempt and disgust for the crappy present; nostalgia for a time when things were different, just possibly better; commitment to rhyme and exactly measured lines (fifteen syllables in the first three lines, twenty-four in the fourth); respect helplessly paid to the "dream" which was once entertained and which, because it was so good, helped ruin the present. The stanza is about jazz but about more than just jazz:

> Dead's the note we loved that swelled within us, made us gasp and stare,
> Simple joy and simple sadness thrashing the astounded air;
> What replaced them no one asked for, but it turned up anyhow,
> And Coleman Hawkins, Johnny Hodges, Bessie Smith and Pee Wee Russell lie
>   in Okeh churchyard now.

Light verse no longer feels very light, has gone "high" instead into a version of pastoral that is affecting and moving. But I speak for myself here, as one for whom since the day I first read *Lucky Jim* back then, Amis has been the most entertaining, the most exhilarating of contemporary writers. Who's doing better then? What about you?

The Old Devil

JAMES WOLCOTT

Lunchtime in London. Ambling toward the lobby of the Savoy hotel is the author Kingsley Amis. He has a recognizable stride. It's the boulevard stroll Fred Mertz had in the episode of *I Love Lucy* where Fred, top hat atilt, chugged into a nightclub as an English duffer, doncha know. Not that there's anything ersatz about Amis's dash or demeanor. Seated in the bar of the Savoy for a brief chat about his new novel, *Difficulties with Girls* (Summit), he is every stitch and seam the English gent. A portly gent, it should be said— his belt now takes a long ride around the rotunda. But his face, that of a leading man sliding into character parts, has a distinguished glaze. For someone as fond of drink as Amis is (he's written numerous books on the topic), he shows no signs of the puffy, floaty discoloration often caused by longtime submersion in the sauce. Nothing fishy about his eyes either, which are scrupulous, keen—twin sentries on alert. His eyes man their stations even as he enters a relaxation mode. Amis nurses a nonalcoholic starter called a pussyfoot, then, with a flip of his wrist to consult his watch, announces it is time for a *real* drink: large bourbon with ice. At the thought of having a serious gargle, he immediately perks up, like a houseguest who has heard the ding-ding of the dinner bell. Liberation is at hand.

Kingsley Amis has entered an Indian summer of acclaim. It is as if his deck chair were stationed sunward to catch the dusk. In his late sixties, Amis is mellow proof of the adage that the important thing is to outlive the bastards. With an eclectic output which includes everything from a survey of sci-fi, *New Maps of Hell,* to a James Bond adventure, *Colonel Sun,* from a study of Kipling to a roundup of his own verse, he has secured a wide berth on the shelf, but at the cost of some suspicion that slumming had stuffed his sinuses as a serious comic novelist, reducing his characters' outbursts to a chronic wheeze. The success of *Stanley and the Women* wounded that notion and *The Old Devils* dealt it a deathblow. A lopsided look at love and liquor among the Geritol set, *The Old Devils* won the Booker Prize in 1986.

Amis's acidic rebirth in late age has helped take the steam out of his iconoclasms as a young devil. The tempests that once swirled over *Lucky Jim,*

This article originally appeared in *Vanity Fair* 52 (April 1989): 36–46. Reprinted with permission.

Amis's status within the Angry Young Men, his championing of genre fiction and rejection of F. R. Leavis's great tradition (with characteristic overkill, Leavis supposedly reviled Amis as "a pornographer"), have been construed over time into the settled dust of academic recap. Even the boil over his political shift from Labour left to Tory right has leveled to a low simmer. He has become, in short, an institution—an underlying asset.

In a floating exchange rate where various flavors of the month are up, down, sideways, drifting, Kingsley Amis represents the gold standard in English literature, as Evelyn Waugh did before him. Like Waugh, his belly seems designed to cushion him against runs on the bank. Evidence of his asset value is a compilation of his favorite poems published in England last year called *The Amis Anthology,* a bedside keepsake suitable for preserving crushed rose petals. (The notes retain Amis's thorny touch, however. Apropos of a John Betjeman poem about golf, he remarks, "For the record, I am bored by golf to the point of hatred.") Although Amis appreciates the kind attention he's received in recent years, he's mildly miffed that reviewers keep treating him as a serial mugger, preying on one protected species after another. "What people tend to get wrong is this 'target' thing. 'Who is he in for this time? You know, this last time he had it in for women. This time he has it in for queers. And he has it in for . . .' " Jews, wogs, make a list.

On that list women occupy the top spot. Despite having written sympathetically from the female point of view in the Trollopian *Take a Girl Like You,* Amis has acquired the reputation of behaving in print like a sour-ball S.O.B. beset by bitches. It's a somewhat dubious rap and rep. True, at the end of the labored satire *Jake's Thing,* his impotent Jake chooses to remain limp rather than lay himself open to women and their irrational mood mongering. And then there is Exhibit A, *Stanley and the Women.* After its tough go at finding a publisher in America, accusations were made that feminist cabals had sought to blockade Amis's brand of woman bashing from our beaches. But following much ado in the *T.L.S.* and other places, *Stanley and the Women* belatedly made it ashore. It remains one of Amis's most problematic novels—almost Jamesian in its implicative asides and askew point of view. When I first tried reading it, I found it thick, gray, and wrinkly, a hunk of elephant hide hacked from a lumbering attack of misogynist ego. But in a bitter funk I picked the book off the shelf, began browsing, and suddenly his warped account of dissonance between the sexes all made *perfect sense.* It is a novel that you don't so much read as surrender to as a chill narcotic—you have to be in a susceptible state of disappointment to receive its needle. *Stanley and the Women's* paranoid premise, persuasively dramatized, is that women everywhere are mad and maddening. Their unavowed aim is to make men's lives a steaming muddle. "Not enough of a motive?" shouts a doctor at Stanley, trying to put him wise. "Fucking up a man? Not enough of a motive? What are you talking about? Good God, you've had wives, haven't you?"

But the male bonding that takes place in *Stanley* (us against all them crazy dames) is a funny parody of drunken guy talk, not meant to be taken as gospel. Complaining about women is how Stanley and his chums loonily let off steam. There are worse ways to let off steam. Unlike D. H. Lawrence, whose bearded prophecies leave Amis cold, he doesn't see strife between men and women as an apocalyptic contest of will and submission—blood consciousness, phallic worship, and the eternal feminine battling it out beneath the snake-coiled tree where Eve was tempted. He veers away from absolutism and violence. He doesn't decapitate women in his fiction, like Norman Mailer, or sniff at their flesh as if it were tainted meat, like Saul Bellow and John Updike. He achieves a rough equivalence. His men are hardly prizes. The amoral shittiness of men is as constant in his fiction as the moral shiftiness of women. And those men often get their comeuppance, like the pub owner in *The Green Man* who stages a ménage à trois only to have the two women get so entwined that he's extraneous. Amis's women certainly aren't weaklings. They have far more spike and spunk than the meek mice in Margaret Drabble and Anita Brookner. "What makes you such a howling bitch?" asks the narrator in *Girl, 20* of the horrid Sylvia, who's been carrying on with his married pal, Roy. Her reply:

> "I expect it's the same thing as makes you a top-heavy red-haired four-eyes who's . . . impotent and likes bloody symphonies and fugues and the first variation comes before the statement of the theme and give me a decent glass of British beer and dash it all Carruthers I don't know what young people are coming to these days and a scrounger and an old woman and a failure and a hanger-on and a prig and terrified and a shower and a brisk rub-down every morning and you can't throw yourself away on a little trollop like that Roy you must think of your wife Roy old boy old boy and I'll come along but I don't say I approve and bloody dead. Please delete the items in the above that do not apply. If any."

Any man reading such a passage will check afterward to see if he still has his scalp.

Girl, 20 is middle-period Amis. There was a tailing off of interest after that burst of verbal hostilities, into the implausible mystery of *The Riverside Villas Murder* (great seduction scene, though), the arthritic collapse of *Ending Up,* and the alternative-world fantasizing of *The Alteration* and *Russian Hide-and-Seek*. Amis seemed to be in a long slough. What brought him out of his slide? It's been intimated that it was the breakup of his marriage to the novelist Elizabeth Jane Howard that cracked open the raw, cathartic emotions which found their flow in *Stanley and the Women*. (He currently lives in a curious arrangement with his first wife and her third husband.) It may have been a healing catharsis, for his next novel, *The Old Devils,* had a ravishing presence named Rhiannon and a tremendously romantic ending. "The poem, his poem, was going to be the best tribute he could pay to the only woman who had ever cried for him." For his characters it's the heaviness of being that's unbearable. Lightness is for the young and the dead.

Difficulties with Girls is a drier, lighter affair. It doesn't knock dentures around like hockey pucks, as *The Old Devils* did—it wears a toothpaste smile that's yellowing at the edges. A sequel to *Take a Girl Like You, Difficulties with Girls* concerns the marriage of a young couple, Patrick and Jenny Standish, as they cope with the swinging sixties. They're coping better than one of their neighbors, Tim, who convinces himself after his difficulties with girls (in bed he loses his erection presto) that he's a latent case. He tries to acclimate himself to the homosexual life-style to the point of acting "poofy" at the local pub. Only a night on the town with a homosexual couple down the hall finally frightens Tim back to the straight and narrow. Amis's mild and unmalicious depiction of the gay couple has drawn a few flurries. "One reviewer, who I won't name and who's male, said the trouble with the portrayal of these males, you know, he put it like that, is that it's based on hearsay and not on actual experience. Oh, sorry about that, yeah. Hmmm. Thank you. You know, the trouble about Mr. Shakespeare's portrayal of Cleopatra, it's not based on experience."

No one disputes Amis's authority when it comes to man-woman wrangling. Perhaps the funniest exchange in *Difficulties with Girls* comes after a spot of adultery one afternoon. Patrick, who has just given a married woman named Wendy a spin in the sack, basks in the belief that he's thrummed her lute, uncorked an inner glow. Her hard-set look soon tells him he's quite mistaken.

> "I don't understand. You drove at me so remorselessly, so . . . implacably. You seemed tormented by some kind of hatred, for me, for yourself, whatever, I don't know, I'm just baffled. What is it with you, darling? Won't you tell me, for the love of God?"
>
> If he had not felt slightly indignant at the thought of all that good work going for nothing, he might not have said, as he did, "I know I've asked you this already, old thing, but are you absolutely *sure* you're not an American?"

From *Lucky Jim* to Sylvia's tirade in *Girl, 20* to this postcoital spat in *Difficulties with Girls,* the best parts of his fiction have been playable—actable. Amis learned from Anthony Powell, Evelyn Waugh, and especially P. G. Wodehouse the importance of capturing character through dialogue, framing the action, keeping the staging simple. But much of his histrionics came right out of his own hammy spirit. His handsome actor's face houses big-screen lights and shadows. The poet Philip Larkin has paid tribute to Amis's pantomimic skill in their student days at Oxford, mentioning a photograph showing Amis contorting his face into a fierce scowl as he crouched on the grass with an invisible dagger, miming the role of—Japanese soldier. Even more striking than Amis's jawline jujitsu were his vocal air raids. He was a master of sound-track noises (gunfire, static, pigeons, geese) and foreign gibberish. One of his classics was a morale-boosting speech by F.D.R. fighting to be heard on a faulty radio against an incoming front of interference and band music.

Writers are often mimics, trying on attitudes like masks. But when Gore Vidal, say, imitates Richard Nixon or Ronald Reagan on TV, it's a suave simulation, a parlor trick meant to raise at most a titter. Sweat doesn't bead his marble mask. Amis's classics are more Artaud. Larkin: "Kingsley's masterpiece, which was so demanding I heard him do it only twice, involved three subalterns, a Glaswegian driver and a jeep breaking down and refusing to restart somewhere in Germany. Both times I became incapable with laughter." His son Martin Amis seconds the incapability part, saying that after his father's routines there isn't a dry cheek or dry pair of trousers in the house. "The great mimics are very vehement. I mean, he does one of an airplane taking off, but by the time he gets to the pilot he's completely purple in the face. Putting even his body at risk."

I met with Martin Amis, no stranger to vehemence himself, one night at his home in London. "I don't have to wear nappies," one of his sons told him, "not on Tuesday I don't." Ah, the inimitable logic of children! Martin was staying with his two blond boys while his wife went out to a concert. Dinosaur toys lined a shelf downstairs. Martin himself appears in his father's fiction in *I Like It Here,* asking questions about big beasties. "If two tigers and a lion fought a killer whale, who would win? And him going, 'It just could never happen.' Yeah, but who would win?" He also remembers the thrill of checks arriving. "I used to run upstairs with the mail and say, 'There's a check,' and sit around and open it. It was incredibly exciting. It was a check for £700 or something, which would buy you a house." In later boyhood Martin Amis had his own literary difficulty with girls—smart and sarcastic, his first novel, *The Rachel Papers,* was considered a little too inclined to panty sniffing. (A somewhat sanitized version of the novel was being filmed in England when we met.) It was the addictive-minded *Money* (money as sex, money as maintenance, money as obsession) that put Martin on the map in America.

In his father's house his writing is still a submerged landmass, however. "He doesn't read my stuff. He can't get on with it. The last one he read, I think, was *Success,* thirteen years ago." His father had read a chapter of *Money* when it was printed in a magazine, but showed less patience with the complete novel. "I knew the exact moment he sent the novel windmilling across the room: when a minor character named Martin Amis showed up in the book. He has very firm rules about that."

Kingsley Amis resists and resents self-referentialism in fiction not only because he thinks it's trendy but because to him its tricks are dated. "Because my first novel, which was never published, had a hero called Kingsley Amis."

Its title? *"The Legacy.* It's a writer's title. *The Legacy?* Who wants to know about that?"

Writerliness Kingsley Amis abhors. To be a writerly writer is to be cerebral, cliquish, enclosed, exiled to a bookish realm, be it a Borgesian maze or a Nabokovian hall of mirrors—literary with a capital *L*. To be a readerly writer is to be literary, lowercase. Although Martin clearly admires his father's fiction and his dedication to book reviewing ("He believes in putting something back into literature"), he seems less enthused about the lowercase slack in the recent work. Of *Difficulties with Girls,* he comments, "It's sort of tacky, as if it's being told to you at a pub, that novel." For his part, Kingsley looks with amusement at his uppercase son. "My son's next novel is going to be very long—it's called *London Fields.* Now, that's a writer's title. That's the sort of thing that great novels are called." (The novel is also set in 1999, another sign of greatness calling.)

The tentative title of Kingsley Amis's next novel is more reader-friendly. "I think it's going to be called *The Folks Who Live on the Hill.* After that, you know, bloody Bing Crosby record." Only these are not Bing Crosby's idea of folks. One husband is desolated when his wife runs off with another woman—he wants her back. Another character is a woman with a history of alcoholism. "Anyway, she's off the bottle, you think she's very nice. She's going to say, 'Harry, you see those people walking on the street there?' 'Yes, dear.' 'I'd like them to be in a *war.*' " There are also dead-end discussions in which two baffled men try to figure out exactly what it is lesbians do. From the bits Amis recited, the book sounds like a swing back to the crust and brio of *The Old Devils.* He's at home with these crocodiles.

After *The Folks Who Live on the Hill,* Kingsley Amis is considering his memoirs, to be structured not as a chronological account of his life but as an ABC of anecdotes. "My memoirs are not going to be an autobiography, but an alphabiography, putting them in alphabetical order. Because there are only two things I have a good memory for, poetry and anecdotes. I've got lots and lots of anecdotes." As an example, he mentions the black musician Rex Stewart, cornetist for eleven years in Duke Ellington's band. "I said to him, 'Did you know that King George VI'—actually, it wasn't King George VI, it was Prince George, the Duke of Kent, but I didn't know that then—'had a complete collection of Ellington records on their original American labels?' 'Yes,' he said. 'We all knew that,' he said. 'When we were refused hotel service in Charleston, somewhere like that, we'd say, "Well, George likes us. George likes us." ' "

Like the jazz masters he admires, Amis has learned to pace himself, keep his whistle wet, bend to the notes. He has a shorthand fluency, a flair for slang phrasing that's like the stop-start of fast music. Even a minor novel like *Difficulties with Girls* has a sad moan at the back of its metallic chimes. And there's little danger Kingsley Amis will go God on us, as Evelyn Waugh did. He's wedded to the human stew. Its incessant bubble.

A Touch of Class

Terry Teachout

The one indispensable answer to an environment bristling with people and things one thought were bad was to go on finding out new ways in which one could think they were bad.

—Kingsley Amis, *Lucky Jim*

The trendy Amis, of course, is Martin, whose latest book, *Einstein's Monsters,* is described on the dust jacket as "Martin Amis's impassioned fictionalized protest against nuclear weapons.... The subject is depressing, almost unthinkable. But Amis makes of these stories a life-affirming lament." Such laments, taken in tandem with the equally stylish America-bashing of *The Moronic Inferno,* a recent collection of occasional essays, helped to make of Martin Amis a coming young man of English letters.

Martin's father used to be a coming young man of letters himself. When Kingsley Amis, an obscure poet and lecturer at a dreary South Wales university, published *Lucky Jim,* his first novel, in 1954, critics were quick to recognize in him a comic novelist on the order of the pre-*Brideshead* Evelyn Waugh. But Amis *père* spent the next three decades doing every unfashionable thing imaginable. He tried his hand at various types of genre fiction: ghost stories, spy stories, detective stories. He wrote a column for *Penthouse* called "Kingsley on Drink." He even wrote a James Bond novel.

The only thing Kingsley Amis never got around to doing was tinkering with his style, which has remained more or less unchanged throughout seventeen novels, a collection of short stories, and a diverse assortment of other books ranging from a biography of Rudyard Kipling to a history of science fiction. "What I think I am doing," Amis said in 1976, "is writing novels within the main English-language tradition, that is, trying to tell interesting, believable stories about understandable characters in a reasonably straightforward style: no tricks, no experimental foolery."

In time, Amis's politics would become as quaint as his prose style. The author of *Lucky Jim* was, like the other Angry Young Men who electrified English readers of the Fifties with their vigorous rejection of mandarin literary

From *The New Criterion* 7 (Nov. 1988): 8–17. Reprinted with the kind permission of the author.

ways, a socialist of sorts. But Lucky Jim, as Amis put it in a 1967 essay, gradually turned right, a metamorphosis which shocked and dismayed many of his erstwhile fans. ("How could a chap like me, an intellectual with an interest in jazz and science fiction to protect me from total fuddy-duddyism, *possibly* not be on the Left?")

As Amis grew more obviously conservative, critics who once praised him began to dismiss him as a middle-aged hack incapable of realizing his youthful promise. Eventually, Amis even began to have trouble publishing his books in the United States, a dilemma with an inescapably political dimension. One novel, *Russian Hide-and-Seek,* never found an American publisher at all, while another, *Stanley and the Women,* became a *cause célèbre* on both sides of the Atlantic when word got out that feminist editors at three New York publishing houses, dismayed with the novel's alleged misogyny, had turned it down.

Kingsley Amis's sales, to be sure, have remained perfectly respectable. His last novel, *The Old Devils,* even won the 1987 Booker Prize, England's equivalent of the Pulitzer Prize for fiction, and he continues to get good reviews. But the critical tide now runs against him. John Updike's 1979 review of *Jake's Thing* in *The New Yorker* made the latter-day case against Amis with dismaying clarity:

> [I]t is a rare sentence of his prose that surrenders to the demons of language, that abdicates a seat of fussy social judgment, that is there for its own sake, out of simple awe, gratitude, or dismay in the face of creation. His universe is claustrophobically human, and his ambition and reputation alike remain in thrall to the weary concept of the "comic novel."

This is an interesting, if obtuse, appraisal of Kingsley Amis, for it correctly singles out much of what is distinctive about his work. With a slight change of tone, some readers might even take it for high praise. But while all of Amis's novels are funny, many of them are far from "comic," at least in the specifically limiting sense Updike has in mind. His vision of modern life is surprisingly, even shockingly black, and the laughter of his finest work is the uneasy kind provoked by a sudden vision of the skull beneath the skin.

Like so many other comic writers, Kingsley Amis was born into middle-class drabness. William Amis, his father, was a senior clerk in the export department of Colman's Mustard whose cultural tastes ran to Gilbert and Sullivan and detective stories. "My parents," Amis remembered, "evidently underwent a fairly gruelling nonconformist nurturing in and around a Baptist chapel in south-east London. By the time I came along they had moved a certain distance away from this environment. The training they gave me was strong in morality, rudimentary and quite uninsistent in questions of doctrine apart from a conventional taboo or two."

Amis's father shared the common desire to see his only child ascend the slippery pole of class, and so young Kingsley was sent to a private preparatory school, where he earned a scholarship to St. John's College, Oxford, in 1941. Though wartime Oxford was a sober and austere place, the undergraduate Amis contrived to be known as a militant Labourite, a jazz fanatic, and a virtuoso mimic. Decades later, his classmate Philip Larkin would recall Amis's phenomenal abilities in this last capacity:

> [H]e used it as the quickest way of convincing you that something was horrible or boring or absurd—the local comrade ("Eesa poincher see . . . assa poincher see"), the Irish tenor ("the sarn wass dee-cli-neeng"), the University CSM ("Goo on, seh"), a Russian radio announcer reading in English a bulletin from the Eastern Front ("twelf field mortars"), his voice suffering slow distortion to unintelligibility followed by a sudden reversion to clarity ("aberbera mumf mumf General von Paulus").

Amis was drafted in 1942 and served in the Royal Corps of Signals. After the war, he returned to St. John's College, where he took a first in English in 1947 and, that same year, brought out a volume of poetry called *Bright November*. In 1948, he married Hilary Ann Bardwell, by whom he had two sons "who turned up very fast, one after the other"; in 1949, he accepted a job as a lecturer in English at the University College of Swansea in South Wales.

Amis was soon recognized as a poet of modest but genuine accomplishment. "Kingsley Amis," Philip Larkin said in 1964, "I admire very much as a poet. . . . I think he's utterly original and can hit off a kind of satiric poem that no one else can (this is when he is being himself, not when he's Robert Graves)." Like Larkin, Amis was a charter member of The Movement, the group of plain-spoken English poets whose work, according to Robert Conquest's 1956 manifesto in the Movement anthology *New Lines,* was animated by "a refusal to abandon a rational structure and comprehensive language" and "a negative determination to avoid bad principles."

By the time these words appeared in print Kingsley Amis had already written *Lucky Jim*. Immediately upon its publication in 1954, this comic portrait of an inept young college professor from the lower middle class drew lavish praise from critics and readers in England and America. Even Somerset Maugham was impressed by the book, although he found Amis's scruffy characters disturbing. As he explained in his *Sunday Times* review:

> This is a new class that has entered upon the scene. It is the white-collar proletariat. Mr. Kingsley Amis is so talented, his observation is so keen, that you cannot fail to be convinced that the young men he so brilliantly describes truly represent the class with which his novel is concerned. They do not go to the university to acquire culture, but to get a job, and when they have got one, scamp it. . . . A few will go into Parliament, become Cabinet Ministers and rule the country. I look upon myself as fortunate that I shall not live to see it.

Clearly what distressed Maugham was not so much the novel as the postwar England in which it was set. Just as Kingsley Amis's Oxford had been a dour institution caught in an uncomfortable transition from the plovers' eggs of Charles Ryder to the austerities of a country at war, so was Amis's England turning into something strange and new: a centralized welfare state which, for all the earnest intentions of its founders, remained far from classless.

Young men like Jim Dixon, the hero of *Lucky Jim,* were stalwartly attempting to crash the economic and social barriers of class during the Fifties, and Amis was acutely aware of their struggles. His portrait of Professor Welch, the small-time cosmopolitan, with his madrigal sings and his readings of Anouilh in the original and his dogs named Ego and Id, rings every bit as true as that of Jim Dixon, who freely confesses to having specialized in medieval studies because "the medieval papers were a soft option in the Leicester course."

Where did the young Kingsley Amis learn to turn class differences into a source of biting comedy? For years, the American paperback edition of *Lucky Jim* carried on its cover the following blurb from Arthur Mizener: "No one has been so funny in this vein since Evelyn Waugh was at his best." While Amis has consistently acknowledged the influence of Waugh, he has also been careful not to overemphasize it. "I'm flattered," he said in 1985, "but the analogy is misleading. Waugh wrote very elegant comedy. His people spoke beautifully. Compared with his works, mine look like grim documentaries."

The grim settings and situations of Amis's early novels suggest another, less obvious source. Robert Conquest, writing in *New Lines,* cited "George Orwell, with his principle of real, rather than ideological honesty" as an important influence on the Movement poets, and it is a very short journey from the drab prewar England of *Coming Up for Air* and *Keep the Aspidistra Flying* to the equally drab postwar England of Jim Dixon, a scholarship boy who, like one of Orwell's hapless heroes, might easily have wound up selling insurance door to door or working in a second-hand bookshop had he been born twenty years earlier.

Still, Amis has at all times been a comic novelist, one who shared with Orwell a consuming interest in popular fiction. "The reading on which my writing has been founded," Amis wrote in 1986, "was always various, even indiscriminate, including as it did and taking seriously not only 'straight' novels but adventure stories, ghost stories, spy stories, detective stories, science fiction." When asked in 1975 to name the modern writers who had most influenced him, Amis mentioned Waugh, Anthony Powell, Angus Wilson, the early Joyce—and P.G. Wodehouse.

Asked what advice he would give to a young comic novelist, Wodehouse said: "I'd give him practical advice, and that is always get to the dialogue as soon as possible. I always feel the thing to go for is speed.... I think the success of every novel—if it's a good novel of action—depends on the high spots. The thing to do is to say to yourself, 'Which are my big scenes?' and then get every drop of juice out of them." *Lucky Jim* follows this advice to the letter. Like nearly all of Amis's novels, it begins *in medias res* (" 'They made a silly mistake, though,' the professor of history said, and his smile, as Dixon watched, gradually sank beneath the surface of his features at the memory") and charges directly into an action-packed plot in which set piece follows set piece with the relentless speed of *Right Ho, Jeeves* or *The Mating Season*.

From the beginning, Amis's knack for mimicry proved to be an invaluable novelistic means of depicting the nuances of class. Amis's characters, like Waugh's, are defined by their accents and their use of language. ("He quickly decided on a bluff, speak-my-mind approach as the best cloak for rudeness, past or to come. . . . Deliberately intensifying his northern accent, Dixon said: 'Afraid I got off on the wrong foot with you last night.' ") But while the young Waugh, following the example of Ronald Firbank, allowed his dialogue to speak almost entirely for itself, the young Amis sets his off, Wodehouse-style, with ironic commentary:

> If Welch didn't speak in the next five seconds, he'd do something which would get himself flung out without possible question—not the things he'd often dreamed of when sitting next door pretending to work. He no longer wanted, for example, to inscribe on the departmental timetable a short account, well tricked out with obscenities, of his views on the professor of history, the Department of History, medieval history, history, and Margaret and hang it out of the window for the information of passing students and lecturers, nor did he, on the whole, now intend to tie Welch up in his chair and beat him about the head and shoulders with a bottle until he disclosed why, without being French himself, he'd given his sons French names.

Kingsley Amis, as this passage suggests, was very much on the rampage in *Lucky Jim*. His own understanding of what he was attacking was not yet fully developed, though, and it is not surprising that *Lucky Jim* was widely read, even by so perceptive a critic as Edmund Wilson, as a fairly straightforward paean to English socialism: "Uncertain and perplexed though they are, [Amis's characters] have still something to build, to win. . . . The only things they have behind them to brace them are the victory of the Labour Government in 1945, the ideals of the Welfare State, and they hold out as best they can, at the cost of much nervous strain, much confusion of social relations, much sacrifice of individual dignity."

To be sure, *Lucky Jim* does pay homage to the egalitarian values of the Labour Party. ("If one man's got ten buns and another's got two, and a bun has got to be given up by one of them, then surely you take it from the man with ten buns.") But Jim Dixon's rebelliousness is less political than personal. He is, for instance, as quick to snap at "phoniness" as Holden Caulfield, his near-contemporary, and inclined to bristle defensively at the appearance of anything having to do with high culture ("The piece was recognisable to Dixon as some skein of untiring facetiousness by filthy Mozart").

Part of what Dixon and his creator were rebelling against, although this fact is not made explicit in *Lucky Jim,* was modernism. Speaking of the Angry Young Men as a group, an older Amis pointed out that "there was certainly no rebelliousness at all of treatment or presentation [in our books]. And we were, in that sense, reactionaries rather than rebels. We were trying to get back, let's say, to the pre-Joyce tradition, really—but not very consciously." For many of Amis's contemporaries, this rebellion would at times be scarcely distinguishable from out-and-out philistinism; Dixon's reflexive dislike of "filthy Mozart" is not so very far away from Philip Larkin's railing against "things that seemed crazy when they were new and seem crazy now, like *Finnegans Wake* and Picasso."

Amis's relationship to high culture, of course, is a great deal more ambivalent than the word "philistine" would suggest. Far from regarding Mozart as "filthy," for instance, Amis is an extremely well-informed music lover, and two of his later novels, *Girl, 20* and *The Alteration,* make convincing use of classical musicians as major characters. Amis's real quarrel, which he shared with Orwell and with the rest of the Angry Young Men, was not so much with high culture per se as with the pretentious upper-crust mandarinism of Cyril Connolly and the *Horizon* group. (Significantly, one of the things about Professor Welch that irritates Jim Dixon most is his interest in things French.)

Jim Dixon's greatest frustrations arise from of his difficulties with women. Like so many of Amis's later novels, *Lucky Jim* contains two contrasting principal female characters: Margaret, the sexual predator who symbolizes everything hostile and disagreeable and confusing about her sex, and Christine, whose behavior is equally confusing but who is prettier, more desirable, and far more agreeable. Like Orwell, Amis is quick to endow this sexual contrast with strong overtones of class conflict:

> The notion that women like [Christine] were never on view except as the property of men like [Professor Welch's son] was so familiar to him that it had long since ceased to appear an injustice. The huge class that contained Margaret was destined to provide his own womenfolk: those in whom the intention of being attractive could sometimes be made to get itself confused with performance.... But renewal always came: a new sweater would somehow scale down the large feet, generosity revivify the brittle hair, a couple of pints site positive charm in talk of the London stage or French food.

In *Lucky Jim,* the conflict is resolved predictably: Jim Dixon triumphs over the barriers of class, getting the nice girl and a better job and thumbing his nose at his snooty enemies. "The shits," Amis said of *Lucky Jim* in 1987, "all get their comeuppance in the end." This unabashedly happy ending is typical of the kind of book Kingsley Amis would write at regular intervals throughout the rest of his career: fast, funny, and not too long, with all the loose ends tied up neatly in the last chapter. But *Lucky Jim* also served as the calling card of an author of real promise, and his subsequent books would make good on this promise, sometimes in thoroughly unpredictable ways.

Given the enormous success of *Lucky Jim,* Kingsley Amis could have easily gone dry or, worse, repeated himself mechanically in sequel after sequel. Indeed, Jim Dixon might have made a rather charming series character, a sort of welfare-state Bertie Wooster. But Amis chose instead to follow up *Lucky Jim* in 1955 with the novel *That Uncertain Feeling,* the story of John Lewis, a Welsh librarian who finds himself entangled in an extramarital affair with a bitchy woman who, having married money, is looking for sexual adventure as well. Like *Lucky Jim, That Uncertain Feeling* is fast and funny, but its tone is far more unsettling, and the best Amis can contrive in the way of a happy ending is his hero's reluctant decision to leave town and take a lower-paying job at (of all places) a coal mine, there to remain faithful to his long-suffering wife and their children.

Throughout his career, Amis would alternate between straightforwardly comic novels like *I Like It Here* (1958) and *One Fat Englishman* (1963) and more adventurous books like *That Uncertain Feeling* and *Take a Girl Like You,* a longish novel dating from 1960 which tells the story of a beautiful young woman named Jenny Bunn and her determined struggle to remain virginal. *Take a Girl Like You,* like its predecessors, is set in Amisland, the sooty, shabby industrial town up the road from Wigan Pier where good jobs grow on other people's bushes and the landladies serve cheap breakfasts. "I kept a very thick and detailed notebook for *Take a Girl Like You*—about a hundred pages," Amis later recalled, and the result strongly resembles an old-fashioned social novel in its sober proliferation of detail. But Amis's purpose is uncertain. The greater length of *Take a Girl Like You* is not accompanied by a corresponding increase in gravity, and the reader ultimately feels that underneath the descriptive padding, the book's real scope is no greater than that of such lighter efforts as *Lucky Jim* or *That Uncertain Feeling.*

By this time, Kingsley Amis had revealed quite a bit about himself in the various essays and articles which were later collected in *What Became of Jane Austen?* (1970). The journalistic Amis is to some extent a theatrical creation, a beef-eating pantomime Englishman who, for all his untutored literary shrewdness, is nonetheless quite pleased to dismiss highbrow books like *Lolita* as "thoroughly bad" and "suffocatingly narrow," opting instead for a diverse assortment of popular wordsmiths ranging from Warwick Deeping to Mickey Spillane:

> It might well be agreed that the best of serious fiction, so to call it, is better than anything any genre can offer. But this best is horribly rare, and a clumsy

dissection of the heart is so much worse than boring as to be painful, and most contemporary novels are like spy novels with no spies or crime novels with no crimes, and John D. MacDonald is by any standards a better writer than Saul Bellow, only MacDonald writes thrillers and Bellow is a human-heart chap, so guess who wears the top-grade laurels?

Though the Kingsley Amis of *What Became of Jane Austen?* is something of a lowbrow poseur, he is also a perfectly sincere fan of genre fiction, and this affection led Amis to produce a book which was at once his first fully successful attempt at expanding the boundaries of the traditional comic novel and his first outright genre novel. Published in 1966, *The Anti-Death League* is a seriocomic spy thriller about Operation Apollo, a top-secret biological warfare experiment conducted by the British Army and aimed at Red China. Amis's large cast of characters exists not merely to exploit the rich comic potential of military life but to dramatize a far more serious problem: how to make sense of a godless world.

The progress of Operation Apollo is disrupted when Captain Max Hunter, an alcoholic homosexual, causes a scandal in the unit by secretly distributing leaflets advertising the formation of an "anti-death league" which has no purpose and no program save to enhance public outrage at the meaningless way some people die. ("*Case No. 1:* A woman of about 30 years old was dishing up the family supper. She took a potato out of the dish and popped it in her mouth. It lodged in her throat and she died of asphyxiation [sic] then and there, in front of her husband and 3 young children who were present at the time.")

Hunter's private anguish acquires added immediacy when his friend James Churchill, the hero of *The Anti-Death League,* falls in love with Catharine Casement, who promptly discovers that she is suffering from breast cancer. The absurdity of the world in which they live is emphasized when Operation Apollo is revealed to be an elaborate ruse undertaken for arcane strategic reasons. The message of the novel is stated explicitly by Catharine: "You knew very well that it's up to people not to get on with the bad things God has invented for them. It's their job to show they're better than he is."

Kingsley Amis's early novels are full of dark hints that the world is under the thumb of an actively malevolent creator. ("You atheist?" Yevgeny Yevtushenko once asked Kingsley Amis. His reply: "Well, yes, but it's more that I hate him.") *The Anti-Death League* is Amis's first full-scale treatment of this theme, and despite occasional lapses into sentimentality, it remains an impressive achievement, both for its emotional depth and for the ingenious way in which it uses the techniques of the thriller to serve more ambitious satirical ends. Kingsley Amis is still angry, but he is no longer so naive as to think that the world can be made noticeably better by taking a few extra buns from the rich and giving them to the poor.

In 1967, Kingsley Amis published an essay called "Why Lucky Jim Turned Right" in which he announced his acceptance of the conservative vision of human nature and its limits. ("Many of the evils of life—failure, loneliness, fear, boredom, inability to communicate—are ineradicable by political means.") Amis's political conversion was initially stimulated by his growing awareness of "more and more voluminous and unignorable evidence" of the evils of Communism, much of which was doubtless brought to his attention by his friend and colleague Robert Conquest. But his greatest contempt was reserved not for committed Communists but for the hopelessly phony "wets" of Sixties England:

> I mean the kind of person who . . . professes neutralism while reciting Hanoi's line; who says the East European satellites are really swinging places that have stopped bothering with politics; who used—when it was more newsy—to go on about Ian Smith's Fascist regime; who thinks student freedom is impaired when a college applies its statutes; who buys unexamined the abortion-divorce-homosexuality-censorship-racialism-marijuana package; in a word, the Lefty.

These concerns would become the subject matter of the 1968 novel *I Want It Now,* a fast-moving situation comedy in four sharply contrasted tableaux which focuses on the bumpy courtship of a glib young talk-show host on the make and a sexy, slightly deranged American heiress. *I Want It Now* takes on two ambitious subjects: the irresponsible rich and the trendy Left. Ronnie Appleyard is much like Jim Dixon, but he lives in a post-*Lucky Jim* world whose increased upward mobility has made it possible for refugees from the lower middle class to aspire to infinitely more stately mansions—at the price of their souls.

For all its underlying seriousness, Ronnie Appleyard's story in *I Want It Now* is told within the modest compass of the comic novel. Appleyard's frenzied efforts, like those of Jim Dixon, bring him happiness in the end; he keeps his job, gets the girl, and even becomes a less wet, more humane person into the bargain. ("I was a shit when I met you. I still am in lots of ways. But because of you I've had to give up trying to be a dedicated, full-time shit. I couldn't make it, hadn't the strength of character.") Similarly, Amis's next novel, *The Green Man* (1969), for all its considerable interest, remains safely within the precincts of the ghost story. With *Girl, 20* (1971), however, Amis takes as great a forward stride as he had five years earlier with *The Anti-Death League.*

On the surface, *Girl, 20* looks suspiciously like yet another of Amis's Wodehousean pastiches: short, brilliantly concentrated, full of sharp verbal satire and richly comic set pieces. But the humor in *Girl, 20* is ferociously dark, even more so than in *The Anti-Death League,* and Sir Roy Vandervane, the anti-hero of the novel, is the most complex character Amis has yet created. Sir Roy is a musician of real, if second-rate, talent. But he is also a first-rate phony, for his politics are casually leftish (by now a reliably bad sign in any Amis character) while his private life is entirely subordinated to the increasingly desperate pursuit of nubile, ever-younger women.

The amorous adventures of Sir Roy and Douglas Yandell, the music critic and amateur pianist who serves as narrator, keep the focus of *Girl, 20* squarely on women and their discontents, a perfectly natural development for an author whose first marriage had recently ended in divorce. Accordingly, the portrait of love in the Sixties sketched by Amis in *Girl, 20* is altogether forbidding. In *The Anti-Death League,* Amis allowed his principal characters the solace of love in the midst of chaos. Not so in *Girl, 20*. Kitty, Sir Roy's wife, is doomed to a life of unhappy solitude; Penny, his daughter, becomes a heroin addict; Sylvia, his seventeen-year-old mistress, is a practitioner of "moral vandalism" who is clearly psychopathic. Even Vivienne, Douglas Yandell's charmingly eccentric girlfriend, walks out on him at the end of *Girl, 20* because, despite his solid, even stodgy aesthetic values, Douglas lacks the moral strength fully to commit himself to a romantic relationship.

In its fusion of high comedy and serious intent, *Girl, 20* represents an apotheosis of the Wodehouse-style comic novel. It also marks the high point of Amis's use of language as a medium through which the social and cultural follies of English life can be savagely guyed. ("It was . . . a quarter, or chamber concerto for violin, with parts for sitar, bass guitar and bongoes. Across the top of the first sheet *Elevations 9* was written, perhaps by way of title. I felt a particular loathing for that 9: either there were eight other *Elevations* or the numeral was arbitrary, a piece of decor, which was nearly as bad.")

Perhaps inevitably, the novels which followed *Girl, 20* were all less successful in their various ways. *The Riverside Villas Murder* and *The Alteration* are well-made genre novels, the first an old-fashioned detective story, the second an exceptionally clever "alternate world" fantasy about what England would have been like in 1976 if the Protestant Reformation had never taken place; *Ending Up* (1974), a tale of old age and physical decline, is a mordant but slight variation on Muriel Spark's *Memento Mori*.

Jake's Thing, by contrast, is a clear attempt to recapture the darkly comic mood of *Girl, 20*, this time taking as a point of departure the adventures of a middle-aged man who, finding himself impotent, dives crotch-first into the therapy racket. The subject is promising, allowing Amis to focus on the affectations of postwar English culture and the war between the sexes, two of his favorite targets. But the treatment is too obviously studied; one feels that Amis is self-consciously "doing" the world of psychobabble in *Jake's Thing* and that his satirical shots are insufficiently incisive for so gifted a marksman.

More disturbing is the obvious coarsening of Amis's prose style. The author of *Jake's Thing* is no longer capable of the lapidary concentration of *Girl, 20*. His ear is less sure, his style less pithy. This loss of tautness can be found to an even greater degree in *Russian Hide-and-Seek,* a fantasy about

England under Soviet rule. *Russian Hide-and-Seek* may have been turned down by American publishers for political reasons, but it remains Amis's weakest novel for artistic ones.

In *Stanley and the Women,* published in 1984, Kingsley Amis moves for the first time since *The Anti-Death League* beyond the narrow technical confines of the comic and genre novels. Longer and more serious in tone than *Jake's Thing,* this book is the climax of Amis's growing tendency to regard the war between men and women as a permanent and unwinnable battle; indeed, *Stanley and the Women* almost seems at first glance to be the finished novel for which *Jake's Thing* was merely a preliminary study.

Stanley Duke, the hero and narrator of *Stanley and the Women,* is a middle-aged businessman with a good job and a seemingly happy second marriage. His teenage son, Steve, suddenly develops symptoms of what turns out to be schizophrenia, and Stanley's second wife simultaneously reveals that she no longer loves him. When Steve goes to a female psychiatrist, the reader is led to expect a brutal attack on feminism. Instead, Stanley goes much farther, arguing that not merely feminists but all women are amoral, untrustworthy monsters. There is no "good" woman character in *Stanley and the Women,* for both of Stanley's women, not to mention Steve's therapist, turn out to be predators of the very worst kind. The familiar predator-nice girl pairing of Amis's earlier novels has turned into something far more disturbing: predator-predator.

Midway through *Stanley and the Women,* Stanley Duke suggests that "women were like Russians—if you did exactly what they wanted all the time you were being realistic and constructive and promoting the cause of peace, and if you ever stood up to them you were resorting to cold-war tactics and pursuing imperialistic designs and interfering in their internal affairs." As readers of "Why Lucky Jim Turned Right" know, no comparison, coming from Amis, could be more damning. And the case against women is made even more directly at the end of the novel when a sympathetic male psychiatrist delivers the following speech:

> Good God, you've had wives, haven't you? And not impossibly had some acquaintance with other women as well? You can't be new to feeling the edge of the most powerful weapon in their armoury. You must have suffered before from the effect of their having noticed . . . that men are different, men quite often wonder whether they're doing the right thing and worry about it, men have been known to blame themselves for behaving badly, men not only feel they've made mistakes but on occasion will actually admit having done so, and say they're sorry, and ask to be forgiven, and promise not to do it again, and mean it. Think of that! Mean it. All beyond female comprehension. Which incidentally is why they're not novelists and must never be priests.

Stanley Duke is not wholly without a crude kind of sympathy for women. "The root of all the trouble," he says, "is we want to fuck them, the pretty ones, women I mean. Just try and imagine it happening to you, everyone wanting to fuck you wherever you go." But Stanley derives no comfort from his limited understanding of the feminine dilemma. At the end of *Jake's Thing,* Jake Richardson, offered a miracle cure decides that he would rather remain impotent than have to put up with women. The end of *Stanley and the Women* is bleaker still: Stanley becomes reconciled with his second wife. "While she hurried on about having been so desperately frightened and upset and one thing and another," he says at the very end of the book, realizing that he is trapped in a hopeless, universal dilemma, "I turned towards Cliff, who did the brief lift of the chin South London people use to mean Told you so or Here we go again or Wouldn't you bleeding know. People elsewhere too, I dare say. Perhaps all over the world."

The uncontrolled rage of the male characters in *Stanley and the Women* is as disquieting as the continuing lack of focus in Amis's prose, and the knowledge that Amis's own second marriage (to the novelist Elizabeth Jane Howard) had ended in divorce shortly before the publication of *Stanley and the Women* necessarily colors one's reading of this horrifying fictional portrait of a second marriage gone sour. Not surprisingly, many reviewers of *Stanley and the Women* went so far as to accuse Kingsley Amis of sharing the misogyny of Stanley Duke and his friends. "A novel," Amis retorted, "is not a report or a biographical statement or a confession. If it is a good novel, it dramatizes thoughts that some people, somewhere, have had. Haven't most men, at moments of high exasperation, thought, 'They're all mad'?"

The real message of *Stanley and the Women* probably lies somewhere between these two poles. Amis returns again and again in his novels to the theme of the extreme difficulty, if not hopelessness, inherent in human relationships; *Stanley and the Women* takes a more jaundiced (and less convincing) view than usual of the degree to which women are the cause of the problem.

Stanley and the Women is dedicated to "Hilly," Amis's first wife, to whom he grew more closely attached with advancing age. Amis's 1987 entry in *Current Biography* has as its penultimate sentence the following bald statement: "Amis lives in a self-contained ground-floor flat in a house in north London that he shares with his first wife and her third husband, Lord Kilmarnock." *The Old Devils,* written in 1986, suggests that these changes in Amis's life wrought a welcome transformation in his writing as well.

The scene of *The Old Devils* is Wales, locale of *That Uncertain Feeling,* and the action of the novel concerns the gradual reconciliation of a pair of aging lovers who parted nearly forty years before. There is no diminution of harshness in Amis's satire, but the world of *The Old Devils,* for all its disillusion and brutality, is one in which even the very old can achieve redemption of a limited but genuine kind through the power of love.

This is a note which has been missing from Amis's "serious" novels since *The Anti-Death League,* and it is made all the more powerful by the fact that he sounds it with a restored technical authority. In *The Old Devils,* the slackness of Amis's last few novels has hardened into a more persuasive narrative style. The rapidity and pithiness of his early comic efforts have been successfully exchanged for the subtleties of a broader fictional canvas. The cast of characters in *The Old Devils* is large, the plot accordingly complex, and while there is little of the sheer comic brilliance of *Lucky Jim* or *Girl, 20,* there is in its place an unforced human warmth. Rhiannon, the woman who triggers unexpected depths of feeling in most of the men in *The Old Devils,* is the first female character in Amis's work with the complexity and roundness of Jim Dixon or Max Hunter or Sir Roy Vandervane. No mere misogynist could possibly have imagined her, much less have written so deeply moving a story of old age and romantic love.

Amis's latest novel, *Difficulties with Girls,* recently published in England and due out here next year from Summit, represents a relaxation of the newfound expressive powers of *The Old Devils.* A sequel to *Take a Girl Like You, Difficulties with Girls* is an easy-going examination of the married life of Jenny Bunn, one of Amis's most engaging and sympathetic characters. As the title of the book suggests, *Difficulties with Girls* rings amusing changes on many of Amis's familiar themes. But *Difficulties with Girls,* clever, entertaining, and assured though it is, nonetheless adds little to our knowledge of Kingsley Amis. *The Old Devils* must remain his valedictory statement to date, and it is an impressive one. For a writer to have made so singular an artistic advance so late in his career is a truly noteworthy achievement, one which suggests that Amis's best work may still lie ahead of him.

Some reviewers thought that Kingsley Amis wrote *The Old Devils* as an act of literary contrition after the rage and malice of *Stanley and the Women.* Michiko Kakutani even suggested that "[i]nstead of making fun of his characters' dilemmas, Mr. Amis has chosen this time to write each of them—men and women—from the inside, and this decision . . . burnishes the entire novel with the luster of redemption." But Amis surely needs no redeeming. Though his cultural targets have shifted since the days of *Lucky Jim,* the wit with which he skewers them, and the outraged moral values on which that wit feeds, have remained constant; he is still "finding out new ways" to attack the bad things in an absurd world. Meanwhile, his early satirical thrusts have outlived their original social contexts and retained their sharpness and pertinence.

This is not to say that Amis is a great novelist. In fact, he has gone to some pains to avoid the traps that await the writer who purposefully aspires to greatness. Amis told an interviewer in 1975 that Gore Vidal's novels "suffer from American cleverness: the fear of being thought stupid, or dull, or behind the times. I think that's a very bad attitude for the novelist to adopt." Despite the deliberate modesty of his own artistic attitudes, Kingsley Amis has done virtually everything one might possibly expect of a novelist, particularly a comic one. To read Amis's novels in bulk, rather than merely dipping into *Lucky Jim* or *Stanley and the Women,* is to realize that he has created not a miscellaneous shelf of amusing entertainments but a distinctive oeuvre full of character and complexity.

Comparisons with Evelyn Waugh remain hard to resist. Waugh's classicism, his ruthless detachment, the silent but omnipresent religious underpinnings of his early books: all of these qualities lend to his best work a greater depth and artistic purity. But Amis still remains Waugh's closest postwar counterpart, a genre writer of satirical bent whose output is nonetheless far more serious and satisfying than that of most of his peers and virtually all of his juniors, Amis *fils* included. Some of his novels may well prove to be "major," and one cannot doubt that most of them will continue to be read with real pleasure.

Kingsley's Ransom
Why have the British been bashing the original Amis?

James Wolcott

Late this summer, a literary crime was committed in London: if the victim had been a woman, it might have been called "granny bashing." The elderly gentleman being ganged up on was Kingsley Amis, who, at seventy-three, had brought out his twenty-fourth novel, "The Biographer's Moustache," to little acclaim. The majority opinion was that this book revealed sad evidence of diminished capacity. The *Observer:* " 'The Biographer's Moustache' is reflex writing, full of Pavlovian pedantry." The *Sunday Times:* "A stale, flat, savourless affair." The *Daily Mail:* "Banal, boring and extremely silly." Terribly dated, nearly everyone agreed. Amis, having been a pooh-bah on the public scene for decades, had become an overstuffed father figure, and father figures are made to be toppled. (After beating up on the father figure, the London press then smacked the son figure around, taking special glee in the failure of Martin Amis's much hyped "The Information" to be short-listed for the Booker Prize.)

If the reviews of Kingsley Amis's new novel reached a hostile decision (Pack it in, Pops), the interviews intended to promote it were even nastier. They literally added insult to injury. In August, Amis had one of the all-time bad months. His old friend the solicitor Stuart Thomas died; Amis spoke at the funeral service. At the time, he was a guest at the Swansea, Wales, home of his friends Michael and Virginia Rush, and in none too fine repair himself. When a *Guardian* interviewer, Joanna Coles, and her photographer arrived, Amis joked about a groin pull and grumbled about being dislodged from the sofa to have his picture taken in better light. You might think an interviewer would sympathize with the plight of a septuagenarian in obvious discomfort, but no, Amis was treated as if he were a prima donna holding up production. A more damning portrait was drawn by Glenys Roberts, for the *Daily Telegraph,* who likened Amis to "a cross between Winnie the Pooh and the misogynist American comedian W. C. Fields" and then complained that she was able to tweeze only a few quotes from him. That morning, Amis had taken a

---

From *New Yorker* Oct 30, 1995. Reprinted with kind permission of James Wolcott, contributing editor to *Vanity Fair.*

serious spill on the stairs, landing on his back, and as he waited on the sofa for the doctor, he sloughed off her questions. "It isn't often one goes from London to Swansea to meet a famous figurehead and encounters such a lack of civility for one's pains," Roberts fumed. No, it probably isn't. Given that Amis was physically racked, and dispirited about the death of his friend, he would probably have been better off cancelling the interviews instead of staring out into space in long, Pinteresque silences. The reviews of his interviews proved more scathing than the reviews of his book. The *Evening Standard* took a stern line with the geriatric juvenile delinquent: "Journalists should not let him get away with it.... If it is not possible to come up with anything remotely new or interesting, newspapers should not print this stuff."

Amis's oft-quoted line about bad reviews is that they ruin his breakfast but not his lunch. Yet such a battery of setbacks, public and private, may have been a serious blow even to an old curmudgeon with a thick crust. Amis had cracked a couple of vertebrae in his fall, and shortly afterward he suffered a stroke and ended up in the intensive-care unit of a London hospital. "I fear he may be on the way down," one longtime friend says.

I had no knowledge of this when I read the hostile notices of "The Biographer's Moustache." At the time, I merely found myself experiencing such cognitive dissonance that I ordered the book from England toot sweet. For many of the very sentences that reviewers had singled out as examples of slack execution, faltering powers, or rabid prejudice made me laugh. One critic was baffled by the line "A girl of about thirty answered his ring apparently clad in an excerpt from the Bayeux Tapestry." Another was offended by the sentence "Wishing he had been drunk, Gordon got on a bus apparently reserved for winners and runners-up in some pan-European repulsiveness contest." Another cited this supposed clunker: "Gordon got to his feet as Louise had done and grappled with her briefly in an amatory way, at the end of which she disengaged herself without hostility and telephoned for a minicab." This deadpan diagram struck me as inspired—a perfect Etch-A-Sketch drawing of the activities of a pair of stick figures. Admittedly, I'm favorably predisposed. As someone who has read virtually everything Amis has written, including such little-known curiosities as his study of Rudyard Kipling, I always look forward to the latest Amis novel not as a separate and detachable art work but as an opportunity to spend time in his mental company.

For better or worse—mostly better—Amis loosened the collar of English prose. He loosened its tongue. Not that he did it alone: Anthony Powell mastered the art of taking a sentence the long way round; Ivy Compton-Burnett hung thick nettings of domestic discourse; Henry Green dropped petals in the unimpeded flow of his characters' consciousness. But it was Amis who invested writing with the largest volume of chat. Beginning in 1954, with "Lucky Jim," he made a performance art of the right inflection, and not just in his fiction. The journalistic reviews collected in "What Became of Jane Austen?" and "The Amis Collection" have a slangy, matey tone that is a deliberate slap at both the grim spectre of F. R. Leavis, the forbidding Cambridge don who was said to have decried Amis as a "pornographer," and the belletristic legacy of Bloomsbury, wherein books were discussed in terms of breeding and palate. Amis opinionized in an off-duty mode, his manner frank and relaxed. He would discuss Keats not as a doomed Romantic immortal but as a chap who sometimes got a little flowery. According to Harry Ritchie, a contributor to a 1991 Amis Festschrift, Amis's reviewing has had a powerful influence on postwar English criticism. Now, he wrote, "the democratic wise-cracking of critics such as Clive James and John Carey, inspired by Amis's example, constitutes a new orthodoxy."

Amis's deceptively casual approach was more than a tactical ploy, a way of sneaking in punches; it expressed his conviction that language loses its responsive energy and observant value when it becomes overjewelled and forcibly sublime. He deplored Nabokov's aestheticizing of the mother's car death in "Lolita." After quoting the description of "a porridge of bone, brains, bronze hair, and blood," he remarked, "That's the boy, Humbert/Nabokov: alliterative to the last." He made sport of Evelyn Waugh's "Brideshead Revisited" in a review smartly titled "How I Lived in a Very Big House and Found God," deploring how Waugh's abject awe of religion and the aristocracy turned his once pristine prose into slosh. He even took Jane Austen to task for turning priggish in "Mansfield Park." He saw literature not as a mountain range of Towering Masterpieces but as a series of individual involvements that engage us at eye level and can be divided into those books we fancy and those we don't. Or, as he wrote, "Importance isn't important. Only good writing is."

And good writing can be found anywhere, in any genre. Amis was one of the first active practitioners (as opposed to pop-cult theorists) to see that the traditional literary novel has no monopoly on art. He monkeyed with the class system in literature, treating the categories of high-, low-, and middlebrow fiction as rough equals. Along with his serious comedies ("Take a Girl Like You," "Stanley and the Women," "The Old Devils"), he wrote an innovative mainstream treatise on science fiction ("New Maps of Hell") and an uncondescending study of James Bond ("The James Bond Dossier"), and later tried his hand at his own post-Ian Fleming Bond novel ("Colonel Sun"). He has also plowed the horror graveyard ("The Green Man"), played "what if?" with history ("Russian Hide-and-Seek," "The Alteration"), and dabbled in walking the detective beat ("The Crime of the Century"). Always an antimodernist, Amis rebelled against the role of the artist as deep-sea diver of the inner universe (Flaubert, Joyce, Woolf, Proust, Beckett: take your exemplary pick). He preferred to cast himself as a versatile pro running a modest amusement shop. His stance reflects not only a practical Everyman approach to writing but the distinctive English aversion to looking pretentious. But to Amis's detractors his pretension-avoidance was just a facet of his inherent philistinism and hostility to anything that smacked of cultural enhancement. (Translation: He thinks we're sissies!)

In his new book, Amis plays footsie with fact and fiction; "The Biographer's Moustache" was written parallel with the completion of the authorized biography of Amis by Eric Jacobs, which was published in England earlier this year. The biography, a dutiful, uninspired job, did turn up an interesting fact about Amis's childhood—that his mother, worried about his nourishment, spoon-fed Kingsley his meals until he was twelve or thirteen years old. "Then a new regime took over, though only slightly more adult," Jacobs writes. "After some minutes toying with the food on his plate, Kingsley would say, 'Mum, would you sort it out for me?' Mum then divided what was left into two parts, the food that definitely must be eaten and the rest that Kingsley could leave if he wished." This mollycoddling explains Amis's reliance on others for his routines, and his sense of himself as a little monarch. The critic Paul Fussell saw much of Amis in the sixties; he and his then wife, Betty, who is a food writer, knew what it was like to live under his rule. Betty Fussell recalls, "Kingsley's rituals. We all lived by them when we were with Kingsley—man, woman, and child—because we had to. They were the order of the day, as inviolable as military commands or church liturgies." Even on holiday, people had to abide by Amis time. She writes, "Breakfast with the papers was punctually at 9 A.M., even if Kingsley had fallen dead drunk into bed at 4 A.M. after a liquid intake that reduced the rest of us to Jell-O for the next 24 hours."

Kingsley's maintenance routine has continued despite changes of address. He shares a house in north London with his first wife, Hilly, and her third husband, Lord Kilmarnock—an odd living arrangement, which Amis himself has admitted smacks of an Iris Murdoch novel. Hilly brings him dinner every Monday, Wednesday, Friday, and Sunday. On Tuesdays and Thursdays, his daughter Sally pinch-hits. And what Amis's critics didn't seem to appreciate is that Jimmie Fane, the biographical subject in "The Biographer's Moustache," is also something of a stuffed goose. Like his creator, Fane has a lot of bluff in his makeup. Paul Fussell, who has written a thorny valentine to Amis called "The Anti-Egotist: Kingsley Amis, Man of Letters," told me that one of his chum's most admirable traits is that, "compared to Americans, he doesn't have an ounce of sincerity about him—everything he says is figurative." Likewise Fane. Everything he does is for foggy effect.

In this portrait of the artist as aging matinée idol, Amis is mostly making fun of his own inflatable persona—puncturing his own gasbag. Fane is a toady to the rich, a meal sponger, a wine snob, and a word bore ("These days I'm told the creatures have the impertinence to call themselves *gay,* thereby rendering unusable, thereby destroying a fine old English word with its roots deep in the language"). He diverts himself by playing pranks on his hapless biographer, the aforementioned Gordon—one of those earnest nonentities who make useful foils in English fiction. Gordon's abuse at the hands of Fane and his brief, wrenching affair with Fane's wife, Joanna, serve as his sentimental education. Never again will he partake of aristocratic nooky. At the end, Gordon recognizes Jimmie Fane for the shit he is—a "massive and multifarious shit." Nor does Fane's fiction pass inspection; the seemingly rich ambiguities of his early prose are laid bare by Gordon as "abject piss, well beyond any excuse of a comprehensive change of taste, simple passage of thirty years or more, etc." It's as if Amis were imagining the worst that could be said about his own output—imagining himself consigned to limbo.

A number of reviewers complained about the lack of engine in the novel's narrative. Fair enough; yet story has never been Amis's strength. (The plot of "Lucky Jim" didn't roar down the railroad tracks.) Amis's non-genre novels have always been ambulatory exercises in mulling things over. Where so much of current literary fiction either aims for damnation, combing the alleys in search of sex demons and serial killers, or strives for affirmation, seeking the rainbow over the bridges of Madison County, "The Biographer's Moustache" muddles through the middle latitudes of normalcy, which are laced with random nuttiness. Amis's characters don't scan the world through photo-realist lenses, putting a price-tag on every item of furniture and fashion; they take things in a general lump.

But beneath their surface inertia is what Fussell calls Amis's "highly rapid ironic intelligence." Amis's novels are always operating at two speeds simultaneously—a slower narrative speed and a faster judgmental clip. Behind their putty faces, Amis's characters formulate thoughts and store grievances; they mimic "all's well" even as their minds articulate like mad. The tension builds slowly and is discharged in a cloudburst of pique and frustration—like the exchange in "Girl, 20" when the narrator asks a friend's young mistress what makes her such a "howling bitch," and she replies in a snap:

> I expect it's the same thing as makes you a top-heavy red-haired four-eyes who's never had anything to come up to being tossed off by the Captain of Boats and impotent and likes bloody symphonies and fugues and the first variation comes before the statement of the theme and give me a decent glass of British beer and dash it all Carruthers I don't know what young people are coming to these days and a scrounger and an old woman and a failure and a hanger-on and a prig and terrified and a shower and a brisk rub-down every morning and you can't throw yourself away on a little trollop like that Roy you must think of your wife Roy old boy old boy and I'll come along but I don't say I approve and bloody dead. Please delete the items in the above that do not apply. If any.

(For a misogynist, Amis often gives the women the choicest comebacks—if not the last word, then the knockout next-to-last word.)

The machinery of "The Biographer's Moustache" is sleepy, and the invective is more contained (though there is a passing reference to "his bloody lordship and his piss-artist elephant's-bum-faced four-eyed boiler of a wife"), but the book transports the reader along to a brilliant set piece in the ancestral home of a dotty duke—a sort of P. G. Wodehouse Blandings Castle novel in compact form. Here Jimmie introduces Gordon to sylvan haunts similar to those of his youth:

> The view before them was certainly unusual in that, to the eye of a town-dweller at least, it contained nothing of the twentieth century no power lines, no metal fences, no machinery, no advertisement. . . . Nevertheless the scene made no more than a puny appeal to Gordon personally. It was green, brown here and there but mostly green, motionless, silent, unpopulated and asking for the addition of a passage in curlicued italics about man's quest through the ages.

This country interlude saves "The Biographer's Moustache." It reminds you that a novel is not a blueprint for better living or a spiritual guidebook but an organism, with its own breathing patterns. For all the talk of Amis's patented misanthropy, the book is almost suspiciously free of malice.

"The Biographer's Moustache" is agreeable minor Amis, somewhere below "Lucky Jim" and "Stanley and the Women," and above "I Want It Now" and "Difficulties with Girls." Given his age, drinking habits, and shaky health, it's a wonder Amis bothers banging out a book at all. It isn't as if he had anything additional to prove. If you pick up "Lucky Jim" today, you're impressed by how much it has retained its original fizz. Written over a period of seven years, during which Amis was peppered with encouragement and advice from the poet Philip Larkin (to whom the novel was dedicated), this academic comedy, published in 1954, about Jim Dixon, a young instructor at a podunk college, remains the classic test case: how does a bright mind cope with creeping boredom? Trying to pass as a capable young man, Dixon indulges in a full repertory of facial expressions (hearing his name called, he makes his "shot-in-the-back face") and anti-cant exercises. (When he reads a paper that begins, "In considering this strangely neglected topic. . . ," he asks himself, "This what neglected topic? This strangely what topic? This strangely neglected what?") "Lucky Jim" also contains Amis's prototypical hangover scene: "His mouth had been used as a latrine by some small creature of the night, and then as its mausoleum."

In an era in which Bret Easton Ellis and Susanna Moore run a chop shop of body parts, Jim Dixon's escapades seem as innocent as Archie comics. But the success of "Lucky Jim" provoked a furor that (unlike the furor over Ellis's "American Psycho") disclosed and defined a deep crack in the prevailing culture. Dixon may have been an incorrigible dear, but the social type he represented struck many as dastardly. Somerset Maugham, who admired the book, nevertheless washed his hands of its antihero, this "white-collar proletariat." Dixon and his ilk are ill-mannered layabouts, Maugham said, who frequent alehouses—"they are scum." Amis was lumped with the Angry Young Men, who included John Wain, John Braine ("Room at the Top"), and, most famously, John Osborne ("Look Back in Anger"). In a perceptive essay, "Class War in British Literature," Leslie A. Fiedler declared that the Angry Young Men's mission was to overturn the tea table where the genteel spirits of Auden and Eliot presided. They had no patience for exquisite taste, for "the Sitwells and Russian ballet"; that world bore no relation to the ugly, red-nosed mass-culture world around them. Snorts of laughter were their weapons in this war. Of the Angries, only Amis demonstrated creative staying power. (Osborne, for example, became a fulminating fop, like some deranged version of Captain Peacock on "Are You Being Served?") Amis had the stubbornness of the artist who learns how to ration his intake of experience and process it for later release. He paced himself to produce facsimiles of life in bite-size pieces.

After a spotty period in the early eighties, in 1986 Amis won the Booker Prize for "The Old Devils," that jangly group portrait of lust and swollen livers among the Geritol set, and then, in 1990, he was knighted. With one eye on the exit, he published his "Memoirs," which mixed anecdotes he had dined out on for years with a few revisionist put-downs. The Russian expert Robert Conquest, an old friend of Amis's and his collaborator on "The Egyptologists," told me that he'd noticed an anecdote about himself in the manuscript of Amis's memoir which wasn't true; after he pointed this out, Amis substituted Philip Toynbee's name—"which I don't think was accurate, either."

Amis has recently completed a new nonfiction book, and he was deep in the bag of yet another novel before his illness. Very few American writers continue to plug away past the point of glory, but Amis has been harnessed to his work habits. He would rise each morning for a small meal of yogurt and honey, put in three hours of work, break for lunch, then write for another hour in the afternoon. "That's four hours a day, every day, seven days a week," he informed the *Guardian*. Yet this steady application is more than a sturdy example of neo-Victorian work ethic, akin to the production schedule Trollope kept. Morale is a fragile mechanism. The diligence of Amis's daily routine expresses a strong psychological drive to keep the motor running, as if Amis believed that if he came to a halt a greater power would seize possession: his life would be impounded. "The moment you stop writing, you're turning your face to the wall," he told Joanna Coles, of the *Guardian*.

One of the most interesting revelations in the grudging interviews Amis gave was that he still dopes himself to sleep at night. "I pill myself up. Very relaxing, pills and Scotch. I sleep very well. It's partly drugged sleep, of course. But better drugged sleep than no sleep." On being asked if he could sleep without his dosage, he replied, "I don't know, I'm not going to take the risk. I don't like lying in bed tossing and turning. I used to be scared of the dark." (Readers of "The Old Devils" will recall the character Charlie, who suffered from this same fear.) By giving himself knockout drops at night, Amis is hastening sleep and blotting out intimations of mortality before they can muster an appearance. He chooses a small oblivion to ward off a bigger one. If his fiction sometimes reads like a groggy dream with the cobwebs still clinging, perhaps this is because it's the product of so much fermented anxiety. Like Hemingway near the end, Amis, in recent photographs, resembles a desolate hulk; his body has become a haunted house. "There is no personal God. There is no point to life," he told Glenys Roberts, of the *Telegraph,* with "utter finality," adding, "Though there is a point to art." And what is the point? To give other people pleasure, he said, with what Roberts deemed "uncharacteristic generosity."

In the current climate, beauty and pleasure are doomed to be obscured by character issues, which are in turn governed by attitudes toward race, class, sex, and politics. The posthumous reputation of Philip Larkin has been pitted by the publication of his letters and Andrew Motion's biography, which document his racist jingles, reactionary gibes, miserliness, damp palm for soft porn, and unwillingness to commit to the women in his life, all adding up to an image of a mama's boy in a dirty old man's raincoat—not the picture of a lyric poet you want to carry in your locket. Even Fussell, a staunch cultural conservative, says that he has become "disaffected with Larkin's character," which he now finds "hateful." Amis has always been more open about his cranks and antipathies than Secret Agent Larkin, so there'll be less shock at whatever indiscretions are later divulged, but not necessarily lighter reprimand. Inklings of the toxic leakage to come can be found in Jacobs's biography, a prize exhibit for future prosecution being a photograph of Amis on the beach which shows the words written in lipstick on his back by his wife Hilly, who was fed up with his philandering: "1 FAT ENGLISHMAN I FUCK ANYTHING." The caption notes, "They split up shortly afterwards." Amis went on to marry the novelist Elizabeth Jane Howard, with whom he had been having an affair. When that marriage dissolved, years later, the divorce was bitter and public. Robert Conquest recalls Howard's denouncing Amis in the press: "You'd pick up the paper one day and there'd be the headline 'How Kingsley Ruined My Life.' Then a few days later would be the headline 'How Kingsley Ruined Our Holidays.' " The Jacobs biography also reprints the draft of an unfinished, unpublished poem Amis sent to Conquest, a Kiplingesque ditty that ends:

> The usual sort of men
>   Who hold the world together
> Manage to face their front
>   In any sort of weather.
>
> With rueful grins and curses
>   They push the world along;
> But women and queers and children
>   Cry when things go wrong.

The paradox is that it's often easier to pardon true, frothing bigots, like Céline or Ezra Pound, because they seem so lashed by pathological furies; their sort of prejudice can be analyzed as the black ash of a charred heart. Next to them, Amis and Larkin merely sound cheeky. They're firing poison blow darts.

Yet compared with such hearties on this side of the Atlantic as Hemingway and Norman Mailer, Amis isn't so macho. The Amis man does not seek conquest of women and dominion over his shining field of endeavor; like his creator, the Amis man wants to settle into a comfortable rut. He is a longtime combatant in the sex wars, who no longer has the energy or the inclination to do more than kvetch about the minor irritations of his captive fate. (The last page of "Stanley and the Women" declared a domestic truce.) And a small rivulet of remorse trickles through the rut the Amis men travel from home to office to pub. It springs from Amis's personal history, from his persistent sorriness over the breakup of his marriage to Hilly. He snapped at the *Guardian* reporter who asked if he ever wondered whether things could have been otherwise: "Of course it could have been otherwise, but you don't think of that at the time, do you?"

No, you think of it later, and try to make amends. In the final line of "The Old Devils," Malcolm sits down to write a poem to an old love—"The poem, his poem, was going to be the best tribute he could pay to the only woman who had ever cried for him." Amis's biographer notes that the novel "You Can't Do Both," the predecessor of "The Biographer's Moustache," is an extended note of regret addressed to Hilly, and a subplot in "The Biographer's Moustache" involves restitution to a woman from the past. But it is more than guilt that sends Amis's heroes on these good-will missions. They're also expressing a fear attendant on death. The saddest fate in an Amis novel is to be alone, ailing, and unvisited. Amis men may resent being dependent on women, but they would miss having someone to talk to even more. Kingsley Amis has kept writing because he knows that death is when you reach the end of your words.

An Interview with Kingsley Amis

Conducted by Dale Salwak

Since his first novel, *Lucky Jim* (1953), Kingsley Amis has become widely known as a novelist, poet, social and political commentator, and literary critic. Born an only child in suburban London on April 16, 1922, he was educated at the City of London School and St. John's College, Oxford, and served in the British Army (1942–45) as an officer in the Royal Signal Corps. He married Hilary Ann Bardwell in 1948, dissolved the marriage in 1965, and married the novelist Elizabeth Jane Howard in the same year. He has taught at various universities, including Swansea, Princeton, Cambridge, and Vanderbilt. Now a full-time writer and journalist, Amis lives in Barnet, Hertfordshire.

Mr. Amis and I met on January 24 and 30, 1973, at the Travellers' Club in London. The sessions included two hours of taped interview each day. I must extend my deep appreciation to Dr. Gordon N. Ray, President of the John Simon Guggenheim Memorial Foundation, for arranging my interview with Kingsley Amis; to Myrtle C. Bachelder at the University of Chicago, for financial aid in making my trip to London possible; and to Kingsley Amis, who treated me with the utmost generosity.

Q. Considering your background and education, did you find it particularly difficult breaking into the establishment as a young writer?
A. No. I want to record an emphatic no to that one. I started off with no social advantages at all. I acquired two very substantial ones. Having been to Oxford and having gotten a good degree at Oxford helped a great deal. And I'd heard there was a thing called the London literary racket which people used to talk about very much in the early 1950s, and that it was all an interlocking network in which Jones would review Smith's book favorably and vice versa, in which jobs were given to people you'd been to school with, and so on. That may have been going on but I never saw it, and it never did me any harm. I found my progress unimpeded by any external matters of that sort. Perhaps people have been stabbing me in the back all the time without my noticing it. But it showed me that what I had thought when I was

From *Contemporary Literature* 16,1(1975): 1–18. Reprinted by Permission of The University of Wisconsin Press.

younger (in my teens and twenties)—the view that Britain is a very rigid, structured, separated society, and that it is very difficult to break through from one class to another—was quite untrue. In my youth, England was not very stratified and it's less so now. It's always been alleged that the English, particularly the English as distinct from the other British, have an upper-class accent and various kinds of inferior accents, but even that is going now. It would be very difficult at any rate for a nonexpert to differentiate the way Princess Anne talks, for example, from somebody who is earning twenty pounds in a boutique.

Q. Looking back on your own career, can you reconstruct for me the way in which the "Angry Young Men" arose?
A. As always, I think it was all certainly not one or two things. Rather, it was a combination of accidents. One was that it so happened that three or four writers (myself included), none of whom were from upper-class backgrounds or had been to public schools in the British sense, emerged at about the same time. And they were all roughly of an age, and it so happened that there had been a kind of delayed action effect after the war. John Wain appeared, it so happened, in 1953. I think there was a feeling of exhaustion after the war. The older writers were still writing, but for some reason no new writer of any fame, any note, had appeared for seven or eight years. I think this was partly because people were busy putting their lives together again.

I was twenty-three when the war ended, and I spent the next few years trying very hard to get a good degree at Oxford, overwhelmed by getting married, finding almost simultaneously there were suddenly two babies in the house, and getting a job and working hard at it. There was this lag of eight or ten years after the war when nothing happened. Then by a series of coincidences, within three years, John Wain appeared, I appeared, John Braine, John Osborne, Iris Murdoch, and Colin Wilson all appeared. And others. Now that looks like a movement, and I can quite see, since there was this business of nonupper-classness (middle-class, middle upper-class perhaps, but certainly not upper-class) people could be forgiven for mistaking this for a sort of minor revolution or turning point in English writing. I don't think it really was that, but it had the look of being one.

Another reason why the thing was made to look like a movement is the fact that the novels and the plays were to a large extent about people at work. The hero of *Hurry on Down* wants to know where he fits in, where he's going to get a job, and changes his job a lot. The hero of *Lucky Jim* isn't sure what he wants to do, but we see him at work and a lot of his difficulties come directly from his job. Jimmy Porter in *Look Back in Anger* isn't employed very much but how he earns his living is important. *Room at the Top,* perhaps to a greater degree than any, is about a man getting on in the world. In other words, someone said that the weakness of the English novel of the twentieth century up to the time he was talking about (could be 1939) was that nothing happened until after 6:00 P.M. or on Saturday and Sunday. It wasn't that the people written about were of the leisure classes, it was just that we never saw them doing anything, apart from committing adultery and getting drunk. What they did at the office or at the factory, except for a very few self-consciously proletarian writers, we know nothing about.

Q. What are your feelings about the political novel? Norman Mailer has made a way of life out of this for the past ten years. George Orwell occasionally used the convention of the novel for political statements. Do you see any similarities between yourself and Orwell?
A. I'd be flattered to think there were any similarities between myself and Orwell. I think that with the exception of *Animal Farm,* which is an incredible freak of nature—unique—I don't regard Orwell as much of a novelist at all. A fine writer and a man with marvelous ideas, but look at his novels. *Coming Up for Air* is absurd as a novel. *1984* has got some marvelous ideas, but no narrative pressure. You get one situation and then another situation and another, and that's about it. It's repetitive. You get it also in his best novel, *Burmese Days,* which is nearest to being a novel. A man is in a hopeless situation, meets a girl who he thinks is going to pull him out of the hopeless situation, and she lets him down. Same thing as in *1984.*

As regards Mailer, I think that's a wonderful example of self-ruination by going in for politics. When I read *The Naked and the Dead* I thought wow, look out chaps, here's somebody on the scale of Dickens or Eliot, better watch him closely. But I needn't have worried, because he's systematically destroyed his talent by being rather silly. Very intelligent man, brilliant gifts. He was a novelist in the very sense that Orwell isn't—he could narrate and develop. All this semi-political rubbish has made Mailer just a hollow shell. I can't read him anymore. This is what often happens to American writers; they cease to become writers and become institutions. Too successful, too much money and something happens to them. There is so much temptation to become a national figure that you can become one, as has happened to Mailer and to James Baldwin (in a rather different way), although I don't think Baldwin had anything like Mailer's natural talent. Or you can disappear like Salinger, whose doom I lay squarely at the door of the *New Yorker* magazine for paying him the retainer. There are some people who flourish on being paid retainers because it stops them worrying about how they're going to pay for the groceries next week. Very few, however. I think most people need a little pressure like that.

Q. What is there to write about in England today?
A. Anything. That question brings up the whole question of what the novelist is up to. And this brings up another thing which I think is in favor of the British writer here—he is not distracted from his proper task, which is to write about human nature, the permanent things in human nature. I could

reel you off a list as long as your arm, beginning with ambition, sexual desire, vainglory, foolishness—there's quite enough there to keep people writing. Of course the terms in which these qualities express themselves must be contemporary, unless one's writing a historical novel, and I see nothing against that. If you say, for instance, I'm so interested in the anatomy of ambition or jealousy that I'm deliberately going to take it outside the present context, so there'll be no distraction, and I'm going to go back to the eighteenth century—there, nobody's going to say what a true comment on the present scene, because I don't want them doing that, I want them to concentrate on my subject. The dress in which these abstractions are clothed must be contemporary, unless the writer is detaching them deliberately, and the contemporary details must be right.

But it's not the job of the novelist to represent the contemporary scene in any sense. He may turn out to be doing that, if he's any good he may turn out to be portraying the contemporary scene, and perhaps later be a source for social historians, but that's not a thing you can try to do. If you try to do that you become either propagandist or trivial. Dickens, for instance, had certain things which he wanted to say about his contemporary scene, although most of that, the sort of social reforming element in Dickens, was a little bit behind the social clock. He would not take up a cause unless it had been pretty heartily taken up by the people in advance. What primarily interested him, I'm sure, was how extraordinary people are. What extraordinary things they can do and say when they are very hypocritical, when they're very respectable, and when they're very mean. And, incidentally, of course he will show them being hypocritical and mean and so on in a contemporary fashion, wearing contemporary clothes in all possible sense of the term.

Q. Turning specifically to your novels, are you consciously aware of using comedy as a critical device?
A. In a sense, yes. It's essential from my point of view that the bad people should be ridiculous as well as bad. In my novels there are good people and bad people, which is very rare these days. There's often a lot wrong with the good people, and one must also lay off by making the bad people say good things or be right about things that the good people are wrong about. There are bad people, and it is essential to make them ridiculous. So that Professor Welch [*Lucky Jim*], who is a bad person because he treats Dixon very badly, is ridiculous because it is essential that he should be. Bertrand is rather a bad person—pretentious, rides all over people's feelings, women's feelings especially. But he's also a ridiculous person. The bad people have got to be funny, so that's critical if you like. But then of course when it comes to the good people the thing becomes a little more complicated, and also the question of whether the good people are really good becomes complicated, too.

To make a good character prominent is very difficult. This has been a perennial, incurable problem ever since literature existed. I think that one would find in my books that it's much more likely that an important good character would be a woman rather than a man. I think that Jenny Bunn is a good character, and Patrick Standish is a bad character [*Take a Girl Like You*]. He's in a way, I think, the most unpleasant person I've written about. I have sympathy for him, yes. He has his good points—when he pays for the other girl's abortion, for example. As a good character, Jenny is quite opposite to what Patrick could ever possibly be like, a good character who comes to grief and who has faults that one cannot get moral about. They are faults of foolishness, perhaps, indecision, but she is a person with wholly good instincts, generous, great humility, too much really. There's also Julian, who is all that Patrick ought to be and isn't, because although immoral sexually, let's say (many people would disapprove of the way he conducts his life), Julian actually knows what one should do and what one can do and what one should not do. And it's Julian who denounces Patrick for his behavior.

Those are in a sense my two favorite types. One is the person who is naive and shrewd (Jenny), in other words inexperienced, sees things for what they are, would never be wrong about a person even though she might be taken in by some things about them. The other admirable person is the person who is like Julian, entirely his own man, not preyed upon by anxieties, guilts, doubts, but nevertheless, in fact, is sufficiently so that he can afford to behave morally. I mean by that, he would never have treated Jenny as Patrick did because he'd just have decided he had to leave her. He too might have been confronted by Simon [*I Want It Now*], but would have said, "Sorry, this is too much; there'll be another one along in a minute."

Q. In "A Memoir of My Father," you speak of the early training in morality you received. Could you elaborate?
A. All the standard Protestant virtues (of course I know these overlap with Catholic virtues and Jewish virtues, and so on) were put forward and taken for granted—conscientiousness, thrift, hard work, patience particularly. That is to say, one mustn't expect to run before one walks nor to be a success at anything to start with. Everything worth doing is going to take time and trouble, unstinting and unceasing trouble. These were very good lessons. But God never came into the conversation. God was never actually referred to or appealed to, and there was no question of displeasing God by my actions or trying to please him. My parents would take me to church on Armistice Day, sometimes at Christmas, but these visits got less and less frequent as they grew older. In the last ten, perhaps twenty years of their lives, they never went into a church. They had suffered, they said, from forceful religious indoctrination, being forced to go to chapel when young, and I think my father regarded himself as a rebel in a mild way, mild certainly from today's standards. He had broken away from a very inflexible Christian kind of upbringing. When I saw my grandparents they too seemed to have come out on the other side. God didn't come into the conversation much.

Q. Anthony Burgess, in his review of *I Want It Now,* comments that with the appearance of this novel a moral philosophy begins to emerge. How much stock do you put in a remark like that?
A. Quite a lot. Again, I think it's improper perhaps to talk about one's self in such terms, but I've always been a moralist, which doesn't mean of course that I behave any better than anybody else. If I weren't a moralist I might behave even worse than I do in ordinary life. I think—and this goes back to dad and mom and so on, if you like—that because of my strong views that some kinds of behavior are admirable and others are despicable, hence I have this fairly rare phenomenon that there are good and bad characters. And very often they're not at the center of the stage, but minor characters who are completely good (Moti in *The Anti-Death League,* for instance) and completely bad (Dr. Best).

I think that it's become more obvious, if you like, that there's a moral concern at work. But I would have thought that it had been there from the start. If Jim is such a slime, why doesn't he tell Margaret to leave, as he could do. Admittedly they work in the same department and it would be awkward. Bertrand would have no trouble at all getting rid of Margaret. Jim hates it and at the same time laughs to himself about it, which is a thing some people miss; the only way he can bear it is by joking to himself about it. There is a responsible concern, and if you like, at the end he says, well there are limits, and as a Catholic would say, the individual's duty is to save his own soul first.

Q. Do you see any time during your career when you have consciously modified the way you look at things?
A. Yes, I think so. At any rate that's what it looks like. There's been an increase in the dim view which is taken of life, and the element of horseplay and high spirits decreases. But I'd say that I've always been a writer of serio-comedies, and I wouldn't be fair in ignoring the Margaret theme in *Lucky Jim.* I'm not claiming any merit for this, only trying to describe what it is—an attempt at studying a neurotic person who brings pressure to bear by being neurotic. It's true that Jim's response to this can be taken by the reader as amusing, as comic, but he doesn't think it's comic. He talks about it to himself, reflects about it. What he is trying to do is cheer himself up, to make it more bearable by trying to be funny about it. But that's quite a serious bit.

Even in *I Like It Here,* which has very little to say about anything, there are two fairly serious moral moments. One is when Bowen goes over to Strether's side, having regarded him first with uneasy contempt, and becomes protective. The incident which is supposed to show this is when he adjusts Strether's false teeth that had been half-knocked out of his mouth. The other thing is when he discovers something more about his wife than he thought, that she couldn't be a blackmailer's girl, something he'd never put to himself before, and that that was the most important thing about her.

Q. I notice that Jim Dixon makes a distinction between the "nice" and the "nasty" people, and that that distinction is referred to in your later novels. What does Jim mean by the "nice" life?
A. That is an attacking rather than a propounding remark, against *nostalgie de la boue*. It's a critical remark, saying don't let's pretend that it's a good thing to starve in a garret, that the painful experiences are good for you, the disagreeable experiences are good for you. Let's just face the obvious truth that you're probably a better person and nicer to your fellows if you are reasonably contented, reasonably well off, and have a reasonably comfortable time. It's not a materialistic remark, nor is it a spiritual uplift remark, but it's an attacking remark.

Jim and I have taken a lot of stick and a lot of bad mouthing for being Philistine, aggressively Philistine, and saying, "Well, as long as I've got me blonde and me pint of beer and me packet of fags and me seat at the cinema, I'm all right." I don't think either of us would say that. It's nice to have a pretty girl with large breasts rather than some fearful woman who's going to talk to you about Ezra Pound and hasn't got large breasts and probably doesn't wash much. And better to have a pint of beer than to have to talk to your host about the burgundy you're drinking. And better to go to the pictures than go to see nonsensical art exhibitions that nobody's really going to enjoy. So it's appealing to common sense if you like, and it's a way of trying to denounce affectation.

Q. Jim also manages to emphasize the division of classes and is constantly reminded of his lowly status. Is this an exaggeration?
A. He'd be the first to exaggerate it to himself, and I don't know how conscious I was of this at the time, but he's blaming his origins for things that his origins aren't to blame for. He's rather an uncouth person anyway; he could easily be more couth without his origins being changed. But I think that the proportion of that in *Lucky Jim*—the social climbing aspect—is not very important. For instance, Gore-Urquhart, who is Jim's eventual savior and benefactor, is certainly a man of the people who has made his way, but of heavy Scotch accent and therefore not one of the Scotch upper crust.

Q. In *That Uncertain Feeling,* an important question is raised when John Lewis turns down the promotion, presumably for reasons of integrity. However, Jean berates John for turning down the job and says economic security is more important. Is this ever resolved?
A. I think that Lewis' scruples about turning down the promotion because it has been rigged are only half-scruples. I'm pretty sure if we could run the thing through again up to the point at which the promotion is offered, and Lewis had had a sudden burst of self-confidence, he'd say, "I'll take the money." What is at work is partly scruples, but not enough alone to make him act in a scrupulous way.

What is also at work then is an attack of sexual panic. Despite his views of himself—which are partly ironical, as a striding, sneering Don Juan—when he finds himself behaving like that he realizes he hasn't got what it takes; he's afraid of getting really involved with Mrs. Gruffyd-Williams, and he's afraid of what this will do to his marriage. It's very largely a selfish fear which he then dresses up partly with scruples. But he uses them as a cover for his feelings of panic. He's in deep water, he's out of his depth, he's in a situation he can't handle. Then he strides in to Jean and says, "I'm a knight in shining armor, my integrity is at stake, I've turned down the promotion." He receives a well-earned kick in the stomach by Jean's obviously sensible retort, "What about the money? And what's so scrupulous about you in other fields?" That is a rebuke that Lewis has fully earned.

Some of Lewis' guilt feelings are sincere. He talks near the end about not giving up, not surrendering to one's desire for comfort, for sex, pleasing one's self all the time, and realizes that given his character, one can't hope to keep all those selfish desires in check all the time, but what he must not do is to stop trying to keep them in check, which means at least he won't be behaving badly all the time. This is, for him, a very realistic conclusion to come to.

Q. *Take a Girl Like You,* on the other hand, seems a little more complex.
A. Yes. I began that in 1955, and put it aside to write *I Like It Here* because it was obvious that *Take a Girl Like You* was going to take a long time to write. I was already behind in a sense. I was very nervous after it. I started making notes for it in Portugal in 1955, then put it aside in 1956, and wrote *I Like It Here,* then took up *Take a Girl Like You* again. I was very nervous because it was going to be a new departure for me; I even made about twelve drafts of the first chapter. I compared the first with the latest, and realized the only difference was that the later draft was ten percent longer. So I went on with it at an increased rate.

People say, "I laughed like hell at your book," and in a sense this is the nicest thing anyone could say. But when somebody said to me about *Lucky Jim,* "Thank you for your serious book," I thought, "Ah, you see what I intended." When *Take a Girl Like You* came along, it was saying, to put it very crudely, I hope they'll go on laughing, but this time they won't be able to escape the notion that I'm saying something serious. I don't mean profound or earnest, but something serious.

Q. You speak of becoming grimmer in your view of life. Do you see any change in values, in Jenny's speech at the end of *Take a Girl Like You,* for instance?
A. That's meant to be a very sad moment, because in fact, compared to Standish's behavior, she's a better person than he is, and the Bible-class ideas are better than his, even though they are quite inadequate. This is her trouble—she is presented with a great moral imperative or prohibition, without

being able to understand the reason for it, without being able to work out the reason for it, and without wanting it, without being temperamentally on the side of it. Although Jenny is working-class, this would not be the right term for the earlier heroes. I think Dixon would say indignantly, "What, working-class? I'm middle-class." I imagine Dixon's father as being a small shopkeeper, or a man in some commercial firm, a lowly position but still white-collar person, obviously lower strata. Lewis' father—I doubt if he ever went down into the mine—is probably an office worker.

The same sort of thing applies to Bowen. Jenny, however, had to be working-class, not for any kind of political or social reason, but purely for strategic literary reasons, in that she had to feel on arrival, and the reader must feel this, too, that she is out of her element altogether, and she feels that her element is inferior to the one that she's in. In fact, it's not, but she feels it. This has got to be emphasized by first a geographical shift—she has come south (things have gotten more mobile since 1958 in England, however). In those days for a working-class girl to come south was something of a step to take. Therefore, she is socially isolated; there's no one to go to see, everybody's a stranger, has advanced ideas, more money than she was accustomed to, and they all seem more glamorous than people at home, certainly. So she'd have to be working-class.

Also, since the book is about the bit of morality—what happens when people can't give any emotional backing to their beliefs—this wouldn't be plausible except from a working-class milieu where people are more backward in that respect. I'm expressing neither approval nor disapproval when I say backward—backward in a chronological sense. You'd certainly find people with that sort of morality in Wales during that period. But I'd just done Wales, so she had to come from somewhere else. I could have made her Scotch, but that would have raised other problems I didn't want. I already had a Scotchman in the story, and so forth. Northern England is a very varied place, but it is believable that in the smaller towns, in Yorkshire for example, a girl could have been like that, born in 1938 or so.

Q. Beginning with *Take a Girl Like You,* I notice more of an emphasis upon sex. In light of your review of *Portnoy's Complaint,* in which you said the novel was "unfunny," how do you feel about sex in the novel?
A. Sex is a very important topic and most people are interested in it. I don't mean by that that it does no harm to one's sales; there is that, that is so. But it's also an immensely painful topic, and for that reason to laugh about it is important. This does not mean laughing *at* it, but its comic aspect is the only one one can hope to put into fiction. But to write about actual sex activity—what people do in bed, as opposed to people's sexual interests, schemes, seduction campaigns—except comically, I think, is impossible. I'd find it impossible. The moment I feel myself about to write a sentence which gives evidence of my sexual excitement, I stop. I don't much want to actually, but I would

never do so because of how I feel when I feel that a writer is doing that to me. I become embarrassed. I've nothing against pornography provided it's well presented as pornography, provided the writer says, "Look, you and I are going to have a jolly romp together, I'm going to tell you a story all about what people do in bed, and you're supposed to become sexually excited about it. Okay?" Fine. But if he says, "I'm telling you now a serious, also perhaps funny story, but anyway my aim is to entertain you and possibly to edify you," and if he starts trying to excite me sexually while he's doing that, it turns me off.

The other thing is if it's written about seriously, not pornographically but seriously—this is when I think the most embarrassment arrives. In some of the works of D. H. Lawrence, for example, there are serious attempts to portray a marvelous f—. I don't think it can be done. It's much funnier in its effect than anything I could possibly produce, but it also produces embarrassment. I don't mean sexual embarrassment, but the embarrassment one feels when one's heard something out of place, the wrong sort of thing is said.

Regarding the increase of sex, there is quite a lot in my latest novel, *The Riverside Villas Murder*, which is in part about an adolescent boy and the woman who lives next door. There's none at all in the novel I began recently, at least I can't see there being any. This is partly what a lot of writers do, their desire to elude categorization, to disappoint expectations. So I'm a funny writer, am I? This one, you'll have to admit, is quite serious. Oh, so I'm primarily a comic writer with some serious overtones and undertones? Try that with *The Anti-Death League* and see how that fits. So I'm a writer about society, twentieth-century man and our problems? Try that one on *The Green Man*. Except for one satirical portrait, that of the clergyman, it is about something quite different. So there is a lot of sex? Try that on the one I've just begun, in which sexual things will be referred to, but they've all taken place in the past because of the five central characters the youngest is seventy-one. So you dislike the youth of today, Mr. Amis, as in *Girl, 20?* Try that on the one I'm writing now where all the young people are sympathetic and all the old people are unsympathetic. This can be silly, but I think it helps to prevent one from repeating oneself, and Graves says the most dreadful thing in the world is that you're writing a book and you suddenly realize you're writing a book you've written before. Awful. I haven't quite done that yet, but it's certainly something to guard against.

Q. Roger in *One Fat Englishman* is certainly shown to be a ridiculous character, largely because he is taken out of his-social element. However, near the end it seems you express sympathy for Roger. Is this part of your concern with treating all characters fairly, even the bad ones?
A. One can't write about anybody that one hasn't got some sympathy for. A reviewer remarked that "Roger behaves badly in more different ways than is usual, even for an unsympathetic character in a novel, but that I can't help feeling that the author likes the character, and so do I." Yes I do, I do feel a lot

of sympathy for him because, I think, he's awful all right, and he knows it, and this is no excuse. But it does point to a perennial human problem, I think, that I tried to pin down in Roger's character and experiences—that if one behaves badly, it's no help to realize it.

Roger is a bastard to a very large extent, and he understands it, and yet he can't be different. One isn't asking for sympathy for him exactly, but we all have our crosses to bear, and being a bastard and realizing it is a kind of cross which he bears. Right at the end, the author steps forward, so to speak, to sympathize with Roger, and Roger weeps because although nobody says so, he was actually in love with Helene, or loved her as much as he is capable of loving anybody, and now he's lost her. So yes, I sympathize with him, I invite the reader to also, without condoning anything that he does.

Q. How did you feel about *The Egyptologists* after completing it?
A. I've always enjoyed it. To fill you in, Robert Conquest wrote the original draft which had the idea in it, and most of the characters in it, and a lot of the dialogue, and the science fiction dream, the Nefertiti statue, and so forth. I put in the plot, I introduced the women in fact, and the television debacle. But again, you see that horrible old morality keeps peeping up from time to time, when Schwartz falls in love with the treasurer, or starts to, and goes away. She sees that you can't run your life like that, it won't do for her, because it's a choice of what she is—she's either too starry-eyed about what life can be, or too decent and sensitive a person.

Q. Concerning Dixon's distinction between the "nice" and the "nasty," is Ronnie saying the same sort of thing in *I Want It Now* when he calls himself a "shit," or when Churchill in *The Anti-Death League* looks at the world and sees everyone as "nasty?"
A. I think they overlap a bit, but I think that Churchill is voicing what Moti would call selfish self-indulgent *contemptus mundi*—why is the world so bad—as a way of making his (Churchill's) sufferings seem more important. I think that covers that remark, because Moti is not the voice of the author exactly (how could he express the author's view totally, being an Indian with a totally different religious background). However, in that scene he is putting what the author would say when he says we must all try to become men.

As regards Ronnie, I think this is rather separate on the whole. He's making a remark purely about himself, and I think when he says he hasn't got the determination or the guts to be a full-time shit, to be a successful shit, I think this is perfectly true. It's like the man who doesn't sincerely want to be rich—he hasn't got the continuity of effort. In fact, Ronnie likes pleasure, and this is the thing about him from the start—at least I kept trying to introduce this notion. It's not a conscience at work. He has this habit of being efficient by saying what he thinks sometimes, a very bad practice if you want to be a success (never say what you think; rather, always think before you speak).

But Ronnie also likes pleasure, and he likes women, and this is emphasized several times, and power seekers, in my experience, don't like women. They may sleep with a lot of them, but that's a different matter altogether. And almost at once he starts liking Simon (much later he realizes he can't do without her). If he wasn't capable of liking her, none of it would have happened. He'd have said, "Oh the hell with this, this is too much trouble. I'll find someone else." Obviously there's something wrong with that book, because a lot of people said they find that Ronnie's sudden conversion is unconvincing and suddenly he starts behaving well. I thought that it was unconvincing because it was so obvious that that's what he'd do, because the early part of the novel is full of pointers in that direction.

Q. How seriously, then, should we take Ronnie's conversion at the end?
A. I don't think it's a conversion. Rather, it's the plot that comes into importance here. If things had been different (what we say about any drama or literature) none of this would have happened. As Milton says—to compare the great things to the small—if Othello had sacked Iago in Act I of *Othello*, Othello and Desdemona would have got on perfectly well for the rest of their lives. That's a grand example but I give it because it's such a well-known one. If Ronnie had been different, he wouldn't have bothered with Simon at all. Right from the start of their relationship he is concerned with her, before he knows that she is rich and this is very important.

The turning point in the novel comes far too early from my point of view. He sees her at the party, he likes her, tries to take her on, is separated, she reappears in the street without any shoes and such, he tells her to clear off, she says she has no money. He then says he has to do something about this girl, and after they've been to bed (unsuccessful as it is), before he finds out that she has money, he's very angry when she won't go but is also concerned, I think. It's not as if a last minute Dickensian change of heart occurred, where Scrooge suddenly says, "Come on, let's bring out the turkey and the plum pudding and let's all be generous to each other." I would like to think that it's there from the start.

Q. I notice that your novels often conclude with the two central characters turning to each other for support: John Lewis and Jean, Ronnie and Simon, and Churchill and Catharine, for instance. Is this intentional, or did it just work out that way?
A. I hadn't really considered the point before. Perhaps it happens to work out that way. Two going off together is a very common ending for all sorts of movies and books and so on, and perhaps that had its influence on it. But I suppose it's a rather sentimental feeling, if you like. Among all the disasters that have taken place and all the people that have been disappointed, these two have at any rate got each other, which is some sort of consolation. Also, if you like, the idea that one can't be happy on one's own, you can only be

happy with another person, and so I suppose in a sense I am saying that by these endings.

Q. How earnestly should we take the supernatural in *The Green Man?*
A. As earnestly as possible, I would say. It all really happens; none of what is recounted happens only in the hero's mind. It's all literal in that sense. I think we can fit the supernatural part into the natural part by saying that the hero is made aware of his own deficiencies by finding out that the reason he's being picked on by the dead wizard to fulfill his designs is that the wizard feels Allington's character is essential for the wizard's purposes, Allington being a man who doesn't care for people and manipulates them for his pleasure. That's the link between them. I think it should be taken very seriously; I took it very seriously. And naturally I enjoyed doing it, and brought in some devices that had been in my head for years. I'd always been interested in the supernatural in fiction; here was a chance to do a ghost story.

As always, when you start to construct with plot it turns into something else, such that the ideas about the supernatural that you had in the past seemed to have somehow produced ideas in the natural world that fit in with them. I'm a very firm believer in the idea that the unconscious does two-thirds of the work. For example, the idea about opening the window and seeing it is light inside and yet dark outside, and the idea that everything stops outside, and that you can't move, can't leave the room because you can't get through the air molecules (it's like concrete). That too had been in my head somewhere. The idea that it is dark outside became an obvious link in the chain of supernatural circumstances. And the idea that everything stopped outside became attached to the idea of God or His emissary putting in an appearance. In what other way could God visit a mortal human being except by making everything stop outside? Otherwise, somebody might come in and we can't have that. It's God's security measure that makes everything stop, if you like.

Q. Is your portrayal of God in *The Anti-Death League* different from the being in *The Green Man?*
A. These are two very different incarnations. In *The Anti-Death League,* it isn't an incarnation at all in a sense. This is a view of the malignant God, who is very well described in Empson's *Milton's God* where he states practically, I think, that the orthodox God of Christianity is very wicked, and gives reasons for this. He sees God playing in *Paradise Lost* not altogether a dissimilar role from the role God plays in *The Anti-Death League* (although, of course, Empson's book was written before my novel ever appeared). I think if you were to look at that, this would throw some light on *The Anti-Death League.* In the novel, God is showing his malicious, malevolent side.

The Green Man takes a rather different view, and I'm not sure if they are really reconcilable. *The Green Man's* God is slightly malignant, doesn't at all object to inflicting suffering, but that is not his main concern. He's running a game that's much more complex than that. He's admitting that he's not omnipotent, and that what may strike Allington as very arbitrary is in fact forced upon him because of the rules of the game. The chap in *The Green Man* does get tempted occasionally (let's throw down one dinosaur into Picadilly Circus and see what will happen), and that's the sort of thing with the being in *The Anti-Death League* (let's give her a cancer, smarten them up a bit; so that priest thinks he's in communication with me does he—all right, let's sort out his dog). Of course I incarnated God in *The Green Man* as a young man simply because he can't be an old man with an enormous white beard. The idea of a young, well-dressed, sort of aftershave lotion kind of man, I think, made him more sinister. That was the intention, anyway.

Q. Turning away from fiction for a moment, what do you find satisfying in the writing of poetry?
A. It's a higher art, and there's still even today a certain almost mystical status which attaches itself to a poet which the prose writer hasn't got. Many of us would be poets full time if we could, but we can't. Auden can do it, although he writes a lot of interesting prose as well. If one's mainly writing fiction, one would think that all one's creative energy goes into creating fiction. Some subjects, however, are not suitable for fiction. I'm delighted when I can write a poem.

There are several compensations for growing older as a writer, as you get to know yourself better, in your writing inclinations and so on. One gets more cunning, improves one's technique slightly as one gets older. You realize you get a little bit better at making transitions, such as realizing what a handy word "later" is (saying, for example, "What a marvelous old chap that fellow was," Roger said to Bill, later—thus eliminating the need for describing the end of the party, the departure of guests, and so on). You come to identify more precisely when to start a novel, and this is again not a conscious thing. It suddenly dawns on you that you know enough about your characters to start, and you understand your central situation to start. That means a certain amount of what you are going to say is already arranged in your mind. The same applies to political journalism, for example. Having written the first sentence, one ought to be able to take a rest, because one has done half the work. The great besetting fear is finding yourself with nothing left to say. I've tried to hedge by trying to write different sorts of books, partly because I like ghost stories, detective stories, spy stories. *The Riverside Villas Murder* is a detective story, set in 1936 in the middle of the great period of detective stories. My latest novel which I'm working on now is very orthodox.

Q. I understand you also wrote a novel, still unpublished, during the early 1940s while attending Oxford. Can you tell me something about it?
A. It's not really interesting. A novel that I'd admired enormously, and which is quite unknown (an English novel), called *The Senior Commoner*—about

life at Eaton—made a tremendous impression on me. It's one of those curious novels in which absolutely nothing happens at all. Smith goes to see Jones and they talk, and then Jones goes away and runs into Brown and then Brown goes away and runs into Smith. It's about school life with no story to it.

I fell under the lure of this. There is a very crude and absurd story in my novel, called *The Legacy,* which again has a moral line in it in that it starts off with a young man who has inherited some money on conditions that he enters the family business (which is frightfully dull—accounting or something) and marries the girl his elder brother approves of by a certain time. He wants to be a poet and he has a nice girl, but by the end says to hell with poetry and marries the nasty girl and that's all that happens. I suppose there are some mildly amusing bits of observation, when he goes to live in a boarding house for a time and the people in the boarding house are studied. It's really no good and not funny.

Q. John Gross wrote a fascinating book entitled *The Rise and Fall of the Man of Letters.* How do you feel about being classified as a man of letters?
A. To him the man of letters is the man who gets most of his income from journalism and writing memoirs of people, collecting their letters, and all that type of stuff. I think that for me nothing really important had taken place since about 1880, in the sense that while lots of interesting books have been published, I think of myself like a sort of mid- or late-Victorian person, not in outlook but in the position of writing a bit of poetry (we forget that George Eliot also wrote verse), writing novels, being interested in questions of the day and occasionally writing about them, and being interested in the work of other writers and occasionally writing about that. I'm not exactly an entertainer pure and simple, not exactly an artist pure and simple, certainly not an incisive critic of society, and certainly not a political figure though I'm interested in politics. I think I'm just a combination of some of those things.

The Curious Theodicy of Kingsley Amis

Lawrence Graver

Having achieved a reputation as an eccentric satirist of provincial manners, Kingsley Amis has produced in his latest novel an eccentric theodicy. The benevolent Providence who crowned Jim Dixon and transformed Jenny Bunn's defloration into a festival has now turned vicious; and Amis' people (often decent but comically inept) take on a new dignity stemming from their courageous efforts to deal with the malice of an unfamiliar God.

God's malignity has a military base. Several officers preparing for the top secret Operation Apollo at a camp in rural Britain are unsettled by suspicions of espionage in their ranks and by the horrifying ingenuity of their assignment (the details of which are kept from the reader until the close of the book). The main figure in this teasing spy story is the hapless Captain Leonard, a mechanically trained security officer born to follow false leads, whose attempt to solve the conspiratorial riddle provides the novel with its main line of action. Yet it is clear from the beginning that Amis is using the fashionable espionage story as a frame for other explorations. As the plot develops, the responsibility for terror becomes generalized, almost metaphysical, echoing Robert Frost's chilling question:

> What but design of darkness to appall?
> If design govern in a thing so small.

The image of a malevolent creator is familiar enough in modern literature. For Hardy, he can be a dotard given to jokes in bad taste; for Conrad, a failed artist, "perhaps a little mad," for Beckett, the inquisitorial father of decaying circus clowns. Amis, however, finds God a far less extravagant and theatrical figure; for the purposes of *The Anti-Death League* He fades into the background. What remains dominant is His creation: a world in which "a toothache is more powerful than an orgasm," contingency the only permanent order, and death the final, ambiguous gift. "I know there's nobody there," the hero says:

From *The New Republic* Aug 13, 1966. Reprinted with permission.

"But there are such things as patterns, even when we know nobody willed them. Runs of bad luck, as I said. And a system that runs itself is still a system. You don't have to believe in a weather god to find a climate unbearable."

Most impressive in *The Anti-Death League* is Amis' ability to make his climate seem past bearing by mounting a series of gray, commonplace events: a cat scrimmages with a bird, a homosexual's eloquent proposition is spurned by a friend, a girl develops a small lump in her breast, a young courier is crushed under a lorry. These grim strokes accumulate, creating the pressures of claustrophobia and imminent menace, making people feel like flies "when the swatter comes down."

To convey the sense of threat most forcefully, Amis builds his novel around an elaborate metaphor drawn from the language of botany, pathology, astronomy, and thermonuclear war. Part One of the three-part structure is called "The Edge of a Node," and "node" is used in the expansive sense of a knot, a tumor, and a lethal place, "a bit of life it's death to enter." As the plot develops, each of the main characters is brought, by the ruthless logic of contingency, to various points at the edge or dead center of the node. Finally, when the frustration and violence become unendurable, someone anonymously writes an abusive poem against God (a hectoring address by the deity Himself "To a Baby Born Without Limbs"), founds *The Anti-Death League* ("incorporating Human Beings Anonymous"), and demolishes a local priory with an atomic rifle.

The novel's hero (though not the founder of the League) is James Churchill, a twenty-four-year-old lieutenant, soured by the discovery of gratuitous cruelty and suspicious of theories about the blessings of fortitude and the redemptive qualities of suffering. Despite a powerful, innate capacity for joy, he feels overwhelmed by human frailty, as if "the necessity of getting through the ordinary way . . . were detuning his heart, screening and muffling its capacities." But, like Lucky Jim, who pledges to persist in thinking bad things bad, Churchill angrily refuses to accept meaninglessness: "Why should I? . . . No good reason. Lots of bad ones. Laxness and cowardice. Inability to concentrate on what's important." For a short time, he rediscovers joy by falling in love with Catherine Casement, a survivor of two broken marriages, now at the point of acknowledging that "there is nothing about her life that she liked." But the lovers are defenseless against life's only order—still another run of bad luck—and Catherine is hospitalized with cancer.

Churchill has a vision of "a geometrical replica of the lethal node he had described. . . . :

> "It was in the form of a broad horizontal disc, vague and granular at the periphery, thickening towards the middle. Through the exact centre a taut vertical thread ran both ways to mathematical infinity. You entered the node, or it

moved across you, until you arrived at the thread. Thereafter, instead of moving or seeming to move on towards the farther edge of the disc, you could only move up or down the thread. Presumably if your motion across the disc were along a chord instead of along the diameter you could continue to travel laterally until you reached the far side of the circumference and emerged. [Five of his friends] were travelling along chords at varying distances from the center. But Catherine had been on the diameter and had reached the center and the thread. And he too, Churchill . . . was on the thread."

The mood, then, is dismal, lightened only occasionally by an act of self-assertion, or a familiar thrust of Amis' idiosyncratic humor. One character, in a delightfully drunken ambience, tries to become "inarticulate with dignity," or thinks that "only by having been to bed with somebody is it possible to attain the pitch of conversational intimacy; that is needed as prelude to getting them into bed." Such humor, though familiar, is not terribly consoling. People can—in the words of the heroine—rise above God by refusing to employ the instruments of torture. He has given them. But they remain fragile and without significant powers of self-determination. The sum of human pain, as Swift once said, is inestimable.

What is one to make, then, of a sour, philosophical Amis? The answer depends, in part, on where one placed his strengths to begin with. If you prefer the comedian with powers of anarchic laughter, *The Anti-Death League* is Amis without Andy, offering virtually nothing. There is a grotesque psychologist named Best, generically related to Bertrand Welch, and a few acerbic observations about the lunacy of military life, where traditions grow "like weeds after the rain." But the larger ironies of Operation Apollo transcend the comic, and the novel's virtues—as I have suggested earlier—are different.

If, however, you prefer Amis as a moralist, the case becomes more complicated. In earlier books like *Lucky Jim* and *Take a Girl Like You,* his most impressive achievements are local and specific, arising from the immediate impact of social pretense, fatuity, or comic self-revelation; and his most interesting theme has been the odd, often evasive way people muddle toward freedom against the restrictive effects of arbitrary social power. One trouble with *The Anti-Death League* is that the arbitrary power is no longer social but metaphysical, and Amis is less confident about its origins, more commonplace in his responses to its terror. Despite the strength and urgency of his convictions, he is not continually interesting on the subject of faith and the nature of evil. After several of the startling paradoxes wear off, his voice loses its characteristic doubleness, becoming morose and repetitive. Since the blame for the fate of the characters remains externalized, the strong air of complaint (invigorating at the start) grows tiresome from familiarity by the end of the novel. Instead of deepening, Amis' protest stays on one level, aimed at the same formidable target.

A similar charge of singularity can be made against the characters. Some years ago, Amis described a fully developed character as one viewed from "all points of the compass, with respect, irony, impatience, and sadness." Strange to say, the celebrated irony and impatience seem to be going out of his voice, at least as far as his attractive characters are concerned. With the exception of Best and Leonard, the people in *The Anti-Death League* are viewed with excessive sympathy, an unexpected indulgence from a writer who has often been labeled nasty. (In a self-conscious way, Amis seems to be using *The Anti-Death League* to announce new departures. Not only does he machine-gun L. S. Caton—who has passed *à la Hitchcock* in and out of the early novels—but he has compassionate things to say about homosexuals and classical music, two subjects much maligned by people in his previous fiction.)

The characters also suffer under the novel's brutal determinism and its heavy reliance on plot. In an early poem, Amis speaks of the tendency of narrators to forget the barbaric origins of the legendary material and to

> "change our cruelty/
> Into the quaint naughtiness of story."

One would want a different set of terms for Operation Apollo, but the point remains relevant. The multiple plot is so spectacular, so cunningly carried off, that the characters are finally flattened by their situations. The exigencies of story demand forty pages and the services of an unceremonious *deus ex machina* to tie things together (and quite literally, for he arrives at a maneuver by helicopter).

As an entertainment, inspiring uneasiness and making us care about the characters, *The Anti-Death League* is an assured success. As a book about complex people suffering under God's dark design, it is more vulnerable. The gain is in range and daring, the loss in surefootedness.

Kingsley and the Women

JOHN MCDERMOTT

> Women are really much nicer than men:
> No wonder we like them.
>
> —"A bookshop idyll"

The publication of *Jake's Thing* (1978) was seen by most, indeed nearly all, reviewers as Amis's sad but inevitable arrival at a terminus long foreseen in his work—an arrival, moreover, that showed he had gone off the rails. Briefly, this thesis maintains that from about the point where Amis "sold out" by writing James Bond novel, which is also about the point where he spoke out in favour of American involvement in Vietnam, the right-wing quality of his social and political views has been matched by a tendency in the novels that is reactionary in substance and (and partly therefore) unpleasant in tone: *Girl, 20* attacks pop music, trendiness and the cult of youth; *The Alteration* describes, not totally with disapproval, a right-wing totalitarian state, and *Russian Hide-and-Seek* describes bleakly a totalitarian state on the Soviet model. And the non-fictional output shows a continuing and deepening preference politically for right over left, and critically for *lisible* over *scriptible* (with a liking for the sound of neither term); a market-economy attitude to the funding of the arts; a book on (good God!) Kipling, and an interest in language recently characterised by a Professor of English Studies as "Kingsley Amis banging on about 'hopefully.'"

With *Jake's Thing* (the thesis runs), Amis has turned his lamentations to the heresies of feminism, "against women," as the *Sunday Times* notice puts it, "against those females who encroach upon the male's 'thing.'"[1] This is not quite right, though; the novel features women very prominently, certainly (and very sympathetically, as it happens), but is not centrally concerned with sexual politics.

The spotting of this preoccupation with women (two wives, two ex-mistresses, one mad woman and one close-to-mad woman have significant roles) has led to two distorting tendencies in reviews of the book. The first sees

---

From *Critical Quarterly* 27 (Autumn, 1985): 65–71. With permission by Editorial Board of *Critical Quarterly*.

lines of connection, unrefracted by any notion of artifice, between Jake's personal and domestic circumstances and Amis's. Philip Gardner, in the only full-length study of Amis so far, speaks of previous "authorial self-restraint" now followed by "a release of control, a relaxation into resentful realism, welcome no doubt to its author," and Amis has had to insist that "Jake's problems are not mine."[2] Some may find this not only curiously tasteless, but also curiously inconsistent in a critical climate which is much concerned with the impersonality of authorship and the artificiality of texts. Gardner's reference to Amis's "ability to involve the reader in the consciousness of major characters whose predicaments brilliantly or darkly mirror his own" continues a tradition of criticism that sees some of the novels (*Lucky Jim* and *One Fat Englishman,* for example) less as fictions than as reports in the thinnest disguises, and as standing in very simple relation to the facts of the writer's life. One does not, of course, have to take the writer's word for it, but a piece like Amis's "Real and made-up people" (*TLS,* 27 July 1973) is more convincing than these "confessional" approaches which suggest that there is brought to bear in consideration of the literary Amis an awareness of the *extra*-literary Amis in a way that is not true of, say, the extra-literary Burgess or Golding or Howard or Amis *fils.*

The second, more important, distortion has been a misreading of the book, seeing in it Jake's/Amis's attitude to women as of central importance. In tone these judgements vary from the mild ("Many people, especially women, seem to have detected the accents of male chauvinism in this work") to the extreme ("The humour, so often sour, misogynistic and even misanthropic"). In a *Listener* end-of-the-year piece for 1978 Amis is described as "author and newly-discovered misogynist."[3] A classic distillation of the thesis mentioned above is given in Peter Ackroyd's review for the *Sunday Times:* "in successive novels Kingsley Amis has chronicled his distaste for boring academics, for foreigners (especially Americans), for the rich, the young and the very old. Now, in *Jake's Thing,* he turns against women, who dominate the book with a variety of lachrymose and threatening attitudes."

Leaving aside the synopses of the earlier novels, there are two principal errors in all this. The first is that ungenerous portraits of women, or, to put it rather differently, portraits of unlovely women, are a recent development in Amis's fiction. This is far from being the case. If Amis *is* a misogynist; he is not a *newly*-discovered one. A long-standing strength of the novels has been the convincingness of his unlovable women as well (and this is harder to achieve) as the lovableness of his lovable or estimable ones, of whom there have been plenty—Christine, Carol Goldsmith, Jenny Bunn, Helene Bang, Catherine Casement and Lady Hazel; Mrs. Trevelyan isn't half bad as murdering adulteresses go; "Dame Anvil is good to look at, and strong-willed" in an admirable cause; and there are some very appealing young girls, such as Amy Allington and Hilda van den Haag. But the other sort of women starts as early as *Lucky Jim,* and nowhere in the canon is there a woman who more dangerously combines malice with neurosis than Margaret Peel. Her apart, one might mention Lady Baldock, the Diana of *The Green Man* (who is in some ways a forerunner of Eve Greenstreet), and Kitty Vandervane, though the extremes of her behaviour are presented rather with sympathetic affection, as her anxieties are demonstrably well founded.

From a writing career of over thirty years and of seventeen novels, it is little enough on which to base a charge of misogyny. Literary Amis is, if anything a ladies' man, and in *Jake's Thing* the only really nice people are women—certainly not Jake or Geoffrey or Rosenberg or (by a mile) Ed.

Indeed, the women have much the better of it. The lines quoted from "A bookshop idyll" at the top of this article have been taken as "deflating" over-emotional woman. If we replace them in their context

> Should poets bicycle-pump the human heart
>   Or squash it flat?
> Man's love is of man's life a thing apart;
>   Girls aren't like that.
> We men have got love well weighed up; our stuff
>   Can get by without it.
> Women don't seem to think that's good enough;
>   They write about it.
> And the awful way their poems lay them open
>   Just doesn't strike them.
> Women are really much nicer than men:
>   No wonder we like them.

the passage is seen as ironical, and the poem as a whole deflates the *male* ego.

And if one surveys the fiction as a whole, it becomes evident that one of Amis's most characteristic figures, and strengths, is the hero-as-shit. The Welches *père et fils* are not, admittedly, heroes, nor is Johns, but they are useful early markers, as is Dixon himself who for much of the novel is too craven to make his private and public attitudes jump together and tell the Neddies where to get off; John Lewis's involvement with Elizabeth is a mean affair, betraying friend and class as well as wife; Patrick Standish has charm but not (much) goodness; Roger Micheldene "considered himself qualified in gluttony, sloth and lust, but distinguished in anger"; the Egyptologists organise themselves solely for purposes of deception; the inaptly named Dr. Best is the nastiest person in *The Anti-Death League;* Ronnie Appleyard and Patrick Hamer are well matched in a flyting of vanities (though Ronnie gets better); Maurice Allington really loves no one until appreciating his daughter late in *The Green Man;* Roy Vandervane is without dignity, and does his best to betray the cultural tradition he is well placed to defend and sustain: Bernard Bastable is very nasty.

Amis has his gents, too, of course: Dixon at his best, Julian Ormerod, Ronnie when he discovers he genuinely loves Simon, Ayscue above all. Many

Amis men are engaged in trying to be, in some ways, better, including Jake (with his desire to help the mad woman, his forbearance with and regret over Kelly, his generosity to Brenda and Geoffrey in the matter of the house) and the recent Stanley.

As a special case one may point to the homosexuals in Amis's fiction, themselves always sympathetically presented, apart from the absurd Reverend Sonnenschein. With that exception, these characters (Hunter, Colonel Manton) are shown with, and as having, a fuller-than-average measure of kindness and sound judgement. It is worth noting in the light of this local convention of the Amis world that in *Jake's Thing,* which has two such characters, one of the longest laments about women, coupled with a lament for the ignorance of the young, is assigned to the appealing, *reasonable* Damon Lancewood. And it is in talking to this wise gay that it is made clear not only that women are nice but that the negative view of them belongs to Jake and not the author, who presents the women of this novel extremely sympathetically. If Jake is having a rough ride, so is Brenda, and the references to Alcestis and Iphigenia make it clear that she, like Kelly, is rather a victim than a source of unfairness.

But what the long list of bad men shows is that in any taking sides between nice things and nasty things, men overwhelmingly outnumber women among the nasties. In terms of the "misogyny" thesis, therefore, what is most striking in the alleged "ambiguous and increasingly malicious portrayals of women" (*Sunday Times* again) is its sheer wrongness. A characteristic dynamic of Amis plots is that wives who have run out of hope finally abandon husbands who are hopeless: Martha leaves Dick Thompson; Mrs. Bastable left Bernard; Carol Goldsmith seems likely to throw in her lot (unofficially at least) with Gore-Urquhart; Jean Lewis *would* have left John if it weren't for the children and the money, and of course it is Brenda who leaves Jake.

Clearly, on the evidence of the novels, misogyny is not Amis's thing, and, unless it is *de facto* a defining characteristic that speeches hostile to women are put in characters' mouths, it is not easy to see that misogyny *tout court* is the central issue of *Jake's Thing.*

So, what is? What is it Jake has a thing about? He is an extreme instance of a familiar Amis type, largely moved by boredom and anger. Obvious precursors are Bernard Bastable and Roger Micheldene, but the outlines of the type were set as early as *Lucky Jim.* Thought it may be merely fortuitous that Jake Richardson (i.e. Jacques son-of-Richard) sounds like a re-formulation of Jim Dixon (i.e. James son-of-Dick), these two academic historians have something more than nominally in common. More than the similarity of Dixon's "strangely neglected topic" to Jake's "bit of nonsense about Syracuse," and the fierce interior monologues that are the equivalent of Dixon's faces, they see the world in similar lights; frustration and boredom provoke fantasies of violence unspoken and unperformed:

"... The young fellow playing the viola had the misfortune to turn over two pages at once, and the resulting confusion ... my word ..."
  Quickly deciding on his own word, Dixon said it to himself.

(Lucky Jim, p. 8)

"Why so? You may have forgotten, but you once gave me an assurance that you had no objection to exposing your genitals in public."
Imprecations suggested themselves in such profusion and variety that Jake was silent quite long enough for Ed to say ..."

(Jake's Thing, p. 176)

... nor did he, on the whole, now intend to tie Welch up in his chair and beat him about the head and shoulders with a bottle ...

(Lucky Jim, p. 85)

To distract himself from restraining himself from kicking Geoffrey in the balls, Jake said, "What's whatsisname like? ..."

(Jake's Thing, p. 158)[4]

And there is the same affectation of philistinism—Dixon's "filthy Mozart" and Jake's "a passage of Horace stole into his mind unbidden, so he booted the bugger out again." Each, moreover, feels himself the target of a woman's rigged suicide attempt.

What distinguishes them, of course, is a matter of tone. However dire Dixon might consider his predicament, his frustrations are relieved by his being released from Welch, by achieving a job which he thinks he can do well (achieving it over a despised rival), and by stealing the despised rival's girl. What's more, he is young and has all before him, whereas Jake not only loses his wife to a despised sort of rival but also—it is several times stressed—has begun to be conscious of, and worried by, his own mortality. It is the existence of "something wrong" that takes him to his doctor at the beginning of the novel, and "excessive shitting" that takes him back there at the end. Anxiety about his body is accompanied by anxiety about his mental state. When, recently returned to Oxford, he thinks about opening his suitcase, he displays the dithering and confusion that characterise Marigold in *Ending Up* as well as the deplorable Geoffrey. His admission to Kelly—"I'm just old and past it"—may simply be a way of being kind to that unhappy girl, but the sense of growing old is a recurrent one: "... step by step Jake's anxiety mounted, some of it now detaching itself and identifiable as anxiety about his anxiety. What the bugger was wrong with him? He hadn't had a hangover for thirty years but he could have sworn that this was a radical departure. Well, thirty years were thirty years, weren't they?" (p. 208).

It is not to be wondered at that a man becoming acutely conscious that his life will not, after all, last for ever should feel that consciousness most acutely in the areas where that life has been most actively lived. For Jake these are his work—"the work, in the sense of his subject and his attitude and contributions to it, gave less grounds for satisfaction ... he hadn't revised his lectures and his seminar material except in detail, and not much of that, for how long?"—and sex—"in my time I've been to bed with well over a hundred women." On a smaller scale, even his garden has "begun to be too much for him, not physically but mentally or morally."

It is not the case, as suggested by at least one reviewer, that Jake's " 'thing' is threatening to shrivel up with a kind of nostalgic impotence"; he is still capable of performing, and does, both on "the night of *Thunderball*" and with Eve. The eagerness of his sexual appetite as a young man grants him membership of the club to which Ronnie Appleyard and Patrick Standish belong. What has come between the thrusting Ronnie of *I Want It Now* and the indifferent Jake, who doesn't want it now, is the novels' increasing preoccupation with death (*The Anti-Death League, The Green Man, Ending Up*), particularly when they are describing sexual activity. The poem "Fforestfawr" is relevant here, as Dai Evans arranges a tryst with his mistress just after his father's funeral, and another, "Nothing to fear," quite an early poem, describes a man's wait for his mistress in a borrowed flat:

> —it's a dead coincidence
> That sitting here, a bag of glands
> Tuned up to concert pitch, I seem to sense
> A different style of caller at my back,
> As cold as ice, but just as set on me.

This versifies the out-of-the-trepidation that mars Patrick's pleasure as he waits for Jenny Bunn to turn up and be seduced. Patrick cheers himself up with the thought that there was "quite a good chance of his never actually being called upon to die at all. Those medicos would probably come up with something in the next decade or so."

Jake faces the consequences of the failure of this piece of wishful thinking. His colleague Wynn-Williams simply falls down dead. His exact contemporary, Ernie, the college porter, "licensed to chaff him about his amatory career," shares not only Jake's sense of time passing ("We're all of us getting on, Ernie, you know"/"*Aitch!* Don't remind me, sir—we are indeed. And hay") but a sense of the decay of institutions also ("Nice little lot of young gentlewomen come up to our university these days, eh sir?"). More is involved here than an alleged loss of sexual power. Ernie, with the oddities of his regional speech, testifies to the vigour of Jake's past: "Nay nay, Mr. Richardson, you know what I'm talking abate. Plenty of people remember the way you used to weigh the girls, I can tell you. A ruddy uncraned king you were. You fancied something—pay! you got it. And I bet you still know how to mark 'em dane." Jake confirms the truth of this: "Ed got it wrong, it's not that I can't, I can but I don't want to. With anybody . . . If I fancied anyone, I'd fancy you, believe me. I'm just old and past it."

Jake is a man ageing in a world he sees (as ageing men will) as changing, and looking what is nearly his "last on all things shitty." The book is full of signs of unwelcome change and decay—in language ("Cheers" and "Wanker!"), in machinery ("You got your coffee out of a machine, and having done that you couldn't get it back in"), in expense ("he laid out his fifty quid or whatever it was for a second-class ticket" from London to Oxford), in educational standards ("I think it might pay you for instance to remember that Mediterranean is spelt with one T and two Rs and not the other way round"), and in the seeming annexation of Britain by Arabs, Asians and the Japanese who even invade his college: "Jake knew where he was at once without liking it there."

Thus, the prospect of a chemically resuscitated sex drive is not to the point. The catalogue of deplorable things that women are, "all according to him," with which the novel ends, should be viewed in the context of Jake's thinking about his life generally. He finds it "quite easy" to say "No thanks" because what is on offer is a solution to what is not (by itself) the problem. Jake's thing is accidie. Brenda goes from him to Geoffrey because Geoffrey is "interested . . . pays attention," whereas Jake "couldn't be bothered" telling her about Kelly because "it would have been . . . boring."

This passage occurs early in the novel:

> Looking out of the window, he remembered with no great vividness doing the same thing one night some shortish time after Brenda and he had come to live here. Then as now there had been plenty to see, mainly by the street-lamp that stood no more than twenty yards off: houses, trees, bushes, parked cars, the birdtable in the garden diagonally opposite. Then, too, some of the windows must have been illuminated and it was quite possible that, as now, the only sounds had been faint voices and distant footsteps. After some effort he remembered further his feelings of curiosity, almost of expectation, as if he might find himself seeing a link between that moment and things that had happened earlier in his life. He remembered, or thought he did; there was no question of his re-experiencing those feelings, nor of his wishing he could. What was before him left him cold, and he didn't mind.

Jake's thing is (to resume the point by emphasis) *Jake*'s thing, not Amis's, and, although antipathy to women is a marked symptom of the condition, the thing itself, as is shown by the music of elegy in the passage last quoted, is more than is simply suggested by "misogyny": Jake's thing is that nothing now seems worth the effort. As Ernie would say, it's a lazy feeling.

Notes

1. *Sunday Times,* 17 September 1978, p. 41.
2. Gardner, *Kingsley Amis,* Twayne English Authors Series, (Boston 1981), p. 105. Interview with Auberon Waugh, *Sunday Telegraph Magazine,* 17 September 1978, pp. 33–6.
3. *Spectator,* 25 November 1978, p. 18; *Spectator,* 23 September 1978, p. 81; *Listener,* 21/28 December 1978, p. 839.
4. Page references are to Penguin editions.

Jake and Lolly Opt Out

John Updike

If the postwar English novel figures on the international stage as winsomely trivial, Kingsley Amis must bear part of the blame. Though he himself is a poet good enough to be generously represented in "The New Oxford Book of English Light Verse" (which Mr. Amis edited), it is a rare sentence of his prose that surrenders to the demons of language, that abdicates a seat of fussy social judgment, that is there for its own sake, out of simple awe, gratitude, or dismay in the face of creation. His universe is claustrophobically human, and his ambition and reputation alike remain in thrall to the weary concept of the "comic novel." There was something unabashedly sophomoric about "Lucky Jim" (1953) which bespoke an eternal schoolboy; adult experience appears unremittingly oppressive to James Dixon save for the chemical holiday, the physiological crime and punishment, of drunkenness and hangover. On this one Janus-faced topic Mr. Amis could and can write with inspiration; but as farce and satire "Lucky Jim" lay uneasily between the romantic good humor of Wodehouse and the sublime hardheartedness of Waugh. Compared with a contemporaneous American study of reluctant pubescence, Salinger's "Catcher in the Rye," it lacked not only private psychological intensity but, oddly enough, true comic edge. For there is no need to write "funny novels," when life's actual juxtapositions and convolutions, set down attentively, are comedy enough.

Amis's newest novel, "Jake's Thing" (Viking; $9.95), is in fact a more ample and less artificial grab at life than "Lucky Jim," though little in the book's reception would imply that. On the back of the jacket, the *Daily Mail* is quoted as chortling, "The funniest thing he has done since *Lucky Jim* . . . The book takes an unerring smack at our times." Well, the hilarious central subject of "Jake's Thing" is impotence and, beyond that, acedia, the deathlike condition of not caring; and the unerring smack is not at our times but at Mr. Amis's pained and isolated hero. Jake Richardson, an Oxford don who lives in London (apparently a not unusual arrangement), in an attempt to revive his libido subjects his fastidious sensibility and fifty-nine-year-old body to a series of humiliating psychiatric conferences, sex gadgets, and exhibitionistic work-

From *Hugging the Shore* by John Updike. Copyright 1983 by John Updike. Reprinted by permission of Alfred A. Knopf, Inc. Originally appeared in the *New Yorker*.

shops. Jake has once been a great womanizer, with over a hundred scores to his credit. He is married to his third wife, the overweight and wide-eyed Brenda. He wants, he thinks, to save his marriage. The muffled engine of the plot, the underplayed *primum mobile,* is the depth of anguish and affective embarrassment which glues this conservative, elderly man to psychologists and fellow-patients whom he despises; against the background of this poignance, nothing looms as very funny. Mr. Amis attempts to milk for a few mechanical laughs the juxtaposition of a snoopy cleaning lady with Jake's medically prescribed pornography reading and the introduction into his home of a device called "the nocturnal mensurator." No doubt some of the therapeutic language—"inceptive regrouping," "genital sensate focusing"—is meant to be droll. But the centerpiece of the satire, if satire it is—the lengthy workshop Jake and Brenda endure with the dwarfish psychologist Rosenberg, the workshop "facilitator" Ed (an American, always a bad sign), and eight sufferers from kleptomania, paranoia, inferiority complex, and assorted phobias—comes over as more horrifying than biting, more pathetic than amusing. It is by no means clear that Rosenberg and Ed are charlatans, though Jake comes to believe so, and the English reader might be disposed to expect so. To an American, conditioned to tolerance of all sorts of craziness on behalf of the soul, the extravagant exercises of group therapy seem at least a gallant attack upon virtually intractable forms of human loneliness and mental misery. Brenda, who enters this strange world in the wake of Jake's impotence, comes to argue, "Now Ed has too good an opinion of himself I quite agree, but he does help people, or lets them help themselves which is just as good. I'm sure there are good reasons for saying he couldn't or he shouldn't or he doesn't really but he does." The author in this debate stands a bit off to the side, giving Jake lots of space but Brenda some very good lines—better lines than her supposedly ill-educated, insecure character would warrant—and Mr. Amis's bemusement deepens as his hero, in an increasingly violent succession of verbal explosions, proceeds from wounded impotence to triumphant misogyny.

Jake, once the novel escorts him back to the predominantly male environment of Oxford, takes on some of Lucky Jim's manic recklessness, and through a drunken seduction he narrows in on the heart of his problem, which is the hatefulness of all things female. As long as he is in London, docilely busing back and forth between his sex therapist and his wife, his inklings are no more malign than the private observation; of a female anatomical part featured in a magazine called *Mezzanine,* that "in itself it had an exotic appearance, like the inside of a giraffe's ear or a tropical fruit not much prized even by the locals." But back in the university precincts, where the female minority hoots at Jake as a "wanker" and sends him a plastic phallus in the post, he is led to perceive that "they [women] don't mean what they say, they don't use language for discourse but for extending their personality." The indictment immensely widens, to include "their concern with the surface of things, with objects and appearances, with their surroundings and how they looked and sounded in them, with seeming to be better and to be right while getting everything wrong, their automatic assumption of the role of injured party in any clash of wills," etc., etc., all of which can be subsumed under the lament, in "My Fair Lady," of Professor Henry Higgins: "Oh, why can't a woman be like us?" The ending of "Jake's Thing" is too good—too startling and too inevitable—to give away; but let it be hinted that it echoes with uncanny fidelity the notorious conclusion of Mickey Spillane's "I, the Jury."

The novel's innocent air of not having wanted to come out this way is one of its charms. Much sorrow and some wit flourish in the chinks of the shambles as marital saga, reactionary diatribe, and pilgrim's progress vainly compete to set a consistent tone. The book is made up of twenty-eight jollily titled chapters that feel like consecutive essays. As a continuously developing stream of event and revelation, "Jake's Thing" suffers from contrived jokiness and unsteady perspective; the author seems now immersed in Jake, now on the verge of disowning him, and there are curious patches where the action is summarized rather than relayed, as though the writer had to avert his eyes. As a portrait of a man, however, and the times that enclose and infuriate him, the novel is satisfyingly ambiguous, relentless, and full. Jake has more complaints than the similarly indisposed Alexander Portnoy: he can't get used to seeing Asians and blacks in the streets of London; he can't help noticing that men in dirty overalls seem to have more money to spend than he; he conducts inwardly a running criticism of the architecture, dress, manners, and cuisine he daily confronts; he suffers from moments of seeing "the world in its true light, as a place where nothing had ever been any good and nothing of significance done." He is in a rage. Yet he is also dutiful, loyal in his fashion, and beset; we accept him as a good fellow, an honest godless citizen of the late twentieth century, trying hard to cope with the heretical possibility that sex isn't everything.

The Old Devil

GABRIELE ANNAN

Difficulties with Girls, Kingsley Amis's eighteenth novel, finally reveals him as the W.C. Fields of English letters. His comedy has always rested on his own droll taking-the-mickey technique. His prose swarms on to the page like clowns into the ring and clambers all over the characters food, clothes, interiors, and inadequately camouflaged intentions, mimicking their speech, facial expression, and body language:

> While he spoke, Porter-King had been moving his lighter up and down in the general area of his right hip, perhaps polishing it against the ginger-coloured dog-tooth check, more likely because he fancied there was a little pocket in his jacket round about there.

Or:

> "Mr. Valentine—" began Patrick when the three were settled.
> "I wonder," said the man referred to, sounding as if he really thought it might go either way, "if I could persuade you to call me Tim?"

These examples come from *Difficulties with Girls.* But the merry hooliganism of Amis's early novels has dwindled to a tetchy weariness, a kind of sod-you melancholy. Even the reprise of Jenny Bunn from *Take a Girl Like You* doesn't seem to have cheered him up. Amis women divide into two categories: manipulative bitches and a much smaller one where compassion, humor, and understanding combine with extreme sexual desirability. The original Jenny has always been top of the second.

In 1960, when *Take a Girl Like You* appeared, she was twenty, and the story ended with her losing her virginity to the lecherous but quite decent Patrick Standish. Now it is 1968: Patrick and Jenny are married and have moved from a country town to London, and Patrick from school teaching to publishing. He is slobbier than before and more sophisticated. Jenny is as innocent as ever and much more pathetic because she has grown used to being deceived and neglected, longs for a baby, and can't get pregnant. At

From *New York Review of Books* 36 (June 15, 1989): 12–14. Reprinted with Permission from *NYRB*. Copyright © 1989 Nyrev, Inc.

twenty-eight she is as squeamish as she was at twenty. When Patrick tries to explain to her what homosexuals actually do, she can't bear to hear it. Her dealings with them are another matter: Steve and Eric, perpetually bickering in the next door apartment, afford opportunities for Amis to take off gay behavior and talk, and for Jenny to be faultlessly tolerant and compassionate. She has become altogether faultless, a Victorian pulp heroine, especially in the penultimate chapter where Amis indulges himself with a positively Victorian tableau:

> A narrow sunbeam rather theatrically lit up part of the front of the building, missing by some yards the figure of Jenny at the sitting-room window. One of her pot-plants was near her on the sill and she might have been attending to it just before, but she now stood looking fixedly downwards through the glass, perhaps not seeing much. Soon she dropped her head further, paused and slowly turned away in a movement that expressed for Patrick [unseen by her in the street below] all he had ever seen of resignation, disappointment and loneliness. He tried to swallow, and said "Like the base Indian" in a voice that made an old bag in a green check trouser-suit swing round and stare at him in an affronted way.

The next chapter and the book end with Jenny discovering she is pregnant.

> Patrick's face was covered with tears. He came and put his arms round her and just squeezed, and they stayed like that for some time.
> "How wonderful," he said. "For us both. I'd stopped hoping or imagining. You clever little thing." He kissed her hands. "You've done it. Changed everything. You've saved us."
> Jenny was happy. She was going to have him all to herself for at least three years, probably more like five, and a part of him for ever, and now she could put it all out of her mind.

Or have we been led down a corridor of reflecting ironies, running from the theatrical sunbeam through the green check trouser-suit, the base Indian, and Patrick's tears, to end up at Jenny's modest but still probably excessive hopes? If so, the corridor is mined: there are bits of unexploded sentiment lying around. There were quite a lot in *The Old Devils,* two novels back; now they constitute a real danger.

The most sympathetic of the women in *The Old Devils* was understanding, kind, sexy, and well into middle age. Being older made her better able to look after herself than Jenny is; not just with men, but as a character in fiction. Jenny is just too much: devastatingly attractive (everyone tries to pick her up), "she looks, as well as beautiful, like someone who finds sex entirely natural and enjoyable, and to do with love." These revolting words are addressed to her by Patrick, and so they too may be meant as another irony. One hopes so. But they're still true; and Jenny is also monogamous and forbearing beyond belief: only right at the end, after a particularly elaborate betrayal by Patrick, does she contemplate leaving him; but then the prospect of the baby changes her mind.

A perfunctory story, but there is a subplot: the title *Difficulties with Girls* refers only ironically to Patrick's difficulties, which are the opposite of what is usually meant by difficulties: too much success, not too little. Real difficulties—or at least he thinks so—are experienced by Tim, another of the Standishes' neighbors. Tim finds women attractive, but after he's been to bed with one he goes off her. He doesn't really like female company. This is normal for Amis men, but it worries Tim. His analyst suggests he may be homosexual, and to test this hypothesis he gets Steve and Eric to take him to a gay club. Imbroglios and fist fights result, but eventually, egged on by Jenny, Tim returns to his estranged wife, another Griselda like Jenny but not so pretty. Tim is Jenny's counterpart in innocence, only in his case innocence is a comedy turn.

Amis has lined up a row of bullet-riddled old targets: the London literary scene with special reference to publishers and their ghastly parties, psychiatry, and modern education. The little brats in the children's hospital where Jenny teaches whine and pick their noses because their parents have brought them up on permissive theories of child rearing; while Patrick has had to give up teaching altogether because his subject—the noble study of classics—is being phased out of the curriculum. "Well, what would you?" he says. "The bloody world's moved on without consulting us, as Horace had it." Even sex isn't what it used to be; though there, according to a best-selling septuagenarian lady novelist, the decline set in earlier, with D.H. Lawrence: "He invented having to get it right when you went to bed with somebody," she grumbles.

A very moot point in a novel where the main issue seems to be getting it right between the sexes. Jenny is the male chauvinist pig's dream girl, forever making cups of milky coffee for her circle of male admirers, tormentors, and lame ducks. She gave up teaching full-time in order to have more time to be a good wife. So she has more time to be lonely and miserable. Amis seems to approve her decision. Or does he? His apparently most antifemale novel, *Stanley and the Women* (1984), was interpreted by Professor Marilyn Butler as a defense of women against men. Amis is said to have thought she was barmy: nevertheless, there are no difficulties about reading *Difficulties with Girls* as a savage attack on male selfishness and exploitation of women.

Amis's beery literary persona and tweedy diction have helped to persuade us that he's a misogynist. But he is really a misanthropist. Women are ghastly but men are ghastly too; so we should as far as possible forgive each other our ghastliness. And there are one or two good women around to encourage and redeem—Madonna figures like Jenny. Up to a point, it's really a quite Christian position, with the transcendental part left out.

Kingsley and the Women

Hermione Lee

"Go on about not liking women," someone encourages the Amis-surrogate in *Jake's Thing*. He does. And how he does! Of all the specimens Amis subjects to malediction and anathema—Americans, other foreigners, people of the next generation, the literati, psychoanalysts, interior decorators, academics, homosexuals—women come first. His titles reduce them to species—*Take a Girl Like You; Girl, 20; Stanley and the Women;* and now *Difficulties with Girls.* His plots, equally obsessional, fix on one or another area of lamentable or disgusting human behavior (most things human disgust him)—sexual irresponsibility and greed, impotence, madness, old age, jealousy. But whatever the central male character's "uneasy feeling," his complaint will sooner or later give him grounds for giving or receiving a diatribe on "not liking women":

> They don't mean what they say, they don't use language for discourse but for extending their personality, they take all disagreement as opposition, yes they do, even the brightest of them, and that's the end of the search for truth, which is what the whole thing's supposed to be about. (*Jake's Thing*)

> "Not enough of a motive?" His voice had gone high. "Fucking up a man? Not enough of a motive: What are you talking about? Good God, you've had wives, haven't you? And not impossibly had some acquaintance with other women as well? You can't be new to feeling the edge of the most powerful weapon in their amoury. You must have suffered before from the effect of their having noticed, at least the brighter ones among them having noticed, that men are different, men quite often wonder whether they're doing the right thing and worry about it, men not only feel they've made mistakes but on occasion will actually admit having done so, and say they're sorry, and ask to be forgiven, and promise not to do it again, and mean it. Think of that! Mean it. All beyond female comprehension. Which incidentally is why they're not novelists and must never be priests." (*Stanley and the Women*)

From *The New Republic* 201 (July 31, 1989): 39–40. Reprinted by permission of *The New Republic*, © 1989, The New Republic, Inc.

Like-minded Anthony Burgess, enthusiastically reviewing *Stanley and the Women* in 1984, greeted Amis as the leader of a counterrevolution, the Norman Mailer of Hampstead. "Lady reviewers," said Burgess, adopting an Amis-style derogatory category, "will express whimsical wonder that the great lessons of the new feminism have not sunk into yet another obdurately piggish male brain. They've sunk in all right. Women wanted the big division, and by God they've got it." But a less welcoming and less exuberant reading can be made of Amis as a writer armadilloed inside his overlapping plates of fear and loathing, bigotry and scorn, still "going on" in the same way about the same things.

Some readers find this lovable and reassuring. There's an English habit (as Alan Bennett has pointed out) of getting fond of everyone—train robbers, venal politicians, failed dictators, bad actors—if they only live long enough. And post-Booker-prize Amis *père* is beginning, I suspect, to be treated with that kind of cozy warmth, as a splendid monument of British satire, an engaging old devil. Perhaps he will be knighted. This kind of fond veneration seems to me misplaced. For one thing, he has a tremendously strong and vicious set of teeth and very high savage comic spirits, so he should not be taken for granted. For another, his comedy (now more than ever) is not affable. It is desperate. To reread him feels to me more like a life sentence than a long friendship.

It's suggestive of his reiterativeness that *Difficulties with Girls* returns, nearly 30 years on, to the characters of *Take a Girl Like You*. Sexy, high-principled northern working-class lass Jenny Bunn ended up in the first book, for all her principles, drunk and unconscious, being raped by her predatory, handsome, self-regarding suitor Patrick Standish. As though this weren't enough punishment to have meted out to one fictional character in revenge for her niceness, Jenny Bunn has now become Mrs. Standish. They married because she was pregnant, then she miscarried. Since then (eight years later, in 1968) she has not been able to give Patrick, as she puts it to herself, "his money's worth."

Patrick, in this direly conventional analysis of biological imperatives, has been consistently unfaithful to her since their marriage. The opportunities for this have widened since his move, Lucky Jim-style (but without the sense of good fortune), from his job as a classics teacher in a Hertfordshire school to a London publishing house. The novel's sluggish and cursory plot, mainly located in their desirable new South London apartment block, "Lower Ground," centers on Patrick's infidelities and Jenny's unhappiness, with analogous "difficulties with girls" provided by the violently quarreling homosexual couple next door, and by another potential neighbor, an eccentric calling himself Tim Valentine, who has left his wife because he thinks he's gay. Comic set pieces are provided by publishing parties and conspiracies, and scenes in the local pub, presided over by a jovially fascist landlord.

Amis's comic brilliance has always taken two main forms. One is his bravura handling of violent farce, never surpassed since *Lucky Jim,* and here gone as limp as Jake's thing. The other is his implacable dossier on cant and affectation. Based on a long and unbending set of rules about what does and doesn't belong to "the realm of the fully intolerable" and what has and hasn't been taken over by the "terrible craps" (such as *liking trees*), the dossier consists of wonderfully splenetic and unforgiving readings of false language, bad taste, and grotesque pretensions. However reprehensible the main character, he is always the Amis-surrogate whose assumptions are lined up like his author's, as when Patrick says of a social event, "You're reading too little into it," or remembers that his reasons for disliking some woman had "something to do with talking, or with words. Well, it would have."

As usual, then, *Difficulties with Girls* consists of the annotation and explication of terrible mannerisms. Tim Valentine's catastrophic sneeze and experiments with queenliness; the sexy neighbor Wendy Porter-King's vapid emotional garbage ("Life seems to have begun at last in a strange way"), and her husband's accessories ("Round his neck he had knotted a mauve-and-yellow scarf to show this or that about himself"). No one 'scapes whipping; any desirable woman passing by in the street is fodder for the dossier:

> one with a greedy mouth, wearing a mostly white dress that buttoned down the front and had its row of buttons seriously pushed out of line from within, walking fast and in a kind of self-centered way on glistening red high-heeled shoes, chafing to track down some other poor bugger and fuck him up. Over to him, thank God.

But something is wrong. More wrong, that is, than what is already wrong, from the whimsical lady reviewer's point of view, with that quotation. The mannerisms aren't very funny, and more important, they don't seem especially accurate. There are some ordinary gestures against the swinging 1960s—the publisher's cynically trendy list, "Poets in Progress" and "Media Monitors," a guru in Eaton Square ("Krishna Ram Das has made you see the world is good"), a visit to a Soho porn shop ("Was it bondage, sir?"). But the satire reads more like a reiteration of settled prejudices than the earlier kind of deadly precision job on, say, provincial sexual mores in the late 1950s in *Take a Girl Like You*. Some of the diatribes—on the political "struggle-for-power" between the sexes, or the dangerousness of psychoanalysis—echo very similar passages from novels set in the mid-1970s and 1980s.

Why, then, the return to the late 1960s? The reason for this is not at first obvious, because it's so hard to believe. But by the end of the book (a jealous fight between the gay couple, Tim's return to "normal," and Jenny's pregnancy, which she and Patrick both welcome as the "saving" of their marriage), there's no mistaking it.

Women (in case you need reminding) are awful. Homosexuals are disgusting. This is frequently emphasized in the scenes where Patrick is persuading Tim that there is "nothing wrong with him," and that he should avoid "that world" because it "is incredibly nasty and incredibly dangerous," or where Jenny, whose puritanism is meant to be sympathetic, is wondering what homosexuals *do:*

> If it was *entirely* up to them, why did she go on feeling that what they did (she disliked getting even as far as that way of putting it) was unpleasant every time she thought of it, and just as unpleasant, absolutely as unpleasant, when she thought of it now as when ever she had thought of it the first time?

In every homosexual partnership, there is a "woman" (one of "nature's ladies"), as the "male" homosexual neighbor, Eric, explains to Patrick:

> You and I are by nature, by our respective natures, males who are irresistibly attracted by a non-male principle. In your case, straightforward, women; in my case not straightforward, not women—*but,* non-male, except anatomically. And it's the clash between male and non-male that causes all the trouble. They're different from us. More like children. Crying when things go wrong. Making difficulties just so as to be a person.

The title tells us that this is the clue to the book. And this explains its dating. It is set in the year of the act that legalized homosexual activity between consenting adults. This gives Amis his best example of the damage done by the libertarian 1960s (a now standard right-wing view in Britain). One of his targets has always been "openness": the psychoanalyst's work at disclosing what is hidden, the adulterer's "irresponsible" desire to confess, the predatory woman's addiction to emotional heart-searching (referred to by Patrick as "cock-tax"). The argument here seems to be that 1960s libertarianism was responsible for the worst kind of openness, leading to what Basil Ransome in *The Bostonians* (similarly about 500 years behind his times) called "the damnable feminization of the age."

Amis is too cunning not to have exceptions to his rules, and in his weaker novels, like this one, his strategies show through revealingly. The awfulness of women is "allowed" for by the exceptional niceness of Jenny, whose resignation to betrayal and insult is touching, and who is clearly meant to appeal to us for her dutiful endurance of her husband's behavior, her delighted gratitude when he feels like making love to her, and her belief that a woman should never make a scene.

The blimpishness of Patrick's views ("No to all immigrant restrictions, eh? They haven't got to live with 'em," etc.) is craftily set off by a range of far, far more bigoted minor characters, done of course with relish, whom even Patrick is allowed to find extreme. But the most characteristic strategy is the loathing and the humiliation that Amis pours into his anti-hero. Patrick's adulteries are stupid, his work is contemptible, and his treatment of Jenny beneath contempt. Even in *Take a Girl Like You,* he had to think back many years before "he could find a time when he had felt all right—not happy or fulfilled or in tune with things or any of that junk, but simply *all right*." Now his average states of mind are on a scale somewhere between "ennui and dejection" and a terrible, panic-struck fear of dying.

Like his late friend Philip Larkin, Amis is a great celebrator of English misery and bad feeling. His best writing maintains that the world "in its true light" is

> a place where nothing had ever been any good and nothing of significance done: no art worth a second look, no philosophy of the slightest appositeness, no law but served the state, no history that gave an inkling of how it had been and what had happened. And no love, only egotism, infatuation and lust. (*Jake's Thing*)

The "Lower Ground" that the Standishes inhabit is a defensive position, but it is also an underworld of bile and dismay. The worst thing about hell, so they say, is the repetitiousness, the inability to escape from oneself.

Amis Lite

Charles McGrath

The title of Kingsley Amis's new novel, "Difficulties with Girls" (Summit; $18.95), could as well apply to all his long fiction—seventeen novels that form an extended and almost obsessive satiric examination of the ways in which men fail to get along with women. Amis is often dismissed, like Peter De Vries, as one of the last practitioners of that lightweight and marginal genre the "comic novel," and his books are certainly funny, but they employ few of the conventions of high comic writing. They have none of the mandarin polish of Beerbohm or Firbank; none of the airy silliness of Wodehouse; none of De Vries' word-play and literary allusions. There is about Amis's prose a kind of ornery plainness—a flat refusal to be arty or highbrow—and the books carry, along with the jokes, a ballast of pain and melancholy.

In recent years, Amis has perversely made a point of finding humor in subjects that are difficult or unpleasant; three of his four novels before this one dealt corrosively with impotence, madness and misogyny, and the debilities of old age. Originally labelled an anti-establishment type, an Angry Young Man, he is frequently accused these days of having gone over to the other side, but actually he belongs to neither camp, and remains a kind of odd man out in contemporary fiction: a stubbornly unfashionable (and at times deliberately old-fashioned) writer who takes a dim view of liberal and Tory alike, and has made a lifelong study of nastiness and prejudice and hypocrisy—of the ways we betray one another.

In this country, Amis's reputation rests mainly on his first book, "Lucky Jim," which was published in 1954 and may be his most consistently funny novel. I know chunks of it almost by heart, like Jim's drunken attempt to conceal a bedroom smoking mishap by shaving the rug, and they still make me laugh. But "Lucky Jim" is not entirely characteristic of Amis. The hero lucks out, after all: he escapes his boring teaching job and his neurotic girl-friend, and moves to London, still an innocent—and possibly still a virgin. John Lewis, who is the hero of Amis's next book, "That Uncertain Feeling," is neither. Married, with two children, and trapped in a dead-end job in a provincial library, he embarks on a guilt-ridden affair with a predatory

---

From *The New Yorker* 65 (June 12, 1989): 121–124. Reprinted by the kind permission of the author. © 1989 Charles McGrath. All rights reserved.

socialite, only to wind up in an even drearier and more provincial job in a Welsh colliery. After "Lucky Jim," in fact, there are no innocents in Amis, unless one counts Jenny Bunn, the sweet and trusting heroine of Amis's fourth novel, "Take a Girl Like You," who comes down from the North to work in a nursery school near London and spends much of the book fighting off a randy classics master named Patrick Standish—and in the end even Jenny gives in, or is forced to give in.

In book after book, Amis's great subject turns out to be not love or romance—those staples of traditional comic writing—but sex. Sexual desire is the engine that propels most of his plots, sex is the subject most often on his characters' minds, and the sadness that pervades his books is largely a postcoital sadness. Amis was one of the first British writers to take sexuality for granted and to write about it frankly, and yet sex in his books remains something vexing and problematic. It's not exactly shameful, the way it could be for so many earlier English novelists, but neither is it liberating, as it is Lawrence. Often, sex in Amis is just bothersome—a necessity for which the price you have to pay is invariably too high. But sometimes it's close to an affliction.

Jenny Bunn and Patrick Standish turn up again in "Difficulties with Girls," which is, in effect, a sequel to "Take a Girl Like You." They're married now, and living in a modish apartment block in London. Jenny works part time in a hospital, caring for children, and Patrick has given up schoolteaching in favor of a job with a second-rate publishing house. His chief difficulty is the common Amis complaint: a sort of constant, oppressive horniness. As Jenny sadly notes to herself, the mere sight of a pair of breasts is enough to "turn the scale" with Patrick, and when he isn't going to bed with other women—or thinking about it—he's often patronizing a shop near Charing Cross Road that specializes in girlie magazines. (Some enterprising graduate student should look into the leitmotiv of naughty reading material in Amis—from the racy tabloid that John Lewis keeps handy under a sofa cushion, to the magazine *Mezzanine,* with its photos of genitalia like "giraffe's ears," which the hero of "Jake's Thing" is forced to study as part of his therapy, and Patrick's *Twosome* and *Titter.* The one thing that no Amis character in need of a quick thrill would ever be caught dead with is a *book.*)

Much of "Difficulties with Girls" is concerned with the effects of Patrick's priapic condition on the Standish marriage, and on Jenny in particular, but there is also a subplot involving a neighbor of the Standishes, Tim Valentine—a prison visitor by occupation, or so he says—whose problem is almost the opposite of Patrick's. He suffers from some form of performance anxiety, and has been convinced by a psychiatrist that he must subconsciously be a homosexual (or "proof," to use the term most often employed in the book). Eventually, Tim falls in with a gay couple named Eric and Stevie, and the theme of sexual difficulty should probably be extended to include them—or, at least, Eric, the "husband" of the pair. He more or less sums up the book, in fact, when he tells Patrick, "It's the clash between male and non-male that causes all the trouble. They're different from us. More like children. Crying when things go wrong. Making difficulties just so as to be a person." (Eric's troubles with Stevie culminate in a not very convincing murder attempt, and, in general, the homosexual scenes are the weakest in the book. They're not openly homophobic, as some critics have claimed; they might be more interesting if they were. Instead of the brilliant invective that Amis can so often summon up to offend liberal pieties, here is only a kind of broadness approaching caricature—the kind of giggle that turns up all the time on "Benny Hill.")

"Difficulties with Girls" is set in the London of the late sixties, and yet, aside from a couple of references to the sexual revolution and to a fellow who has renamed himself Krishna Ram Das (one of the Somerset Ram Dases, someone points out) and is dispensing mantras from a house on Eaton Terrace, there's little period description or flavor. It's as if Amis hadn't bothered to remember what the sixties were really like—or couldn't bear to. The flat that Patrick and Jenny live in, with walls so thin they can hear the neighbors, belongs more to the yuppified London of the Thatcher eighties than to the communal sixties, and Patrick's publishing house is caught in a prewar time warp, bringing out overwritten tomes about ancient Babylon and the usual slim volumes of vapid poetry. There are virtually no young people in this book, no references to sixties clothing or music, and only one mention of drugs—a labored definition of a "reefer." The mind-altering substance of choice here, as in all of Amis, is alcohol, which is consumed in astonishing quantities and almost limitless variety. Amis is to booze what De Quincey was to opium. No one has written with greater relish of the giddy optimism of drunkenness, or more harrowingly of the miseries of the morning after. At one point, for example, Patrick, coming home after a lengthy publishing lunch, finds that a last cognac has "produced in him a tiny refined concentrate of a hangover, mundane stuff like headache and dry mouth hardly there at all, his attention fixed on whether or not a giant fist would fall on him from heaven before his heart blew up."

Part of what made "Take a Girl Like You" so successful was its evocation of that moment in late-fifties England when a certain self-conscious bohemianism became fashionable. The novel is full of precise and telling details: a Mel Tormé album on the record-player; a copy of "Bonjour Tristesse" that one of the characters picks up and leafs through in an idle moment. And it's instructive to consider in this context Amis's "Girl, 20," which Summit has just reissued in paperback, along with "One Fat Englishman." The latter is an odd and almost creepy book about the travels in America of a loutish English publisher, a man who is practically Appetite personified. But "Girl, 20"—about a middle-aged composer and conductor who, in his need to stay youthful, chases after a startlingly obnoxious seventeen-year-old girl, takes up all sorts of trendy causes, and eventually turns to "innovative" music—is sharp and funny and unexpectedly touching. First published in 1971, it's really Amis's valediction to the sixties—filled with stinging putdowns of the cultural and intellectual pretensions of that decade, and animated by vivid passages such as this one, where the narrator, a newspaper music critic, talks about a concert of experimental music:

> The element I was trying to breathe seemed not so much gaseous as fluid, or even some rarefied form of gelatin that shuddered constantly under the swipes of immense invisible ping-pong bats. It smelt of tennis shoes, hair and melting insulation, and was fearfully hot. If the place itself had the look of the hastiest possible adaptation to human occupancy, the audience—five hundred strong? a thousand?—might have been making it their home for weeks. . . . Every few feet were plastic carrier bags, radios, footwear and clothing discarded momentarily or for good, coloured newspapers of strange format, textiles that might have been blankets or stoles or things intermediate, and the already substantial piles of general litter. Here and there I could make out an ordinary human being.

By contrast, the sixties of "Difficulties with Girls" are a bland and featureless era, and as a result the book has an oddly dated, disconnected feel. Amis's novels tend to dramatize their concerns rather than talk about them. They rely heavily on dialogue and confrontation—on pub scenes and restaurant scenes and party scenes, which give the characters the chance to score points off one another, and give the author, a master mimic and ironist, the chance to plant outrageous tirades in the mouths of others. "Difficulties with Girls" is no exception, but, because the world of the book seems at times less than real, the issues it raises—Patrick's infidelity in particular—never take on much urgency or consequence, and the plot is memorable less for any over-all development than as a vehicle for a series of little set pieces. One of the most satisfying of them has to do with Patrick's pursuit of Deirdre, an aging Irish novelist, who is writing her memoirs about her years with "Willie Yeats" and "Bernie Shaw" and "fellows of that kidney" in the hope that Alec Guinness will star in the movie version. Over a vinous lunch (during which she nearly drinks Patrick under the table), she drops a few hints of what the manuscript contains, including this answer to Patrick's question about what H.G. Wells was like:

> Oh, he was on and off like a little sparrow, my dear. It may sound odd to the present generation, but I don't think any of us minded at all, or even noticed. You didn't then. Rebecca did, of course. She was always the girl for noticing and minding. The voice of the future, they called her, and they were right. My grandnephews and -nieces tell me that's the general way of it in this day and age, noticing and minding everything. I suppose the truth is there's never been many as much fun as H. G.

Another set piece involves Patrick's affair with a neighbor, the horrid Wendy Porter-King, whose pillow talk is enough to set the teeth on edge. "The sky is blue and I feel gay," she says fatuously, and later, after Patrick feels that he has acquitted himself particularly well, she tells him, "I don't understand. You drove at me so remorselessly, so . . . implacably. You seemed tormented by some kind of hatred, for me, for yourself, whatever, I don't know, I'm just baffled. What is it with you darling? Won't you tell me, for the love of God?" Listening to her, Patrick becomes convinced that she must secretly be an American.

Set pieces aside, "Difficulties with Girls" is a milder, slighter book than anything else Amis has written recently, and, perhaps more to the point, a milder, slighter book than "Take a Girl Like You" (which of all his novels may be the most generous and ample), and the question inevitably arises: Why a sequel at all? Why relocate Patrick and Jenny in what is clearly for Amis an uncongenial period? If there's an element of nostalgia here, it must be less for the innocence or utopianism of the sixties than for the youthfulness and expansiveness of Amis's earlier writing, and maybe even for the kind and open nature of the revived Jenny Bunn, who is that rarity in Amis, and in all fiction, actually—a character both truly good and truly interesting.

The cruelties of real time, as opposed to novelistic time, are such that if Jenny and Patrick were to be transported to 1989 they would now, like Amis, be middle-aged—almost as old as the geezers in "The Old Devils," Amis's previous novel, who are endlessly preoccupied with their teeth, their bowels, and their hearts, and with carefully tending their secret stores of resentments and jealousies. "The Old Devils" is a remarkable and affecting book; it's tired and grumpy in the same way its characters are tired and grumpy—a brilliant match of tone and theme. And the vision it offers of what's in store for all of us is so bleak and unforgiving that in the end one of the characters decides to devote what time is left him (allowing for daily visits to the pub, that is) to memorializing the past by translating an old Welsh epic poem and inserting references to a lost love. Something of the same impulse, though on a less tragic scale, seems to lie behind "Difficulties with Girls." It's a book that takes the big and difficult themes of recent Amis—impotence, infidelity, craziness—and views them in an earlier, simpler, more benign light. The story ends happily, almost on a fairy-tale note—itself an oddity for Amis— and it contains in Tim Valentine a character of so many tics and such exaggerated foolishness that he could have wandered in from some other kind of novel altogether. (Were it not for his embarrassing sexual problem, he might be on leave from a meeting of the Drones, for example, or a country-house weekend with Bertie Wooster and Gussie Fink-Nottle.) There are moments, in fact, when "Difficulties with Girls" is on the verge of breaking into farce or comic nonsense: moments when it aspires to be the kind of lighthearted "romp" that Amis's critics accuse him of writing.

But Amis must know that going back is always a chancy undertaking, and that sequels rarely live up to their originals. "Difficulties with Girls" suggests that it's Amis's anger and impatience—even his intolerance—that have given his writing its edge. Like the beer his characters toss down with such enthusiasm, his work is better when it's dark and bitter.

Closing Time

David Lodge

Kingsley Amis's first novel, *Lucky Jim* (1954), did more than inaugurate a British version of the campus novel already established by Mary McCarthy and other American writers. It made its author, willy-nilly, the standard-bearer for a whole new school of British novelists, who refused the mythopoeic streams of consciousness of the great modernists, and the somewhat specialized social and spiritual preoccupations of their successors, like Greene and Waugh, in favor of an observant and irreverent rendering of the texture of ordinary life, especially provincial life, in Britain, as the nation sluggishly tried to free itself from the constraints of the prewar class system.

This fiction was the prose equivalent of the poetic "Movement" of the Fifties, to which Amis also contributed, and *Lucky Jim* was dedicated to the most gifted and original of the Movement poets, Philip Larkin. Amis, indeed, had more in common with Larkin than with novelists like Alan Sillitoe and John Braine with whom he was journalistically linked under the heading of the "Angry Young Men." It was not really anger that fueled Amis's writing, but rather an acute sensitivity to affectation and hypocrisy in social and personal behavior. This he was able to convert into farcical comedy and a very distinctive prose style, superficially inelegant, but in fact full of artful and amusing rhetorical device. Kingsley Amis belongs to a very British tradition of novel writing that goes back to Dickens, Smollett, and Fielding, which uses irony and humor to explore serious subjects, such as madness and death. Even in the lighthearted and high-spirited *Lucky Jim* there is the troubling theme of Margaret's hysteria, and as Amis went on publishing novels (which he has done with remarkable regularity) they have become progressively darker in tone, their comedy steadily blacker.

Comedy and humor, however, do not always travel well, and one has the impression that readers in other countries, including the United States, are somewhat baffled by Amis's work and the esteem in which it is held in Britain. In this respect he is again representative. "If the postwar English novel figures on the international stage as winsomely trivial," John Updike

From *New York Review of Books* 5 (March 26, 1987): 15–17. With permission of Curtis Brown on behalf of David Lodge. Copyright © David Lodge 1987.

uncharitably declared in a review of *Jake's Thing* (1978), "Kingsley Amis must bear part of the blame . . . his ambition and reputation alike remain in thrall to the weary concept of the 'comic novel' . . . there is no need to write 'funny novels' when life's convolutions, set down attentively, are comedy enough." More recently, Kingsley Amis met even stronger resistance in America: his *Stanley and the Women* (1984), widely acclaimed in England, could not for some time find an American publisher, allegedly because a feminist cabal among New York publishers, outraged by the novel's misogynism, conspired against it; but one can't help feeling there must have been some pretty strong literary reservations among male editors as well.

Amis's latest novel, *The Old Devils,* may get a more sympathetic reception, for it is much more evenhanded in its treatment of the war between the sexes than anything else he has written, and it has very little of the rather artificial comic plotting that wearied John Updike. I would hazard a guess, however, that many American readers will be puzzled why it was a popular and for once uncontroversial choice for the 1986 Booker Prize. *The Old Devils* is Amis at his most mellow, most disarming, but it is still an intensely, defiantly, almost inscrutably British novel.

I say "British" rather than "English" because, although Kingsley Amis himself is very much an Englishman (indeed presents himself as almost a caricature of one these days), *The Old Devils* is set in Wales and is partly concerned with the concept of "Welshness"—in itself a source of potential puzzlement to the foreign reader. Politically and socially, Wales is more closely linked to England than either Scotland or Northern Ireland, but it has a long and distinctive cultural tradition of its own. Its sense of self-identity is, however, split between cultural nationalists (mainly from the North) who struggle to preserve and extend the Welsh language as a weapon against English "imperialism," and those, mainly living in the industrialized south, who regard themselves as no less Welsh because their mother tongue is English and tend to resent the fanaticism of the nationalists.

Most of the characters in *The Old Devils* are Welsh of the second type. All of them, with some minor exceptions, are old. Old age, and the problems of coping with its indignities, frustrations, and regrets, is the real subject of the novel; but the theme acquires a special piquancy, and poignancy, from its Welsh setting. Amis himself taught English Literature for many years at the University College of Swansea, and the novel was apparently inspired by, and partly written in the course of, a return visit to his old haunts.

The story, such as it is, is triggered by the decision of Alun Weaver to retire from his successful television career in London as a kind of "professional Welshman" and return to his native South Wales with his wife Rhiannon. Alun was the friend of a famous poet, now dead, called Brydan (who closely resembles Dylan Thomas) and has been living off this association for years. The arrival of this couple arouses mixed feelings among their old friends, now old in a double sense, partly because it revives memories of various youthful liaisons and indiscretions, and partly because the randy and egotistical Alun immediately sets about blowing some of these embers of faded passion into life again.

The circle includes Malcolm, a sentimentalist with feeble poetic aspirations and fond memories of Rhiannon, and his wife Gwen, one of Alun's old flames; Sophie, another old flame, and her husband Charlie, a rather childlike boozer; Peter, an overweight ex-academic once deeply entangled with Rhiannon, now married to the shrewish (and English) Muriel; and two other couples, Garth and Angharad, and Percy and Dorothy. Garth keeps boasting about his health and quizzing the others about theirs, and Dorothy gets uncontrollably and volubly drunk at every opportunity. Since all the other characters have more or less alarming physical symptoms to worry about and drink is their chief pleasure in life, this makes Garth and Dorothy particularly tiresome company. But one of the themes of the novel is the necessity of putting up with boring and exasperating friends because you have known them for years, and it is too late to escape from them.

The novel establishes its "note" in the first chapter, with Malcolm gingerly eating breakfast.

> He had not bitten anything with his front teeth since losing a top middle crown on a slice of liver-sausage six years earlier, and the right-hand side of his mouth was a no-go area, what with a hole in the lower lot where stuff was always apt to stick and a funny piece of gum that seemed to have got detached from something and waved disconcertingly about whenever it saw the chance.

As he is boarding a bus on his way to the Bible and Crown, the pub where he and his cronies gather every day, "his left ball gave a sharp twinge, on and off like a light-switch, then again after he had sat down." In the pub he is so anxious to head off an anticipated question from Garth about the state of his bowels that he gives away the exciting news about the Weavers' impending return more quickly and casually than he had intended. Also present is Charlie Norris, preoccupied with drinking his way out of his customary hangover ("His second large Scotch and dry ginger was beginning to get to him and already he could turn his head without thinking it over first. Soon it might cease to be one of those days that made you sorry to be alive"). They are joined by Peter, whose request for slimline tonic with his gin seems a pathetic gesture toward reducing a belly so vast that putting his socks on in the morning is a major operation.

An enormous quantity of alcoholic beverages of various kinds is consumed by these men in the course of an average day, and although Sophie claims that she never realized how much Charlie drank until the night (there was only one in recent memory) he came home sober, she and the other wives are not far behind their menfolk. At the same time that the men are assembling at the Bible ("You wonder why on earth you go," Malcolm muses, "especially when you've got there and find it's exactly like it always is, and then you realize that's why you went") their spouses, having gathered under the pretext of a coffee morning, rapidly push the cups and saucers aside and get down to the serious business of seeing off several litres of Soave and Frascati. When some of these characters get together at the seaside later in the novel, they lunch off "pickled fish with plenty of gherkin and chopped onion, the whole firmly washed down with aquavit and Special Brew and tamped in place with Irish Cream." The main source of suspense in this novel would appear to be the question of who will die first, and whether it will be from heart failure or cirrhosis of the liver (it would be unfair to reveal the answer here).

The unhealthiness of these lives is partly connected with a lack in their marriages. Peter and Muriel have not touched each other for ten years. Charlie sleeps in a separate cot so as not to disturb Sophie when he comes drunk to bed or wakes in the night with the horrors. Malcolm is treated by Gwen with affectionate contempt, sometimes just contempt. Angharad's once potent sexuality has been destroyed by a drastic hysterectomy and Dorothy was never known to have had any. Only Alun and Rhiannon seem still to have an appetite for life and love as well as drink, and in Alun's case it is vitiated by a streak of selfishness that leads him to disgrace himself in the eyes of all the others.

Although the surface texture of the novel is amused and amusing, one feels that it is a very fragile integument covering an appalling abyss of pain, despair, and anxiety. There is a dark irony in the spectacle of people for whom "the evening started starting after breakfast" (all Amis's rhetorical cunning is in that apparently redundant "starting") who are both oppressed by the mounting evidence of their own mortality yet incapable of occupying the time left to them with anything more creative than boozing, reminiscing about the past, and grumbling about the present. Alun, admittedly, plans to write a novel in retirement, but the vanity of this ambition is exposed in one of the best sequences of the book. Charlie, urged to give his honest opinion of the opening fragment of Alun's manuscript, tells the writer what he secretly knows already:

> "The whole tone of voice, the whole attitude is one that compels bullshit. If I say it's too much like Brydan I mean not just Brydan himself but a whole way of writing, and I suppose thinking, that concentrates on the writer and draws attention to the chap, towards him and away from the subject. Which I suppose needn't be Wales in a way except that it always *is,* and somehow or other it's impossible to be honest in it."

The human condition as depicted in *The Old Devils* is not so far removed from the bleak vision of Samuel Beckett as it might seem, or as Mr. Amis might like to think. Devils are dead metaphors, and the Bible a meaningless metonym for a pub. It would seem one is not, in Yeats's phrase, a soul fastened to a dying animal, but just a dying animal. When one of the characters dies, the reaction of the others is either devastating banality or impotent irony:

> "No, he had it coming. . . . There wasn't a damn thing he or anyone else could have done about it. Not a thing."
> "Oh fabulous," said Peter, breaking a long silence. "Well, that certainly softens the blow and no mistake. Blessing in disguise, really, looked at in that light."

Two things soften, or are intended to soften, the darker implications of the story. One is the marriage of Rosemary, the Weavers' daughter, to William, the son of Peter and Muriel. Their wedding concludes the novel and is intended as a conventional symbol of continuity and renewal—too conventional, I must say, for this reader. The characters of the young couple are not sufficiently realized to make the hope invested in them by their parents seem more than sentimental. More persuasive—indeed, genuinely moving—are the relationships of Rhiannon with her two old admirers, Malcolm and Peter, on whom she has the effect of Eliot's April, mixing memory and desire, stirring dull roots with spring rain. This is slightly embarrassing for Rhiannon, especially with respect to Malcolm, but Rhiannon gamely submits to being taken by Malcolm for a sentimental outing to some site of their courting days which she has quite forgotten; while to Peter she extends a hand of forgiveness and friendship.

The Old Devils is unusual among Amis's novels in being narrated partly from the point of view of women—principally Rhiannon, but also Gwen and Muriel for a time. The perspective shifts frequently between these three and the four principal male characters, Malcolm, Charlie, Peter, and Alun. It is not always easy to remember who is who, and married to whom, and there is presumably a point to this. As we grow older, we grow more like each other, our anxieties and desires become restricted to a narrower and narrower range (the fear of death and of loneliness, the desire for animal comfort and peace of mind). In this phase of life, ordinary, unaffected human kindness counts for a lot. It is because Alun and Garth lack this generosity of spirit that the novel ultimately comes down hard on them. Amis has always been a very traditional moralist.

And what has all this to do with Wales? In a sense, nothing. The theme of old age could be explored in any regional context, as well as in the imaginary landscape of the later Beckett. But there is an elegiac quality about the topography of South Wales, romantic scenery interspersed with the relics of decayed industry, that makes it an appropriate setting. And in this novel the subject of Wales and Welshness is locked into an ironic double-bind that is characteristic of Kingsley Amis's work. It is very hard to find in the novel an attitude to Wales that is both positive and authentic. All enthusiasm for things Welsh, all celebrations of the Welsh language or the Welsh character, are made to seem bogus—but only the Welsh are allowed to say so. From anyone else such criticism would be arrogant and unwarranted. The consequence is that, as Rhiannon says to Peter, "Wales is a subject that can't be talked about. Unless you're making a collection of dishonesty and self-deception and sentimental bullshit." The same, it seems, goes for death—the skull beneath the genially smiling surface of this novel, Mr. Amis's best for many years.

Kingsley Amis

V. S. Pritchett

In his new novel, "The Old Devils" (Summit; $16.95), Kingsley Amis returns to the comedy of "Lucky Jim," but thirty or forty years on. The setting is South Wales, and the time has come for sizing up the traditional state of culture shock in which Celt and Saxon are entangled: where the Saxon is blunt, the singsong Celt is carried away by his imagination and his secretiveness. Times have changed for both parties to the intrigue. They are seen on private journeys from late middle age to old age, and facing social change. The coal miners' cottages are now often occupied by weekenders; hotels are tarted up for tourists. Italian and Indian restaurants now put one Welsh dish on their menus. Where is the old, "authentic" Wales?

The novel opens with two diverting and matching scenes. In the first we see a group of aging men, friends since their schooldays, proud of their sporting history, who regularly meet in an underheated, more or less private room at a pub called for some conjectural historical reason the Bible & Crown. Dedicated whiskey drinkers, some of the friends are enormously overweight, so that getting up from a chair when it is their turn to "shout" for another round is agony. The old devils grunt in the insinuating silences between their talk, which is mostly about their illnesses, the state of their bowels, and the pills they have taken. Two of them are mildly scholars; one owns a tavern; another works at a tinplate mill on the coast; another is a builder—but only of grandiose town halls. An item of news is released—perhaps not startling news, for what counts in suspicious Wales is "not what you knew but who could prove you knew it": a famous Welshman, the TV star Alun Weaver, and his wife, Rhiannon, have come back from years of success in London to live in their native town. How will they settle in? Hasn't he made a fortune by his talks on the box about the most famous of all Welsh poets, Brydan (who is probably drawn from Dylan Thomas), and by selling Welsh culture short to the vulgar British and the credulous Americans? Was Brydan a saint or a fraud? Was he authentic? Has Alun Weaver, a minor poet himself, cleverly got on the bandwagon of a dead man's fame? Alun is handsome; in his time, he was the best-known local Don Juan. And what about his delightful

From *The New Yorker* 63 (April 27, 1987): 102–104. Reprinted by permission of Sterling Lord Literistic, Inc. Copyright 1987 by Victor S. Pritchett.

wife? There was a disastrous scandal when she was a student and had to leave the town because she had been obliged to have an abortion. Her lover was not Alun Weaver, and now the matter is forgotten—times have changed. Still, to have married the slippery Alun Weaver!

While the corpulent old devils are at the Bible & Crown, the same news is being discussed by their wives and others at what is notionally "a coffee morning" in Sophie Norris's spacious drawing room, near the golf links. Coffee cups are more or less untouched. Ashtrays are filled with cigarette ends, and the ladies are drinking glass after glass of Soave Superiore, and moving on to Pinot Chardonnay. Before long, they will be more than eying a magnum of Orvieto. There are few silences at the ladies' party. One tipsy lady, Dorothy, is ruining their chance of going over the burning question of how Alun Weaver and his wife will "settle down" by going on about her trip to Russia and her discovery that the Welsh, Russian, and Red Indian languages have much in common because they have an aversion to the verb "to be." Sophie, the hostess, sees that the lady must be stopped but muddles it:

> Dorothy's heavy-duty mode took an appreciable time to come round from, so that when she paused for a second or two, as she did after the Red Indians, nobody had anything to say at first, until Sophie just scraped in on the last of the amber by asking to hear about the trip to Leningrad.

We realize that Sophie, who when she was young was known as "one of the surest things between Bridgend and Carmarthen," is not bright. Note: "the amber" is the British name for the yellow, warning traffic light. That image is a key to the shock effect of Amis's elaborate prose and his comedy. He has a wicked love of organizational verbiage. States of feeling are evoked as "areas"; if conventional, they will be called "standard." Confidences become "soft-soap sessions." For Amis, language has the ongoing, shortcut know-how, the echo of traffic, but is not for that reason to be despised. He is far from being facetious. His genius may owe something to the ornate Kipling. One of Amis's characters enjoys Kipling's word "frowsty" as a state of mind, and would echo Kipling's "A good cigar is a smoke." And Amis has Wodehouse's gift for spinning out strings of malign afterthoughts. Evoking the marriage of one of the old Welsh devils and an Englishwoman noted for her plainspoken, down-putting Yorkshire manner and her scorn for Welsh evasion, he writes:

> After all these years they really understood each other very well. Her saying that in an ordinary tone meant that hostilities were suspended and more, that that subject was now free, cleared for bringing up at any later stage without penalty. Further yet, as might not have been instantly clear to anyone but him, it constituted an apology, or the nearest she was ever going to get to one.

The return of the Weavers does stir up memories of tender feelings in one or two of the old devils. The narrative breaks up into a number of journeys about Wales in which the characters are revisiting sentimental scenes of their youth. The gentle Malcolm, who years ago was in love with Rhiannon, takes a trip with her along the coast to a spot where they had had a tender meeting. She breaks into tears—because he remembers it all and she does not. Young people nowadays, she reflects, can do what they like, but in her time they couldn't. Alun Weaver's trips are very different. His exploits as a Don Juan have their ad-hoc leaps into the unintended. They are matters of nerve. For example, he takes it into his head to drop in on his old flame Sophie. She has a talent for educated abuse. His vanity is flattered: insults are a good sign. Almost without a word, the seduction takes place. We don't see it; we know it has happened because he asks how much time they have left and because she returns to milder insult as they are saying goodbye. Even better, we know it by his reflection:

> All sorts of stuff, for instance what had been taking place a little earlier, seemed much as before, or at any rate not different enough to start making a song and dance about. . . . The most noticeable characteristic of the past, as seen by him, at least, was that there was so much more of it now than formerly, with bits that were longer ago than had once seemed possible.

At the center of the novel is Alun Weaver travelling with a disorderly party to Birdarthur to see the tomb of Brydan. The beautiful village is packed with gift shops in vulgar exploitation of the poet's fame. Here, self-deceived and now anxious, Weaver tries to settle to serious, honest writing. The old scholarly Charlie tells him firmly that he has no talent: his love of public performance, his identification with Brydan have destroyed it. While Weaver struggles to write, Dorothy, the most demonstrative of drinkers, is causing trouble in the village. Night has come, and, to add to the general anxiety, Charlie vanishes. There is a search. The old gentleman is found at last, having got lost on his way home—he has been afraid of the dark all his life! Indeed, when found, he collapses with what looks like a stroke. It isn't, but there is a warning here for the sporting old devils: someone will certainly die.

There is a violent and confused row at the Bible about an official document issued by the Lower Glamorgan Water Authority—a row in which Alun Weaver is asked "what he meant by it, who he thought he was talking to and similar questions," and is attacked as "a second-rate bloody ersatz Brydan." Then Tarc, the publican, shouts, "Out, the bloody lot of you. . . . Starting with you, Squire Weaver. . . . I've been dying to get rid of you buggers for years." He means it. He is sick of them. Out they go. Learned old Charlie sees the whole thing as grand opera in German: "In a ritualistic monologue of great power and beauty ('*Heraus sie alles sofortig*') Tarc invokes his immemorial right to banish the Ancients from their refuge, ordains and salutes their passing one by one and compels the removal of their age-old trophies." The Irish see themselves as saints; the Welsh see themselves as operatic giants. The old devils drift off to a freezing ill-lit house filled with ghastly dusty portraits and a virtual library of bottles of strong drink. Here Alun Weaver quietly, almost decently, raises a glass to his lips and, in the most authentic manner, drops dead in front of them.

"The Old Devils" is crowded with people who are keenly watching one another, who know one another well, but who give away as little as possible about themselves, who love to live as rumors. A crowded grand finale is necessary. What better than the classic deflating fête champêtre of a wedding under the changing Welsh sky, in which the younger generation warn their wayward elders about their behavior; in which in-laws meet new in-laws, with scornful eyes on one another; and in which old passions are recalled. Alun Weaver's widow, the beautiful Rhiannon, will meet again the man she really loved years before. That scolding, snobbish Yorkshire wife will walk out on her Welsh husband and go back to England, where people are plain and straightforward and know how to boss their garden plants, and where women have given up the non-U and ridiculous custom of wearing their best hats at weddings or funerals. Connoisseurs of weddings will note the maneuvers that occur when photographers try in vain to get the crowd in some sort of sheeplike order—an "area" that is distinctly not "standard." (The indispensable whispered arrangement about the cost of the wedding is very funny indeed.) And the novel ends with the sight of the poetic Malcolm sitting down to work on his translation of a long poem by Cynddelw Mawr ap Madog Wladaidd (c. 1320–?1388)—"more of an adaptation, actually," for in it he is making Rhiannon the central figure: a tribute, because if she has not given him love she has given him a poem. Kipling, who had his sentiments about a gallant tradition, would have approved. And so would Wodehouse. The old, robust masculine tradition of British comedy from Fielding and Smollett continues in our own vernacular.

Amis Behavin'

William H. Pritchard

Thirty-three years ago Kingsley Amis published "Lucky Jim," the most auspicious debut of an English comic novelist since Evelyn Waugh's "Decline and Fall" in 1928. The book was so funny and so successful that Mr. Amis's subsequent novels—like Norman Mailer's after "The Naked and the Dead"—were faulted for not living up to its high standard. In fact, the 15 novels that followed "Jim" were richly entertaining in quite distinct ways, as they experimented with genres like the spy, ghost or mystery story, the futuristic fantasy and the black comedy ("Ending Up"—an instance of such comedy, its subject old age—was his most assured success after "Jim"). Recently, with "Jake's Thing" and "Stanley and the Women," Mr. Amis has engaged in a sending-up of assorted pieties and ideologies, from psychoanalysis to internationalism to feminism to contemporary "improvements" in landscape, cityscape, pubscape.

Now, with the age theme to the fore and with women and men suffering equally under its stroke, comes "The Old Devils," winner of England's Booker Prize for 1986. His most ambitious and one of his longest books, this is neither a sendup nor an exercise in some established genre. It sets forth, with full realistic detail, a large cast of characters at least six of whom are rendered in depth as well as on the surface. "The Old Devils" is also Mr. Amis's most inclusive novel, encompassing kinds of feeling and tone that move from sardonic gloom to lyric tenderness.

The devils in question are a group of Welsh married couples in their 60's (Mr. Amis was born in 1922), whose firmly established daily routines on the parts of both sexes consist in talking a lot while consuming enormous, indeed unbelievable, quantities of drink. These routines are complicated by the return from England of Alun and Rhiannon Weaver, members of the group from decades past and implicated with several of them through affairs of the heart, the body or both. To nobody's surprise, Alun—a successful literary publicist of things Welsh who has sold out whatever real literary talent he possessed—takes up with vigor his career as seducer of two of the wives, while Rhiannon is thrown into sentimental and extremely poignant relations with two of the husbands, still lovers of her in their different ways. Divided into 10 parts, each

From *New York Times Book Review* (March 22, 1987): 14. Reprinted with permission of the author.

of them focusing on one or more of the characters, the novel proceeds through ironic comedy to the point where Alun, the subversive scapegoat, or *pharmakos* (as the critic Northrop Frye would call him), is rejected. Sudden death by a stroke claims him (he chokes on his whisky and water), and the society resumes its "normal" functioning, even with a change or two for the better.

Alun Weaver is a particularly vivid example of a recurrent type in Mr. Amis's fiction, the rogue male who is often though not always a womanizer, usually though not always a heavy drinker, but invariably endowed by his creator with plentiful verbal resources. When such a hero stays at the center of the narrative (as in "Jake's Thing" or "Stanley and the Women") in either first or third person, he dominates it to the extent where other characters can't compete with him. They may be more virtuous, but the rogue is more interesting (or, depending on your perspective, more repellent), since we know so much of his consciousness and participate so closely in his performance. Readers appalled by the misogyny vigorously expressed in "Stanley and the Women" were suffering partly because they couldn't get outside the first-person narrator's consciousness, which covered everything like a tent. In "The Old Devils" Mr. Amis has solved his problem of narrowness by a more dramatic kind of presentation in which the aggressive speech and sentiments of the rogue are responded to, with different degrees of approval and disapproval by the other old devils.

In the Glendower—a tavern-and-grill place owned jointly by one of the foremost old devils, Charlie Norris, and his brother Victor—Alun has the following exchange with a waiter:

> "What is the vintage port?" asked Alun.
> "Port is a fortified wine from Portugal," said the waiter, having perhaps misheard slightly, "and vintage port is made from—"
> "I didn't ask for a bloody lecture on vinification, you horrible little man." Alun laughed a certain amount as he spoke. "Tell me the shipper and the year and then go back to your hole and pull the lid over it."

Alun's response, aggressively inventive to the edge of viciousness, provokes mixed feelings in us, and these feelings are shared by his companions. In a similar moment, after Alun abuses a boring minor devil named Garth Pumphrey, once a veterinarian, Charlie says to Peter Thomas, the fattest and nicest of the oldsters: "Not very nice, that just now, was it? . . . In fact not at all nice. It's odd, that was exactly what you've always wanted to say to him, you hoped somebody would one day and then when they do it's nothing like the treat you'd been banking on. Bloody . . . bloody little cowshed mountebank was it? M'm. There's trenchant, eh?"

The book's real trenchancy lies, as with any of Mr. Amis's novels, in the language, especially as it renders the physical infirmities, the embarrassments and humiliations of getting old. In the first pages, Malcolm Cellan-Davies sits down to eat his breakfast of toast and diabetic honey: "He had not bitten anything with his front teeth since losing a top middle crown on a slice of liver-sausage six years earlier, and the right-hand side of his mouth was a no-go area, what with a hole in the lower lot where stuff was always apt to stick and a funny piece of gum that seemed to have got detached from something and waved disconcertingly about whenever it saw the chance."

Reading such prose, one is constantly surprised by something extra, a twist or seeming afterthought signifying an originality of mind that is inseparable from the novelist's originality of language. At age 61 Yeats wrote bitterly in "The Tower" of "this absurdity . . . this caricature,/ Decrepit age that has been tied to me / As to a dog's tail." Mr. Amis fleshes out and domesticates the caricature by showing us Peter's plight, a fat man who can't cut his toenails in the house for fear his wife may discover telltale fragments of them:

> "After experimenting with a camp-stool in the garage and falling off it a good deal he had settled on a garden seat under the rather fine flowering cherry. This restricted him to the warmer months, the wearing of an overcoat being of course ruled out by the degree of bending involved. But at least he could let the parings fly free, and fly they bloody well did, especially the ones that came crunching off his big toes, which were massive enough and moved fast enough to have brought down a sparrow on the wing, though so far this had not occurred."

After various felicities, we encounter that final stroke of mastery, the assurance that in fact Peter has not yet unintentionally brought about the fall of a sparrow. The caricature of decrepit age, passively endured by one of its sufferers, has been opportunistically converted into an occasion of imaginative pleasure.

The novel is filled with mordant, but also affectionate and nostalgic, feelings and observations about Wales (Mr. Amis taught at Swansea in the early 1950's, and his second novel is set there) expressed in typically Amis sentences like the following about a deconsecrated church: "This one had been converted not into a pornographic cinema but, less offensively some might have thought, into an arts centre." Best to read carefully, so as not to join the "some" who assume that an arts center is clearly better than the offensive cinema. But along with the expected clevernesses, there are welcome surprises, not to be counted on in an Amis novel, like a woman (Gwen, married to Malcolm) being convincing about how awful men are when they pretend to listen to women: "Tell us what you think, love—no go on, I really want to hear. And then when you did tell 'em, well it was quite a long time before I started noticing the glaze in their eyes. They were being good about you talking." The best surprise of all happens twice, in two dramatic sequences—Rhiannon with Peter, then with Malcolm—that are unashamedly moving in their expression of loss and of memory's tricks. There has been nothing quite like them in Mr. Amis's previous fiction (though see his poem to his father, "In Memoriam W.R.A."), and their presence makes the book, for all its skill in caricature, much more than a caricature.

As I read and reread "The Old Devils" (it gets better on a second try), I found myself wishing that Philip Larkin—who called Mr. Amis "quite the funniest writer I had ever met"—could have stayed alive to read it, especially since so many moments in it recall specific Larkin poems as well as his general ethos. When Rhiannon and Malcolm visit a shut-up Welsh church on a remote promontory, we think of Larkin's "Church Going"; or they encounter a crowd of bathers that might have stepped out of "To the Sea." At another point, Charlie Norris rewrites a line from "Dockery and Son" into "Life was first boredom, then more boredom, as long as it was going your way, at least." And the novel's title surely recalls Larkin's great poem about age, "The Old Fools." But the kinship is stronger than any matter of specific references: both Mr. Amis and Larkin are deeply humorous writers, and—as Robert Frost liked to say about himself—never more serious than when humorous. In "The Old Devils" Mr. Amis has tried to be seriously humorous about the impossible subject of death, as he was in the little poem that concludes his collected poems: "Death has got something to be said for it; / There's no need to get out of bed for it; / Wherever you may be, / They bring it to you, free."

The close of the novel has a mythy feel about it, a marriage between young people who are viewed with respect, even admiration, by the novelist. There is the sense that life goes on, with the young entertaining hopes as high as those some of the old devils once entertained. Peter's son tells him at his wedding reception that, strangely enough, his relationship with his bride has been nothing less than splendid: " 'Absolutely no snags or problems of any kind at any stage right from the start. My God, I've just realised it was love at first sight. Doesn't that sound ridiculous?' 'No,' said Peter." This is undoubtedly the most affirmative "No" Mr. Amis has ever had a character utter, and it comes as a fitting end to a book that, along with its eloquent and wonderfully comic presentation of life's awfulnesses, is very much on life's side.

Do Not Go Sober

James Wolcott

> Perhaps being old is having lighted rooms
> Inside your head, and people in them, acting.
> > —Philip Larkin, "The Old Fools"

Kingsley Amis's *The Old Devils* is so dense with booze that the book seems sunken, subaquatic, its retired Welsh sots trying to remain standing in an aquarium stocked with gin and drifting hunks of scenery. They don't always succeed. "Siân Smith fell down on her way out but soon got up again and made it into the hall." Even sitting can be a trial. "There came a noise that began rather like a fart of heroic proportions but soon proved to be made by the exhaustive ripping of the canvas seat of Peter's chair under his buttocks." These pratfalls are set within a movieish swirl of clinking bottles, lingering smoke, and confidential asides ("I never realized how much he drank till the night he came home sober. A revelation, it was"). By morning, Amis's wasted wrecks feel as if heavy furniture has been pushed around in their heads. Everyone recalls the hangover in *Lucky Jim* ("His mouth had been used as a latrine by some small creature of the night, and then as its mausoleum"), and a casualty here wakes up taking similar inventory ("He felt as if about two-thirds of his head had recently been sliced off and his heart seemed to be beating somewhere in his stomach, but otherwise he was fine . . ."). Another dreams amorously of Mrs. Thatcher, who tells him that "without him her life would be a mere shell, an empty husk." Teenagers who crave kicks might envy the lifestyle of these aimless ruins, with their pensions and pills. This crew can get oiled until their eyeballs float and there's nobody around to tell them, "Mind your elders." They *are* the elders. Nearly everyone they had to mind is kaput.

Not that they're merry sods, waving mugs in time to songs at ye olde alehouse. Their principal place of congregation is an adjunct room to a pub called the Bible, once home for a squash club and decorated now with old photos nobody's bothered to take down and a couple of leftover ashtrays. Its defunct air suits its male regulars (the wives tipple at home), themselves smugly past-it. It's a place where men go to pretend. "Queers aside," thinks

From *The New Republic* 196 (March 30, 1987): 33–35. Reprinted by permission of *The New Republic,* © 1987, The New Republic, Inc.

Alun, a TV smoothie who has returned to Wales after a posh career in London, "men above twenty-five or so were never drunk however pissed they might be." Cold air keeps creeping in on this clique, bringing 'em back to personal history, inescapable thoughts, that old sow mortality. Booze as they might, Amis's ornery types are sandbagged in being. But what being! *Ending Up,* an earlier Amis tale of age and collapse, was an elaborate mousetrap of black humor snapping the spindly necks of its set-up cast. *Stanley and the Women,* trying so hard to provoke, was little more than a cranky fit—phlegm passing itself off as bile. But *The Old Devils* has a tough honest crust and scuttling sideways humor. Nowhere in it does Amis attempt shapely sentences or lyrical, dying falls. His is an aesthetic of the antibeautiful. The book's astringency feels just right. It's the best novel on the delinquencies of the old since Muriel Spark's *Memento Mori.*

The sheer cussed readability of *The Old Devils* is a constant reward. Bam, right from the start Amis tunes in to the morning chat of one of his couples as if it were a long-running radio show. Malcolm, the male half of this team, smokes a single cigarette in the morning to get his insides going. He doesn't hold with the laxatives that his wife, Gwen, recommends. "He thought it a bit thick for a man not to be able to win an argument about his own insides, even one with his wife." Along with Malcolm and Gwen, the couples treading time in *The Old Devils* are Alun and Rhiannon, Charlie and Sophie, Garth and Angharad, Percy and Dorothy, Peter and Muriel. There's also a young pair consisting of William (son of Peter and Muriel) and Rosemary (daughter of Alun and Rhiannon), whose wedding takes up the novel's least riveting chapter. I've provided a line-up because a number of reviewers in England, where the novel won the Booker Prize, have complained about not being able to tell the players without a scorecard. P.J. Kavanagh in the *Spectator:* "Somehow it became almost Russian in its confusing welter of Christian names, it was difficult to remember who was speaking, or who was married to whom." Comments like Kavanagh's shouldn't deter. At a time when so many novels are vehicles for a single vote (*Edisto, The Counterlife, Tough Guys Don't Dance,* whatever), Amis provides a distinct party mix. He moves a small troupe of actors across the page, and their voices never fritz through crosswiring, as in George V. Higgin's lowlife broadcasts. They have their own individual swing. Take, for instance, Alun's suave solo on one of the book's favorite bogus themes, The Spirit of Wales.

Asked what it is like to be back north, he replies, "Many things grave and gay and multicolored but one above all: I'm coming home. That short rich resounding word means one simple single thing to a Welshman such as I, born and bred in this land of river and hill. And that thing, that miraculous thing is—Wales." This parody of Dylan Thomas at his most mellifluous and fruity (a Dylan Thomas figure named Brydan hovers over *The Old Devils* like a plump, puking cherub) is almost too easy, and Amis is shrewd enough not to overdo it. He hits his relaxed stride in more extended sessions, like this man-to-man talk between Malcolm and Alun on the topic of Malcolm's Shortcomings:

"You're the feeblest creature God ever put breath into," said Alun. "Why any woman should have spent thirty-three minutes married to you, let alone thirty-three years, defies comprehension. You've no idea in the world of what pleases a woman: in other words"—he seemed to be choosing these with care—"you're not only hopeless as an organizer of life in general, you're a crashingly boring companion into the bargain and needless to say, er, perennially deficient in the bedroom. Correct?"

"That about sums me up. Oh, I'm also cut off."

"Cut off?"

"Cut off from real people in my own little pathetic fantasy world of dilettante Welshness, medievalism and poetry." Malcolm drained his glass.

"*Poetry?* You ought to be ashamed of yourself, a great big hulking fellow like you...."

Mimicry has always been one of Amis's specialties, vocal and facial. The poet Philip Larkin recounted that at Oxford Amis had a rich repertoire of riffs. "Kingsley's masterpiece, which was so demanding I heard him do it only twice, involved three subalterns, a Glaswegian driver and jeep breaking down and refusing to restart somewhere in Germany. Both times I became incapable with laughter." It was Larkin who encouraged Amis to put more faces into *Lucky Jim* (Larkin himself seems to be making faces in *The Old Devils*. Echoes abound, from a rephrasing of one of his most famous lines—"Life is first boredom, then fear" becomes "Life is first boredom, then more boredom"—to a replay of their shared love for old jazz: "Through a roaring fuzz of needle-damage the sounds of 'Cakewalkin' Babies' emerged.")

The mimicry that Larkin admired was and is more than imitation. Amis has a brilliant handle on how theatrical bits of business infiltrate daily life until they become casual shtick. " 'Rhiannon Rhys, as she was when I first met her,' said Malcolm fluently, raising himself in the seat like a panelist answering a question from the audience...." When Amis shows his couples in the privacy of their own homes, it's like taking a peek backstage. Alun's snowy mane, for example: "Most of his friends were pretty sure that he improved on nature in this department as in others; not many of them would have guessed that Rhiannon put the whitener on for him while they giggled and had drinks." (Alun and Rhiannon are this book's Lunt and Fontanne.) Amis is also apt on how clothes become costume. Meeting Rhiannon for a day-trip, Malcolm climbs out of the car wearing "a hacking jacket whose dark red, green fawn checks ... were too large by an incredibly small amount." From that foxy detail alone we know that Malcolm foolishly fancies himself a rakish blade. (Malcolm's peaked cap also gives Rhiannon pause.) Amis has always been marvelous on the subtle gradations of the slightly off.

For Amis, slightly off isn't a bad state to be in, considering the surrounding mess. Happiness he locates at the margins, away from the madding crowd and media megahype. Like Larkin (with whom he shares a distrust of the transcendent sublime—e.g., his poem "Against Romanticism"), he sees the century choking on its own unrest and coughing up weeds. No Shelleys await to lift the planet high. Useful purpose is petering out, not only in the old devils but in Wales, the world. The brawny flex of the industrial age is finished:

> Now, where once ships by the dozen had lain, bringing timber, ores, pig-iron, fetching coal, coke, spelter, there was just the harbor dredger, looking as if it had not yet been out that year, and a single dirty little freighter flying the blue, white and red of Yugoslavia.

And in the absence of trade and enterprise, what's left? Tourism, mostly—a quaint makeover of the country so that it's acceptably chichi for cosmos on holiday and locals itching for a little flash. As Charlie puts it neatly, "Everywhere's trendy now unless it's actually starving." Equally ersatz is the attempt to bottle the ruddy flavor of Wales into such a self-conscious package that the place becomes more a slick site for a TV series than a lived-in heap of associations.

But behind the racy promise of chic or the peeling bark of antiquity, something intangibly real remains. "Anyway, it was Wales all right," thinks Rhiannon when she arrives by train:

> There was no obvious giveaway, like roadsigns in two languages or closed-down factories, but something was there, an extra greenness in the grass, a softness in the light, something that was very like England and yet not England at all, more a matter of feeling than seeing but not just feeling, something run-down and sad but simpler and freer than England all the same.

In passages this gently ruminative, Amis reaches a level of response that he hasn't attained since *Take a Girl Like You*. And near the end of the novel there's an episode involving one character's fear of the dark that has a zero-pathos purity of fellow feeling.

Kingsley Amis being something of an old devil himself (asked what he was going to spend his prize money on, he replied, "Booze, of course"), it's hardly surprising that the book has an air of complicity. What is surprising is that the air is so cool and clear. Despite the age of its cast, *The Old Devils* doesn't tiptoe near the sunset waters of *On Golden Pond* to engage in gallant reverie. Its rambling yet pointed dialogue, snapshots of decay, and noisy misdemeanors are very much in the present tense. Amis's old devils don't look backward, to youth, or forward, to death, but just far enough ahead to get through the livelong day. Each morning becomes a matter of getting the machinery going. Few novels contain this much crowded sensation. Fewer still show such fidgety control of their funny-sad effects. Like Alun, Amis has a stay-awake mind that sees through muck and stupor. Sobriety sits in his forehead like a Cyclopean-eye, always open for business. Business here is brisk.

London *Times* Obituary: Sir Kingsley Amis

Sir Kingsley Amis, CBE, novelist and poet, died yesterday aged 73. He was born in south London on April 16, 1922.

Kingsley Amis was an essentially private man who spent a great deal of his life in the public eye and managed rather to enjoy it. His first published novel, *Lucky Jim,* won him immediate acclaim in 1954, as well as the Somerset Maugham Award. It established him as a master of invective and a man well able to raise a guffaw from his readers, especially the male ones. For the next 40 years Amis produced a regular flow of books which established him as the leading British comic novelist of his generation. The tone varied considerably but Amis picked his targets carefully and his aim was deadly accurate. He wrote about what he knew well and made sure that he did not too much like what he saw about him.

In March 1991 the limelight became especially strong with the publication of his *Memoirs.* As he moved through his sixties Amis deliberately put on a cantankerous face to the world: the old buffer became the old curmudgeon. He had developed a reputation, only partly deserved, of being rude to those who disturbed his wellbeing, such as incompetent waiters, and to those whose opinions he derided, notably of the political Left. The image he cultivated was much enhanced by his *Memoirs,* which blew up a fine old literary dust.

No book he wrote, not even *Lucky Jim,* attracted so much publicity on its first appearance. In a spate of profiles Amis, usually photographed in his shirt sleeves with his baggy trousers supported by massive braces drawn up somewhere around his sternum, managed for the quality press many a glare that would have done credit to Evelyn Waugh himself. Word quickly got around that Kingsley Amis had done another demolition job, this time of well-known names not only among the dead but also among—crimes of crimes—the living. One leading newspaper called the book morally repugnant and thoroughly vindictive.

Only when that dust had settled did *Memoirs* become recognised at least by some for what it was, an assembly of highly collectable anecdotes which would have entertained any dinner party (not comprised of maiden aunts) or

From *The London Times,* 23 October 1995. Reprinted with permission of *The Times,* London. © *The Times,* London, 1995.

literary saloon bar. The storyteller was back at work, but revealing very little about himself apart from his dislikes: reluctance by others to stand their round of drinks came very high on the list. Indeed, in the preface there was a warning sentence: "I have already written an account of myself in 20 or more volumes, most of them called novels." The limelight was there, but amidst the profiles in print and on television the private person remained hidden.

Amis could well have argued that there was not now a great deal to hide. By the time he entered his seventies his life had become rigidly set. During the week he moved between his home in Primrose Hill, which was the self-contained ground floor of a house shared with his first wife Hilly (now Lady Kilmarnock), and the Garrick Club. At weekends, when the Garrick was closed, a pub down the road called the Queens substituted. Amis wrote in the morning, arrived at the Garrick about 12.30, never sat down to lunch there before 2pm, had a few drinks afterwards, wrote again a little in the late afternoon and very rarely went out in the evening.

His hatred of travel, if anything, magnified. He only left London in August to holiday with friends in Swansea when the Garrick was closed. Kingsley Amis, who had regularly played at being an old man, had at last become one. Trouble with his legs and feet prevented him from walking more than a few yards; the bouts of melancholia, which had been with him off and on for much of his life, increased, often prompted by the death of another old friend. That usually meant the loss of one more drinking companion.

A little of the limelight returned when it emerged that he had agreed for a biography to be written despite the publication of *Memoirs* a couple of years back. The author was Eric Jacobs, a journalist and fellow member of the Garrick. Amis was probably encouraged by the fact that the "research" would involve a number of convivial lunches both at the Garrick and the Queens. Despite his infirmities and persistent hypochondria Amis was still able to take in a good quantity of wine and whisky without apparent ill-effects. Jacobs more than once complained that he had difficulty in keeping up with his quarry—in alcohol.

Kingsley Amis came out earlier this year but already its subject's reputation was in decline, especially among the younger, liberal-leaning literary critics. Their venom was fiercely directed against *The Biographer's Moustache* (1995) which Amis, ever ready to turn recent experiences to good use, published shortly after the Jacobs study. The story of a literary hack commissioned to write the biography of a Grand Old Man of Letters, who spends more time hobnobbing with dukes than adding to his oeuvre, attracted some splenetic reviews. By Amis standards the book was slight, but he was sharply wounded by the mauling he received. The bounce and self-confidence began to evaporate.

Kingsley Amis was born in Norwood, south London, into a family that had in his own words come down a bit in the world and "slipped a rung." He began his education at Norbury College, which "only had two famous alumni. Me and Derek Bentley." (Bentley was executed on a murder charge.) He went on to City of London, his father's old school, and won an exhibition to St John's College, Oxford, where he arrived "in impeccably proletarian style" in 1941. Military service, in the Royal Corps of Signals, intervened.

At Oxford, after the interruption of his war service, he formed a number of crucial friendships. The first was with Hilary (Hilly) Bardwell, who was an art student and then a model—head only, no stripping—at the Ruskin School of Art. A two-year affair ended in an Oxford marriage in 1948 when Hilly was already pregnant with Amis's first son, Philip. They remained together, despite peccadilloes on both sides, until the early 1960s and were divorced in 1965. Amis draws on Hilly as a principal character in two of his novels. The married period features in *Take a Girl Like You* and the reunion under the same Primrose Hill roof is thinly disguised in *The Folks that Live on the Hill*.

The second great Oxford friendship was with the poet and librarian Philip Larkin, one of the few people apart from Hilly for whom Amis had almost unreserved admiration—"the best poet I know apart from Housman." Larkin and Amis were united in a love of jazz and their glee in debunking other writers, especially those on the Oxford syllabus. Larkin went through early drafts of *Lucky Jim* suggesting alterations, he was the dedicatee of the finished product and a street where he lived for a time even provided the surname of the hero, Jim Dixon. The friendship of the two men was to remain until Larkin's death and Dixon was to become recognised, quite quickly, as one of the great comic creations of 20th-century fiction.

The novel was published in 1954, by which time Amis had been a lecturer in English literature at University College, Swansea, for five years. He ended up there, he claimed, because Swansea made its academic appointments rather late and avowed that he was lucky to get the job. But he stayed until 1961, when he transferred none too happily to Peterhouse, Cambridge. Several of his Swansea colleagues reckoned to have identified themselves, probably quite correctly, in Jim Dixon's march through the pomposities and incompetences of provincial academic life. But Amis survived the spleen of those affected by his lampoons, just as Jim Dixon managed to survive being classified (incorrectly) as one of the angry young men who were fast becoming fashionable. Amis rather liked South Wales, returning to it often, and found that some of those who lived there provided excellent raw material. It was to be the setting of one of his funniest—and sourest—novels, *The Old Devils,* which won the Booker Prize in 1986. Amis treated the award-giving dinner with appropriate dyspepsia. The success of *Lucky Jim* and a legacy left to Hilly raised the Amis lifestyle above the subsistence level given to a university lecturer.

Amis novels in the familiar yellow and black jackets of his first publisher, Gollancz, followed every two or three years: *That Uncertain Feeling* (1955), *I*

Like It Here (1958) and, probably funniest of all, *Take a Girl Like You* (1960). They were written with fine comic assurance and in some cases were popular enough to be filmed, though not with any great success. The year 1963 brought *One Fat Englishman,* which drew on his experiences as visiting lecturer at Princeton University, an episode also described acidly in *Memoirs.* He was to return to America ten years later, in 1967, this time to Vanderbilt in Nashville, Tennessee. On occasion he could be quite warm about America, saying that he would have gone there more often had he been able to overcome his fear of flying. But that he never achieved and as he got older all forms of travel, including simple train journeys, filled him with apprehension—or so he said.

By the early 1960s Kingsley Amis was fully involved with the novelist Elizabeth Jane Howard. They met for the first time at the Cheltenham Literary Festival in the autumn of 1962. Amis made a pass at his blonde and sophisticated fellow panellist and was straightaway accepted. He moved out of the family home and in with the twice divorced Elizabeth Jane, whom he married in 1965. It was in part a literary association: he helped her with her novels and she helped him with his. But it also soon became a stormy one. Neither seemed willing to bridge the gaps between them of taste and class: she liked polished dinner parties and he preferred conversations in pubs. There were regular arguments about Amis's drinking habits. Amis left a record of the relationship in one of his most misanthropic novels, *Jake's Thing,* and they separated for good in the early 1980s.

In the mid-1960s Amis moved from Gollancz to Cape (he was to end up with HarperCollins) and branched out from his regular terrain of comic novels with their strong underlying vein of censure. *Colonel Sun: A James Bond Adventure* (1968), which took over where Ian Fleming left off, was a thriller he published under the pseudonym of Robert Markham. Previously, and also pseudonymously, he wrote *The Book of Bond* by "Lt-Col. Tanner." There was an indifferent but larky collaboration with his friend Robert Conquest, *The Egyptologists.* But Amis, the professional critic who analysed how others wrote, was adept at mastering established genres. *The Green Man* (1969) was an accomplished ghost story in M. R. James style, under-appreciated when it first came out but winning some belated admiration when it became a television serial in 1990. *The Riverside Murders* (1973) showed that he could write a detective story along with the best of them. His fascination with science fiction had already been displayed in *New Maps of Hell* (1961).

There was Amis the poet, a man who felt that his collections of verse were underestimated, and Amis the editor of poetry with *The New Oxford Book of Light Verse.* There was Amis the literary critic and Amis the expert on Kipling, *Kipling and his World.* Most especially, there was Amis on drink. Alcohol, usually consumed in large quantities, played an important part in most of his novels and he wrote a number of books on the subject. He was a wine bibber—and a spirit bibber for that matter—who knew what he liked and was vituperative about what displeased him. His restaurant column for *Harpers & Queen* was eccentric, diverting and long-lasting.

Beneath the clubbable bonhomie, regularly on display at the Garrick (or Irving, as it became in *The Folks that Live on the Hill,* 1990), and the talent to amuse with funny faces and well turned anecdotes, there was a powerful vein of melancholy. *Ending Up* (1974) is one of his shortest novels and one of his bleakest, a study of the viciousness the elderly show to one another. Thames Television's attempt to put it on screen was much too soft. Amis had only just entered his fifties when he wrote it and possibly he thought it better in the future to put on the mask of the old curmudgeon. Bile was replaced by anger in *Jake's Thing* (1978), directed at psychiatrists, the monstrous regiment of women in general and Elizabeth Jane Howard in particular.

Amis acquired the reputation of being a misogynist and there was plenty of ammunition for his critics in *Stanley and the Women* (1984) and *The Old Devils.* The latter was the masterpiece of his curmudgeon period. It was also highly successful as a television series. He was no favourite of feminist writers and was glibly dubbed "a man's humorist". For a time that probably pleased him: he knew quite a lot about women and delighted in the least pleasant aspects of his knowledge. But he also knew that the tide of taste was turning against him. *You Can't Do Both* (1994) has a hero, Robin Davies, whose life resembles quite closely that of the young Amis. It carries a new mood of half-regret for past misdeeds and, notably, it is dedicated to Hilly. But even such realisations had not prepared him for the vituperation which greeted *The Biographer's Moustache*. Like Maurice Allington in *The Green Man,* Amis felt he was being haunted by some very unpleasant spectres.

Kingley Amis was appointed CBE in 1981 and knighted in 1990. He is survived by his three children from his first marriage (Philip, the novelist Martin and Sally) and by both his former wives.

Can a Feminist (Still) Read Kingsley Amis?

SHARI BENSTOCK

> He thought what a pity it was that all his faces were designed to express rage or loathing. Now that something had happened which really deserved a face, he'd none to celebrate it with. As a kind of token, he made his Sex Life in Ancient Roman face.
>
> —*Lucky Jim*

I found my way to feminism through Amis's *Lucky Jim*. It was 1977, an exhilarating year for feminists, especially women in the academy. In the United States, 1977 saw the publication of Ellen Moers's *Literary Women* and Elaine Showalter's *A Literature of Their Own,* two landmark texts for American literary feminism. Friends were reading Adrienne Rich's *Of Woman Born* and teaching Virginia Woolf's *A Room of One's Own* in recently established Women's Studies programs. The following year, the University of Illinois Press brought Zora Neale Hurston's *Their Eyes Were Watching God* back into print. In England Germaine Greer, author of *The Female Eunuch* (1970), was still the feisty darling of the British media, which provided her occasions to mock the class system and the monarchy and to reveal on Radio 4 that she used men for sexual purposes and then threw them aside when they no longer pleased her.

But in 1977 I was only on the margins of a world in which women charted their own destinies. I was not yet ready to untangle the roots of anger and despair that bound my womanhood. I was living with my husband, an exchange professor of literature at a redbrick university located midway between London and Oxford. That setting encapsulated for me something of the emotional landscape in which Amis's antihero, James Dixon, who for so much of the novel appears to be anything but "lucky," undergoes his academic trials. Had we not spent a year in Britain attending sherry parties in the commons room and hosting dinners in our little house near campus, social events where I met all the academic types Amis lampoons in *Lucky Jim,* it might have taken me longer to discover my own feminism (which is American inflected by French theories of subjectivity) or to understand why this

---

This essay was written specifically for this volume and is published for the first time by permission of the author.

novel so profoundly depressed me in all the places it should have entertained me. When Jim is caught out "flapp[ing] his lips" (38) after he is forced to take the first tenor part of the madrigal performed at Professor Welch's musical evening, I first laughed at his predicament, then found myself in tears. His social failures in settings where everyone else seems to know the codes and enjoy the game are mirrored by his sexual failures. He is caught between the manipulative and not adequately attractive Margaret Peel and the beautiful but "schoolmistressy" Christine Callaghan, while the older, wiser, married Carol Goldsmith looks on. He eventually wins the most attractive of the three women, but for most of the novel Dixon plays a losing hand at love. Why did his creator stack the cards against him? I wondered.

With one or two exceptions, the men in the novel are by turns boorish, pedantic, incompetent, emasculated, malicious, even destructive—nonetheless they retain positions of professional power. The women are either seeking such men or have already found their power within the housewifely role, as has Mrs. Welch. She brought to her marriage "a good-sized income of her own" (66), yet is referred to as "Mrs. Neddy," a diminutive of her husband's given name. Together, they are the "Neddies." Suggestive of cuddly cute pets, this sobriquet belies the couple's social power in the airless world of academe as well as Mrs. Neddy's insistent efforts to prop up her husband's authority as head of household and chair of the Department of History. The single exception to the formulaic woman-seeking-a-man is Miss Cutler, who runs the lodging house where Dixon lives. Her past life is portrayed in a series of four framed photographs on the dining room walls, each of which denotes a loss or absence: her nephew in the uniform of a Pay Corps lance-corporal; her cousin's two nieces; the country house of her former employer; herself dressed as a bridesmaid "in the fashions of the First World War" (166). A spinster of a certain age, Miss Cutler leads a life of service to a changing clientele of single men who rent rooms from her.

Among the married couples, only the Goldsmiths appear to have a union in which there is some level of equality and honesty; Carol Goldsmith tells Dixon that her husband knows of her extramarital affair with Bertrand Welch: "I wouldn't dream of doing anything behind his back," she confesses. At this revelation, Dixon falls silent, "reflecting, not for the first time, that he knew absolutely nothing whatsoever about other people or their lives" (123). Looking more closely at Carol, he observes evidence of aging in her lined face and notices "a black gap beyond the canines" (123). Poor dentistry and signs of eventual mortality dispel the attraction he might have felt for her. But it is Carol who gives Jim key advice on his contorted love life ("Put Margaret out of your mind for once," 124) and who accurately diagnoses his feelings for Christine: "Your attitude," she explains, "measures up to the two requirements of love. You want to go to bed with her and can't, and you don't know her well. Ignorance of the other person topped up with deprivation, Jim. . . . The old hopeless passion, isn't it?" And in the end, after he has lost his university post and learned the true circumstances of Margaret's suicide attempt (that she had asked *both* men she was courting to come to her flat on the evening she took an overdose of sleeping pills), Jim suddenly gets lucky. He wins the beautiful and wise Christine, a 20-year-old with maturity, authority, and clarity of vision well beyond her age, and also a position as a private secretary to Christine's uncle, Julius Gore-Urquhart, at £500 a year—an amount of money that, Virginia Woolf assured us, guarantees essential security and financial independence.

My 1977 reading of *Lucky Jim* altered elements of Amis's story as a test of verisimilitude. Assuming that Dixon's seeming powerlessness represented a version of social, if not sexual, castration, I silently feminized him: Jim became "Jane." At dinners and drinks parties I searched the crowd for a likely "Jane." To my surprise, she was nowhere to be seen. The women I met, most of them academics or the spouses of academics, impressed me as independent, forthright, perceptive, no-nonsense people who announced straightforwardly their values, priorities, and commitments and appeared unintimidated by their husbands and senior male colleagues. These women had spunk, as my grandmother would have said. One of them, a single woman about my age (32), commuted daily to the university by bicycle from a nearby village. When I remarked at the end of a late-evening party on her courage at making the 10-mile ride in the dark, she whispered conspiratorially: "The trick is to stay well to the center of the lane." She appeared to dismiss the possibilities of rape, robbery, or murder enroute to her cottage. I, by contrast, could not find the "spunk" to make the 40-minute train trip to London alone in broad daylight.

When social chat at these occasions drifted beyond the borders of academe, it usually turned to politics, where Margaret Thatcher, entering her first term as prime minister, took center stage. Of course, there were lots of jokes about her coiffure, her false upper-class accent, the extraordinary range of her piercing voice, and her humble beginnings. Someone always recounted the tale of how a greengrocer's daughter rose to power by winning local by-elections in the 1950s and slowly transformed herself, by hard work and hardheadedness, into the Iron Maiden of British politics. She was not a woman, we all tacitly agreed, but a man in a green silk suit. We winked and smiled as someone recalled that "Mrs. Thatcher" credited her political success to her father's encouragement (and his small-business economies) and to her husband, Jim, an academic and reputedly a good cook, who managed the kitchen even after their move to Downing Street. Indeed, the joke was on stay-at-home Jim—who was also rumored to console himself with the gin bottle on nights when his wife was battling the back-benchers in parliament.

I was forced to rethink my attitude toward Jim Dixon; clearly, it would take more to disempower him, to subject him to the embarrassments and humiliations he faces in Amis's novel, than merely to feminize him in a country where women were apparently the stronger of the two sexes. If the struggles of Jim Dixon could not be explained entirely by the feminization factor, perhaps he needed another marker of otherness to account for the precariousness of his professional position and his escalating fear of his colleagues. The predictable category was social class, beloved of British satirists. I searched *Lucky Jim* for telltale signs: a grating accent combined with poor table manners and a preference for pubs and ale. Indeed, Amis makes Dixon a northerner with a "flat" voice that marks him an outsider in a system where all ears are tuned to regional and class differences. And the table manners he displays at Miss Cutler's breakfasts leave something to be desired. But the academic setting, as I was learning, both blurs and accentuates markers of individuality. If only poor Dixon could demonstrate intellectual prowess (which he secretly longs to do), he might save his job and succeed socially. Dixon's plight, I began to suspect, lay not in his gender or place of birth, in the strength (or weakness) of his intelligence, or in the quality of his education, but in his total alienation from academic culture: he has no will to scale the ivy-covered walls. That is, he has no desire to succeed on the terms set out by the university. The story can only end with Dixon's removal from the academic grove, either by losing his position or by removing him to a better, larger world. Amis plays it both ways, thus avoiding the necessity of explaining the "rage" and "loathing" that Dixon feels for himself and his colleagues and that are expressed in the silent "faces" he makes in response to events.

A comedy, *Lucky Jim* skirts issues of disappointment and sadness and never portrays real tragedy. Thus Margaret Peel's suicide attempt does not portend the tragic but merely the embarrassing—not her own embarrassment, of which she is incapable, but Jim's on her behalf. To examine seriously either Margaret's or Jim's situation would require recasting the story in another literary mode where the reader might learn more of their inner conditions—the painful sources of their social poses or the societal causes of their personal pain. Although offering the occasional glimpse of these other scenes, Amis resists the temptation to explore the darker side of the world he creates. Yet that other side is palpable, felt as a lump in the throat of laughter.

During our year in Britain, I tried to put the comic touch on my own private travails as a displaced academic without (yet) a tenure-track job and with the nagging sense that my life lacked direction and purpose. If I had had Jim Dixon's chance at a university position, I would have made a success of it, I told myself. And yet I abandoned the book on post-impressionist art and early modernist literature I had intended to write during that year. I set the project aside on the grounds that the necessary research could only be completed in London and that coordinating the research and travel with my son's school schedule and my husband's teaching routine had proved impossible. In truth, I was afraid—of the train journey, of losing my way in London (a city I knew well from previous visits), of negotiating the intricacies of a research library. So, I stayed home. In early November, as the days shortened, I set out to write a novel that would recount the trials and tribulations of a woman not unlike myself in her role as a minor administrator in a troubled department at a large university in the American heartland. Needing a model for my academic satire, I sought my husband's advice: "*Lucky Jim* is the classic," he declared.

For me at that time, the novel was neither classic nor comic. I can still see the distressed look on my husband's face when he found me clutching Kleenex over tear-stained pages. I thought Amis's characters offensive and repellent. Turning the pages of *Lucky Jim,* I wanted to wash my hands. Even Jim wants to wash his hands of himself: caught before the bathroom mirror in a rare moment when he is not silently contorting his face in wrathful poses, he glimpses his own "humourless and self-pitying" glance. I found Amis's shabby provincial university pitiable, with its homemade musical entertainments and clichéd lectures on "Merrie England"—but all too recognizable in the dust-laden draperies of the commons room where I sometimes joined my husband for a sandwich and a glass of lager. My gaze took in the Dixons and Welches at other tables.

Dixon, a historian of medieval England, has completed a study entitled "The Economic Influence of the Developments in Shipbuilding Techniques, 1450 to 1485" (15). This subject is purely academic, historically narrow, and even he questions whether it was "worth the amount of frenzied fact-grubbing and fanatical boredom that had gone into it." Desperate to find a means of retaining his academic post (despite his anxious boredom as a lecturer), he submits an essay on this subject to a newly established scholarly journal whose editor later appropriates it as his own. The essay wins the unscrupulous Dr. L. S. Caton the chair of History of Commerce at an Argentinian university. Meanwhile, Dixon loses his university post, only to be transported to London and a new life by the good graces of Julius Gore-Urquhart, the novel's deus ex machina.

The moral I eventually carried away from *Lucky Jim* was this: avoid academe, find another future, hope for the arrival of an Uncle Julius. Virtually all my experiences in the shift from an American to a British academic setting in 1977 confirmed a set of contradictory desires in me: to enter this world, and to run from it. In this, I shared a good deal with Jim Dixon. I especially detested the social settings, so well described by Amis, where self-puffery parades itself and the air is fogged with coercive verbal fillers ("Don't you agree? Wouldn't you say so?" the men asked) that closed rather than opened intellectual and cultural exchange. My words were met with quizzical smiles and counter-challenges. My English women friends returned the challenges gleefully. As the months wore on, I sank into the most severe depression I have ever experienced, laughing and crying all the way—at comic novels, television satires, stage send-ups.

I returned to the American midlands in 1978 to accept yet another marginal administrative post at the university, the manuscript of my novel tucked into a desk drawer, still wrapped in the mailer returned from a New York literary agent recommended to me by a friend. For the next two years, I replayed in real life the scenes I had described in *An Occupational Hazard*. This tragicomedy never found a steady emotional footing as it lurched (as I did in those days) between the comic and the self-pitying. A literary disaster, it nonetheless succeeded as self-therapy and in important ways made it possible for me to write the scholarly books that would follow over the next two decades.

But at that moment, I was still years away from my first "real" position in the academy. From the perspective of my recent experience in England, I could not forecast the transformative powers of feminism in the academy or in my life. I did not recognize my private pain as part of a larger pattern of women's experiences; the personal was not yet the political for me. Like Jim Dixon, I inhabited a world where everyone else seemed to know the rules of the game. A gift from London friends at Christmas 1977 gave me a larger view of that world and helped me set *Lucky Jim* in perspective. It was David Lodge's *Changing Places,* the predictable (and perfect) gift for an American academic couple on exchange in England. The most successful inheritor of the *Lucky Jim* tradition, Lodge had lived long in academe and was well acquainted with its traditions and habits of mind. In the generation that separated Lodge from Amis, the period between the mid-'60s and mid-'70s, the intellectual winds of change from the continent blew across the Anglo-American academy. Lodge was thus able to infuse the stuffy world of Amis's academe with energy and the sense of possibilities. At the same time, he raised the stakes of comedy. Lodge provided a necessary escape hatch from Amis's provincial university: the airplane. He portrayed Phillip Swallow (a less loony and more kindly version of Edward Welch) "changing places" for a year with his American counterpart, Morris Zapp, a lusty, doomed egocentric that only America could produce. In *Small World,* the sequel to *Changing Places,* Lodge created a globe-hopping entourage of literary theorists and glamorous Italian Marxists wearing handmade boots and carrying tooled leather briefcases who traveled (first-class) to further their fame and fortune.

To put it bluntly, Lodge made academe sexy. By contrast with Amis's provincials, Lodge's characters are breezy and charming. The egoist Zapp captures our affections and the kindly Swallow engages our sympathies. Perrse McGarrigle, the young Irish poet and lecturer who plays the Lucky Jim role in *Small World,* is an outsider to the closed, defended world of British universities. Yet his outsider status works for him rather than against him. Like Dixon, he is in search of love, and the groves of academe provide the grounds for his quest. Like Dixon's, his intellectual interests seem a mere pretext for pursuits that are hardly academic. McGarrigle's scholarly methods, for example, are outdated by contemporary standards: he is at work on an influence study but has reversed the order of things by exploring T. S. Eliot's influence on William Shakespeare—a confusion that furthers the hilarity rather than destroying verisimilitude. There are hints of sadness, but these involve losses in love rather than risk of unemployment: McGarrigle loses the girl he loves; Phillip Swallow's marital nest is despoiled by Zapp. Unlike *Lucky Jim,* these stories center on middle-aged men and women who grasp at happiness even as they face the realities of aging and death—the great levelers.

I was entering middle age when I at last scaled the ivory tower of higher learning in 1982, my enthusiasm for research and teaching fueled by feminism and a desire to reform the academy. I was no longer intimidated by the Professor Welches of the world; indeed, I wanted Welch's position as chair of the department. That is, I wanted to rewrite Amis's novel as a success story for "Jane" Dixon, feminist theorist and critic. In my story, she hunts down D. L. Caton, the man who stole Jim Dixon's essay on the economics of shipbuilding in the late middle ages to secure for himself a prestigious academic post at an Argentinian university. Amis let this character slip away, but I believe he could find a place in a feminist academic satire for the new millenium. Perhaps I will inscribe him there, a minor character but one who can (and did) help shift a scene.

Notes

1. Kingsley Amis, *Lucky Jim* (London: Penguin, 1961), 250. Subsequent references identified by parenthetical numerals.

Index

♦

1984 (Orwell), 268
1985 (Burgess), 201–2
Act Without Words (Beckett), 197
Afternoon Men (Powell), 28
Alteration, The (Amis), 9, 109, 248, 252, 259, 285
Ambler, Eric, 181
American Psycho (Ellis), 262
Amis, Hillary Bardwell (Hilly), 14, 15, 140, 245, 254, 260, 264, 65, 266, 329
Amis, Kingsley, *Alteration, The,* 9, 109, 237, 248, 252, 259, 285; *Amis Anthology, The,* 105, 238; *Amis Collection, The,* 121, 123, 258; *Anti-Death League, The,* 7, 25, 27, 36–39, 110, 117, 136, 171, 181–82, 184, 210–12, 223, 226, 250–54, 271, 275–76, 278–79, 281–84, 287, 290; *Biographer's Mustache, The,* 15–16, 130, 257–58, 260–62, 265, 328, 331; *Bright November,* 245; *Case of Samples, A,* 29, 231; *Collected Poems 1944–1979,* 76, 229–36; *Colonel Sun,* 72, 116, 237, 259, 330; *Crime of the Century,* 259; *Difficulties with Girls,* 13–14, 83–85, 103, 136, 139, 170–75, 237, 240, 242, 255, 262, 296–301, 304–8; *Egyptologists, The* (with Robert Conquest), 263, 276, 330; *Ending Up,* 1, 9, 12, 64, 72, 74, 79, 82, 85, 109, 177, 184–85, 218, 223, 226, 239, 252, 289–90; *Folks That Live on the Hill, The,* 14, 110, 136, 242, 329–31; *Girl, 20,* 1, 8–9, 26, 72, 79, 84, 86, 89–90, 93, 107, 109, 136, 177, 181–84, 210–11, 219, 239–40, 248, 251–52, 255, 261, 275, 285, 299, 306; *Green Man, The,* 8, 79, 85, 89–90, 110, 181–84, 209–10, 212, 221, 223–24, 226, 228, 251, 259, 275, 278–79, 287, 290, 330–31; *I Like It Here,* 5, 24, 29–31, 54–59, 68–69, 79, 178–79, 208, 241, 249, 271–73, 329; *I Want It Now,* 7–8, 26, 28, 60, 71, 84, 87, 109, 135–36, 182, 210, 251, 262, 270–71, 276, 290; *Jake's Thing,* 1, 10–11, 64, 72, 79, 85–87, 90–99, 103, 110, 193–202, 238, 244, 252–54, 285, 287–91, 293–95, 299, 303, 310, 319–20, 330, 331; *James Bond Dossier, The,* 259; *Kipling and His World,* 243, 330; *Look Round the Estate, A,* 29; "A Chromatic Passing Note," 107, 232–33;*Lucky Jim,* 1, 3–4, 7, 24, 28–30, 34, 45–50, 53, 60–61, 64, 66–68, 76, 78, 80, 103, 106, 108–9, 123, 136, 141–52, 155, 157–68, 176, 178–79, 185, 187–98, 209–11, 213–14, 217–22, 229, 233, 236–37, 240, 243, 245–49, 251, 255–56, 258, 261–62, 266–67, 269, 271–72, 283, 286, 288–89, 293, 300, 304–5, 309, 315, 319, 323, 325, 327, 329, 332–38; *Memoirs,* 16, 120, 130, 188, 263, 327, 329; *My Enemy's Enemy,* 36; "Something Strange," 30, 36; "My Kind of Comedy," 212; *New Maps of Hell,* 237, 259, 330; *Old Devils, The,* 1, 11–13, 65, 74–75, 79, 85–86, 109, 136–38, 237, 239–40, 242, 244, 254–55, 259, 263–65, 297, 308,

Amis, Kingsley (*continued*)
310–14, 315–26, 329, 331; *On Drink,* 106, 243, 330; *One Fat Englishman,* 6–7, 25, 29, 33–34, 36, 70, 123, 180, 182, 184, 208, 210–11, 249, 275, 286, 306, 329; *Riverside Villas Murder, The,* 109, 232, 239, 252, 275, 279, 330; *Russian Girl, The,* 15, 108; *Russian Hide-and-Seek,* 88, 202, 239, 244, 252–53, 259, 285; *Stanley and the Women,* 11, 73, 79, 83, 85–86, 103, 109, 130, 171, 237–39, 244, 253–56, 259, 262, 265, 298–99, 310, 319–20, 324, 331; *Take a Girl like You,* 1, 5–6, 8, 27, 29, 31–33, 35, 50–54, 64, 69–71, 85, 132–35, 139, 171–72, 179, 206, 210, 212, 218–19, 221–26, 232, 238, 240, 249, 255, 259, 269, 273–74, 283, 296, 299–302, 305, 308, 326, 329; *That Uncertain Feeling,* 4–5, 29, 32, 35, 50, 53–54, 68, 79, 86, 131–32, 171, 178–79, 205, 207–8, 210, 219, 222, 225, 249, 254, 272, 304, 329; *What Became of Jane Austen and Other Questions,* 113–14, 120–21, 248, 249–50, *Why Lucky Jim Turned Right,* 121, 189, 244, 251, 253; *You Can't Do Both,* 1, 15, 138–41, 146, 149–57, 265, 331
Amis, Martin, 70, 86, 89, 103, 286, 331; *Einstein's Monsters,* 243; *Information, The,* 257; *London Fields,* 242; *Money,* 241; *Moronic Inferno,* 243; *Rachel Papers, The,* 241; *Success,* 241
Amis, William, 244
Amis Anthology, The (Amis), 105, 238
Amis Collection, The (Amis), 121, 123, 258
Angry Young Men, 28, 58, 75, 130, 188, 238, 243, 248, 263, 267, 304, 309
Animal Farm (Orwell), 268
Anti-Death League, The (Amis), 7, 25, 27, 36–39, 110, 117, 136, 171, 181–82, 184, 210–12, 223, 226, 250–54, 271, 275–76, 278–79, 281–84, 287, 290
Anti-Egotist, The (Fussell), 104
Auden, W. H., 230, 263
Austen, Jane, 61, 68, 163, *Mansfield Park,* 114–15, 259; *Pride and Prejudice,* 146, 158

Baldwin, James, 268
Barth, John, 35
Bayley, John, 230

Beckett, Samuel, 13, 259, 312, 313; *Act Without Words,* 197
Beerbohm, Max, 124, 304
Bellow, Saul, 239, 250
Bennett, Alan, 300
Bennett, Arnold, 28, 40–41
Bergson, Henri, 142, 159
Betjeman, John, 9, 126, 128, 229, 238
Biographer's Mustache, The (Amis), 15–16, 130, 257–58, 260–62, 265, 328, 331
Bradbury, Malcolm, 10, 11, 81, 88, 99, 131, 171, *Eating People is Wrong,* 213–15, 217; *History Man, The,* 215–16
Bradford, Richard, 103
Braine, John, 45, 80, 99, 309; *Room at the Top,* 42–44, 197, 263, 267
Bright November (Amis), 245
Brookner, Anita, 239
Brothers Karamazov, The (Dostoyevsky), 227
Burgess, Anthony, 7, 83, 99, 124, 131, 163, 172–73, 196, 271, 286, 300; *1985,* 201–2

Carey, John, 259
Case of Samples, A (Amis), 29, 231; "Box of Friends," 29; "Dirty Stories," 29
Catcher in the Rye (Salinger), 293
Changing Places (Lodge), 337
Clarissa (Richardson), 5, 31, 51–52, 69, 209
Coles, Joanna, 257, 263
"*Colette*" (Nabokov), 117
Collected Poems 1944–1979 (Amis), 76, 229–36
Colonel Sun (Amis), 72, 116, 237, 259, 330
Coming Up For Air (Orwell), 246, 268
Congreve, William, 160, 163
Connolly, Joseph, 76
Conquest, Robert, 245–46, 251, 264, *Egyptologists, The* (with Kingsley Amis), 263, 276, 330
Conrad, Joseph, 40, 118
Cooper, William, 29, 124
Crime of the Century (Amis), 259
Cropper, Martin, 81

Daniel Martin (Fowles), 198–202
Darkness Visible (Golding), 198
De Vries, Peter, 304
Decline and Fall (Waugh), 319
Dedalus, Stephen, 29, 43–44, 145
Dickens, Charles, 23, 61, 187, 207, 219, 268–69, 309; *Great Expectations,* 153

Dickstein, Morris, 111
Difficulties with Girls (Amis), 13–14, 83–85, 103, 136, 139, 170–75, 237, 240, 242, 255, 262, 296–301, 304–8
Dostoyevsky, Fyodor, 37; *Brothers Karamazov, The,* 227
Drabble, Margaret, 198–201, 239
Durrell, Lawrence, 41

Eating People is Wrong (Bradbury), 213–15, 217
Egyptologists, The (Amis with Robert Conquest), 263, 276, 330
Einstein's Monsters (Martin Amis), 243
Eliot, George, 23, 113, 123, 172, 263, 268
Eliot, T. S., 41, 198, 233, 337; *Waste Land, The,* 198, 233
Ellis, Brett Easton, *American Psycho,* 262
Ending Up (Amis), 1, 9, 12, 64, 72, 74, 79, 82, 85, 109, 177, 184–85, 218, 223, 226, 239, 252, 289–90
Everett, Barbara, 78

Faulkner, William, *Sound and the Fury, The,* 162
Fiedler, Leslie, 118, 166, 263
Fielding, Henry, 2–3, 30, 45, 48, 50, 56–57, 69, 144–47, 159, 187, 208–10, 217, 219, 309, 318; *Joseph Andrews,* 46, 142, 144–45, 147–48; *Tom Jones,* 4, 13, 31, 61, 66, 141–42, 144, 146–48, 158–62, 210
Finnegans Wake (Joyce), 248
Fitzgerald, F. Scott, *Tender is the Night,* 162
Fleming, Ian, 17, 28, 37, 72, 116
Folks That Live on the Hill, The (Amis), 14, 110, 136, 242, 329–31
Forster, E. M., 40, 124, 231
Fowles, John, 99; *Daniel Martin,* 198–202
Frost, Robert, 108, 236, 281, 322
Frye, Northrop, 159, 168, 320
Fussell, Paul, 104–5, 108, 260, 264; *Anti-Egotist, The,* 104

Gardner, Philip, 286
Girl, 20 (Amis), 1, 8–9, 26, 72, 79, 84, 86, 89–90, 93, 107, 109, 136, 177, 181–84, 210–11, 219, 239–40, 248, 251–52, 255, 261, 275, 285, 299, 306
Golding, William, 41, 124, 131, 198, 286; *Darkness Visible,* 198
Gollancz, Victor, 123

Great Expectations (Dickens), 153
Green, Martin, 30; *Mirror for Anglo-Saxons, A,* 30
Greene, Graham, 40, 90, 309; *Heart of the Matter, The,* 191
Green Man, The (Amis), 8, 79, 85, 89–90, 110, 181–84, 209–10, 212, 221, 223–24, 226, 228, 251, 259, 275, 278–79, 287, 290, 330–31
Grice, H. P., 93
Gross, John, 29, 104, 111, 280; *Rise and Fall of the Man of Letters, The,* 104
Gulliver's Travels (Swift), 212

Hansford Johnson, Pamela, 40, 45
Hardy, Thomas, 118, 236
Heart of the Matter, The (Greene), 191
Hemingway, Ernest, 264–65; *Sun Also Rises, The,* 162
Hinde, Thomas, 206–7
History Man, The (Bradbury), 215–16
Hitchcock, Alfred, *Psycho,* 119
Hoggart, Richard, 32, 118
Howard, Elizabeth Jane, 254, 264, 266, 330–31
Hughes, David, 81
Hulme, T. E., 112
Hurrell, John, 179
Hurry on Down (Wain), 66, 219, 267

I Like It Here (Amis), 5, 24, 29–31, 54–59, 68–69, 79, 178–79, 208, 241, 249, 271–73, 329
Information, The (Martin Amis), 257
I Want It Now (Amis), 7–8, 26, 28, 60, 71, 84, 87, 109, 135–36, 182, 210, 251, 262, 270–71, 276, 290

Jacobs, Eric, 15, 130, 140, 260, 264, 328
Jake's Thing (Amis), 1, 10–11, 64, 72, 79, 85–87, 90–99, 103, 110, 193–202, 238, 244, 252–54, 285, 287–91, 293–95, 299, 303, 310, 319–20, 330, 331
James, Clive, 259
James, Henry, 4, 40, 45, 55, 69, 77, 108–9
James Bond Dossier, The (Amis), 259
Jerome, Jerome K., 28
Johnson, Samuel, 14
Jones, Daniel, 115
Joseph Andrews (Fielding), 46, 142, 147–48

Joyce, James, 41–45, 108, 123, 246, 259; *Finnegans Wake,* 248; *Portrait of the Artist as a Young Man, A,* 42; *Ulysses,* 32, 61

Kakutani, Michiko, 255
Karl, Frederick, 217, 219
Kavanaugh, P. J., 324
Keats, John, 115, 162, 259
Kelly, Edward, 180
Kenner, Hugh, 123
Kipling, Rudyard, 243, 258, 285, 316, 318, 330
Kipling and His World (Amis), 243, 330
Kipps (Wells), 28, 206–7
Kris, Earnest, 165

Langer, Suzanne, 142, 159, 165
Language of Fiction (Lodge), 29
Larkin, Philip, 16, 65–66, 77, 106, 124, 127, 129, 188, 194, 227, 229–30, 236, 240–41, 245, 248, 262, 264–65, 303, 309, 322–23, 325, 329; *North Ship, The,* 230
Laski, Marghanita, 24
Lawrence, D. H., 23, 30, 40–41, 53, 112–13, 122, 239, 275, 298
Leavis, F. R., 4, 30, 63, 141, 238, 259
Lewis, Wyndham, 112, 123
Lodge, David, 12, 29, 68, 79–80, 108, 130, 148, 158; *Changing Places,* 337; *Language of Fiction* (Lodge), 29; *Small World,* 337
Lolita (Nabokov), 116–19, 249, 259
London Fields (Martin Amis), 242
Look Back in Anger (Osborne), 66, 188, 263, 267
Look Round the Estate, A (Amis), 29; "A Chromatic Passing Note," 232–33; "Nothing to Fear," 29; "Out-Patient," 29; "Science Fiction," 30
Lucky Jim (Amis), 1, 3–4, 7, 24, 28–30, 34, 45–50, 53, 60–61, 64, 66–68, 76, 78, 80, 103, 106, 108–9, 123, 136, 141–52, 155, 157–68, 176, 178–79, 185, 187–98, 209–11, 213–14, 217–22, 229, 233, 236–37, 240, 243, 245–49, 251, 255–56, 258, 261–62, 266–67, 269, 271–72, 283, 286, 288–89, 293, 300, 304–5, 309, 315, 319, 323, 325, 327, 329, 332–38

MacBeth, George, 23
MacDonald, Jock, 24
Macher, Irving, 211
MacLeod, Norman, 5
Mailer, Norman, 239, 265, 268; *Naked and the Dead, The,* 268, 319
Mansfield, Katherine, 23
Mansfield Park (Austen), 115, 259
Marcuse, Herbert, 36
Maugham, Somerset, 58, 68, 124, 245–46, 263
McDermott, John, 103, 171–72, 175
McEwan, Neil, 81
McGrath, Charles, 12
Memento Mori (Spark), 252, 324
Memoirs (Amis), 16, 120, 130, 188, 263, 327, 329
Michie, James, 1
Midsummer Night's Dream, A (Shakespeare), 146
Miller, Karl, 122, 172–73, 175
Milton, 198, 277; *Paradise Lost,* 6, 198, 278
Mirror for Anglo-Saxons, A (Green), 30
Money (Martin Amis), 241
Moronic Inferno (Martin Amis), 243
Moseley, Merritt, 104
Mr. Polly (Wells), 206–7
Much Ado About Nothing (Shakespeare), 158
Murdoch, Iris, 41, 66, 99, 122, 124, 206, 260, 267; *Under the Net,* 122
My Enemy's Enemy (Amis), 36; "Something Strange," 30, 36
"My Kind of Comedy" (Amis), 212

Nabokov, Vladimir, 114, 116–17, 242, 259; "Colette", 117; *Lolita,* 116–19, 249, 259; *Pale Fire,* 5, 54
Naked and the Dead, The (Mailer), 268, 319
New Maps of Hell (Amis), 237, 259, 330
Nichols, James, 178
North Ship, The (Larkin), 230

O'Faolain, Sean, 62
Old Devils, The (Amis), 1, 11–13, 65, 74–75, 79, 85–86, 109, 136–38, 237, 239–40, 242, 244, 254–55, 259, 263–65, 297, 308, 310–14, 315–26, 329, 331
On Drink (Amis), 106, 243, 330
One Fat Englishman (Amis), 6–7, 25, 29, 33–34, 36, 70, 123, 180, 182, 184, 208, 210–11, 249, 275, 286, 306, 329

Ordeal of Gilbert Pinfold (Waugh), 54, 62
Orwell, George, 30, 40, 67, 111, 122, 239, 268; *1984,* 268; *Animal Farm,* 268; *Coming Up For Air,* 246, 268;
Osborne, John, 66, 80, 188, 193, 263, 267; *Look Back in Anger,* 188, 263, 267
Othello (Shakespeare), 277

Pale Fire (Nabokov), 5, 54
Pamela (Richardson), 69
Paradise Lost (Milton), 6, 106, 198, 278
Pinkus, Philip, 176
Poe, Edgar Allan, 126
Portnoy's Complaint (Roth), 119, 274, 295
Portrait of the Artist as a Young Man, A (Joyce), 42
Pound, Ezra, 113, 123, 265
Powell, Anthony, 16, 28, 78, 82, 124, 240, 246, 258; *Afternoon Men,* 28
Pride and Prejudice (Austen), 146, 158
Pritchard, William H., 11, 76
Pritchett, V. S., 78, 206–7
Prospect of the Sea (Thomas), 115
Psycho (Hitchcock), 119
Pynchon, Thomas, 35

Quennell, Peter, 112

Rabinovitz, Ruben, 29
Rachel Papers, The (Martin Amis), 241
Richardson, Samuel, 5–6, 31, 51, 208; *Clarissa,* 5, 31, 51–52, 69, 209; *Pamela,* 69
Ricks, Christopher, 6
Rise and Fall of the Man of Letters, The (Gross), 104
Ritchie, Harry, 111–12, 259
Riverside Villas Murder, The (Amis), 109, 232, 239, 252, 275, 279, 330
Robbe-Grillet, Alain, 34–35
Roberts, Glenys, 257–58, 264
Robson, Wallace, 83
Room at the Top (Braine), 42, 197, 263, 267
Rosten, Leo, 16
Roth, Philip, 70, 114, 119, *Portnoy's Complaint,* 119, 274, 295
Russian Girl, The (Amis), 15, 108
Russian Hide-and-Seek (Amis), 88, 202, 239, 244, 252–53, 259, 285

Saki, 29
Salinger, J. D., 67, 123, 268; *Catcher in the Rye,* 293

Salwak, Dale, 103, 110, 134, 180, 184
Santayana, George, 165–66
Saturday Night and Sunday Morning (Sillitoe), 197, 208
Shakespeare, William, 161–63, 174, 337; *Midsummer Night's Dream, A,* 146; *Much Ado About Nothing,* 158; *Othello,* 277
Sillitoe, Alan, 80, 197, 206–8, 309; *Saturday Night and Sunday Morning,* 197, 208
Small World (Lodge), 337
Sound and the Fury, The (Faulkner), 162
Spark, Muriel, 99, 252, 324; *Memento Mori,* 252, 324
Spender, Stephen, 40
Stanley and the Women (Amis), 11, 73, 79, 83, 85–86, 103, 109, 130, 171, 237–39, 244, 253–56, 259, 262, 265, 298–99, 310, 319–20, 324, 331
Stannard, Martin, 126
Sterne, Laurence, *Tristram Shandy,* 5, 54, 141
Storey, David, 99, 206
Success (Martin Amis), 241
Sun Also Rises, The (Hemingway), 162
Swift, Jonathan, 9, 11, 133, 212, 283; *Gulliver's Travels,* 212

Take a Girl like You (Amis), 1, 5–6, 8, 27, 29, 31–33, 35, 50–54, 64, 69–71, 85, 132–35, 139, 171–72, 179, 206, 210, 212, 218–19, 221–26, 232, 238, 240, 249, 255, 259, 269, 273–74, 283, 296, 299–302, 305, 308, 326, 329
Tallis, Raymond, 79
Tender is the Night (Fitzgerald), 162
Thatcher, Margaret, 16, 130, 323, 334
That Uncertain Feeling (Amis), 4–5, 29, 32, 35, 50, 53–54, 68, 79, 86, 131–32, 171, 178–79, 205, 207–8, 210, 219, 222, 225, 249, 254, 272, 304, 329
Thomas, Dylan, 4, 53, 65, 68, 85, 90, 115, 124, 126–27, 222, 310, 315, 324; *Prospect of the Sea,* 115
Tom Jones (Fielding), 4, 13, 31, 61, 66, 141–42, 144, 146–48, 158–62, 210
Tristram Shandy (Sterne), 5, 54, 141

Ulysses (Joyce), 32, 61
Under the Net (Murdoch), 66, 122
Updike, John, 141, 239, 244, 309

Vaizey, John, 82
Vidal, Gore, 241, 255

Wain, John, 66, 99, 206, 219, 263, 267; *Hurry on Down,* 219, 267
Waste Land, The (Eliot), 198, 233
Waterhouse, Keith, 206–7
Watkins, Alan, 76
Waugh, Auberon, 110
Waugh, Evelyn, 28, 40, 54, 61–65, 70, 74, 88, 124–26, 167, 187, 212, 238, 240, 242, 243, 246–47, 256, 259, 293, 309, 327; *Decline and Fall,* 319; *Ordeal of Gilbert Pinfold,* 54, 62
Wells, H. G., 28, 40–41, 124, 206–7, 307; *Kipps,* 28, 206–7; *Mr. Polly,* 206–7
What Became of Jane Austen and Other Questions (Amis), 113–14, 120–21, 249–50, 248

Whitman, Walt, 123
Why Lucky Jim Turned Right (Amis), 121, 189, 244, 251, 253
Williams, Raymond, 32
Wilmes, D. R., 9
Wilson, Angus, 28, 30, 66, 99
Wilson, Colin, 267
Wilson, Edmund, 62, 247
Wodehouse, P. J., 187, 240, 246–47, 252, 262, 293, 304, 318
Wood, Michael, 173, 175
Woolf, Virginia, 40–41, 259, 332, 334

Yeats, W. B., 148
You Can't Do Both (Amis), 1, 15, 138–41, 146, 149–57, 265, 331

The Volume Editor

Robert H. Bell is William R. Kenan Jr. Professor of English at Williams College. He was graduated from Dartmouth College and received his Ph.D from Harvard University. He is author of *Jocoserious Joyce: The Fate of Folly in Ulysses* (Cornell University Press, 1991; University Press of Florida paperback, 1996) and of many articles in scholarly journals. He has also published scores of reviews, features, and humor pieces in magazines, newspapers, and on National Public Radio. In 1998 he was awarded the Robert Foster Cherry Award for Great Teachers.

The General Editor

Zack Bowen is professor of English at the University of Miami. He holds degrees from the University of Pennsylvania (B.A.), Temple University (M.A.), and the State University of New York at Buffalo (Ph.D.). In addition to being general editor of this G. K. Hall series, he is editor of the James Joyce series for the University of Florida Press and the *James Joyce Literary Supplement*. He is author and editor of numerous books on modern British, Irish, and American literature. He has also published more than one hundred monographs, essays, scholarly reviews, and recordings related to literature. He is past president of the James Joyce Society (1977–1986), former chair of the Modern Language Association Lowell Prize Committee, and current president of the International James Joyce Foundation.